THE ENGLISH ARISTOCRACY

THE ENGLISH ARISTOCRACY

1070–1272

A SOCIAL TRANSFORMATION

✤

DAVID CROUCH

YALE UNIVERSITY PRESS
NEW HAVEN AND LONDON

For information about this and other Yale University Press publications, please contact:

U.S. Office: sales.press@yale.edu   www.yalebooks.com
Europe Office: sales @yaleup.co.uk   www.yaleup.co.uk

Set in Janson MT by IDSUK (DataConnection) Ltd
Printed in Great Britain by TJ International Ltd, Padstow, Cornwall

Library of Congress Cataloging-in-Publication Data

Crouch, David.
  The English aristocracy: 1070–1272: a social transformation/David Crouch.
    p. cm.
  ISBN 978-0-300-11455-3 (cl: alk. paper)
1. Aristocracy (Social class)—Great Britain—History—To 1500. 2. Nobility—Great Britain—History—To 1500. 3. Great Britain—History—1066-1687. 4. Great Britain—Social conditions. I. Title.
  HT653. G7C7597 2010
  305.5′20941—dc22

                                                                                            2010038325

A catalogue record for this book is available from the British Library.

10 9 8 7 6 5 4 3 2 1

CONTENTS

ILLUSTRATIONS

ACKNOWLEDGEMENTS

THIS book is the end of a long intellectual voyage, which began in Cardiff in 1978 and, as happens in long voyages, involved several detours. That I have got to the end at all is due to the Leverhulme Trust, which in 1985 conferred a ridiculous amount of money on a brash and untried young ex-teacher surviving in the grim Thatcher years on short-term academic contracts in London. It allowed me (for reader, I was that man) to devote four years' study to the earls of England and compile a huge archive of data with which I am still grappling. It also allowed me to pursue my study of William Marshal – for better and for worse, the definitive medieval aristocrat – published in 1990 and reissued in a second edition in 2002. I feel now that I have fully justified the Trust's generosity, and wish it known how deeply grateful I am for its vision and confidence. The University of London's Institute of Historical Research was likewise generous in housing my project at the time, and since then I have carried it with me to academic homes in Scarborough and Hull. What is gratifying for me is the fact that one of my research assistants in my London days, Nicholas Vincent, has since become one of the most significant and productive medieval historians England has produced. I would like to thank several friends for substantial input into this book in terms of both informed criticism and material. As well as Nick Vincent, these include Mandy Capern, Hugh Doherty, John Gillingham, Lindy Grant, Eric Hemming, John Hudson and Richard Sharpe. There are others over the years who have given me insights that have lodged in my mind and inspired productive internal debate, not least Martin Aurell, David Bates, Paul Brand, Glenn Burgess, David Carpenter, Peter Coss, Julian Haseldine, Derek Keene and Ann Williams. The two anonymous readers for Yale University Press were both helpful and encouraging in their reports. Robert Shore, Yale University Press's copy-editor, saved me from countless obscurities and gaffes. I should also acknowledge the patience of Robert Baldock and Heather McCallum at Yale in waiting for the manuscript of this book for so long.

Hull
31 October 2010

ABBREVIATIONS

AmHR	*American Historical Review*
Annales Monastici	*Annales Monastici*, ed. H.R. Luard (5 vols, Rolls Series, 1864–69)
ANS	*Proceedings of the Battle Conference* (1978–81); *Anglo-Norman Studies* (1982–)
ASC	*The Peterborough Chronicle, 1070–1154*, ed. and trans. C. Clark (2nd edn, Oxford, 1970)
BIHR	*Bulletin of the Institute of Historical Research* (later, *Historical Research*)
BL	British Library
Bodl. Libr.	Bodleian Library
Book of Fees	*Book of Fees, Commonly Called Testa de Nevill*, ed. H.C. Maxwell-Lyte (3 vols, HMSO, 1920–31)
Cal Charter Rolls	*Calendar of the Charter Rolls Preserved in the Public Record Office* (6 vols, London, HMSO, 1923–7)
Cal Close Rolls	*Calendar of the Close Rolls Preserved in the Public Record Office* (London, HMSO, 1892–)
Cal Patent Rolls	*Calendar of Patent Rolls Preserved in the Public Record Office* (London, HMSO, 1891–)
Chanson d'Aspremont	*La Chanson d'Aspremont*, ed. L. Brandin (2 vols, Classiques français du moyen âge, 1923–4)
Charters of the Earls of Chester	*Charters of the Anglo-Norman Earls of Chester, c.1071–1237*, ed. G. Barraclough (Record Society of Lancashire and Cheshire, cxxvi, 1988)
Close Rolls	*Close Rolls of the Reign of Henry III* (14 vols, London, HMSO, 1902–38)
Complete Peerage	[G.E. Cokayne], *The Complete Peerage of England, Scotland, Ireland and Great Britain*, ed. V. Gibbs (13 vols in 14, London, 1910–59)
Curia Regis Rolls	*Curia Regis Rolls Preserved in the Public Record Office* (20 vols, London, HMSO, 1922–2007)
D & C	Dean and Chapter
De Nugis Curialium	*De Nugis Curialium or Courtiers' Trifles*, ed. and trans. M.R. James, revised C.N.L. Brooke and R.A.B. Mynors (Oxford, 1983)
Documents	*Documents of the Baronial Movement of Reform and Rebellion, 1258–1267*, ed. and trans. R.F. Treharne and I.J. Sanders (Oxford, 1973)

Domesday Book	*Domesday Book seu Liber Censualis Willelmi Primi Regis Angliae*, ed. A. Farley and others (4 vols, London, 1783–1816)
Early Yorkshire Charters	*Early Yorkshire Charters* i–iii, ed. W. Farrer (Edinburgh, 1914–16); iv–xii, ed. C.T. Clay (Huddersfield, Leeds and Wakefield, 1935–65)
EHR	*English Historical Review*
English Lawsuits	*English Lawsuits from William I to Richard I*, ed. and trans. R.C. van Caenegem (2 vols, Selden Society, 106–7, 1990–1)
Estoire des Engleis	Geoffrey Gaimar, *Estoire des Engleis*, ed. and trans. I. Short (Oxford, 2009)
Facetus	A. Morel-Fatio, 'Mélanges de littérature catalane', *Romania*, 15 (1886), 224–35; translation in A. Goddard Elliott, 'The *Facetus* or, The Art of Courtly Living', *Allegorica*, 2 (1977), 27–57. References to the Morel-Fatio text
Foedera	T. Rymer, *Foedera, Conventiones, Litterae et Acta Publica*, ed. A. Clarke and F. Holbrooke (7 vols, London, 1816–69)
Gesta Henrici Secundi	*Gesta Henrici Secundi*, ed. W. Stubbs (2 vols, Rolls Series, 1867)
Glanvill	*The Treatise on the Law and Customs of the Realm of England Commonly Called Glanvill*, ed. and trans. G.D.G. Hall (London, 1965)
GS	*Gesta Stephani*, ed. and trans. K.R. Potter and R.H.C. Davis (Oxford, 1976)
HH	Henry of Huntingdon, *Historia Anglorum*, ed. and trans. D. Greenway (Oxford, 1996)
Histoire des ducs	*Histoire des ducs de Normandie et des rois d'Angleterre*, ed. F. Michel (Paris, 1840)
HSJ	*Haskins Society Journal*
HWM	*History of William Marshal*, ed. A.J. Holden and D. Crouch, trans. S. Gregory (3 vols, Anglo-Norman Text Society, Occasional Publications Series, 4–6, 2002–7)
JB	*The Chronicle of Jocelin of Brakelond*, ed. and trans. H.E. Butler (London, 1949)
JMH	*Journal of Medieval History*
JW	John of Worcester, *Chronicle*, ed. R.R. Darlington and P. McGurk, ii (Oxford, 1995), iii (Oxford, 1998)
Leges Henrici Primi	*Leges Henrici Primi*, ed. L.J. Downer (Oxford, 1972)
LM	Stephen de Fougères, *Le Livre des Manières*, ed. R.A. Lodge (Geneva, 1979)
Monasticon Anglicanum	William Dugdale and Roger Dodsworth, *Monasticon Anglicanum*, ed. J. Caley et al. (8 vols, Record Commission, 1817–30)
MP, *CM*	Matthew Paris, *Chronica Majora*, ed. H.R. Luard (7 vols, Rolls Series, 1872–84)
OV	Orderic Vitalis, *The Ecclesiastical History*, ed. M. Chibnall (6 vols, Oxford, 1969–80)

Patent Rolls	*Patent Rolls of the Reign of Henry III* (6 vols, London, HMSO, 1901–13)
Pipe Roll	*Pipe Rolls*, identified by regnal year (Pipe Roll Society, 1884–)
Pipe Roll of 31 Henry I	*Magnum rotulum scaccarii vel magnum rotulum pipæ de anno tricesimo-primo regni Henrici Primi (ut videtur)*, ed. J. Hunter (Record Commission, 1833)
PL	*Patrologiae cursus completus: series Latina*, ed. J.-P. Migne (221 vols, Paris, 1847–67)
Placita de Quo Warranto	*Placita de Quo Warranto temporibus Edw. I. II. and III*, ed. W. Illingworth (Record Commission, 1818)
PP	*Past & Present*
Red Book of the Exchequer	*The Red Book of the Exchequer*, ed. H. Hall (3 vols, Rolls Series, 1896)
Regesta: William I	*Regesta Regum Anglo-Normannorum: The Acta of William I, 1066–1087*, ed. D.R. Bates (Oxford, 1998)
Regesta	*Regesta Regum Anglo-Normannorum*, ed. H.W.C. Davis et al. (4 vols, Oxford, 1913–69)
Registrum Antiquissimum	*Registrum Antiquissimum of the Cathedral Church of Lincoln*, ed. C.W. Foster and K. Major (10 vols, Lincoln Record Society, 1931–73)
RH	Richard of Hexham, *De gestis regis Stephani*, in *Chronicles of the Reigns of Stephen, Henry II and Richard*, ed. R. Howlett (4 vols, Rolls Series,1886–9), iii
RHF	*Recueil des historiens des Gaules et de la France*, ed. M. Bouquet and others (24 vols, Paris, 1864–1904)
Roman de Rou	*Roman de Rou*, ed. A.J. Holden (3 vols, Société des anciens textes français, 1970–3)
Rotuli Chartarum	*Rotuli Chartarum*, ed. T.D. Hardy (Record Commission, 1837)
Rotuli Litterarum Clausarum	*Rotuli Litterarum Clausarum, 1204–27*, i, ed. T.D. Hardy (Record Commission, 1833)
RT	Robert de Torigny, *Chronica*, in *Chronicles of the Reigns of Stephen etc*, ed. R. Howlett, iv (Rolls Series, 1889)
s.a.	*sub anno* (under the year)
Shirley, *Royal Letters*	*Royal and Other Historical Letters Illustrative of the Reign of Henry III*, ed. W.W. Shirley (2 vols, Rolls Series, 1862–66)
Stenton, *First Century*	F.M. Stenton, *The First Century of English Feudalism, 1066–1166* (2nd edn, Oxford, 1960)
Stubbs, *Select Charters*	W. Stubbs, *Select Charters and Other Illustrations of English Constitutional History*, ed. H.W.C. Davis (9th edn, Oxford, 1913)
TNA	National Archives (Public Record Office)
TRHS	*Transactions of the Royal Historical Society*
Wendover	*Chronica Rogeri de Wendover liber qui dicitur Flores Historiarum*, ed. H.G. Hewlett (3 vols, Rolls Series, 1886–9)
WM, *GRA*	William of Malmesbury, *Gesta Regum Anglorum*, ed. and trans. R.A.B. Mynors, R.M. Thomson and M. Winterbottom (2 vols, Oxford, 1998–9)

WM, *HN*   William of Malmesbury, *Historia Novella*, trans. K.R.
                             Potter, ed. and revised E. King (Oxford, 1998)
WN, *HRA*   William of Newburgh, *Historia rerum Anglicarum*, in
                             Chronicles of the Reigns of Stephen, Henry II and
                             Richard I, ed. R. Howlett, (Rolls Series, 1885), i–ii
WP   William of Poitiers, *Gesta Guillelmi*, ed. and trans.
                             R.H.C. Davis and M. Chibnall (Oxford, 1998)

1. Map of Places Mentioned in the Text

INTRODUCTION

A GREAT and still, for the most part, unrecognised process unrolled within the period covered by this book, a development that thoroughly transformed English society for centuries to come. My chosen period begins in 1070, so you may be sure that I am not referring to the Norman Conquest. I am talking of the time after the fuss caused by Hastings began to die down. This is not, of course, to suggest that Duke William's invasion of England was an insignificant event without great consequences for English society, only that another major transformation of the English way of life began around a century later, and it is as yet less than fully appreciated how fundamental this was. I am also not suggesting that the social transformation of the late twelfth century was unconnected to the Norman Conquest. The Norman and Angevin dynasties that ruled England after 1066 were French, and their aristocracy, whether from immigrant or native lineages, was French-speaking. The post-Conquest kingdom of England was integrated within a Francophone cultural area, and much more open to its influences than it had been under the West Saxon and Scandinavian kings who ruled before 1066. The social transformation of the later twelfth century was indeed not a product of England, though England helped produce it. It was a great movement within Western society to which the English had to respond as much as did the Normans, Flemings, Bretons, Burgundians and Gascons.

To call what happened a 'revolution' would be asking for trouble, though the word does at least convey something of what happened, even if the French word *bouleversement* expresses it better. Put briefly, society in 1230 was radically different from what it had been in 1180. But since it took two generations to consummate the change fully, the word 'revolution' conjures up something far too speedy and tumultuous to describe what really happened. Indeed, it had been on the way to happening in 1066. But the period between 1180 and 1230 was nonetheless a key one, because those two human generations became aware of their society in ways people had not been before. They began to perceive it as organised in hierarchical groups, and started to find ways to place themselves within that social hierarchy, a hierarchy of what we would call 'classes'. The key event was when unconscious aristocracy (a social élite definable by modern historians) became nobility (a self-conscious and privileged social élite identifiable to contemporaries) and forced the rest of society to accommodate itself to that fact, a process that took over a century to play itself out in England and elsewhere in western, central and southern Europe.

Ideas of social transformation between 1070 and 1300 are not new in the writing of history. The problem for English historiography is that scholarship since the nineteenth century has mostly focused on the Conquest and the changes instituted by the Normans. In some ways this is hardly surprising. However you read the evidence, there was mass dispossession amongst English landholders after 1066 and a genuine cultural revolution, in which the French language and mores became dominant in all areas of English society. Where nineteenth-century analysis went badly wrong, however, was in seeing the Norman Conquest itself as the social revolution, with new forms of landed tenure producing a new society, a 'feudal' one. The introduction of knight service was seen as the key to the whole process. F.W. Maitland, J.H. Round and F.M. Stenton were the three intellects who cemented this idea so firmly into the heads of English historians that much English social history remains written in those terms, even in the first years of the twenty-first century.[1] And if this is so it is because English medievalists – following Maitland's obsession with the social implications of law and the potential of Domesday Book – have come to define a hierarchical medieval society by land tenure and its obligations. The logical outcome of such a view was that the next social transformation must therefore have occurred when feudal knight service lost its vigour, and it must have happened, so the theory went, at the end of the thirteenth century when 'feudal institutions' were in manifest decay. The name of 'bastard feudalism' was given to this supposedly new form of society, where aristocrats used money, physical intimidation and inducements to corrupt communal institutions and the courts to produce a society run by noble gangsters in gold chains and miniver.[2]

French social historians have also theorised about social transformations or, to use a favourite word of theirs, 'mutations'. Until recently, the dominant French theory was that a major social transformation had occurred around the year 1000, when – so it was suggested – the old Carolingian order collapsed in France under pressure from emerging princes, who grabbed royal prerogatives for themselves, and established their regional authority by castles and the violence of their knights. This theory, principally associated with the historians Robert Fossier and Georges Duby, was still as pervasive in French historiography in the 1990s as the Maitlandish legal-tenurial outlook was in England. It too was dependent on a nineteenth-century tradition: that it was privilege that defined social order, a privilege backed up by violence. The year 1000 has now lost most of its social significance in French historians' minds, though I have suggested elsewhere that it is not wrong to see the emergence of knights and castles in the late tenth century as socially significant, if not in the way the Duby-Fossier school believed.[3]

It is the other social transformation suggested by French historians that is at the heart of this book. In the 1970s, Georges Duby and his pupil Jean Flori sketched out the idea of a transformation in the status of knighthood that becomes visible in the sources for the 1180s. Knights ceased being principally an occupational group, defined by their military function, and by the 1220s were everywhere perceived as being consciously noble by virtue of being 'dubbed' (see below, pp. 51–2). The fact that a particular act was held to confer noble status is of no little significance and is – as Duby was aware – the key to the emergence of a noble class out of an undefined aristocracy in medieval society. Knighthood, as I have said elsewhere, became the mercury in the barometer of social pressure.[4] Anglophone scholarship has absorbed this insight. My own theory, presented in earlier books, is that it triggered a cascade effect in society, where other social groups had to define themselves against what was generally perceived to be a manifestly exclusive noble class. So Western society in the early thirteenth century developed a view of itself as arranged hierarchically in classes of differing levels of prestige. Magnates (or 'peers', as they became called in England by the 1250s) developed a superior knighthood signalled by their use of the banner and other insignia. Common knights or bachelors occupied a lower, but still noble, level of status, as did – at least in France – the squires by the 1230s. In England the process continued into the fourteenth century, where an even lower noble group, the 'gentleman', appeared. And, beneath these, non-noble groups also found their level in the hierarchy: 'husbandmen', 'yeomen' and, at the bottom, 'peasants' all learned to know their place. This was the society of the *ancien régime*, which – despite revolution and parliaments – survived in some form in Britain, and even in France, well into the nineteenth century. After 1832 in Britain, as Jonathan Clark tellingly argued in 1985, the display of aristocratic ideals ceased to be taken as sufficient warrant for social and political deference.[5]

This book examines the emergence of a noble class in English society in the detail it deserves. It is divided into five parts, each reflecting a means by which the idea of nobility was expressed and defined. No one part is more significant than the others. But since the key development is how knighthood came to be taken as a defining border of noble status, then knights, military culture and knighthood open this study. The Western aristocracies, since their emergence in the seventh century, owed much of their power to their ability to exploit their position between the royal court and the country.[6] This was still the case in the twelfth and thirteenth centuries, as it would be for centuries more in England. The second part examines one half of that relationship, the dialogue between the king of England and his aristocracy. It has a relevance to the book's overall theme. The transition from an aristocracy to a nobility in the twelfth century was paralleled by the emergence and adoption of an aristocratic agenda against the king. The thirteenth-century nobility obtained an increasingly acknowledged and formal place in the rule of England, and the apex of nobility was then the right to join in the discourse, to be a 'peer'. The third part of the book looks at the other side of the social equation. An aristocrat had to have a following and a country that looked to him, or her, for leadership. This was achieved by a variety of means: economic inducement, bribery, a conspiracy of deference and, ultimately, intimidation, leading sometimes to violence. The fourth part looks at the more responsible side of aristocratic power, the right to do justice where the aristocrat held jurisdiction. The possession of such rights – particularly in relation to capital justice – became part of what it meant to be noble, and fits into my overall argument. Finally, there is the fifth part, which may seem miscellaneous, but is not. It looks at a series of areas of life where noble status altered human behaviour. These include formalised conduct, the expectations laid on noble males and females, and the peculiarly noble way of expressing one's relationship with the King of Kings, for the nobility had a much more troubled and troublesome place in the Christian scheme of things than did the peasantry. This final chapter brings us full circle, for the rite of *adoubement* into knighthood, as it developed in the twelfth century, was consciously imitative of the way a clergyman was ordained into his orders. It enacted God's sanction of noble status. Every area of medieval life had a conscious religious dimension, and nobility was anything but an exception to that truism.

Space was not available to pursue some areas that might have been included in this volume. The education of the noble, and the literature written for and by the social élite will have to wait for another time. Family structure and lineage could have been examined to some advantage, but are not. However, it can at least be said that the subject has been dealt with at length by myself and others elsewhere. The same could be said about the use of material possessions to define nobility. On these matters, this book builds on my earlier, major studies, to which I refer back. The first was *The Image of Aristocracy in Britain, 1000–1300* (1992), which examined the ways in which nobility could define itself by material culture, using Welsh and Scottish society as a comparison to what was happening in England. The second was *The Birth of Nobility* (2005), which presented both a critical and a comparative examination of several centuries of writing about aristocracy in England and France, and a somewhat wry look at the way two parallel national academic traditions had successfully managed to ignore each other's existence. More importantly, it offered a dialectic between the historiography and a wide range of source material on the four key questions about aristocracy that the historiography had thrown up (conduct, descent, class and lordship). There was no particular reason to deal with them in that order, though at least one reviewer had the absurdity to suggest that I saw conduct – being the subject of the first section – as more important than the subject of the last chapter, which dealt with women. Other reviewers remarked on there being no section entitled 'Conclusion', though in the circumstances there didn't need to be. But if such a thing were needed, it is this book, which I rather hope will be my final word on the subject, though no doubt I won't get away with it quite so easily.

PART ONE

KNIGHTS AND THEIR CONSEQUENCES

CHAPTER ONE

✣

THE KNIGHT IN ENGLAND

CIRCUMSTANCES compel us to begin the story of English aristocracy with the knight, though not for the same reasons as nineteenth-century scholars. They believed knighthood defined a new feudal social order. By contrast, I believe that it lies at the root of the identification of self-conscious nobility and, from the late twelfth century onwards, provided a justification for the higher status of one class of men over another. If knighthood is indeed the mercury in the barometer of social pressure, then understanding its qualities and developments will help us understand how social change happened. Knighthood came to England as a mature idea. Knights had been visible as a social group in French society for maybe a century before they arrived as the spine of Duke William's conquering army in 1066. The question of the origin of knighthood is not the business of this book (thankfully), but a summary of existing views is neither out of place nor unnecessary.

The beginnings of knighthood and the appearance of the castle are contemporary, and this is probably not accidental. Both appear in the north of France in the second half of the tenth century. They were responses to major challenges to French society, both through the rise of regional principalities and continuing external threats. As is well known, mounted warriors had been characteristic of Frankish armies since the time of Nithard and doubtless before. What was new about the knight was that he was a full-time cavalryman defined by his skills and employed for a purpose: primarily to garrison the new castles being built by the princes, counts and seigneurs of tenth-century France. It has often been observed how eleventh-century sources name knights as bands associated with particular castles. This is a reflection of their primary purpose: to be a mobile force at the command of a lord, to help impose his lordship and defend his interests. It was this function that brought down the criticism of the Church on the heads of knights throughout the eleventh century. They were seen as the cause of violence in French society, rather than a natural consequence of that society's restructuring.

There was, of course, more to the knight than garrison duty. Since lords employed *mesnies* (military households) of knights, the possession and parade of a knightly *mesnie* itself became a badge of high status. Great lords in all contemporary societies had military households, but in France the *mesnie* was made up of highly trained cavalry bound together by a new ethos, wider than just a warband's devotion to a particular lord. Knights had a fellow-feeling with knights of other lords, for they were a status group with a developing ideology of their own. Lords as much as knights were trained in the same military skills, and the earliest French seals often (though not invariably) represent princes and counts as knights. William the Conqueror's own seal as *patronus* of the Normans had him in armour on a horse. It is for this reason that the use of knighthood to define the membership of an aristocratic class is so very difficult, as we will see.

All aristocrats may have been knights, but it did not follow that all knights were perceived as aristocrats. Most were employees. Another issue relates to knights as landowners. Although some men did military service – including terms of castle guard – in return for grants of land, it is likely that such tenures applied only to the lucky minority of knights. Most knights, especially the landless ones deriving from landholding families, served for other rewards: bed, board, equipment and cash. This sort would have been more useful to lords than those knights holding land by military tenure. Retained knights (*mercenarii, stipendarii* or *soldeiers*) were flexible in their service and had no outside demands on their time. The limiting factor in their recruitment was their not inconsiderable expense to their employers.[1]

This résumé of the evolution and importance of the knight in eleventh-century French society sidesteps the large and centuries-old debates behind it, but since I (and many others) have analysed that elsewhere, there is justification for taking a short cut. I am presenting here a model of knighthood and its development that is intellectually sustainable, and that will be pursued throughout this chapter. The story for us begins with the Conquest generation of Normans. What can we know of the nature of the Conqueror's knights? The fullest account we have of the life of such a Norman knight in the immediate pre-Conquest period is Gilbert Crispin's portrait of the early career of Herluin son of Ansgot (died 1078), before he quit the world for the cloister around 1034. Gilbert's essay is hagiographical, and designed to boost the claims of Herluin to sanctity. Nonetheless, there is every reason to trust the outlines of his account where it deals with Herluin's secular life before he found a religious vocation. Gilbert (*c*.1046–1117) – as a monk of Bec-Hellouin with an aristocratic background – had known Herluin and was well placed to collect information on him. Gilbert's account fits well with the model of knighthood that has been set out earlier. Herluin was born around 996, the eldest son of a family of Viking colonists with a number of properties south of Rouen. His mother was a woman related to the counts of Flanders, and Herluin was plainly brought up in a French milieu. He was fostered into the household of Godfrey, count of Eu and Brionne, where he received an intensive military training and became friendly with Godfrey's son, Gilbert. When Gilbert succeeded his father, Herluin assumed a leading place in his military household. This brought him wealth and attention, and eventually a knightly following of his own. But his career was still tied to the Brionne household, and when he fell out with his master, who apparently resented his growing fame, Herluin lost access to power and patronage. Nonetheless, his sense of obligation still led him to rally to Count Gilbert when he became involved in warfare around 1030.[2] With Herluin we see how Norman society conformed to the pattern of others in western France, where power resided in a magnate's retinue and military following, and knightly training was a necessity for all who had access to it and wished to succeed in lay life.

Of such were the French conquerors of England in 1066, a large proportion of whom, as we are told by both William of Poitiers and Bishop Ermenfrid of Sion, fought for pay and the anticipation of plunder.[3] Many were like Count Gilbert of Eu and Brionne, whose sons participated in the Conquest: wealthy magnates trained as knights, loyal to their duke and fond of war. Others were more exactly like Herluin, leading retainers of the magnates they had been brought up with, men trained to support their lord with their own swords and those of their followers. And others beside were like the members of Herluin's company of knights, which Gilbert Crispin said amounted to twenty horsemen when he rode to support the count his lord. There was no perception therefore that a knight belonged to a unified social group or class; knighthood was common to all conditions of laymen who wanted to be something in the world, however high or low they stood in the world's esteem. So, in 1081, the Anglo-Breton magnate Wihenoc of Monmouth was described by a clerk of the abbey of Saumur as a *miles*, a clerk who also wrote of those who held land from Wihenoc in Gloucestershire and Gwent as *milites*.[4] Likewise, around 1100, we find that a 'certain noble *miles*, rejoicing in wealth and lands . . . on the appointed day arrived with a numerous company of *milites*', in order to woo the Norman widow Hildeburga of Ivry.[5] In the entries of the English pipe roll of 1130, we find that being 'made a knight' was commonly used as a synonym for coming of age amongst landed families.[6] Knighthood was so pervasive in society it could not then be used as a definition of high status, only of manliness.

There is later evidence that points up the miscellaneous origins of the knights who came to England in 1066. William of Poitiers mentions knights drawn from Maine and Brittany, two Norman satellite provinces, and others from the Île-de-France and even Poitou.[7] A source close to the Senlis family, twelfth-century earls of Northampton, talks of knighthood as arriving in England in the persons of two brothers, Simon and Garnier, from the Beauvaisis. The brothers had contracted to provide a company of forty knights from their province to sail with Duke William in return for wages. Simon, however, stayed to enjoy a grant of the town of Northampton and other lands in the Midlands, while on their father's death Garnier quit England to return to Picardy and take up the patrimony.[8] All these men would have shared a culture of knighthood, which gave Duke William's army some cohesion, but they might not have had much else in common.

KNIGHTHOOD AND THE ENGLISH

It is always intriguing to speculate as to what the native English made of these incomers. The concept of retained household warriors would not have been unfamiliar to them, and they were used to seeing their own warriors on horseback, but the all-embracing knightly freemasonry of the French would have been largely unfamiliar.[9] The words with which they grappled with the concept are revealing. There are instances in the Anglo-Saxon Chronicle for William I's reign that look like attempts to come to terms with a new element in society. The most straightforward is the Chronicle's noting of the coming-of-age ceremony in 1086 for Henry, the king's son. It describes him as being 'dubbed' as a 'ridere', and we briefly see here the application of that word to knighthood in an English context. 'Ridere' never seems to have caught on in England, though it may have been an occasional translation for the French *chivaler* for a couple of generations after the Conquest. The cognate *Ritter*, of course, became the German translation of *chivaler* in the twelfth-century empire.[10] The brief description of Henry's knighting indicates that English writers had come to grips with the concept of knighthood, but that its response was not fully integrated. Earlier there is a reference to the building of castles across England and the filling of them with objectionable 'castelmenn', which might well be another attempt to make sense of knightly garrisons.[11] But in the end the word that came to denote what we call the 'knight' was its onomastic ancestor, the Old English 'cniht'.

The eventual equation of 'cniht' and *chivaler-miles* is revealing as an indication of how English society naturalised the idea of knighthood. Its first occurrence appears to be in 1088 when the Anglo-Saxon Chronicle describes Tonbridge in Kent as garrisoned by Bishop Odo's 'cnihtas'. This might be interpreted as a general reference to Odo's hirelings, but later in the same entry such men as the sons of Earl Roger de Montgomery of Shrewsbury are described as 'gode cnihtas' and 'the betstboren men' of the country. Thereafter there is no doubt what a 'knight' is in England: a retained and paid member of the retinue of a king or magnate, or a noble trained in arms.[12] The choice of 'cniht' as a translation of *chivaler* helps make clear how foreign knights were understood by the English. 'Cnihtas' before 1066 were the household attendants of a greater man, and not necessarily people of great consequence. The term's original meaning of 'boy' or 'attendant' still lingered, though 'retainer' was the dominant meaning by the eleventh century.[13] It may well be that the word 'cniht' as originally used was thought of as a better match for the French word *bacheler* (a word to be found *c.*1100 in the *Song of Roland*), which sometimes betokens a young knight or retainer, and sometimes a household servant.[14] And it is clear that the Latin word *miles* might in early times be used in just the same way, for we find a document of 1100 × 1108 from Rochester, in which William d'Aubigny lists his *milites* and includes amongst them 'Ansfrid the chaplain'. There may here be some relic of the pre-Conquest equation made between *milites* and *ministri* (servants or officers).[15]

Domesday Book is frankly not much help in attempting to pin down the state of English knighthood in the late eleventh century, for all the exhaustive attempts that have been made to make its evidence speak.[16] To begin with, it is a land survey and so has no interest in the considerable body of knights who were retained within baronial households for pay or board. It certainly mentions *milites*, and in great numbers, but rarely in a context that is in any way revealing about the *milites* in question. Its principal use is in establishing how English society in the 1080s was still working to accommodate the alien idea of knighthood. It is obvious that when the returns talk of the thegns of Feckenham in Worcestershire before 1066 having four *milites* holding their land under them, the scribe concerned did not have *chivalers* in mind. But what are we to make of the thirty-four *milites* who in 1086 lived 'amongst the French and English' of Bury St Edmunds, supported apparently by the rents of twenty-two peasants?[17] Were they a mixed group of *chivalers* retained in the town by the abbot its lord? There were certainly 'English knights' mentioned in the survey as a feature of England in 1086, but were they simple 'soldiers' or horseback 'knights'? There is no way of knowing.[18] It can be taken as established that there were certainly hundreds and probably many thousands of such varied *milites* in 1086, and that some of them were not very well off, but that is as far as analysis of Domesday Book takes us. Other contemporary sources are more specific in terms of social levels. The celebrated Italian physician Faricius, writing at Malmesbury in the later 1090s, talks of a comfortably-off Gloucestershire woman of his acquaintance, neither common nor of any noble claims, who in 1093 married a knight, 'a man of her sort of level (*parilitas*) in society'.[19]

By 1100, free English landowners were being shoehorned into the role of the *chivaler*, and some were willing enough to try the fit. There were a number of relevant developments that bore heavily on the English landowner of means. The first was the imposition on the English of the same terms of tenure as their French neighbours. This went with a whole range of customary obligations, including military service to the lord of the fee on horseback or in garrison, and a series of exactions concerning inheritance and reliefs. Three early surveys of knight service illustrate this very well. Amongst the holders of knights' fees of the archbishop of Canterbury in a survey of around 1100 appear the names of Wulfsi of Croydon, Ægelwine son of Brihtmaer, Ulf, Deorman, Ordgar and Wulfnoth.[20] Similarly a Peterborough 'List of Knights' of the first decade of the twelfth century includes the names Leofnoth, Swein, Ragenald, Godwin of Upton and Picot son of Colswein. It also mentions numerous unnamed sokemen 'who serve alongside the knights', though not necessarily in the same capacity, of course. Indeed, none of the named English is actually listed as serving as a knight, but as serving 'with the knights' and, in some cases, 'as far as is appropriate to them'. But since the same qualification applies to several Frenchmen in the list the phrase does not necessarily mean that the English did not serve with horse and arms.[21] Though English names are a minority in the Peterborough and Canterbury lists, they are listed along with Frenchmen as subject to customary service. Perhaps most important of all is an early survey of knight service – one of several early surveys – carried out by the abbey of Shaftesbury. The survey, which appears to be roughly contemporary with the Peterborough list, was compiled in English, not Latin (or perhaps translated from Latin into English soon after it was written). It talks therefore not in terms of *milites*, *feoda militum* and *homagium*, but 'knychtes', 'knychtesmetehom' and 'manredene'. The fact that the English language was finding equivalents for the Franco-Latin vocabulary of knight service by the 1110s is significant, as is the fact that the holders of the estates to which the Shaftesbury survey allots knight service were mostly English in name at the time it was compiled.[22]

The second force acting on the military culture of native English society was the willingness of free English landowners to serve their Norman king in the field, even in France. This was certainly the case already in the 1070s. Loyal English levies under the bishop of Worcester and abbot of Evesham played a critical part in the response to the rebellion of the earls in 1075.[23] In 1079, English-born soldiers likewise played a part in King William's campaigns in the Vexin. Toki, son of Wigot, lord of Wallingford, was with the Norman army at Gerberoy and brought up a horse when the king's was shot from under him; he was killed by a crossbow bolt as he helped the king remount.[24] Toki's presence in the king's immediate vicinity in a cavalry battle in France rather indicates that English soldiers were by then riding amongst the knights and had adopted their identity. They may have been a common sight. Simeon of Durham in the 1090s describes visions of two columns of knights, one of Englishmen, the other of French, the French distinguished from the natives principally by their greater arrogance.[25] Toki's sister had married the Norman magnate Robert d'Oilly, which was a further way of linking the two worlds. Toki is only one of the more high profile of many instances of assimilation into the dominant Francophone culture of the court. Another would have been Edgar Ætheling, the great-nephew of the late Edward the Confessor, who had been put forward to succeed to the throne as a young man in 1066. For all that Edgar was involved in attempts to unseat the Conqueror in 1069, he developed a friendship with his son Robert Curthose, duke of Normandy, in the 1080s and had secured Norman estates from him by 1091. Like Duke Robert and all the greatest dukes and counts of northern France, Edgar felt the pull of crusade and appeared in the capacity of crusader in the early Latin kingdom of Jerusalem. In 1106, he fought with his friend Duke Robert against Henry I of England, though he escaped the consequences of defeat. It is therefore a fair assumption that Edgar (himself half-Magyar) was an Englishman thoroughly acquainted with French military practices and

culture, and part of the French international world. His niece's marriage
to Henry I pulled him further into the ambience of the court. It is also
notable that Edgar's nephew, Earl David I of Huntingdon, though of
Anglo-Scottish blood, was a pillar of Henry I's court after 1113 and a
suggested early devotee of the aristocratic tournament.[26]

Perhaps the most evocative evidence of the Francisation of the English
free landowner in the Norman period concerns a dependant of Earl David.
A charter exists of his household knight, one Osbert of Arden, lord of
Kingsbury in Warwickshire. Osbert was the eldest son of Siward, son
of Thurkil of Arden, a substantial native magnate in Warwickshire and
Gloucestershire. It is unsurprising that Osbert should have found a place in
David's household in view of David's English descent. What *is* surprising at
first sight is that in the 1120s Osbert issued a charter to one Thurkil Fundu –
obviously also an Englishman – by which he granted him a tenement 'for this
service, namely that when I request it in due form he will carry my painted
lances on my horses and at my expense from London or Northampton to my
house at Kingsbury. When I wish to go overseas to the tournaments, I will take
him and bring him back completely at my own expense.'[27] Osbert was not
only riding to tournaments in England but travelling abroad to pursue t
he sport in its heartland in France. The fact that he was in Earl David's
household indicates that his master was also pursuing this French aristocratic
enthusiasm. Nothing could be more revealing of the conquest of the
English mind by French aristocratic norms and culture by the middle of
Henry I's reign.[28]

How big a group of English landowners was being culturally assimilated
into the French world of knighthood in the late eleventh century? It will
never be possible to say how many of the manorial lords of England in the
reigns of the Conqueror and his sons were of English descent rather than
French birth. Domesday Book appears at first sight to offer compelling
evidence of the wholesale dispossession of the native aristocracy by
incomers. Furthermore, Orderic Vitalis's and William of Malmesbury's
writings portray England as the prize of conquest, the land being ruthlessly
redistributed to the invading army to the new king's advantage.[29] The
extinction of the highest levels of the pre-Conquest aristocracy by 1085
through death in battle, exile and execution is not in doubt, though it is not
the main point of interest here. It is clear enough from an analysis of
Domesday Book that the few leading English magnates it names are beneficiaries of the Conqueror's redistribution of lands, rather than survivors of
a pre-Conquest order.[30] But that is as far as Domesday Book takes us and as

usual it fails to shed any light on more vital issues, in this case the extent of the survival of English manorial lords, the group that would have generated a native knightly élite.

The survey is interested in the two upper levels of tenure: those who hold directly of the king and those who hold of these 'tenants-in-chief'. At these upper levels we find predominantly French names, though there are nonetheless substantial pockets of English survival in the West Midlands and the North of England. We could reasonably expect to find even more English survival at the next level of tenure down, but this level of landowning is rarely recorded by the survey. Yet a large proportion of manorial lords in England would have been men of this sort: landowners with a level of intermediate (or 'mesne') lord imposed upon them by the French magnates to whom the king had granted the great estates.[31] The most successful attempt at penetrating the misleading obscurity of the Domesday evidence is the analysis by Christopher Lewis of the names of the Domesday hundred jurors, which actually survive for Cambridgeshire and part of Hertfordshire in the satellite documents known as the *Inquisitio Comitatus Cantabrigiensis* and *Inquisitio Eliensis*.[32] Of these 160 men, who owed their place on the juries to being substantial free landowners, half have French and half English names, which would tend to indicate that the manorial lords in those counties would have been equally split in ethnic origin. What is more, the sorts of English names carried are characteristic of eleventh-century thegnly, not unfree, Englishmen, so the English jurors of 1086 were decidedly of the same status as pre-Conquest landholders. But the Domesday survey of Cambridgeshire tenants in 1086 nonetheless still records predominately Franco-Germanic names at the level of subtenants and omits most of the Englishmen who are listed as being on the juries.[33] Domesday Book manifestly does not tell anywhere near the full story of English survival.

A further problem is the well-known shift amongst families of English descent from giving English baptismal names to giving Franco-Germanic ones. Sometimes names changed even after baptism. Robert Bartlett pointed out how a young lad in Whitby in the later years of Henry I's reign changed his name from the Anglo-Scandinavian Tostig to William because his friends made fun of it.[34] The same king's wife changed her name from Edith to Matilda on travelling south for her marriage, and indeed their child, the future empress – called Æthelic in the Anglo-Saxon Chronicle – was also in due course known as Matilda too.[35] The sons of the wealthy Warwickshire landowner Siward son of Thurkil of Arden (died 1139) were

called Osbert, Henry and Hugh. Their generation, the third after the
Conquest, had adopted an entirely Anglo-French identity. It is only occasionally that genealogical notes reveal the English origins of mid-twelfth-
century manorial lords with unexceptionable French names. So Bury
documents reveal that Adam of Cockfield, a well-known Suffolk knight of
the time of King Stephen, was the son of one Leofmaer and grandson of
Wulfric of Groton, an Englishman of the Conquest generation.[36] Charters
of Colne priory in Essex early in Henry II's reign tell us that the then lord
of the substantial manor of Burgate, Suffolk, William (II), patronised the
priory – the foundation of his overlords, the Veres – because his father,
William (I), was buried in it, as was his grandfather Æthelhelm, who indeed
features as the Domesday tenant.[37] Likewise, late in Stephen's reign, one
Ranulf of Bashley, Hampshire (a knight owing castle guard at Carisbrooke
to the earl of Devon), and his wife, Edith, make grants to Christchurch,
Twynham, for the soul of Godwin, his father, and Raesa, his mother.[38]

Later inquests seem more than happy to recall English predecessors, so
in 1260 the quarrelling family of the county knight Gilbert (II) of Hoby,
Leicestershire (viv. 1286) presented a genealogy that commenced with an
Ulfketel of Hoby, Gilbert's great-great-grandfather, who must have held the
manor in Stephen's reign.[39] Another inquest of 1220 recalls that Sir William
Falconer of Thurcaston, Leicestershire, had as grandfather and predecessor
at the time of Henry I, an Englishman called Stanheard.[40] Indeed, there may
have been a thirteenth-century vogue for unearthing or even inventing
pre-Conquest English ancestors. The romance Gui de Warewic was commissioned around 1200 to celebrate the union between Earl Waleran of
Warwick's son, Henry II of Warwick, and Margaret d'Oilly. It rejoices in the
English antecedents of the d'Oilly family: Guy is modelled on the historical
English magnate Wigot of Wallingford. It also celebrates the Englishness of
the Arden family of Warwickshire, principal tenants of the earl: inventing a
'Harold of Arden' to be Guy's mentor in arms and his steward.[41] Early
thirteenth-century genealogical literature associated with the earldom
of Huntingdon makes much of the descent of the earls from Earl Waltheof
and Earl Siward of Northumbria, Waltheof having the extra cachet
of being, of course, a saint of the Church.[42]

Taken together, the evidence strongly suggests that as many as half of
the manorial lords in Henry I's England were of English, not French origin,
and even those whose paternal line was French might very well by then
have been from mixed marriages. The continuing Englishness of the political community in Henry's reign is further attested by the fact that when the

king made his bid for power in 1100, he issued an Old English as well as a Latin version of his Coronation Charter, appealing directly to a substantial Anglophone landed community.[43] There was still French aristocratic migration into England in the first third of the twelfth century, but it is unlikely that it was sufficient to drive the proportion of English down significantly.[44] Indeed, the supposed mocking characterisation of Henry I and his queen, Matilda, as 'Godric and Godgifu' by Norman elements of the royal court in 1102 tends to indicate that they felt threatened by the emergence of a decidedly and increasingly confident Anglo-French aristocracy.[45] The other indication that supports this conclusion is that the post-Conquest English rapidly adopted French names and French aristocratic culture, a development that tends to obscure how English was England in 1100. Some understanding of this can be found in the French *Roman de Thèbes* (*c*.1150 × 1163), which imagines the defenders of Thebes being joined by distinguished if anachronistic foreigners: 'There was an Englishman called "Godriche", who was accomplished and courtly. "Godriche" was a fine knight and maintained a rich household (*conrei*), no one else had a finer except the king himself – his bridle, saddle and spurs were all solid gold. He rode on "Swallow of Lincoln" (*Arondelle de Nicole*), whose speed was faster than the flight of a bird and who galloped along in little bounds. It would be a fool who sought a swifter mount and none, brown or bay, could match him in a race.'[46] To the French writer of this historical geste, English identity was evident, but subsumed into a continental noble culture.

THE RISE OF THE COUNTY KNIGHT

It was this mixed group of insular manorial lords that became increasingly prominent in the course of the twelfth century, as knighthood became perceived as a marker of nobility rather than simply a sign of status and adulthood. These lords – English- or French-born – aspired to knighthood, which provided a common culture for the élite amongst them, a culture that they shared with the almost exclusively French magnates who peopled the royal court. In this social structure, England was not unlike any major region of France at the beginning of the century. But the development of English knighthood was nonetheless significantly different from what it was in northern France, largely because it was defined within a society that was still framed by a pre-Norman past.[47] What knighthood had in England, which it did not have in France, was a political focus outside the courts of magnates, princes and kings. As I have suggested elsewhere, a peculiar characteristic of nobility in England was that it became centred on membership of local communities, and the most distinctive of these was the shire court, one of the legacies of pre-Conquest society to Norman and Angevin England.[48]

The writs and proclamations issued by the Norman royal chancery provide abundant evidence that the shire courts and their officers, to which the writs are addressed, remained vital to English governance for long after the Conquest. They were more than simple customary law courts. The shire court was an assembly at which a whole range of concerns might be aired. It may have been a duty and even a burden to appear at it, but it was also a recognition of a man's status to be seen amongst his fellow landowners and recognised as a man of affairs. At the beginning of the century such men were called *barones*, such as the *barones comitatus Seropesberiensis* addressed in a letter of Bishop Richard de Beaumeis of London at some time around 1123, when the bishop informed them of a request made of them by the sheriff in a case recently held in the county court at Bridgnorth.[49] An account of a shire court of Norfolk and Suffolk held in the later 1140s at Norwich talked of 'the many *barones* of the county . . . and many other accomplished and prudent men and witnesses (*concionatores*)' present. The assembly called on the *barones* of the shires who were present to pronounce upon the nature of the liberties of the abbey of Bury.[50]

The word 'baron' (Fr. *ber*) signified simply at that time 'a mature man of affairs' and might equally be applied to a group of burgesses or the frequenters of a baronial or royal court, such as that of the exchequer (see below, pp. 48–51).[51] But since the mature and politically influential men of the county might very well be knights, it is not surprising to find that eventually the leaders of the county court came to be called its 'knights'. An early consciousness that the leaders of local society were 'county knights' is evident in the writings of Orderic Vitalis in the 1120s. He recalls the hostility of the *pagenses milites* of Shropshire to their rebellious earl when Henry I's army closed in on him. These 'county' knights turned on their lord and his retained household knights.[52] We do not know whether these men were English, French or a mixture of both, but they clearly perceived a common interest in resisting the dangerous ambitions of the dominant local magnate. Orderic is not always safe to trust even on matters close to his own day, but he had been in England for an extensive stay before he wrote this passage, and was himself born in Shropshire.

Within a generation of the events at Bridgnorth, *milites* were being treated as prominent men of affairs. The French-language chronicle of

Shobdon priory (later Wigmore abbey), Herefordshire, talks in the 1140s of the shire court of Hereford being comprised of the bishop and his men, Hugh de Mortemer and his followers, the prior of Shobdon 'and many others: *chivalers*, clerks and laymen, assembled from every side'.[53] By the time of the Assize of Clarendon (1166), this was certainly an accepted idea. The assize refers to the personnel of the shire courts in much the same way as the Shobdon chronicle: the sheriff, his officers, the seneschals of the barons, and all the knights and free tenants (*franco tenentes*) of the shires. By now, the 'barons' are meant to be taken as the king's barons, the magnates.[54] By 1170 and the Inquest of the Sheriffs, the oath in each shire of their circuit is to be given by its 'barons, knights and free men'. By 1176, the Assize of Northampton fully recognised the predominance of the opinion of the county knights in matters of weight in the county court. Twelve knights of a hundred were to swear before justices to the offences against the king's peace (c. 1). They are referred to later in the same clause as the *legales milites* (the 'law-worthy knights') of the shire, a phrase that ties their status to a responsibility for law, order and justice in their county.[55] The shire itself saw things that way. On 9 March 1189, a final settlement between two disputants was reached before the sheriff of Wiltshire in the full county court. The concord drawn up in the court has seven named witnesses 'and the other knights who were there present'. The knights mentioned here were the leading men whose attestation was worth recording.[56]

Knights might very well act as local leaders. When, in 1214, representatives of the county of Devon went up to Westminster to argue against their sheriff for the privileges the shire had secured from King John ten years earlier, the delegation comprised six knights and a Cluniac prior. It transpired during the hearing that it had been the knights of the various hundreds of Devon who had led the resistance to the sheriff's demands that they had argued were contrary to the terms of the king's charter, which, plainly, they had as a body kept in safe storage for consultation.[57] The local leadership of knights was acknowledged by the king himself. In 1212, confronted by widespread unrest, King John had sent writs summoning six knights from each shire to meet with him in London. They came as representatives of their shire to hear the king's views on the situation in his kingdom, and presumably also to give their own views, if asked. The next year a similar summons made it clear that all the knights sent from the shires were to assemble before the king in a single place at one and the same time.[58] The king was taking a step that consolidated what his predecessors

had done. Henry II had made knights into figures of local authority responsible to the king. Now his son was negotiating with the self-same local body.
As Sir James Holt has said, the origins of the national representative parliament lie in this perceived need to communicate with the localities through
their recognised leaders.[59]

THE NUMBER OF KNIGHTS IN THE THIRTEENTH CENTURY

The nature of the local élite communities created by the early Angevin
kings' legal measures is not easily penetrated, despite the increase in documentation these same measures inspired. There has been quite a lively
debate on this topic over the last two decades which has tended to focus on
the issue of the overall number of knights. This may well have been at least
4,500 in any year in John's reign, and certainly more than that if the indeter-
minable number of retained and landless knights in magnate households
were taken into account.[60] This focus on numbers is for a variety of reasons.
The falling away of the number of knights after John's reign is taken as an
established maxim. It has indeed been confirmed by empirical studies of the
knights of the counties of Warwickshire, Bedfordshire and Staffordshire,
though there remains some argument as to whether the dramatic nature of
the fall became visible around 1220 or 1240. Peter Coss has some telling
arguments that it was around 1240 that the royal government began to react
to the evaporation of the administrative class that Henry II's assizes had
created.[61] Accepting Denholm-Young's reasonable figure of a mere 1,250
knights in England in Edward II's reign (on the basis of those whose coats of
arms were registered by heralds in the parliamentary roll of 1312) unveils a
catastrophic falling away of numbers in three generations.[62] It has been
suggested on several grounds that the critical drop came in the first decades
of Henry III's reign, when knightly families deliberately refrained from
seeking the dignity for their sons, or the sons resisted taking up the dignity.
It is certainly a significant fact that, despite the baronial cause energising the
political classes in 1258, barely four hundred knights can be found to have
been actively involved in the rebellion of 1264–5.[63]

Two principal reasons for the thirteenth-century decline are now
accepted.[64] The first is that the demands on knights to maintain a noble
lifestyle put knighthood beyond the means of many families who might
have taken it up in the twelfth century. The expectation and consequent
cost of appropriate arms, dress, entertaining, households and residences
became prohibitive at a certain level.[65] Second, the administrative burdens

on knights were increasing. As a result, men who could afford to live the life of a noble knight still chose not to seek knighting, so as to avoid the onerous duties that would land on their shoulders. These explanations are not mutually exclusive, and their conjunction would certainly account for the dramatic nature of the decline in knights. That the crisis was seen by contemporaries as just that is evident from the measure taken in 1224 by Hubert de Burgh's government to fine (distrain) tenants of full knights' fees who were not knights. Thus measures were being taken to force men to be knights. In 1232 and 1234, the distraint was extended to tenants-in-chief whose resources were deemed sufficient to support knighthood, but who had not taken it up. In 1241, a more desperate measure was proclaimed, when all men with an annual income of over £20 were ordered to take up knighthood, whoever they held their land from. It was a measure designed to include within the bounds of knighthood and its obligations most of the significant landholders of England. Lists of such delinquents were from 1246 being appended to the rolls of the justices in eyre by sworn verdict of the shire.[66] But such efforts to increase the numbers of knights by force proved unsuccessful, especially as the king was willing with his other hand to take money from eligible candidates to exempt them from distraint. In May 1258, the Petition of the Barons concluded that it was the king's fault that the knightly community, once so important to shire governance, was collapsing: 'the lord king freely grants to the knights of his realm acquittances, so that they shall not be put on assizes, juries or recognitions, with the result that, in many counties, for lack of knights it is not possible to hold any grand assize, so that pleas of this kind remain unfinished, and petitioners never obtain justice.'[67]

That such exemptions were issued to men who simply did not want to be burdened with local office can occasionally be proved. An example is Anschetil de Martinwast (died 1274), whose principal manor was Noseley in Leicestershire. He succeeded his father, William de Martinwast, in 1246. William had been a wealthy knight heavily engaged in county business, and indeed was a former sheriff of Northamptonshire. Anschetil's close relatives, the successive Martinwast lords of Hallaton, Leicestershire, were also active local knights. Anschetil did not, however, seek knighting on his succession to his father's manors and indeed secured exemption from distraint in 1251 and 1252.[68] It was not until 1256 that he finally got knighted, and then on his own terms: he secured an exemption from assizes, juries and recognitions, and from being made sheriff. But Anschetil was no reluctant backwoodsman. By the 1250s, he was in fact a member of the affinity of Earl

Simon de Montfort of Leicester, and, by 1256, his seneschal. Anschetil was interested in office and its profits; it was routine obligation he was out to avoid.[69] In August 1258, the Montfort connection brought him to prominence when he was appointed as one of four knights to inquire into the excesses lately committed in his native county of Leicestershire. In October 1258, he was appointed one of the joint keepers of the counties of Leicestershire and Warwickshire.[70] Anschetil was clearly perfectly unconcerned about how knighthood might express and enhance his noble status. He had the resources to maintain a noble lifestyle and make connections with greater men, knight or not. It was the routine business of the shire he wished to avoid, and so he used his connections and money to evade the objectionable ceremony of knighting.

The knightly community focused on the county court is therefore seen by the 1230s as being small and, indeed, shrinking rapidly. The belief is that the regular meetings of the county and hundred courts attracted a core of active business-minded knights and magnates' stewards, who were usually themselves knights. There was undoubtedly a wider pool of knights than these hardy businessmen available to the courts. Sheriffs and justices could usually at least find sufficient names of active characters to make up the panels of twelve knights for grand assizes or the panels of four needed to visit defendants who claimed to be ill, so as to verify their excuses for non-attendance. But whether these nominated knights would actually turn up was quite another matter; often they did not. One of the best-studied counties so far is Warwickshire. Here, there might have been a pool of several dozen resident knights in the second decade of the thirteenth century. But only a small proportion of these was involved in the business of the shire.[71] A study of the seneschals of the dominant local magnate of the time, Earl Henry II of Warwick (died 1229), has, however, discovered that the astute young earl made a point of recruiting his household knights out of this very group of active county knights, and indeed appointed them his seneschals. In this way the earl would have secured considerable influence over the county court, its business and possibly also its verdicts.[72] His action indicates the potential importance of this small community of local knights, not just for the shire but for the magnates who had ambitions to extend their local control within it.

By the 1230s, therefore, the social transformation that is the subject of this book had happened, as we can tell from its fallout. By 1220, knights were very much recognised as noblemen, the leaders of society in their counties. As I have demonstrated elsewhere, they were expected to have appropriate noble seals, residences, households and accoutrements. To embrace knighthood was to place oneself in an exclusive social category.[73] To do so meant incurring substantial costs and, in England, onerous duties too. The costs were a major obstacle and headache. In 1272, the terminal date of this study, Ingram of Oldcotes, a landowner of an established Nottinghamshire family, surrendered his life interest in his manors to one Roger d'Arcy. Roger was to make Ingram a knight and fund for life his household of squires and grooms, as well as his needs in horses and suitable clothing: Ingram was seeking the wherewithal to pursue a noble lifestyle and evade the tedious duties of landholding.[74] Not every landowner was willing to go this far, and so the numbers of knights began to shrink, something that we are fortuitously able to observe in England, where we cannot in France. Knighthood was now a challenge to society. Each individual had to assess how he should react to it. To embrace knighthood brought automatic status and the deference of neighbours, who must call its possessor 'messire'. Those who would not take it up, but who shared noble aspirations and a desire for status, had to find ways of securing it for themselves. Thus the cascade effect began, which we will analyse later, in Chapter 5.

CHAPTER TWO

✛

MILITARY CULTURE

O NCE we are clear about the rise of the knight in medieval English
society, and the consequences of that rise, the culture that the knight
or *chivaler* embraced becomes all the more important, for it helped define
noble status. The knight, as has been said, appeared in the later tenth
century as a necessary human adjunct to the new technology of castles. He
was a novel manifestation of the post-Classical idea of society as being
organised for war, and the warrior being its proper leader. By the second half
of the eleventh century it was well established that a range of military
customs bound the knight, whether he was landed or landless. There is
more evidence, naturally, about the former than the latter, and it is with the
customary military obligations laid on the landed knight that I wish to
commence.

The first question about such obligations is when they entered England. In
one sense it is easy enough to answer. The lifestyle and obligations of knighthood entered England bodily in 1066, for all that some French aristocrats and
their retinues were in the Confessor's England well over a decade before
Hastings. Attempts to trace a continuity between pre-Conquest military
service and post-Conquest knight service have been made, but have never
proved convincing; nor is the question a particularly important one, unless you
are interested, as was Edward Augustus Freeman, in seeing Norman England
as a continuation of the Anglo-Saxon English state.[1] Knights in the mid-
twelfth century had little interest in what went on before 1066. If they ever
thought about it, they concluded that tenure began with the Conquest, as did
the Norfolk knight Ralph fitz Torald of Wood Dalling, who stated in the 1150s
that he held his lands, rents and churches 'of my inheritance from the
Conquest of England (*a conquestu Anglie*)', and made grants for the soul of the
Domesday lord, Peter de Valognes, 'who enfeoffed (*feudauit*) my grandfather of
this fee'.[2] For Ralph and his like, 1066 was the social Year Zero.[3]

Most landed estates after 1066 were burdened by the king with knight service (though a proportion of them were held for other forms of service, some domestic and some administrative, called 'serjeantries'). A magnate's honor was held for a negotiated number of knights owed to the royal army when summoned, a total called the *servitium debitum* ('service due'). It is an open and probably unanswerable question as to *how* these totals were reached. It is a more promising query as to *when* they were imposed. In 1166, it was already believed that they had been fixed from the time of the conquest of England a century before, but since the process of conquest was not anywhere near complete until the 1080s, the totals obviously could not have been negotiated in 1066 or 1070 or at any one point in the Conqueror's reign, but progressively as Mercia and then the North were absorbed under Norman control.[4] Furthermore, some of the great magnate honors of the twelfth century were still in the process of construction well into Henry I's reign, with the earldom of Leicester not formed until as late as 1107. It is not unreasonable to believe that the Conqueror at one or several points in his reign sat down with his secular and ecclesiastical magnates in council and ironed out ad hoc totals.[5] But it has not been possible for any of the historians who have considered this question to suggest precisely when that may have been. It is, however, clear that such totals must have been changed and renegotiated over the decades after the conquest. Indeed, the totals of the *servitia debita* of the magnates' honors were constantly being renegotiated through the twelfth and into the thirteenth century, especially as the English royal administration began collecting information about them for tax purposes in 1166, and constantly thereafter, as in the thirteenth century the *servitia debita* went on to become the basis for assessing the yield of the English taxation system throughout the middle ages.

No doubt there was an element of negotiation between lords and their subtenants about totals too, which must have been changed as need demanded and new fees were added. So when the bishop of Worcester made his return to the inquest of 1166 as to the holders of fees on his lands and their antiquity, he helpfully chose to turn it into a historical exercise. He looked at the evolution of the subinfeudation of his lands in three stages. First, he dealt with the 37½ fees that were created 'of old' (*antiq-uitus*). Then he moved to the four fees created in the time of Bishop Samson (1096–1112), and then to the further four created in the time of Bishop Theulf (1115–23). Clearly, Bishop Roger (1164–79) believed that the original 37½ went back to the reigns of the two Williams, when the bishop was

Wulfstan II (1062–96), the Englishman who must have initially negotiated with the Conqueror the first *servitium* imposed on the see's lands.[6] Clearly also, unlike most lay magnates, the bishop had the records available at Worcester to reconstruct the way the *servitium* had changed over the years. Many magnates in 1166 were driven to conduct inquisitions amongst the senior members of their following as to how much service was owed by and to their honors, a process that has been attributed to the fact that magnates never expected to receive the full service from their men, or perform their full service to the king, so kept no record of it.[7]

What I want to concentrate on here is the way that the demands involved in military service illustrated and reinforced a knightly identity, and whether the demands made on landowners by the magnates who were their lords supported a military culture. As has already been suggested (see above, p. 6), the men who took up land on military terms were a mixture. They would have been Frenchmen taking up new estates on terms familiar from their homeland. But maybe as many as half of them would have been English sitting tenants accepting new terms on their ancestral lands. As we have seen from the Shaftesbury survey of the 1110s, an English-language vocabulary had already by then formed to translate the various customary obligations laid on the native landowner who was now classified as a knight. One that Englishmen would have had little trouble accommodating would have been the universal ceremony of homage, performed to a lord on entering his service or acquiring from him an estate. William of Poitiers in the 1070s had no difficulty believing that the English earl Harold of Wessex would have understood the significance of an act of homage when he did it to Duke William in 1064. The English word 'mannredenn' was already there to employ as a translation.[8]

In a society where loyal service was a principal lay virtue, homage was not an empty ceremony, however often the faith it evoked was breached in the observance. Homage remained a deeply symbolic act enacting the bond between lord and dependant, the mainspring of society. It was a bond whose nature was debated by contemporaries. An intriguing mid-twelfth-century discussion survives concerning the theory of homage and its breach from the point of view of the dependant. A man who has joined hands with another, it says, does so chiefly to offer his new lord military aid and other assistance, but homage is a two-way process: 'he has to look after my interests as if they were his own, while I must do the same for him.' The view is also expressed there that the link created by homage is void if the lord fails in that obligation, and there is no moral wrong in divesting oneself of such a disadvantageous allegiance in such a case, providing it is done in due form.[9]

The act of homage covered a wide range of eventualities, too many to be dealt with here, though a number of instances can be given to establish quite how wide was that diversity. A principal instance was when a young knight came of age and into his inheritance, as a rite of passage: thus, in 1166, a young Cambridgeshire heir, Alan fitz Gilbert, was described by his lord as 'being an immature youth as yet unable to make homage'.[10] It was usually performed by tenant to lord, but might be performed to the lord's own hono-rial lord, as was the case when, in the 1160s, Earl Richard fitz Gilbert of Striguil (died 1176) took the homage of a newly enfeoffed tenant of his subtenant.[11] The dependency that homage evoked might not necessarily involve military service. At some time in Stephen's reign, at Leominster, one Robert of Hurstley wanted to transfer to his nephew and namesake an estate that he held by hereditary right from the priory there. So he surren-dered Hurstley, Herefordshire, to the abbot of Reading, of whose house Leominster priory was a dependency, and the abbot then relayed seisin (real possession) of the estate to the nephew, receiving his homage and oath of allegiance or fealty. In this case, the service required from the estate was a rent of half a mark, not military duty.[12] Homage was done by new heads of religious houses to their lay advocates, as when the prior of Ware did homage to Countess Petronilla of Leicester (died 1212).[13] No less military an act of homage could be imagined.

Homage in all cases was a very personal act: joining hands and affirming a relationship with a superior. It could be an impressive and exalting occasion. On 25 July 1155, William fitz Alan celebrated coming into his honor by a handsome donation of a major church to Haughmond abbey, it being later recalled by one of his vassals present that it was done 'on the day he took homage from his men at Bridgnorth before all the assembled barons and knights'.[14] Likewise, Guiscard Leydet II (died 1221), a leading tenant of the honor of Pleshey, celebrated the occasion in August 1197 when his younger brother Robert came of age on campaign with King Richard the Lionheart and did homage in the presence of the king and Count Baldwin IX of Flanders (probably in Normandy) 'when King Richard had returned from Berry and taken Vierzon', listing as present several English earls and barons.[15] It was important to note when and where it had been made. In his estate papers Sir Thomas Hotot II of Clapton (died c.1278) kept careful notes of homages done to his two lords in 1254 and 1268, and similar notes of homage done to him by a major tenant in 1273.[16] The personal element could be less celebratory. A jury recalled in 1223 that two generations previously, probably just before 1166, the baron Robert of Ewyas had fallen out with his principal Wiltshire tenant, Godfrey Scudamore, and refused to accept his homage for the five fees Godfrey asserted he had inherited, claiming more service was owed. Eventually the king, at the intercession of his uncle, the earl of Cornwall, and of Hugh de Lacy, a friend of the Scudamores, obliged Robert to accept Hugh de Lacy's homage for the fees, so that he could in turn take Godfrey's and place him in seisin without Robert and Godfrey having to join hands in a friendly gesture of acceptance.[17]

Once homage was performed, the oath of allegiance given and possession of an estate delivered, military service was usually (though not always) expected. A major part of it might be castle guard, if there was a central castle in the honor in which the knight's fee stood. Very little is known about the mechanics of garrisoning a private castle in the period of this study. The best-documented instance is that of Richmond in the North Riding of Yorkshire. This formidable castle was in existence before 1086, and was built early in stone. Its position made it a castle with a distinct military purpose in the subjection and defence of northern England. In Domesday Book, its dependent Yorkshire lordship was described as a *castellatus* (castellanry) of 199 manors.[18] Two schedules of castle service owed by the tenants of the honor who served the castle have survived from the twelfth century. We find from these that, around 1130, the knights of Richmond were organised into six groups, who each provided guard for two months. Each group answered for between twenty-two and thirty knights' service, which would be the nominal strength of the castle garrison. The lands that contributed this knight service were by no means all in Yorkshire, but were drawn widely from the North and East Midlands, and even Herefordshire.[19] Richmond may by no means have been typical of a magnate castle and its dependent knights. To begin with, service there was for two months. Elsewhere a period of forty days might be required, as for the knights of the Briouze castle of Brecon and the castles of the earldom of Gloucester in Henry II's reign.[20]

It is not easy to determine how prevalent castle service was amongst the aristocracy of England. But few major honors did not possess a castle. Moreover, within the large honors, there might also be castles held by the greater tenants where subtenanted knights did castle guard. Stenton long ago pointed out the forty days' castle guard (three weeks in time of peace) owed by a subtenant at a castle at Weston Turville, Buckinghamshire, which belonged to Geoffrey II de Tourville (died *c.*1173), one of the major tenants of the earldom of Leicester.[21] Another instance is provided by the castle of

Brandon, Warwickshire, a dependent fee of the earldom of Warwick. In *c.*1138, the earl, as part of a marriage settlement with Geoffrey II de Clinton, its young lord, transferred ten of the seventeen knights' fees Geoffrey owed him to do service at Brandon, instead, one assumes, of doing it at Warwick.[22]

The reality of castle guard was obviously a significant part of knightly life within great honors in the earlier twelfth century, though we will never know precisely how significant. But this active arrangement must have been eroded fairly soon, with the probable exception of castles in the Welsh March, where warfare was more frequent.[23] Before the end of the twelfth century, castle guard owed at Richmond was being commuted for cash payments, and the £21 1s. 2d. expected per annum by the earl was – one assumes – spent on hiring soldiers with fewer outside commitments to interfere with their willingness to do service, especially as regards those unfortunates whose dependent lands were hundreds of miles from Richmond.[24] In 1215, the barons of Magna Carta reminded the king that it was still possible that a man might exercise the option to perform his period of guard, or delegate it to a capable substitute of his own choice, in which case no one ought to be automatically assumed to want to pay to be rid of the duty.[25] Nonetheless, it is no surprise that, in the 1230s, Lawrence of Holbeach, a Lincolnshire landowner, was paying 2½d. annually to be rid of the fraction of knight service he owed *ad wardam castri de Richemund.*[26] The only real evidence of the communal life that the performance of such a duty would entail comes in 1208, and from outside England. In that year, King John, as lord of the honor of Glamorgan, with more than a hint of asperity instructed the barons and knights of Glamorgan to put their houses in the bailey of Cardiff castle in repair, 'and perform there castle guard the way you ought to do and are in duty bound, just as you love your fees'.[27] In these terse instructions from a chief lord you can find an expectation that the knights dependent on a castle should take responsibility for its defence, and maintain a certain solidarity in its performance. It is also apparent that tenants were perceived by their lords as backsliding and obstructive in doing so. It is perhaps significant that we have a picture from Gerald of Wales of the garrison of that self-same Cardiff in 1156 as being made up of a large paid *mesnie* (*stipendiaria . . . familia*) as much as of enfeoffed knights.[28]

TIME OF WAR

Service in time of war was another matter from service in peace. Medieval society possessed an acute consciousness of when civil disorder had crossed into a state of general warfare. It recognised it as characteristic that the state of war suspended many of the niceties and conventions of normal life. So we find in the twelfth and thirteenth centuries the idea of a *tempus guerrae* used to account for events that would not normally happen: in the 1220s, people remembered Stephen's reign as a time of 'grant guerre' when disorder (*desrei*) reigned.[29] This consciousness can be found in England soon after the Norman Conquest. In 1070, the papal legate, Ermenfrid of Sion, noted the state of *publicum bellum* that had existed in England after the landing of Duke William in England, continuing as far as his coronation as king. He prescribed a moderated penance on those of his followers who had killed during it because of their obligation to serve in his host. The phrase, which might be translated as 'open' or 'public' warfare, was already well established by 1066 in the Church's view of war.[30]

It is not just clerical sources that dwell on this as the regrettable way of a world dominated by a military aristocracy. The military aristocracy itself tells us the same. So, in 1166, Walter du Bec recalled that in the time of Henry I he owed knight service for his estates in Norfolk, but that a large outlying estate he held in Cornwall worth the sum of £30 annually, and which may have been held at the time by his mother, was forcibly taken over by Earl Reginald *tempore gwerrae*, that is, between 1140 and 1148, when civil war raged in that part of England. It was a time of forced military deprivations and Walter wanted it brought to the king's attention that the disseisin had not been made good. Several other landowners of 1166 talked in the same way of the bad times of the previous reign.[31] Not many years after this, the pipe rolls following the campaigns of 1173–4 record the outbreaks in the Midlands and East Anglia as a time of *gwerra*, levied by the earls of Norfolk, Huntingdon and Leicester, when theft and arson were prevalent.[32] Likewise, in the later 1230s, the Buckinghamshire knight Bartholomew de Sackville referred back to the *gwerra* of 1215–17, when sheriffs made inroads into the liberty of his father's manor of Fawley, which he was attempting to recover.[33] His lord, Earl William Marshal II (died 1231), also referred back to the same *gwerra*, in which he had looted and inflicted damage on possessions of Reading abbey which neighboured his manor of Caversham, where he compensated the monks.[34] Looking back on his already long reign in 1261, Henry III took some credit for the fact that the country had been so little afflicted with periods of 'hostility and general war' over the past forty-five years, for maintaining a state of civil peace was the king's task.[35]

When there was such a 'time of war', the knight was of course both a principal agent of disorder and the only safeguard from it other than the strictures of the Church. He owed service 'in the army and on horseback' (*in exercitu et chevalcheia*), as the formula often went.[36] The mechanics of the performance of that duty have monopolised a lot of academic attention over the years, though since the 1980s it has become increasingly evident to scholars that paid knights, rather than enfeoffed knights, were decidedly preferred by the Norman and Angevin kings of England when it came to raising forces in both peacetime and war.[37] Paid knights served indefinitely in their lord's household, and the terms of their service were flexible. Geoffrey Gaimar celebrated the military household (*privee maisnie*) of King William Rufus: 'all were *riches chevaliers*, and know that the king paid them much!' Geoffrey noted that the knights Rufus retained (*reteneit*) became wealthy very quickly. They were rich and well equipped (*bien aturnez*) and there was no poverty amongst them. Geoffrey numbered the *soldeiers* (paid knights) the king could summon by writ to be as many as three thousand.[38] This freedom contrasted very much with the army assembled by customary summons. Knights serving as a condition of the tenure of their estates were limited as to where and when they might serve. It was only in time of war that their service was obligatory on receipt of a summons. They could choose not to stay on beyond their contractual period of free service; if they did remain, they had to be paid.[39] So it was that, in 1159, in assembling his great army against Toulouse, we are told that Henry II, 'considering the distance and difficulty of the route, rather than trouble the knights of the countryside, the townsfolk and peasantry', took scutage of sixty shillings a fee across his realm, and 'took with him his chief barons and a few men, but innumerable paid knights'.[40]

The earls and barons of England were nonetheless important in wartime, for they remained the core of any army a king might raise. Their resources and leadership were needed, and it was assumed that they would join the king's army with some force or other. We are not well placed to know how magnates dealt with the need to raise forces for a royal army when they received a summons. One indication we have from a charter of John, count of Eu and lord of Hastings, concerning a campaign in 1166 is that he raised money from his tenants 'for the wages of knights and service in which I am bound in the king's war', just as the king did for his *familia*.[41] It is, however, clear that – except when taxation by scutage was the issue – their *servitium debitum* was more or less irrelevant to a magnate. The best evidence for a magnate's response to military demands in the twelfth century is an inquest the exchequer conducted in or soon after 1170 into the exactions Earl William d'Aubigny I of Arundel (died 1176) had made on his Norfolk lands in response to summonses to go on numerous campaigns between 1157 and 1168. Earl William, a loyalist veteran of Stephen's wars, had campaigned in Wales on all three of Henry II's expeditions there, and himself spent a considerable time as keeper of the Welsh March. He had followed the king against Louis VII to Toulouse in 1159 and to the Norman March in 1160. He would, in 1173, by then in his sixties, lead the men of East Anglia against Flemish invaders. The inquisition tells us he and his officers were assiduous in collecting money from aids levied on his boroughs and demesne estates, and scutage from his tenants. He anticipated expenditure by raising loans from the Norfolk Jews, which his tenants were required to acquit. The earl was in every way a professional soldier and it can only be concluded that his principal concern here was to raise large amounts of cash to employ an effective paid retinue, not enforce customary knight service. He no doubt expected refunds of pay and expenses from the king (as he certainly would have done in the case of money he raised for his diplomatic journey on the king's behalf to Germany), but he was also concerned to field an effective force to acquit his obligation.[42]

Belief that *servitia debita* were symptomatic of a working military system largely depends on a single document: the apparent survival of a writ of the Conqueror to Æthelwig, abbot of Evesham, summoning the five knights the abbey owed for a campaign. If one accepts that this writ is a forgery from the late twelfth or thirteenth century – when the sole copy appears in an abbey cartulary – the whole idea of a 'system' of military service in England collapses.[43] Other than this, the earliest such reference comes in a Norman act of William the Conqueror of 1081 × 87, which mentions that another abbey's tenants might be liable for a summons to military service by writ (*per brevem*).[44] These writs certainly indicate that the king issued demands to his tenants-in-chief for their military support, but we do not know the terms on which he did it. We also know that the lords in response issued their own writs of summons, so that they would have the resources to answer the king. A very early private charter of Robert fitz Hamo, lord of Gloucester, dating from between 1088 and 1106, to a man to whom he had granted a tenancy by serjeantry states that 'when I instruct [him] by my letters (*litteras meas*) he should appear for my service'.[45] Such a reference may seem precocious, but it is a feature in other early serjeantry grants, including one original Warwickshire example of the late 1120s or early 1130s.[46] Fiction reflects this. In the northern French romance *Le Couronnement de Louis*, which dates from around 1130, Count William of Orange sends out his writs (*ses briés*) to his knights summoning them to join him for military service.[47] In another such literary incident in the *Chanson d'Aspremont* (*c.*1190), Duke Girart of Burgundy summons his army in haste and causes his writs (*briés*) to that effect to be sealed and sent.[48] The fact that counts and dukes communicated with their tenants by sealed instruments is such a literary topos in the twelfth century that it must reflect the common experience of northern European aristocracy.

But although it seems that writs of summons were routinely issued by kings to their magnates, and magnates to their knights in the late eleventh, twelfth and thirteenth centuries, very few texts actually survive, even of royal summonses, which is one reason why the military mobilisation they represent is so obscure to us. Summonses were ephemeral documents written up for a particular occasion and purpose, with no archival value. One thinks here of the more than two hundred letters (*letres*) summoning his knights and barons supposedly drawn up by the clerks of Count Richard of Poitou in one night at Amboise in 1188 as he travelled in haste to escape his father, King Henry II.[49] Even royal examples are rare. But where they do survive they offer further evidence against any accepted system of service. A recent discovery is a summons of Henry II of England which can be dated to that same fatal campaign of 1188 in which the king fell out with his son, Count Richard. It is the earliest known text of an individual writ of military summons and runs as follows:

> Henry, by the grace of God, king of England, greets William Marshal. I request that you come to me fully equipped as soon as may be, with as many knights as you can get, to support me in my war, and [that you let me know] how many and of what sort of troops will be in your company. You have ever so often moaned to me that I have bestowed on you a small fee. Know for sure that if you serve me faithfully I will give you in addition Châteauroux with all its lordship and whatever belongs to it [as soon as] we may be able.[50]

At the time it was issued William Marshal (called by his contemporaries 'the Marshal') was a very wealthy man, though he held a comparatively small amount of land from the king, a single estate at Cartmel in Westmorland. The summons could only strictly apply to the Marshal himself. But the king expected him to appear with the rest of his military household and, although he offers no cash in return for this service, he did propose the handsome inducement of the great honor of Châteauroux in Berry, whose heiress was at the time in royal wardship. The king also makes an ironic personal comment about the Marshal's persistency in badgering him for more land. The form of summonses probably took a while to stabilise.[51] But even so, they are remarkably informal documents when they do appear. Only a little more formal than the Marshal summons is the general summons contained in a letter of Richard the Lionheart to Archbishop Hubert Walter in 1196.

> We instruct you to cause all those who have baronies-in-chief in Normandy to cross the sea without delay. You should also summon everyone who owes us the service of a knight in England, except for William de Briouze, William d'Aubigny and the barons of the Welsh March, that they all may join us overseas in Normandy the Sunday before Pentecost with horse and arms, ready for service, and that they should come ready for a long time in our service, so that they need not encumber themselves by too many knights nor bring more than seven with them at most. Also you should summon the bishops and abbots who owe us knight service so that they should oblige us with knights in a way that will do them credit and earn our thanks.[52]

Here again the king is not levying the full service owed to him by his barons, but only a fraction of it. His reason is that such a small number will be less of a logistical and financial burden for his barons. Nor does he say what length of service will be required: the only indication we have for that for the entire twelfth century is a charter of John Marshal, father of the above-mentioned William, who says that two months' unpaid service is the likeliest stretch of time required in wartime.[53]

THE EXCLUSIVE CULTURE OF THE *MESNIE*

The culture and centre of knighthood would – on this evidence – not be found amongst those whom Robert de Torigny called 'agrarios milites', knights who were principally landowners and businessmen but who held land by customary knight service. Rather, it would be in those retained military households assembled by earls and barons to escort them as a support to their dignity, to be their minders in tournaments and their contribution under their banner to the king's wars. Much has been written about this culture, which to Georges Duby was predominantly one of youth.[54] Since war is a young man's game, there is some obvious truth in this idea, though medieval warriors, not least William Marshal (died 1219), could stay in the field a remarkably long time. Marshal – whose first outing in warfare was in 1166 – led his knights at the battle of Lincoln (1217) at the age of seventy-one. Count Robert of Meulan and Leicester (died 1118) fought as a young man at Hastings and then at Tinchebray, forty years later. We have already seen that Earl William of Arundel was in his sixties when he commanded the defence of East Anglia against Flemish invaders in 1173. Robert fitz Walter of Woodham (died 1235), the leader of the baronial army against King John in 1215, is known to have been born in 1148.[55] In the households of such iconic elders, a masculine consciousness of loyalty, endeavour and hardiness would have been bred, which appears crystallised in the 1220s amongst the recognised components of chivalry.[56] A mid-twelfth-century lament from a bereaved household (*conrei*) on the death of its young lord encapsulates the *esprit* evoked here:

> Dear lord! Now you are dead, who will retain your great company? You gave us our equipment, our rewards and great estates; you retained your large military household and kept it cheerful and active, giving us our necessities: mules and palfreys, arms, braided harness and saddlecloths, greyhounds and noble hawks! You gave us sleek horses, gold, silver and rich silks. Your knights were happy because you never let them be in want of anything. You gave them great wealth and everything they wanted. You loved your knights and took good care of them. Those who served you had no cause to regret it, for they never lacked anything. There was never a man so accomplished as you were, nor one so generous. You were wise in council, noble in appearance, accomplished and clever – qualities very rare to find in a man of your rank! What a start you had made in your career! It could be said of you in all truth that had you lived you would have surpassed kings and dukes. But you are lost and gone, fair lord, and have left us grieved and outraged. Now we have no land nor rent and must go back home as soon as may be. Yet we must not talk of return, since we cannot go where you have gone. How will we see either king or queen again without you? We will have to go somewhere else where there is more concern for us.[57]

The odd mixture of materialism and emotion in this lament is very striking, and we cannot acquit the author of a deliberately ironic intent. But the emotions at least can be paralleled. The distraught *mesnie* of the Young King Henry would have said exactly the same on his premature death in 1183. The biographical *History of William Marshal*, sponsored by his household

banneret and executor, John II of Earley (died 1229), was a response to
the death of just such a lord by his bereaved family and household, a lord
called in the 1230s by the next generation of Marshal knights 'that noble
man of holy memory . . . indeed the very best lord and good man'.[58]

It is necessary at this point to return to the materialistic motives of the
household knight. Knightly equipment had always been expensive, and was
rapidly getting more so in the 1150s and 1160s, when enclosed helmets, mail
leggings, horse armour, boiled, leather plate armour and uniform heraldic
robes began to appear. These were technological improvements to knightly
life that probably had more to do with the tournament field than the battlefield.[59] Knights who followed their lords to the tourney in northern France
needed such noble trappings, and had to look to their lords to provide them,
as in 1166–7 did the twenty-year-old William Marshal to his cousin and
lord, William de Tancarville, and, failing him, to his uncle, Earl Patrick of
Salisbury.[60] Twelfth- and thirteenth-century magnates, with their retinues
of anything between five and two dozen select knights, gave not just military equipment but also warhorses, palfreys, money, gifts and annual grants
of 'robes', that is, lengths of expensive cloth, sometimes lined with fur, to
be fashioned into noble garments and mantles.

Giving robes seems to have been a particularly important way of binding
the *mesnie* to its lord. There is good evidence that it was going on in the
Norman period.[61] The courtier-clerk Walter Map claimed around 1180 to
have seen account rolls in which were recorded the robes Henry I of
England (1100–35) granted to his allies and dependants three times a year
(which would imply it was done on the three great feasts of Christmas,
Easter and Pentecost).[62] William Marshal recalled for his men that his father,
John Marshal I (died 1165), demonstrated his wealth by giving out robes to
his inflated *mesnie* in Stephen's reign (1135–54). The Marshal himself had
laid in eighty lengths of high-quality scarlet cloth lined with miniver to give
out to his household knights and dependants at his own Pentecost court in
1219, and he did not allow his mortal illness to interfere with this ceremony
of lordship. Indeed, his biography tells us that he had a stock of even more
such robes in his London warehouse if they were needed to make a good
show. One of Marshal's colleagues at court employed a full-time tailor in
London.[63] By that same year of 1219, as we know from a statement of the
justices in eyre in Yorkshire, such ceremonial grants of robes were regarded
as the definitive way for a baron or earl to express his status and lordship
over men (see below, pp. 50–1). In 1236, for instance, a clerk came to a settlement with the baron William de Beauchamp of Bedford for his support. One

of the clerk's conditions was that he should receive annual robes from his lord 'just like one of his knights'.[64] The taking of robes was – like performing homage – a definitive act by which a man acknowledged his dependence on a greater, as in the case of one William of *Edrichesleia* in 1293, who was a seneschal of John of Mancetter 'and took his robes'.[65]

Since recognised periods of warfare were so rare in England, compared to France, many, and perhaps most, twelfth- and thirteenth-century English knights never drew their swords in battle, unless, like William Marshal, they went abroad to fight. As warfare and military culture justified their status, this may have been inconvenient for those who were enamoured of their knighthood. The long peace in England during the reign of Henry I was remarked upon in 1136 by the supporters of the new king, Stephen, saying their man was the best placed to continue it.[66] William de Tancarville warned the young William Marshal, when the youth wanted to return to England in 1167, about staying on there: 'for it was in no way a fitting place to stay, except for the vavassor and those who had no wish travel the world'. Tancarville observed that Englishmen who wanted adventure and tourneying were packed off to northern France 'to frequent the company of knights', and Marshal could only agree to the truth of this.[67] A similar French view of English ineptitude in arms comes from a canon of Reims in 1160, who contrasts the English with the valiant Capetian French thus:

> English king! Your war trumpets and bugles are hot air, you can only win by deceit. It is not up to me to praise or condemn if warfare is not to the English taste, or if they are nervous of swords. That they spin plots (*telas*) rather than throw javelins (*tela*) is the English way; you may find a bottle in their mouth, but never an edge on their sword. They are more interested in their bellies than battle, in beer rather than bows, in wine cups rather than weapons.[68]

The military culture of the *mesnie* was, as these references reveal, a cross-Channel phenomenon, and it focused on aristocratic enthusiasm for the tournament. The tournament was already a central fact of Francophone aristocratic life in the eleventh century and, as we have seen, the English-born knight with any aspirations to a noble lifestyle was soon absorbed into its world. A royal chaplain, Ralph Niger, employed at one time in the court of the Young King Henry of England (died 1183), the greatest tourneyer of his age, had some sour things to say about his sometime lord's principal amusement: 'Knights have long squandered their inheritances and energy – and most of all, their souls and lives – in tournaments, in pursuit of empty praise and popular fame, and have brought to nothing military expertise in wickedness. For feuds causelessly become battle, and vanity, greed and foolishness are blended into a mixture of simple wickedness.'[69] The Church's line was in general just what Ralph said: a *torneamentum* was a *tormentum*, its *militia* (knightliness) was *malitia* (wickedness). King Henry II of England apparently agreed, and for all his sons' enthusiasm for the sport, he closed down the English tournament circuit that had once flourished at York, Northampton and London during the reigns of the Norman kings. However, a few years after the old king died, his son Richard revived it, at the petition of a group of his leading earls, with several sites being licensed across his kingdom.[70] By the 1250s, certain English towns owed their entire fame to being tourneying centres. So a list of urban centres of around 1250 characterises Blyth (Nottinghamshire) as a place of tourneys, Yardley (Northamptonshire) as a place of jousting, and Northampton itself – a tourneying venue now for well over a century – as where the younger knights (*bachelerie*) assembled to compete. Other popular sites throughout the thirteenth century were at Brackley and Stamford (in or on the border of Northamptonshire), which made that Midland county the very centre of the sport in England.[71]

The European heart of the tournament, however, lay across the Channel in Picardy, Flanders and Hainault, where the great regular tournament sites of north-west Europe were clustered, at places such as Ressons-sur-Matz, near Compiègne, or Trazegnies, near Valenciennes. Young English aristocrats were not infrequently fostered into the leading noble households of this region. William Marshal was one such, and his Norman cousin and lord, William de Tancarville, was renowned as a tourneyer in the 1160s. Even more significant was the fostering of the boy William de Mandeville (died 1189), earl of Essex from 1166, into the household of the great rival of the Young King as tourneyer, Count Philip of Flanders and Vermandois, in the years when the count dominated the tournament fields of northern France. William became very close to the great count of Flanders, who knighted him and assisted his rise in the court of Henry II, his first cousin. The earl's reputation as a tourneyer is indicated by William Marshal's nomination of him to be one of the four Anglo-Norman champions (along with Marshal himself) to meet those of France in August 1188.[72] At much the same time, Earl William d'Aubigny I of Sussex fostered his younger son, Godfrey, into the household of Duke Godfrey III of Brabant, his namesake and first cousin. In 1173, young Godfrey appears in Brabant amongst the duke's *mesnie* (*familia*) as 'Godfrey the Englishman, the duke's cousin'.[73] There is a further parallel in Baldwin de Tosny, son of Roger de Tosny of Flamstead and Conches (died *c*.1161), who was brought up by his uncle Count Baldwin IV of Hainault, his mother's brother, and perhaps his godfather.[74] William (died 1189) and Robert de Breteuil (died 1204), the two elder sons of Earl Robert III of Leicester (died 1190), appear in the Norman household of their father's first cousin Count Robert II of Meulan (died 1219) in the 1170s, indicating that they spent some time fostered there.[75]

When the romance of Guy of Warwick was composed for the household of Earl Waleran of Warwick around 1200, its eponymous Oxfordshire hero launched his career by a grand tour of the continental tournament fields, starting in France. It did not seem to occur to the author that there was a circuit worth pursuing in England. For him, Guy had to be seen making it good abroad: 'there was not a field as far as Spain on which he was not seen tourneying, and he raised himself above all men in reputation.'[76] The pull of the foreign tournament tour for the English knight did not end with 1204 and the separation of England and Normandy, even though it becomes harder to find examples of fostering abroad thereafter. Indeed, the 'lonc sejor' (as the northern French tournament season was called) becomes the thirteenth-century knightly equivalent of the Grand Tour for the eighteenth-century nobleman. Just as English money was much appreciated in Enlightenment Italy, so its considerable value to the economy of the French tournament circuit was noted by the herald Sarrazin when in 1278 he attacked King Philip III's prohibition of the sport in his domain.[77]

The Clare earls of Hertford and Gloucester are an excellent case study. Earl Richard, born in 1222, was to be found as a youth at tournaments in England in the 1240s, and probably in France as early as 1250. His younger brother, William de Clare, knighted at Christmas 1250, also undertook a tourneying tour of France in the summer of 1252. It was a disaster, leading to William's public humiliation and impoverishment. Earl Richard followed him on the circuit the next year and dramatically recouped his brother's losses, only to come to grief on a subsequent tour in the winter of 1253–4 in company with William de Valence, being badly beaten up at a tournament in Poitou and having to pay a large ransom.[78] The Lord Edward, son of Henry III, was another Englishman on the 'lonc sejour'. He first appeared on the tournament field of Blyth in 1256, as a youth of seventeen. He turned up on the fields of the north-east of France and the western Empire between 1260 and 1262, but seems not to have been particularly successful, and indeed was wounded in 1262.[79] Despite this, on his succession to the throne he lifted the prohibition on tourneying in England, and indeed Sarrazin, the French apologist for the tournament, regarded him as the leader of the sport in his day. When the king met his French royal cousin, Philip III, at Compiègne in 1279, he came with a large tourneying entourage which took the field, though Edward himself remained a spectator. It included the earls of Gloucester and Lincoln, and the barons Hugh de Courtenay of Devon, Ralph d'Arcy, John de Vescy, Roger of Clifford and Hugh le Despenser, each with his own *mesnie*.[80] There is hardly any evidence of French knights returning the compliment and seeking tournaments in England.

The tournament world was therefore the pinnacle of demonstrable chivalric aristocracy, and its very apex was in France, not in England, a view that the English nobility itself agreed with in the twelfth century, and was still acknowledging long after Normandy and Anjou were lost to the Capetians. The need to find sponsorship and employment in magnate retinues, to travel and be seen with the great, to attend the receptions, banquets and gatherings that accompanied the tournament in both England and France, all these things defined noble military culture as a possession of only the select few in England. The aspiration to join such circles and the few opportunities to do so, even for young men of established knightly families, was a limiting factor on the spread of nobility below the knight, though, according to Henry de Laon in the mid-thirteenth century, wealthy squires in France were by then staking a claim to be seen on the field with the knights. Since English squires were even less likely than English knights to do the tour in France, that fact may explain why it was that their rise in status dragged so far behind that of their French counterparts. Military culture thus helped define and limit the size of the noble classes in our period.

CHAPTER THREE

THE SHIFTING BORDERS
OF NOBILITY

IF, as I suggest, the knight rose in the late twelfth century to be unmistak-
ably noble just by being knighted, the consequences of that development
spread in two directions. The first was that the very small but economically
dominant aristocratic group here called 'magnates' had to accommodate the
fact. All lay magnates were knights, but now they were obliged to share their
high and noble status with the members of their retained military households. There are unmistakable symptoms in magnate behaviour as early
as the 1180s that the rise of the knight was resented and defensive measures
were taken to bolster a perceived encroachment on their status by a lower
social order. The other consequence was in the opposite direction. If
nobility lay in the act of knighting a man, those of the same, or even superior, economic level who chose not to be knighted had to accept a non-noble
and inferior standing. Again, there are unmistakable indications that many
had difficulty with this, and that the difficulty was much wider spread in
society than the problem that noble knighthood posed to the tiny number of
magnates. The ultimate consequence of all this was the hierarchical stratifi-
cation of Anglo-French society into self-conscious and recognised status
levels here called 'classes' and the emergence of a particular and long-
lasting European society which at its other end is called the *ancien régime*.

The word 'class' is used a lot in British scholarship about medieval
society. This is not surprising in the context of the nineteenth and twentieth centuries' interest in classifying and deconstructing society by social
and economic analysis. Earlier historians of the middle ages lived in an
intellectual world dominated by the assumptions of Condorcet and Marx,
and were even occasionally aware that they did. So we find in modern works
not infrequent reference to the 'knightly class', 'merchant class', the 'gentry
class' and the 'peasant class': groups defined by function (in the case of
knights and peasants) or in more open-ended socio-economic terms to do

with level of income and standing within society, such as the middling group of free landowners that British historians (and it is only they) call 'the gentry'.[1] The perception that there were such groups in medieval society is not inaccurate. Medieval people were quite happy to discuss them as contemporary groups they themselves perceived (with the exception of the 'gentry'). Thinkers within the Church – in particular – were by the early twelfth century already vociferous in lecturing on what they perceived as the objectionable features of knights, merchants, magnates and peasants as representative groups (as well as laying into their own clerical colleagues for their moral inadequacies). Already by 1100, the Church had a long history of looking at society as a unity divided by function between those who prayed, those who fought and those who worked the land. Though the basis of that widespread functional scheme was theological, nonetheless it could be used to lecture the world in general on the shortcomings of groups within it, such as clergy, princes, military aristocracy and agricultural labourers.

Underlying this understanding is a deeper perception in British historiography that medieval English society was organised into a hierarchy of such groups. This tendency is less justifiable. To begin with, it relies on a legalistic understanding of English medieval society as organised round the principle of tenure. The main catalyst for this view was Sir William Blackstone's influential legal handbook *Commentaries on the Laws of England* (1765–9), which inculcated in those educated in law, a group including many nineteenth-century historians, the idea that the characteristic feature of medieval society was tenure by knight service. This defined medieval society as a 'feudal system', with tenure as the link between social groups. When, in the late nineteenth century, this assumption encountered the intelligence of Frederic William Maitland (1850–1906), a devotee of Domesday Book, it mutated into a perception of medieval society as a hierarchy of tenure organised like Domesday Book into groups ranked below the king: tenants-in-chief, subtenants and peasants. This view dominated British historiography for most of the twentieth century. It was rarely questioned, even by historians such as Rodney Hilton (1916–2002), who wrote within a tradition that explained the relationship between classes as based on control of resources, not tenure.[2]

This chapter is not written within the Maitland tradition. I myself do not see much evidence of any common perception in eleventh- and early twelfth-century sources that society was then arranged in a hierarchy of *groups*, or classes, let alone groups defined by tenure. The sources are very much alive to ideas of hierarchy and individual status, but that is a different matter. As I have already suggested, one of the great developments in Anglo-French society during the period of this book was a slow crystallisation of social levels, which becomes very evident before the end of the twelfth century and intensifies in the next. By 1300, society was seen as one of levels descending and widening, with the lay population belonging to one or other category: earls, barons, bannerets (magnate-knights), knights, squires, freeholders and bondsmen. I will also be suggesting here that it is the intensifying perception of exactly what it was to be noble that was the principal factor in this broad transformation of society. For, as the border of nobility crept downwards from the king, generation by generation, it created levels of status in a social hierarchy. Social identity became fixed, and social – as much as material – aspiration became possible.

MAGNATES: EARLS, BARONS AND PEERS

The earliest group to become socially identifiable, and indeed conscious of itself, was that which historians tend to call 'magnates' (from the Latin for 'great people'). In fact, *magnati* was one of a family of Latin synonyms that writers from the eleventh to the fourteenth century used to describe the group of landowners whose interests embraced a realm and who were consequently close to its prince (*principes, primores, proceres, maiores, nobiliores, illustres, primates* and *optimates*, to name but the most common). Magnates are a constant feature in chronicles and histories throughout the period of this book. This was for several reasons. Lay magnates had castles and military followings which made them highly visible and formidable in their own right. A monarch needed them for the support they offered. It was the magnates and their military households who made up the core of any medieval army. Because they were dangerous, a prudent king or queen would always attempt to have the majority of magnates on his or her side in any potential conflict. They were therefore conceded a voice in the affairs of the realm, by which they became the royal 'council'. The function of a magnate to offer aid and counsel to the king his lord will be dealt with elsewhere (see below, pp. 65–71). As the twelfth century progressed, the magnates became more recognisable as a body in dialogue with the king, with its own agenda to follow. For much of the reign of Henry III, the magnate group was the dominant partner in the dialogue. In terms of this chapter, it clearly gave the magnates a class identity, against which others had to define themselves. Part of that identity was expressed by title and associated privilege, which is the aspect I wish to explore here. Three titles are associated with this dominant group within the period of this study: earls, barons and bannerets.

THE EARL

England had one recognised type of titled magnate in the pre-Conquest period, the 'eorl' as the vernacular had it. The title was derived politically (if not etymologically) from the Scandinavian *jarl*, which displaced the more ancient English equivalent title 'ealdorman' in the reign of Cnut (1016–35). In Latin, the English vernacular 'eorl' was generally rendered as *dux*, which we translate as 'duke'. The earl before 1066 was indeed intended to be perceived as a ducal figure, along the lines of a Carolingian regional leader or prince, and superior to the contemporary French *comites* (counts).[3] But this state of affairs could not survive the Conquest. It seems clear that William the Conqueror had firm views about the place of titled regional magnates within his new realm. Before the Conquest, his title as ruler of Normandy was given variously as *comes* or *dux Normannorum*. He was used to ruling over lesser *comites* in his native principality, and it apparently did not suit him as ruler of England that his titled subordinates should be *duces*. There is some evidence that the Conqueror initially intended to continue the pattern of earldoms he found in England, placing his henchman, William fitz Osbern, in Harold's earldom of Wessex, the Anglo-Breton Ralph de Gael in East Anglia, and his own half-brother, Odo of Bayeux, in Kent.[4] In this period, from 1066 to 1071, there were still English-born earls in Mercia and the North. Charters in the years immediately after the Conquest still describe earls as *duces*, whether William fitz Osbern or Waltheof, and indeed when the Bayeux 'Tapestry' was embroidered around 1070, Earl Harold of Wessex features as *Harold dux Anglorum*.[5] But slowly the word *comes* is offered as translation for the English 'earl' in both royal and private charters. In an act of the Conqueror for Exeter Cathedral in 1069, all the earls and counts present are *comites*, even the English earls Morcar and Edwin. A remarkable bilingual Kentish writ of Odo, bishop of Bayeux, translates the English 'Odo biscof Baius and eorl of Coent' as *Odo Baiocensis episcopus et* comes *Cantie*.[6] Whether this shift in Latin vocabulary was a decision of King William or his chancery, or a more general perception of a new social reality by contemporaries, earls were never 'dukes' again after 1070, except in literary sources. The equivalency of count and earl was even made retrospective. The noble Wulfnoth, son of Earl

Godwine of Wessex, who was sent to Normandy in 1051 as a pledge of good faith by King Edward, lived out his life in confinement in Normandy before 1066 and at Winchester cathedral priory after the Conquest. He was eulogised following his death around 1094 by its prior under the name of *Wulnothus comes*.[7] When, in 1086, Domesday Book recalled a pre-Conquest earl, such as Tostig Godwineson, it was as *comes*, not *dux*. It also called the wives of pre-Conquest earls 'countesses' (*comitissae*), for instance Godiva, wife of Earl Leofric of Mercia, although English had no equivalent female title for earl.[8]

Comital status was deeply cherished and appreciated by those who had it in the eleventh century. Soon after his succession to the county of Meulan in France in 1081, the young Norman aristocrat Robert de Beaumont (died 1118) styled himself with a certain sense of self-celebration as 'I, Robert son of Roger de Beaumont, now by the grace of God raised up as a count in worship (*honor*) and power (*potestas*)'.[9] This was the same Robert de Beaumont who was to acquire the earldom of Leicester from his friend King Henry I of England in 1107. His remarkable double-sided seal was thereafter to show him as count of Meulan on one face, and as earl of Leicester on the other. The word *comes* was used to describe both dignities.[10] The equivalency between French 'count' and English 'earl' is established both by the common Latin vocabulary, and other such instances of double identity. Alan III, count of Brittany (died 1146), who acquired the earldom of Cornwall in Stephen's reign, made a practice of calling himself in his charters 'Alan, a count of Brittany and England', or 'a count of England and a native and count of Brittany'. He too on occasion claimed God's grace for his title.[11] On this equivalency, it is worth noting a comment of a century later, attributed to Earl Roger Bigod III of Norfolk by Matthew Paris in 1249, when animadverting on his enemy, the count of Guînes in Picardy: 'I am as much a *comes* as he is!'[12]

The claiming of God's grace for one's estate in this world was not confined to counts; kings and bishops did it even more frequently. In the case of kings and bishops, the grace might have been argued to be derived from a liturgy of anointing. This was not the case with counts. But any ruler over men with pretensions for his lordship to be considered rightful and just in his authority might well consider that it was therefore God's grace or providence that made him a lord, and so might aspire to God's sanction for his (or even her) title.[13] For whatever reason, the practice is rarely found in England after the mid-twelfth century. William III d'Aubigny, earl of Arundel (died 1221), used divine grace in his title in a charter for Durford priory, as does Hamelin, earl of Warenne (died 1202), in two charters of the 1180s, though they are for an abbey in Picardy.[14] Perhaps the most singular oddity in this respect is an act of Hervey Bagot, lord of Stafford, who describes himself as 'Ego Herveus *gratia dei* dominus de Staffort' in an act issued to a Norman abbey between 1180 and 1214.[15] Though the occasional French seigneur does the same, I know of no other English instance of it.

The high status of an earl could not easily be erased. When, in 1122, Henry I, earl of Warwick (died 1119), was commemorated by the monks of St-Pierre-des-Préaux, whose community he had joined in his last weeks or months on earth, it was as *Henricus comes et monachus*.[16] Yet the theory was that the monastic profession extinguished all secular connections as the new monk went through what amounted to a pre-mortem funeral, with an enactment of Christ's burial and resurrection.[17] Twelfth-century sources betray a variety of beliefs about the status of an earl. There is the view of Simeon of Durham in the 1120s that an earldom and its status were conferred by the king, which his contemporary Orderic Vitalis endorsed, adding that the loss of the county meant the loss of the title.[18] Yet for all this apparent decisiveness, Simeon is a useful witness to the contradictory attitudes to the earl in post-Conquest England. He wrote two related tracts on the succession to the earldom of Northumbria after the fall of the Scandinavian kingdom of York, one of the few medieval attempts to rationalise what being an earl involved. These project the view that the eleventh-century earls were a succession of men, some inheriting the office, others promoted, or even removed, at the king's will. On the other hand, he also assumes that, to be an earl, a man had to be in a line of descent from other earls. So Earl Gospatric son of Maldred claimed the office 'as he aspired to the honour of the earldom by right of his mother's blood'. After Gospatric's deprivation in favour of Earl Waltheof, he fled to Flanders and eventually Scotland, where he was granted the fortress of Dunbar in Lothian.[19] Here – as we know from other sources – he continued to claim the status of an earl, as did his descendants into the fourteenth century.

Simeon's attempt to rationalise the succession to the earldom of Northumbria is based on a supposition that the king was the arbiter of the dignity. In supposing this, Simeon appears to have been motivated by a desire to portray the North as a region integrated within the kingdom of the English. Though he is basically right in saying that in both pre- and post-Conquest England the king could make or break an earl, this is not the whole truth. Simeon had to admit that within the Northumbrian succession, some of his earls had to deal with other men in Northumbria called, 'earl'. So he has Earl Osulf taking Oslac as an associate earl in Yorkshire, as if an earl could create others like him. The truth may just be that there were multiple dynasties in the North out of the king's control which Simeon could not fit into his scheme. It is likewise clear, as I have said, that it was understood by some that an earl needed to be descended from a line of earls as a precondition for holding the office.

In fact, there is plenty of evidence other than Simeon's hints to indicate that, in the twelfth century, the king was not the sole arbiter as to who undertook or deserved the dignity of earl. The 'earldom of Richmond' is a case in point. The Breton comital dynasty deriving from the early eleventh-century lord Count Eudes of Penthièvre was very early on engaged in the conquest of England, with four sons of Count Eudes – all called 'counts' – acquiring a variety of lands in Cornwall, East Anglia, Lincolnshire and the North after 1066.[20] But though these counts customarily called themselves 'counts of Brittany' in the Norman period, they were insistent that they were also 'earls of England'. The foundation narrative of the Cambridgeshire priory of Linton, written before 1100, talks of Count Alan Rufus (died 1093) as founding the priory for the souls of his father and kinsfolk in England, 'where he was then made an earl by the king of the English'.[21] But earl of what? The charters of Alan's nephew, Alan III (died 1146), are insistent that he was 'a count of Brittany and England', but the point was that unlike other earls he had no shire.[22] Instead he claimed to be, and was recognised by King Stephen in 1136 as, 'earl of Richmond', his principal castle in Yorkshire.[23] We get some further insight into an earl's own attitude to his status in the case of this Alan, who in 1140 was sent by King Stephen to oust Reginald, one of King Henry's bastards, from Cornwall, over which the empress, his half-sister, had made Reginald earl. Once he had successfully reclaimed Cornwall from Reginald, he summoned the shire court to Bodmin and there, amongst other things, he issued a charter that commemorated the soul of his uncle Brian 'of whose inheritance I have the land of Cornwall'.[24] This same charter described him as both earl of Cornwall and Richmond, and said that he was earl 'by the grace of God', with no mention of King Stephen's grant. For Alan, his earldom was a matter of hereditary status and providence as much as any royal disposition.[25]

Royal writs addressed to shire courts in the reigns of the Norman kings occasionally address the earl of the shire, if it possessed one. The Norman earl continued to receive the pre-Conquest payment of the 'third penny', that is, a third of the profits of justice in shire and hundred courts. It was described in 1141 by King Stephen 'as what the earl should get', and by Earl Simon II of Northampton (died 1153) not much later as 'the third penny which goes with my earldom'.[26] This prerogative was jealously guarded by earls, and became attached to the dignity in the public mind. Indeed, a study of charters of King Henry II creating earls concludes that the third penny was the sole definitive indication of the award of the status of an earl.[27] Unsurprisingly, an earl would thereafter fight hard to gain the 'third penny' if it was withheld by obstreperous sheriffs or the exchequer, a concern we find with Robert III of Leicester in 1170 and with his colleagues and successors for a century thereafter. It was not so much the money an earl fought for as a recognition of his standing, however useful the money might be. Earls were insistent on their right to receive it into the late thirteenth century.[28] But Alan III of Richmond is one of a number of mid-twelfth-century earls who were divorced from any association with a shire that accounted at the exchequer and so could not expect the third penny.

Pembroke is a particularly relevant case. Though outside England, it had an earl in the person of Arnulf de Montgomery until his dispossession in 1102. Even after his dispossession and exile, Arnulf retained the style of *comes*.[29] In 1138, King Stephen's favourite, Gilbert fitz Gilbert (died 1148), was granted Pembroke and the title of earl. Gilbert was another of Stephen's creations who expressed the view that providence as much as the king had made him earl. He talked of his lands in Wales as 'those parts which divine goodness has annexed to my authority'.[30] When, in 1154, Pembroke was taken back into the royal domain, its dispossessed young heir, Richard fitz Gilbert (died 1176), retained – without apparent royal sanction – the title of earl. Like the Richmonds, he fixed on a castle as his alternative seat. In this case, it was his Monmouthshire castle of Chepstow (Striguil). When his wife, Aoife, the heiress of Leinster, had to choose a title, she simply called herself 'Aoife, the Irish countess, the wife of Earl Richard'.[31] Similarly, the dispossession by King Henry II of the Senlis family of the disputed honor of Huntingdon-Northampton caused the young heir, Simon III de Senlis (died 1184), settled now in Lincolnshire, to choose to call himself simply 'Earl Simon' without any territorial designation; either that or he alluded to his father's dignity and to his kinship with the great earls of Leicester. Only rarely did Simon assume the contested title of Northampton, and that probably not until after the restoration of his father's earldom in 1174.[32] So alongside the administrative legacy and dimension of the earldom was the simultaneous belief that it was a personal dignity which was not necessarily erased by royal dispossession.

Claims to comital status could last many generations and surface in odd ways. The earldom of Pembroke was eventually revived in 1199 when King John 'belted' (see below, p. 47) his then favourite, William Marshal, as earl under that title and (after a delay) handed to him the castle and lordship by right of his wife. But even before 1199, Marshal was insisting in his charters that, even if he was not an earl, his wife, Isabel, Richard fitz Gilbert's daughter by Aoife, was a countess. Before his belting in 1199, some sources called Marshal an 'earl', and while he was still alive others called his son, the younger William Marshal, an earl too. It was not unusual as late as 1200 either in England or France for the sons and heirs of counts to be credited as counts in their fathers' lifetimes.[33] A very evocative self-accreditation with comital status is provided by the earls of Hereford. As far as Henry II of England was concerned, the grossly inflated earldom created by Earl Roger ended with his death. Roger was succeeded in turn by his brothers Walter, Henry and Mahel, the last dying childless in 1165. None of his brothers was given or claimed the title of earl. Instead they went by the title of 'royal constable'. At length, in 1200, Mahel's great-nephew Henry de Bohun was recognised as earl of Hereford by King John. Some time before 1220, one of the new Earl Henry's clerks drew up a charter in which he reviewed previous generations of the family. Earl Roger's brothers all appear there, but not as 'constables': they are 'Earl' Walter, 'Earl' Henry and 'Earl' Mahel.[34] Another such example of wilful self-accreditation as earl is found in the case of Henry fitz Count (died 1222), the illegitimate son of Earl Reginald of Cornwall (died 1176). Henry was a loyalist to King John and he used the turbulent circumstances of the reign to obtain control of the county of Cornwall. Once established there, he issued charters describing himself as 'Henry earl of Cornwall, the son of Earl Reginald', a title that was not recognised by either King John or Henry III's regency council.[35] Such instances of self-creation as earls did not entirely disappear as the thirteenth century progressed. King Henry III's half-brother, William de Valence (died 1296), was given control of Pembrokeshire and a proportion of Leinster by right of his marriage to Joan, granddaughter of Earl William Marshal I. Valence's charters usually describe him as 'lord of Pembroke' or 'lord of Pembroke and the brother of the lord king Henry' until as late as 1285. But from 1283 he is referred to by others, and eventually himself, as 'earl'. It is likely that his wife's usual style of 'countess of Pembroke' convinced the world he was an earl, but he was only formally recognised as such very late in his life.[36]

The fact that earldoms had lives of their own throughout the period of this study explains why kings often took a close supervisory role in the management of the dignity, most usually by restricting it to a very tiny élite amongst the magnates. Some historians have therefore seen an 'anti-comital' policy in the way kings were reluctant to create and continue earldoms (with the odd exception, such as Kings Stephen and Edward III).[37] I would myself suggest that this was not so much a matter of policy, but rather a reflex reaction of suspicion to the level of aristocracy that posed the most obvious threat to royal dignity. Royal resistance to replacing ealdormen after death or exile has been detected by historians as early as the time of Æthelred II of England (978–1016). The Conqueror appears to have taken action to demote the status of earl in 1070, and created very few earls in his reign. The pre-Conquest idea that each shire in England was under an earl's supervision was already defunct by 1075. Neither of the Conqueror's sons made many earls, and when Henry I died in 1135, there were only seven men credited as earl in England, fewer than when the Conqueror died. This situation was literally revolutionised between 1138 and 1140 by King Stephen, who deliberately expanded the number of earls so that there were few shires in England that did not have some association with an earl. His early creations of earldoms up to 1138 had begun as patronage and reward, but by 1140 they had become something more. Stephen's intention in doing this has been much debated, but the most likely explanation (to me) is that he intended earls after 1138 to have a universal military and administrative role as a response to the first serious political crisis of his reign. It is best accounted for as an attempt to tie some of the greatest of the landed aristocracy into the security and administration of the shires where their influence was concentrated, though a few earls (such as Oxford and Hertford) had little or no landed base in the counties from which they took their title.[38]

Henry II thus inherited a larger number of earls on his succession to England than had any of his predecessors. Some earldoms were suppressed after 1154, but not in any systematic way. The only methodical element in Henry II's approach to the earldoms of England was a not unprecedented reluctance to accept their automatic hereditability.[39] By 1156, York, Hereford, Somerset and Worcester had lost their earls; most, however, even those created for Stephen's intimates (such as Arundel, Derby and Hertford), survived. What did disappear rapidly was Stephen's experiment in subordinating sheriffs and shire administration to the earl. With the exceptions of Cheshire and Cornwall, there were to be no 'administrative' earls in Angevin England, and earls were no longer addressed in charters sent to specific shire courts.[40] The dignity of earl was to remain closely supervised until the end of the thirteenth century. Not all earls succeeded in obtaining the third penny of their shires, whose concession remained a mark of royal favour. When a man with a claim to the title of earl entered King Henry II's hall – we are told by Ralph de Diceto – he would have his title scrutinised and authorised before being announced at the door by a herald. This happened in 1180 to William de Mandeville, earl of Essex, when he approached the king to ask for the additional comital style of Aumale, which he claimed from his marriage to the heiress of William le Gros.[41] A further, and more conclusive, check was the ceremony of 'belting' a sword, representing the passing of an earldom to a new grantee, or even an heir. Although first mentioned in the 'belting' of Bishop Hugh de Puiset of Durham as earl by King Richard in 1189, the ceremony must have been older. It closely resembles the *adoubement* conferred both on knightly retainers new to a lord's service, or on aspirants to knighthood, and it also involved the ceremonial use of a 'sword of the county', a symbol of comital dignity in Western society since the eleventh century. It was not until the end of the thirteenth century that the king relaxed the right of belting an earl on his inheritance of the dignity, the last occurrences being the successions to Lincoln and Cornwall in 1272.[42] Lastly, kings issued charters to new earls, which gave them a chance to set out the terms on which they were to be held. The earliest of these for England survives from Stephen's reign, when in 1140 the king conferred the *comitatus* of Hereford on the earl of Leicester.[43] No doubt charters of conferment were issued earlier than this. A charter was issued in Scotland by King David before 1139 to Earl Duncan of Fife on his elevation, and the practice is unlikely to have been older in Scotland than in England.[44]

The particularly sensitive place of the earl in the emerging nobility of England is well attested by the surviving bulk of evidence, and by the abundant indications of the ambition of magnates to secure such status, even in the teeth of royal opposition. Earls were the most visible and influential members of the magnate group at the head of society. Their status was acknowledged, proclaimed, debated, ritualised and sometimes resisted. As with bishops and their consecration, the occasional earl dated charters by the year of his possession of the office.[45] Before the end of the period of this study, what were originally items of royal insignia – such as the jewelled and gilded coronet – were being aspired to by earls and countesses. The coronet was, according to one twelfth-century source, a symbol of *seignorie* (lordship) as much as *royautie*.[46] Likewise, a *virga* (Fr. *verge*) or rod, fashioned from precious metals, was recognised as a symbol of command and lordship applicable to nobles of such high status. It was being borne as insignia by some German and French counts before the 1180s.[47] Items such as these, and the more ancient use of the ceremonial sword and belt, affirmed the status of the earl above the rest of the aristocracy.[48] With the advent of the earl, an exclusive social level was established, and its epiphany helped define the status of those magnates who did not possess comital status, as we will now go on to see.

THE BARON

The great majority of men referred to as *magnati* in eleventh-century sources were not earls and bore no title, hereditary or otherwise. By the end of the twelfth century, however, they were being generally referred to as 'barons' (*barones*) and their estates were 'baronies' (*baroniae*). The word itself derives from the Franco-Germanic *ber*, which essentially means a 'mature, experienced male', as opposed to a young and unproven one. For this reason one can talk in medieval French of *baruns chevaliers* without incongruity: it simply means 'manly knights'.[49] The word 'baron' had no exclusive application to aristocrats. In French, the word can apply to warriors, lords, bishops and saints, though in the plural it often means 'leading followers'. So, around 1138, Geoffrey Gaimar can imagine King Edgar of England holding a council and say, 'he had there *cuntes* (earls), *baruns, chasez* (household dignitaries), archbishops and abbots'.[50] The word had made a transition into Latin (*baro*, pl. *barones*) well before the period of this study and in Latin its meaning eventually became more focused than the French cognate. In the eleventh century, it retained its general sense of 'leading man'. So the *barones* of a lord were his (male) followers, and the term might serve as a synonym for other generalised descriptions, such as *homines, fideles* or *vassali*. So, in the 1140s, Matilda de Senlis referred to a transaction she had carried out before her son, the Essex baron Walter fitz Robert, lord of Dunmow, 'and his *barones*'.[51] As with the French cognate, *baro* would do for any circumstance where a word for 'leading man' was required. This might be in an urban context. So the leading citizens of Bristol were *barones*, possessing estates called *baroniae* in the middle of the twelfth century. The leading citizens of the port of Sandwich were also *barones* in 1127, and the word was applied to all the leaders of patrician families of the Cinque Ports in due course.[52] Likewise, the leading men of a shire assembled in its court were likely to be called its *barones*, as was the case with the 'barons of Shropshire', also in 1127.[53] The leading followers of any magnate might also be called his barons. The *Leges Henrici Primi* (*c*.1118) talks of 'the barons of the king, or of other men'. From this comes the misleading concept of 'honorial barons' as a distinct level of social standing in the tenurial hierarchy propagated by Sir Frank Stenton.[54]

However, the principal sense of the Latin word *barones*, which would emerge increasingly in the twelfth century, was of the *king's* leading men, the magnates who were his direct tenants and who were recruited to his court. As early as the reign of Henry I (1100–35), royal charters routinely distinguish earls from the barons in their opening addresses, as if barons were a separate degree of status. The shift can be seen elsewhere. The leading men of the shire courts were being called 'knights' by the mid-twelfth century (see above, pp. 14–15), not 'barons', and the idea of there being 'urban' barons was seen as needing explanation by the 1160s. It was not so much that the word 'baron' changed its meaning, simply that one of its meanings became predominant, and therefore dating its emerging exclusivity is not easy. The 1170s seem to be the decade where perceptions were sharpening. The writer Thomas of Kent around 1180 still displays multiple senses of the term. For him, a *ber* can simply be 'a man', and *barnage* means 'manpower', but he also depicts a king surrounded by *ses barons plus hals*.[55] However, by 1174, when William fitz Stephen, Becket's hagiographer, had to pause and explain to his readers why the citizens of London were called 'barons', the narrowing process must have become noticeable to all, for by then the 'baron' was normally perceived as being a magnate. Though other towns have citizens (*cives*), he said, London in its greatness has barons. Successive generations of writers felt obliged to comment on the peculiarity, with a degree of hostility. The anonymous French author of a history of Normandy and England, who visited the south-east of England in 1217, noted the oddity of 'the burgesses of London who insist on calling themselves barons'. According to Matthew Paris, Henry III in 1248 professed himself sickened by the wealth of 'those London peasants (*rustici*) who call themselves barons'.[56] In 1212, a jury of the county of Shropshire seemed to know what it meant when it referred in a list of tenants-in-chief to some men (Roger de Mortemer, Hugh Pantolf, Robert Corbet and others) as *barones*, and others simply as *milites*.[57]

Just as earls were marked out from the rest of the nobility by distinct rights, and eventually insignia, barons too found ways to identify their status. The most obvious – and perhaps inconvenient – was the entry fine into an estate which was said to be held *per baroniam*. As an indicator of status, the demand for such reliefs lacked regularity until it was fixed at the sum of £100 by Magna Carta. The Coronation Charter of Henry I (1100) implies that the relief had been unfixed in his late brother's reign, as Henry I promised to charge an incoming earl, baron or tenant-in-chief no more than what was reasonable, and the relief continued to be variable in his reign. Although 100 marks or £100 were the most frequent charges in the reigns of Henry II and his sons, it could be a lot more, especially under John's capricious rule. But at least when the baronial relief was fixed it established that a man was a direct tenant of the king, and those who had to pay it who were not earls were barons.[58] As a marker of baronial status therefore, the baronial relief has its problems, but at least it raised a landowner in the king's eyes. Matthew Paris reported that in conversation with Henry III in March 1257 the king was able to recall 250 of them for him.[59] It may be that the king had been put to learn them as a boy, and, if so, it was because the holders of baronies were of personal concern to him.

Any marks of status that attached to the baron generally referred back to his relationship with the king, whether economic (in the case of the baronial relief) or related to the king's expectation that certain men ought to be consulted in the affairs of the kingdom. From the early twelfth century, it was the custom for written summonses to be sent out to assemble magnates to give their 'aid and counsel' to the king. The summonses were sent individually and by name to certain magnates. They went out as much to earls and ecclesiastical prelates as to untitled magnates, but the receipt of such a summons from the chancery might be taken as mark of baronial status. It affirmed a personal relationship between a magnate and the king, which singled him out from the body of the king's subjects. As with many features of medieval life, it was a relationship that might be cemented by an oath, as when the Devonshire baron Henry de Pommeraye swore faith as one of King John's intimates to report any conspiracy against the king that came to his attention.[60]

There were, therefore, several ways that the medieval English mind could justify a perception that the baron belonged to a status level within society. It could be by his behaviour. In 1218, in the aftermath of the Barons' War, a minor member of the Yorkshire family that held the office of steward of Richmond, one John of Thornton, was reported by the justices in eyre in the North for riding out with an armed retinue of fifteen horsemen. In particular, at Christmas 1217, he had somehow occupied Richmond castle and there distributed cloth worth the substantial sum of

100 marks to his retinue 'as if he had been a baron or earl'.[61] The offence against a perceived hierarchy of nobility is obvious: only magnates awarded robes and held Christmas feasts. There were also materialistic considerations. We find the baron inserted into a clear hierarchy of status in August 1194 in the tournament regulations issued by King Richard the Lionheart. In a ranked list of fees for a licence to hold a tournament, an earl would pay twenty marks, a *baro* ten, a landed knight four and a landless knight two.[62] Though based on a perception of likely economic resources, this places a 'baron' at a status level between earl and knight. The formularies of the first half of the thirteenth century duplicate this arrangement in a more social context, describing model correspondence for a hierarchical list of secular groups: *comites, barones, milites* and *libere tenentes*.[63] Barons were visualised as talking to their equals in a different way from the way they addressed or were addressed by knights, with one formulary making the hierarchical thinking clear when it looks at correspondence between notional equals. Its instructions (dating from the 1230s) state that

> if an earl should write to an earl, or a baron to a baron, the more noble and wealthy man should take precedence; if it is a knight writing to a knight, precedence rests on age and military experience, unless it happens that one of them is a sheriff or bailiff; if it is a knight to a free man, the knight takes precedence; if a free man to his fellow (*par*), his fellow should be given precedence unless the other should be a bailiff.[64]

This was a society where a social hierarchy was understood and discussed. The existence of 'barons' acknowledged that there was a need for another recognised and recognisable level between the titled earl and the dubbed knight in order to acknowledge the nobility and wealth of the magnate who was not an earl. Even within those levels there was a jostling for individual status, but the levels were nonetheless there.

KNIGHTS AS A SOCIAL GROUP

This brings us to the next level perceived within the developing social hierarchy of the late twelfth century, the level to which we have already devoted two chapters. The act of knighting (*adoubement*) has been perceived since the 1970s as transformational in the appearance of a self-conscious nobility, and I will not be differing from that view here. The work of Jean Flori and Georges Duby suggested that the knight's status was transformed at the end of the twelfth century.[65] From a situation around 1100 where all male aristocrats were knights, but not all knights were aristocrats, Anglo-French society shifted before 1200 to a stance where the ritual of creating him a knight made a man noble. That view is explicit in the tract on levels of society written around 1180 by the Champenois clerk Andrew the Chaplain, who pronounced that the prince's power to make a man a knight, even if the candidate were nothing but a merchant, ennobled him.[66] It is implicit in many other contemporary sources, particularly the late twelfth-century romances, where men described as *chivalers* are routinely depicted with the resources, aspirations and qualities of magnates. Likewise, the earliest conduct books, which appear in the 1170s, also assume that the *chivaler* is a man of high nobility.[67]

As we have already seen (above, pp. 13–16), by the middle of the twelfth century the knight was regarded as the leading member of local communities in England. It follows that the consolidation of the local eminence of knights would influence their status in other contexts than the county court. When, in 1163, Earl William of Arundel received a summons to campaign in Wales, he found himself at odds 'with the knights of the honor of Arundel' and it was by an inquest of the four 'oldest, most respected and legally experienced' of them that the issue was settled.[68] In a charter dated at Scrooby, Yorkshire, in 1178, the clerk of John de Lacy, constable of Chester, in whose name it was issued, listed the witnesses of his lord's court hierarchically, commencing with five *milites*. When a clerk of Walchelin Maminot, lord of the honor of Ellesmere, recorded late in Stephen's reign in his master's name the doings of a session of Walchelin's court, he said that it was all done 'before myself and my knights' (*coram me et militibus meis*). Similarly, in the reign of Henry II, the deliberations of the court of Osbert fitz Hugh, lord of Richard's Castle, were conducted 'with the advice of my knights, neighbours and men experienced in law' (*consilio militum meorum et vicinorum meorum et legalium hominum*).[69] In the context of a court, clerks seemed to assume by then that the leading men in its deliberations would be knights, and this is reflected in the witness lists of the documents they created. In 1218, a fine was reached in the honor court of the abbots of Peterborough at Castor 'before the knights of the barony of Peterborough'.[70]

It is worth restating here that the idea that a knight had *status* within society just by being a knight was nothing new in the 1160s. It attached to the offspring of some knights too. So it was written of Robert de Béthune, later bishop of Hereford (1131–48), that he was 'a man venerable and acceptable to the Lord, who was born to quite a noble family of the degree (*ordo*) of knight'.[71] The *Dialogue of the Exchequer* likewise discourses in the 1170s on the status appropriate to one who 'is distinguished by the dignity of knighthood', even a knight in distressed circumstances. He must not be imprisoned with common debtors, however poor he may be.[72] But, even in the 1160s, it could be said, as Wace of Bayeux did, that in any assembly of knights there were rich and poor, rude (*villainz*) and courtly (*cortois*).[73] Society's ideas of knighthood were unfixed for much of the twelfth century. All knights had status of some sort, and some were willing to allow that the status was quite high providing the knight's lineage would support it. The idea of a 'noble knight' was not unheard of in the eleventh century. On the other hand, there was no doubting in the contemporary mind that still in the twelfth century some knights were poor and ill-educated in society's expectations of noble conduct, and the status of that sort of knight was consequently low and certainly not noble.

By the early thirteenth century, the negotiable status of knighthood had ended. By 1230, to be a knight was to be self-evidently noble and set apart from other men, as we have already seen echoed in the formularies of that decade. The development had become evident to everyone as early as the 1170s, in the sense that it was being resisted as the existing noble *habitus* was increasingly challenged by it.[74] There is a famous passage in the Battle Abbey Chronicle (a product of the 1180s) where the powerful and wealthy justiciar Richard de Lucy (died 1179) turns on a local Sussex knight in his court, who has offended him by apparently boasting of a round seal of the type commonly employed by magnates (usually over 60mm in diameter): 'it was not the custom in the past for every petty knight (*militulus*) to have a seal. They are appropriate for kings and great men only.'[75] We can therefore see resistance in some minds to the consolidation of the knight as a noble dignity claiming attributes formerly exclusive to magnates. It can be seen in other ways too. The tournament regulations of 1194 distinguish between the standing of a knight who has land, and a knight who makes his living in the retinue of a greater man. But more significant yet was the appearance of the 'banneret' as a degree of superior knighthood.

In England and France, the superior status of magnate-knighthood, the banneret, can only have been produced by a feeling that common knights were trespassing on the status of better men. Evidence for the banneret surfaces in the late 1170s, when knights *portant banières* are known to have been listed separately in a lost tournament roll of the great meeting at Lagny-Torcy (1179). The significance of the banner as an ensign of high status and the power of command is stated unequivocally in 1187 by Ralph

Niger, a former household chaplain of the Young King Henry of England:
'it is the prerogative of a leader to have a banner borne before him, so that
all and sundry might always be able to mark him out and follow.'[76] The idea
that some knights are distinguished by banners recurs in England in the
1190s and in France in the first decade of the thirteenth century. In 1214,
William le Breton, chaplain of Philip II of France, talked of a group of
prisoners after Bouvines as made up of counts and twenty-five 'others of
such nobility that they rejoiced in the insignia of a banner'.[77] By the middle
of the century, the Latin words *miles vexillifer* or *banneretus* had become
current for the magnate-knight, the banneret. The term would not have
come into being had there not been a necessity to distinguish different
degrees of nobility within the knightly continuum.[78]

The idea of bannerets as a social level might be thought likely to conflict
with the formulation of barons as a social group. Both described the untitled
magnate, one referring to his military status, the other his civil. Indeed, some
early fourteenth-century sources unconsciously conflate the idea by talking
of a *baronettus*.[79] However, it seems that 'baron' and 'banneret' were terms that
could be used in a complementary rather than confused way. Sources will talk
of barons in fiscal and political contexts, and bannerets in knightly and military terms. The same sort of men were indicated by the differing terms. From
the 1250s, *milites regis bannericiis* feature in royal records as the superior
knights of Henry III's household, and the banneret's long-term future was
tied up with muster rolls and rates of pay.[80] The chief importance of the
term 'banneret' for us is to reveal unease within the aristocracy about the
usefulness of the status of knight in defining levels of nobility. Where a
knight had a retinue of dependent knights of his own, it was clear that such
a man needed to be differentiated from the knightly herd, especially as the
status level of baron was by now established within a hierarchical society.
Much clearer to the contemporary mind was the way that the gilded spur, the
attribute of knighthood, provided a very firm boundary between noble
knights and those who had social aspirations but who had not been knighted.[81]

That there was such tension is evident in a number of ways in the
thirteenth century. Wealth was the problem. Where a man from a group that
society in general did not consider to be noble had wealth, and thus the
ability to aspire to the material attributes of nobility, he would cause tension.
The mercenary captain of the Angevin wars was a subject of much vituper-
ation in the circles of William Marshal simply because his wealth, military
life and closeness to princes threatened a military aristocracy that did not
think of itself as fighting for money so much as for loyalty.[82] Even worse was

the merchant. We have already seen how the 'barons of London' were regarded with contempt for their supposed usurpation of a noble title. In 1253, a major riot occurred after a quintain contest between the young knights of the royal court at Westminster and a group of young Londoners from patrician families. The courtiers were beaten and in their outrage insulted the London boys as 'scabby peasants' and 'soapmakers' (the smelliest of occupations).[83] Criticism of the merchant as an unworthy recipient of great wealth had been loud for a century by then. Preaching to Henry II's court late in the 1150s, Stephen de Fougères portrayed the good merchant as one who paid his tithes, made his annual confession, dealt fairly with his customers and eschewed usury. Unfortunately, according to him, the merchant was all too likely to charge extortionate interest, sell the fur of a hare as rabbit or felt as brocade, adulterate wine and pimp his daughter to a borrower who dreamed of acquiring a castle and a noble life-style. For Stephen, a premature Marxist, the merchant was thus the natural enemy of the aristocrat.[84] It was a common joke in the later twelfth century that the merchant's only motivation in aspiring to knighthood was to avoid paying tolls at bridges and gates.[85] Nonetheless, the heads of urban patrician families did aspire to knighthood as early as the time of Stephen de Fougères, when Gervase of Cornhill (*civis meus Londoniensis*) became a prominent member of King Stephen's *familia*, and purchased a large landed estate in Kent and Hertfordshire.[86] In the early thirteenth century, the heads of several London merchant families were knights, notably those of the Blunts, Tolosans and Buccointes. It was therefore not improper that their children should compete with the younger court nobility at the quintain. Their aspirations soon led such men, as they did Gervase of Cornhill, to buy up landed estates in the district around London and join the knights of the shires.[87] The fact that this was observed and resented by contemporaries simply affirms that borders to nobility were perceived by the breach as much as the observance. A harsh social satire written in England in the 1220s or 1230s rams home the point. Knights, it says, were men allied with the earls as noblemen in the service of the king and the commonwealth. Merchants were outside this concern, men with neither grace nor social status, who devoted their time to making money and consuming.[88]

THE SQUIRE

The obvious candidate for a level of social status below the knight was the squire. Like the knight, the twelfth-century squire was not necessarily noble by any stretch of the imagination. He was called by a variety of names, in Latin *armiger, scutiger, scutarius* or *scutifer*, and in French *escuier* or *vaslet*. The squire was in most cases no more than a servile attendant.[89] The so-called 'Laws of Edward the Confessor' (*c.*1136) assume that magnates' households should contain 'their *armigeri* and other servants'. But men called by that name might even be employed by someone like Bernard, the royal scribe of Henry I's day, who had two *armigeri*, David and Roger.[90] For the most part, such men may have spent all their active lives as 'squires'. Some were men of means, and others men of little consequence. So we hear of the squire of Ranulf II, earl of Chester (died 1153), a man named Nicholas, who held an estate from his lord in Derbyshire. At the end of the twelfth century, Robert III of Stafford (died 1193) granted a half-knight's fee to one Thomas Noel, 'for the service of keeping my shield'.[91] On the other hand, there were people like Herbert, the *armiger* of the Warwickshire knight Henry of Arden (died 1190 × 96), who was ranked in his household below Henry's baker and reeve.[92] It was not necessary even in the thirteenth century that a squire progress to the state of knighthood, and a mature man bearing that title might be retained in the office of *armiger* in a great man's household, such as the body of squires we find in the earl of Warwick's household in the 1170s and the 1220s, when we are told a household squire was entitled to annual robes and gifts of horses from the earl.[93]

However, the squire was also likely to be considered a candidate for noble status, simply because a number of youths in the service of magnates and knights and in training for knighthood were also called 'squires'. Youths and boys such as these would have been of aristocratic birth, like the young Englishman William Marshal, knighted at the age of twenty in 1166, and described before then as having been 'eight years a squire (*eskuers*)' in the household of his Norman cousin, William de Tancarville.[94] Such youths and young men were a distinct subgroup within the social continuum of squires, and had the potential to be considered noble through lineage. Already in the last decades of the twelfth century sources were registering this and taking it as the dominant sense. The popular twelfth-century Latin poem instructing various groups in career and love, the *Facetus*, says: 'If a boy is keen on a knight's life let him learn to manage a horse by his thighs and hands. He must begin as a *scutifer* living with knights, and if he wants to be a good knight, get accustomed to a hard life.'[95] A romance of the time of the Third Crusade associated with King Richard's court talks of one element of a household being made up of 'the young bachelors we call *escuiers*' and includes amongst them the group called in French *damoiseax*, a vernacular adaptation of the Latin *domicellus*, a diminutive of *dominus*, or 'lord'. An English legal tract of around 1136 helpfully defines *domicellus* as an equivalent of the English title *atheling* (meaning 'most noble'), 'but we use the word nowadays of more people, because we call the sons of barons *domicellos*.[96] The *ensenhamen* (or book of conduct) by the Gascon knight Arnaut-Guilhem de Marsan, a work of the 1170s, features these noble squires (*donzelos*) as elegant and courtly additions to the model household. 'It is good to have *escudiers* bound to your service. Have two who are charming, good-looking, discreet and accomplished. Whatever might be those of others, yours should be becoming, courtly, educated and well spoken. Such fellows have their uses in that they will gain you a good reputation. If you send them anywhere, one could not be ridiculed on their account, for it is said about such servants, "You can tell the lord by his household." '[97]

The movement towards considering squires as a distinctly noble group in a position below that of the knight is evident in northern France in the early thirteenth century, after the knight has been established as self-evidently noble. The one development seems to have provoked the other, in a knock-on effect. In the French region of the Rémois and the north of the Île-de-France, *armigeri* appear as a distinct social group after the *domini*, or knights, in charters of the 1220s. In the Champenois, a similar chronology has been observed, as indeed there has in a survey of several other French regions.[98] The formula for describing knights in their charters had settled as '*Dominus* A. de B. *miles*' in the first quarter of the century. By the 1250s, we find in several regions of France a lesser style evolving of 'C. de D. *armiger/scutifer*', while a squire's wife or knight's daughter might be distinguished as a *domicella*, in the way the wife of a knight would be a *domina*.[99] The evolution of such styles to reflect the perception of a social group of squires acknowledged the fact that in France as much as England many sons of knights chose not to embrace knighthood. Squires nonetheless pursued a noble lifestyle and aspirations, and by the mid-thirteenth century in France unapologetically took armorial bearings. As the social commentator and moralist Philip de Novara observed around 1270: 'the young magnate, knight *or other man-at-arms* ought to strive after honour, and to triumph so as to earn a name for valour and attain worldly goods, riches and an inheritance'.[100] Philip, by then an aged man, had observed in his own lifetime the appearance of social groups below that of knight that were credited as noble.

The lack in England of such a clear social evolution of what modern French allows us to call an *écuyerie* (or 'squirely' group) and *écuyère*

('squireliness') in the first half of the thirteenth century is a notable diver-
gence from what we might expect from developments considered so far.
The groups represented by counts, barons and knights appear to have
evolved in a similar way in both England and France; not so the squire. An
obvious explanation might be that England was progressively distanced
politically from France during the decades when the 'squirely' dignity was
being defined across the Channel. But this may not account for it: English
noblemen continued to tourney with their French colleagues in north-
eastern France during the thirteenth century, while French noblemen
continued to find places at the English royal court. Cross-fertilisation of
social ideas was distinctly possible in those circumstances, and indeed can
be demonstrated to have happened in other contexts, such as tournament
culture. A more likely argument may be that much of the status of knight
in England was closely defined by its administrative leadership in the shires,
which did not exist in France. The status border between the knight and the
rest of the landed classes may therefore have been stronger and less
surmountable in England, since there was no equivalent way of defining
squires by local office and eminence. Squires in England lacked the voice in
national or even local affairs that knights so conspicuously possessed. This
constraint can be seen in other ways. Men calling themselves squires were
routinely taking heraldic devices in France by 1250.[101] The king was forbid-
ding squires in England from doing this as late as 1292, even though in practice it was difficult to prevent the son of a knight from taking his father's
arms, and indeed the prohibition itself tells us that squires *were* taking illicit
heraldry.[102]

   The fact that there were men who were noble (*gentil*) who were not
knights was registered in England as much as in France. The thirteenth
century was a time of generally rising incomes and opportunities for manorial lords, knights or not, and the capacity to claim a noble lifestyle was
implicit in such a society.[103] In the 1240s, Bishop Robert Grosseteste of
Lincoln's instructions on the management of noble households acknowledged that knights were not the only people who could be classed as *gentis
hommes* and receive robes in a great household.[104] And, as we have seen, the
household of the thirteenth-century earls of Warwick contained a group of
body squires, receiving just such fees. William Marshal's biographer noted
in the mid-1220s the rising social expectations on a squire from what they
had been in the 1170s: a squire now needed from their lords not just a
mount, but a packhorse.[105] Nonetheless, the thirteenth-century English
formularies that dictate the way letters should be addressed and written do

not register squires as a social group below knights. They refer instead to *liberi homines* or *libere tenentes* (free men or freeholders), a description appropriate to men who were to be found in shire and hundred courts alongside but subordinate to knights. Yet even in England there still remains some stubborn consciousness that thirteenth-century English squires were part of a social group. It comes out not least on the tournament field, the catwalk of military nobility. We know from the *Dit des hérauts* of Henry de Laon that in France before 1250 squires were equipping themselves as knights and participating alongside knights in the tournament, though Henry did not approve of the squires' presumption.[106] As early as 1234, there is an indication of squires holding 'bohorts' (or military games) in England, where they would have gone equipped as knights and tourneyed much as knights did.[107] We can therefore see that the imperatives that led to the emergence in France of the noble squire in the first half of the thirteenth century were also being felt in England, even if English society did not fully acknowledge squires as a status group below that of knight until the mid-fourteenth century. I believe we can at least say that *armigeri* were being acknowledged as a social phenomenon in Edward I's England, thus adding a further stage to the development of the hierarchy of English social groups.[108]

THE QUESTION OF THE GENTRY

It is not possible to evade the idea of the 'gentry' when dealing with the question of the social hierarchy of medieval England, though giving it any meaning is not an easy task. It is a construct of a social group peculiar to Anglophone historians, and nothing comparable turns up in French historical discourse.[109] As it is generally used by historians of several historical periods, the term embraces the whole run of substantial local landowners populating the English shires. Most writers on the gentry – as it was perceived to exist before 1300 – see the local county knight as the gentry's definitive representative.[110] There is some justification for seeing local communities of knights as a real force in the English social structure of at least the thirteenth century: men who interacted with the dominant local magnates and whom the king occasionally addressed from the political centre which was his court (see above, pp. 15–16). But 'knights' could hardly be described as synonymous with the entire 'gentry', for there were men of some local notability, lords (*domini*) of manors, who were not knights and did not come from knightly families.[111] In fact, thirteenth-century landed society, and (plausibly) that of the preceding century, was complex, and was structured on differing interactions between wealth, status and aspiration. Furthermore, by the mid-thirteenth century, there was a whole range of important local offices – baronial seneschals, coroners, sub-escheators and hundred bailiffs, most obviously – often occupied by men below the rank of knight. The documentation is such for the period after 1200 that the social complexity of a local society can be reconstructed, as Peter Coss has proved by looking at the rich sources that concern the hinterland of the town of Coventry.[112] As a result of Coss's work, we know that this society was not socially stratified below the level of knight, as was that of the later fourteenth century.[113] In the face of such vagueness of social distinction, how could it be said that thirteenth-century society, let alone that of the twelfth century, perceived a category of local gentry?

There is at least some evidence that people during the thirteenth century were occasionally aware of a middling group of landlords who might not be knights, but who held land for which knight service was owed, and – as we have seen – they realised that aspiration to a noble lifestyle and conduct was not restricted to men called knights. In that respect, 'gentry' is a good modern word to use for that group, as it derives from a Middle English word meaning 'men of good family'.[114] To use the word in that sense is unexceptionable. It registers that local élites were a mixture of families of knightly standing, even if some of their members did not get knighted, and other families of some consequence who had long associated with knightly families, but did not seek the distinction of knighting.[115] What bound them was generations of local consequence, intermarriage and perhaps a common interest and agenda. As a comparison, it is worth looking at the picture of French local society around 1160 conjured up by Wace. He perceives the substantial elements of local society uniting in time of threat, and sees the groups of *chevaliers des villes, li bons païssant, vavasor et major* as the leaders in this confederation of interest.[116] Though he does not call this alliance by any term that can be translated as 'local society' or 'gentry', Wace nonetheless registers that there was such an interest group dominating the countryside. Local society in thirteenth-century England might likewise be detected when it felt the need to bind together, at the level of the county, to negotiate with the king on troublesome issues, as in the famous case where the county of Lincolnshire objected in 1225–6 to the sheriff's plan to increase the sittings of the shire court,[117] or for reasons of social discontent, as in this imagined letter from the first half of the century, where a knight is raising awareness amongst his neighbours and peers of the king's threat to allow base men to aspire to marriage with their daughters: 'There have been in [our] shire shoemakers, swineherds and suchlike commoners considered fit to aspire to marry a noble girl. So let us try to thwart in every way this unwise proposal of the lord king, and endeavour to divert the king's will with the humblest of prayers – or with bribes if need be.'[118] Whether we call such local élites 'proto-gentry' or 'gentry', already in the thirteenth century they formed a seedbed out of which was growing the social level called 'squire'. In due course, they would also generate lesser social levels that would take the names of 'gentleman' and 'yeoman'.

It is here we find the defining change in society between 1070 and 1272. A growing coherence in the idea of nobility and the desire to be seen to possess it solidified the magnate group around the king and made it more visible and exclusive. As we will see in the next chapter, the magnate group in England traded on its social and economic dominance to raise itself into a partner in political dialogue with the king. But then the group most in contact with the magnates, defined by its military calling of knight, endured a consequent fission in the generations on either side of the year 1200. Magnates who did not carry the title of earl found civil distinction as king's barons, the nobles closest to the crown, while in the military sphere the same magnate group separated itself from the rest of men called 'knights'. It took a superior knighthood focused on the banner, not the golden spur. Simple or bachelor knights coalesced during those generations as the lower end of nobility, living up to noble expectations of conduct and material life. But by the 1220s in France the same imperatives were forging an even lower noble group, the squires who derived from the same knightly families, but chose not to be knights. In England, the higher bar set between knights and the rest retarded, though did not ultimately prevent, the forma- tion of a noble status level around the squire. And when squires were affirmed as a noble level in England, other groups formed throughout the fourteenth century as each negotiated a place in relationship to the idea of nobility. A stratified hierarchy of social groups coalesced generation by generation in a cascade effect, and so transformed society, leaving traces on our perception of class even to this day.

PART TWO

FINDING A VOICE

CHAPTER FOUR

✦

THE RISE OF CONCILIARISM

Perhaps the oldest and most obvious way of defining an aristocracy is making it party to a dialogue. Who would be the most influential section of a kingdom's population? The answer is that it would be that to which it was worth the king's while to talk. This simple definition raises a few problems. The first is that the lay aristocracy was not the only influential part of the population. The prelates of the Church were powerful men both in terms of the land, resources and followers they commanded, and also because of the moral, pastoral and spiritual authority inherent in their offices. The political agenda of bishops and abbots was going to be different from that of earls and barons. A second difficulty, which will be explored at length later, is the strength of the voice in which the aristocracy spoke. After all, it was a diverse group of men with idiosyncratic views. It was incapable of unanimity, though it might formulate majority opinions. And who was party to the discussions? Kings met nobles at court, but the court might well be closed to many powerful men of whom the king disapproved. Nonetheless, the ancient mechanism that drove a king to seek the open consent and compliance of the lay aristocracy was a major factor in the formulation of a self-conscious nobility and social class within medieval England. A third problem is more historiographical. It is about the consequences of the fact of an aristocratic agenda, and English historians' tendency to try to make an institution out of a reflex.[1]

The mechanism of taking counsel was a perfectly conscious one for both parties, king and aristocracy. Royal acts make a very big thing about the participation of a body of aristocrats in solemn decisions on solemn occasions. The constancy of this fact of political life across the period of this book may be obvious, but it is worth noting outright at the beginning. When William the Conqueror notified the counties and dioceses of his kingdom that ecclesiastical cases should not be heard elsewhere than the communal hundred courts of England, he did so 'by the common counsel and advice of archbishops, bishops, abbots and all the leading men of my realm'. And when his court was used to make a judgement in a difficult case concerning the abbey of Bury, it was done 'in my presence and that of the archbishops, bishops, abbots, earls and my other nobles'. The record of the judgement made a point that it was reached *unanimiter* by this concourse of influential men. The king and his magnates must be seen to speak 'with one mind'.[2]

But though the end result of the deliberations of king and court might be framed as a joint statement, there must have been deliberations of some sort behind it, and possibly disagreement. The court of William the Conqueror preserves an apparent example of this, and it is worth quoting in full. The author was William of Poitiers, a Norman archdeacon, sometime knight and former royal chaplain, who in the later 1070s wrote a history of his patron's life and times. This is how he described the discussions between Duke William and his chief followers on receiving the news that Harold had seized the English throne in 1066:

> Duke William, after taking counsel (*consultatio*) with his men, determined to avenge this injury by arms, and claim his inheritance by force of arms, although many of the greater men argued speciously (*ingeniose*) that the enterprise was too arduous and far beyond the resources of Normandy. At that time Normandy had in its counsels, besides the bishops and abbots, outstanding men of the secular order, shining luminaries who were the pride of that assembly (*in collegio*)... [three counts and four barons listed].... It was thanks to their wisdom and their efforts that Normandy could be kept in safety; supported by these the Roman republic would not have needed two hundred senators, if she had preserved her ancient power in our own time. However, we have ascertained that in every debate all gave way to the wisdom of their prince, as if by divine inspiration he foreknew what was to be done and what avoided. 'To those who live righteously God gives wisdom'.[3]

There is more than a little artificiality about this passage. Its citation of Ecclesiasticus is a deliberate identification of the Conqueror in his retrospective wisdom with Solomon. Such a comparison would suggest itself to any cleric at his court. As can be seen from the Bayeux Tapestry, William in state occupied a 'faldstool', or seat shaped with lion-heads in allusion to Solomon's throne. Similarly the exaltation of the Norman aristocracy above the Roman Senate is hyperbole, both in numbers and constitution.[4]

But was the dissent of these latter-day conscript fathers from their prince merely another artifice; an attempt to boost yet further the vision and determination of the Conqueror? There is some evidence that it was not. A portion of the Norman aristocracy was reluctant to participate in the Conquest and took little share in its spoils, which may well indicate that there had indeed been dissent between duke and council.[5]

HENRY I AND THE GROWTH OF DIALOGUE

It is important to establish that an aristocracy in council with its prince might not be entirely compliant with his wishes or silenced by his frown. As we will see later, this willingness to dissent accounts for the development of a dialogue between king and court aristocracy throughout the twelfth century, which eventually became an independent aristocratic agenda for the government of England. The relationship between king and aristocracy becomes clearer in the reign of Henry I (1100–35). The nature of Henry's court is far more accessible to us due to the sudden increase in the survival of administrative documents (including the financial account compiled by his exchequer in September 1130) as much as to the number of contemporary historians at work. Henry began his reign in the aftermath of his brother's unexpected death in a hunting accident. He had to survive the defection of the majority of the Anglo-Norman aristocracy to his elder brother, Duke Robert of Normandy, in 1100–1, and the subsequent invasion of England. His security as king depended on the destruction of his brother's rule in Normandy, which he achieved with the battle of Tinchebray (1106). Even so, he had to deal with assassination attempts and periodic rebellions centred on Normandy. It was only in 1125 that he began to appear invulnerable as king of England, and it was only with the death of his nephew William Clito in 1128 that his dissident aristocracy lost a focus for rebellion.

Exposed and overmatched in the many political crises in his life – which included a dangerous feud with his brother William Rufus in the 1090s before he became king – Henry developed a keen sensibility of the importance of the aristocracy to his ambitions and security. This comes out in several ways, particularly at the beginning of his reign. William Rufus was killed on a Thursday. Having brought the corpse of his brother to Winchester for burial on the Friday, Henry was in Westminster by Saturday and was crowned at the abbey by the bishop of London on Sunday, 5 August 1100.[6] By that day, he and his advisers had drafted and promulgated a charter which the chancery soon afterwards issued in multiple copies to be read out at the county courts of England. It was not so much a 'charter' as a policy statement directed at the realm he aspired to rule, but the principal concerns it addressed were those of his magnates. He acknowledged that in his late brother's reign England 'was oppressed by unjust exactions', but now his affection for his new subjects had caused him to address what he implied must be widespread complaints. As the clauses of the charter unroll, we discover that these included the unconstrained charging of reliefs, or succession dues for heirs when they came into their lands; restrictions and financial demands laid on barons who married off females in their families; the marrying of noble girls who came into the king's wardship without consultation; interference with the free enjoyment of widows' lands; forced remarriage of widows and the removal of their children into royal wardship. Henry pledged to address all these concerns. He would not interfere with a dying baron's wishes in the disposal of his lands, and would leave the division to his relatives if the baron himself were incapable; and he would not confiscate the entire wealth of a baron who fell foul of the law.[7]

Here we have for the first time in English history a political platform generated out of the complaints of the national élite.[8] We could hardly say it was the product of a dialogue between king and aristocracy at this point, as William Rufus had apparently been indifferent to his aristocracy's discontent once he was established on the throne. Rather, it arose from Henry's own experience as a member of his brother's court, and the mutterings and seethings of his fellow barons. Nonetheless, by listening to these complaints and replying to them, Henry instituted a dialogue. We can have no doubt that the baronial discontent went a long way back. Henry's own charter said that one complaint, about unrestricted financial penalties on those in the king's 'mercy', went back to his father's reign. Henry was willing to offer hostages to the anger of his barons, and one of his first actions as king was to order the arrest and imprisonment of his late brother's principal agent in England, Ranulf Flambard, bishop of Durham, who, John of Worcester says, had oppressed the *ditiores* (wealthiest) as well as the poorest of the realm.[9] But it would seem to be the propertied élite rather than the rest whose approval Henry was seeking by his action on that critical weekend in early August 1100.

Henry was keen to project a fiction that he had the support of the magnates of his realm on his seizure of the throne, though in fact the only baronial assent he could have had was that of the small entourage Rufus had brought hunting with him. Nonetheless, all the surviving forms of the coronation charter solemnly opened with the statement: 'I have been crowned king of England by the mercy of God and the common counsel of the barons of that same realm.' Versions based on what seems to have been an exemplar held at the royal archive at Winchester, composed by a partisan of the new king in the closely contemporary legal collection *Quadripartitus* and the *Leges Henrici*, concluded that the king's declaration was made 'by the witness of the archbishops, bishops, earls, barons, sheriffs and noble men (*optimates*) of the whole realm of England at Westminster, when I was crowned'.[10] The fiction behind this is amply demonstrated by the fact that on the day of Henry's coronation the archbishop of York is known to have been at Ripon in Yorkshire and the archbishop of Canterbury in exile in Burgundy. Nor was that the end of Henry's co-opting of an absent baronage. Within a week of the coronation, messengers were arriving at Lyon seeking out Archbishop Anselm, bringing letters from the king, the community of Canterbury and another from 'the barons of the realm (*principes regni*)', all soliciting his prompt return to England.[11]

Here for the first time in the historical record is an (admittedly stage-managed) attempt to portray the lay élite of England as a body of men capable of expressing a single mind, and to do it in writing. The king needed a partner in power, a satellite reflecting the light of his sun. He therefore chose to identify his right to rule (in part) with the will of the aristocracy, and put his own views in its mouth.[12] The significance of the baronial letter to Anselm should not be underestimated, however illusory its content. In fact, there is some indication that there was a baronial view on the succession question of 1100 quite independent of the king. When, in July 1101, at Alton, Hampshire, Henry confronted his brother Duke Robert marching on London, a battle failed to occur, despite some defections from the king to Robert. Several contemporary sources say that it was avoided by the actions of the chief men around the warring brothers, who brought them to a reconciliation.[13] From this it seems that the majority opinion amongst the barons was that internecine warfare was to no one's benefit, and they were prepared to pursue civil peace as a political aim. It is a view that will surface again and again in the twelfth century.

The modern studies of Henry I's subsequent court as king emphasise how he made efforts, sometimes extraordinary efforts, to attract a majority of the influential men of his kingdom into it, or at least those influential men he thought would be useful to him.[14] Histories of his reign refer to this on numerous occasions. So we find Hugh the Chanter, the chronicler of the

Canterbury-York dispute, describing the king summoning to a court held in London at Michaelmas 1113 the prelates, leaders (*principes*) and nobles (*primores*) of his kingdom 'to treat with them about peace, the state of the realm and other business'.[15] We find there some traces of a debate (although on ecclesiastical issues), and of advice being offered to the king and taken by him. But for the most part the king wanted acquiescence from his baronage, and in England after 1101 he certainly secured it, for all that he had continuing troubles with the Franco-Norman part of the aristocracy of Normandy.[16] Warren Hollister produced an informative study of the king's relationship with William II de Warenne, earl of Surrey (died 1138). Earl William chose the wrong side in 1101 and his English lands were confiscated. But rather than break him – as he did others – the king returned his lands in 1103 and used further land grants and acts of favour to convert the earl into a loyal supporter of his regime. Earl William fought for Henry at Tinchebray (1106), supported him during the Norman rebellions between 1118 and 1124, and became a constant inhabitant of his court.[17]

Henry I's desire to recruit and control his aristocracy through his court is attested in some surprising ways. The royal clerk Walter Map claims in the 1180s to have seen a list of the barons of England Henry himself had created, by which he could monitor the allowances paid them at court.[18] In light of the preservation of other lists of court customs from Henry's reign, we can easily believe Map on this. This list of barons is the first glimpse we see of an aristocracy defined as those men worthy of the king's notice, and it is not the only such example from Henry's reign. There is abundant evidence from sources of the 1130s and 1140s that it was then an established custom that the king summoned those barons and prelates he wanted to attend particular courts by a letter individually addressed to them.[19] Such lists and letters do not by any means completely define the aristocracy as a social class, because the king was perfectly capable of excluding certain landed magnates from his presence.[20] What they undoubtedly do do, however, is recognise that the king had with the landed magnates taken a partner in political discourse in England by 1100.

It is clear that there was a real dialogue between king and aristocracy. Henry asked for the support of the body of his aristocracy in several ways, and in so doing opened the possibility of refusal. This was particularly the case when the king wanted money from his realm. When he levied one of the occasional customary taxations on the realm that he was allowed – such as an 'aid' for the marriage of his daughter – he needed the co-operation of those who would be responsible for paying the bulk of it: his magnates. So we find in one of his acts the suggestive phrase that his barons had 'given' or 'granted' such an aid in 1114. The clerk who compiled the so-called 'Laws of Edward the Confessor' not long after Henry's death took it as axiomatic that a king would seek his barons' consent before levying an aid. The author recalled that William Rufus, faced in 1096 with the need to raise a huge sum to meet his crusading brother's price for a lease of the duchy of Normandy in his absence, sought (*petiit*) an aid from the 'barons of the whole country'.[21] It scarcely needs adding that the issue on which Henry most wanted the agreement of his magnates was the arrangement he attempted to make for the succession of his daughter to his throne. He tried to fix the deliberations and consent of the court with an oath in 1127, but though it was made, the true views of the magnates were betrayed by the refusal of all but a few to stand by it in December 1135.[22]

OVER THE KING'S HEAD: THE CRISIS OF STEPHEN'S REIGN

The reign of Stephen (1135–54) was a critical one for the development of aristocratic identity in England, in the sense that, during it, the English aristocracy developed its own distinctive 'voice', what Jolliffe called the 'impersonal will of a body of councillors' with which the king had to deal.[23] It was already established that the aristocracy had views that needed to be accommodated, and support that needed to be solicited. Stephen's opportunistic accession shows some trace of this, though, in the end, the events of Henry I's own accession in 1100 were not duplicated. Since the principal Anglo-Norman barons were all congregated in Normandy when Henry I died, their chance to negotiate for their support and state their views was compromised. The sources indicate that aristocratic conferences were held in eastern Normandy in the aftermath of Henry's sudden death, and that the assembled barons decided to offer Normandy – and no doubt England too – to Theobald of Blois, only to discover that they had been pre-empted in their decision by Theobald's younger brother, who had slipped across the Channel and secured London and coronation. Few barons disputed the fact of Stephen's accession or honoured the oath imposed on them to support the succession of King Henry's daughter.[24] As a result, Stephen did not find it necessary to fight for Normandy or to offer anything other than general promises to the aristocracy, who attended his first great court at Easter 1136 in gratifying numbers. Stephen's coronation charter is a bland and brief document making no more than general promises, as the new king did not feel he needed to negotiate with his barons.[25]

The striking development in Stephen's reign, as we now understand it, is the slow descent from the position of great strength the king occupied in 1136 to one of parlous weakness by 1141. A number of historians have analysed why and how this came to be. But the most convincing explanations relate to Stephen's failure in managing relations with his aristocracy: he failed to make his court the arena for ambition that his uncle's court had been; he had no ability to balance factions at his court as he tended towards factional favouritism. In the end, nervous of their rivals and frustrated, his magnates took their struggles to the country and dialogue with the king collapsed.[26] With the distintegration of Stephen's court in 1139, one would have thought that the aristocracy's capacity to generate a corporate agenda would have collapsed too, as every magnate looked out for himself. Perhaps the most surprising thing about the reign is that – although self-seeking and private warfare predominated in the country – this so-called 'anarchy' was not the full story. Some of the most powerful of the magnates generated an agenda for peace. As Ralph Davis proved in 1967, manifestations of this began in the aftermath of the death of Earl Robert of Gloucester (October 1147) when the greatest of the earls on either side in the struggle (William of Gloucester, Roger of Hereford, Ranulf of Chester, Robert of Leicester and Simon of Northampton) came together to agree a network of private treaties that Davis memorably called 'the Magnates' Peace'.[27]

This corporate behaviour is manifested in even more significant ways. There is an ideological dimension to the magnates' actions in the late 1140s which indicates they were enacting that aspect of noble behaviour that gave responsibility for the protection of the defenceless and upholding of justice to the righteous ruler, whether sovereign prince or simple lord.[28] The key episode is what happened at Wallingford early in August 1153. Duke Henry had arrived in England, had gathered his adherents and gone on the attack. He marched his army to Malmesbury to take the royal castle and so clear the way for the relief of Wallingford. A confrontation with Stephen had led to the surrender of Malmesbury and a truce. With the truce concluded, the duke marched on the royal siege-works at Wallingford, the formidable castle that blocked routes up and down the river Thames. The king struck back, managing to trap Henry Plantagenet and his smaller army, but as Stephen was preparing his final coup against his rival, the king's army simply refused to fight the duke. In the words of the *Gesta Stephani*: 'The leading men (*primi*) of each army and those of deeper judgement were greatly grieved and shrank, on both sides, from a conflict that was not merely between fellow countrymen but meant the desolation of the whole kingdom.' They made a truce preparatory to wider discussions of peace, and the armies disbanded of their own accord, leaving king and duke supposedly annoyed at the turn of events.[29]

We may assume that the bishops were the men of 'deeper judgement' (*profundiores*) playing an important part in articulating the armies' discontent with the war, but it was the military leaders who took control. Earls and barons in either army talked to their colleagues and so settled the problem over the heads of the principals. It was these men who engineered the peace settlement as it was negotiated through the autumn of 1153. Their agenda has reached us and the items on it can be reconstructed. In fact, we can see the magnates articulating and acting on it even before Wallingford, which rather tells against the view that the details were ironed out after the event by Archbishop Theobald and Bishop Henry of Winchester.[30] Months before the magnates forced a peace conference in August 1153, we find indications of their awareness that a peace settlement would involve the restoration of the tenurial status quo to what it had been in 1135, on the death of Henry I. The royalist earl William of Arundel was in touch with Duke Henry through his brother-in-law before June 1153, negotiating continued possession of the lands they had acquired which had formerly been royal demesne. On changing sides in June 1153, Earl Robert of Leicester likewise took precautions to secure the duke's consent to alienations made without royal consent in the years of civil war.[31]

The accession of Henry II in 1154 therefore took place in a political environment in which the magnates of England had secured a powerful joint voice. The new king probably had little choice but to make the best of it. The widespread nature of his realms meant that he needed these men's acquiescence to his rule in England, since he was going to be an absentee king; therefore, he was willing to sanction and project a conciliar approach. This was evident even before his accession to the throne. On leaving for the continent in March 1154, Henry appointed his uncle, Earl Reginald of Cornwall (died 1175), as his vicegerent in England.[32] As a new king, Henry was deeply sensitive to his dependence on his earls, and the potential threat they posed. We see several instances of this in 1155. Before the end of his first year as king, Henry appointed the most influential and learned of them, Robert II of Leicester (died 1168), as one of the chief justiciars of England, employing the late King Stephen's friend and servant Richard de Lucy as his colleague.[33] He needed such support if he was to reclaim the lands and assets alienated to the magnates in the last reign. He had already drawn a line at the end of 1153 with the confiscation of Waleran of

Meulan's earldom of Worcester, erected by Stephen for Waleran at the expense of royal interests in the county. To do this, Henry had needed the acquiescence of Waleran's brother and agent, Robert II of Leicester, the same man who became his justiciar in 1155.[34]

CONCILIAR RULE UNDER THE ANGEVINS

It was an urgent necessity in the first half of Henry II's reign that the rule of England should be conciliar, not least because the king was mostly going to be in France. The sparse sources for the beginning of his reign make a proud feature of the great courts that Henry held in his first year and go into some detail as to what was discussed at them. So we learn from a Canterbury source that at the end of 1154 the king held his first Christmas court in Bermondsey priory, 'where – in discussion with his magnates (*principes*) concerning the state of the realm and what needed to be done to restore peace – the king advocated the expulsion of foreigners from England and the demolition of the worst of the castles across the whole country'.[35] Domestic policy gave way to broader concerns the next year. Robert de Torigny reported that 'King Henry of the English, holding council around Michaelmas at Winchester, discussed with his nobles (*optimates*) the conquest of the kingdom of Ireland and grant of it to his brother William. But since his mother the empress was unhappy about it the venture was postponed for the time being.'[36] Henry II was concerned to be seen in council doing business. It may largely have been for the appearance of the thing, but the context of his succession and its aftermath indicates otherwise.

Henry especially needed the support of his court against particular members of the aristocracy. In February 1155, we see him attempting to widen his actions against certain selected magnates. One of the most flagrant profiteers of Stephen's reign at the king's expense had been Count William of Aumale and York. Faced with a hostile king and court at York, William surrendered his English earldom, but here the king hesitated. Count William kept important gains from the royal demesne in Yorkshire, even if he lost the soke of Falsgrave and its castle of Scarborough.[37] The king had to be open to compromise, so as to maintain baronial support. But sometimes the magnates did not support the king's ambitions to restore his patrimony, and then we glimpse the limits of the new regime. Most revealing is the reaction of Earl Roger of Hereford in March or April of 1155 to the king's plan to resume grants of royal demesne made to him in the previous reign. Earl Roger's local power depended on control of former royal towns and castles in Gloucestershire and Herefordshire, and he would not stomach their loss. He therefore quit the royal court, put his castles in defence, summoned his knights and allies, and recruited Welsh mercenaries. The king buckled under this defiance and sent the bishop of Hereford to negotiate a settlement, which was put in the form of a document confirming Earl Roger's title to what he held of the former demesne, with the tacit exception of the Lacy honor of Weobley, which Roger had appropriated in the 1140s.[38] For all that Henry II has been characterised as aggressive and uncompromising towards his aristocracy in his first year as king, he clearly recognised that he had to be circumspect. In Earl Roger's case, the king was just not strong enough to take him down, and perhaps he sensed that the rest of the magnates were not with him. His luck resolved the Hereford problem, for the earl died before the end of 1155, allowing the king to resume royal assets and deny them to Roger's heirs. Henry II was by no means powerless against the magnates in 1155, but his targets had to be chosen with care. If he compromised with William of Aumale and retreated in the face of Roger of Hereford's resistance, he was able, or allowed, to make examples of others. The lesser Marcher baron Hugh de Mortemer attempted to defy the king as Earl Roger had done, but was besieged in Bridgnorth castle and forced to submit. Yet he was small fry and isolated from wider support.[39]

Our best insight into the way the magnates of the court were harnessed to the king's bandwagon can be seen in the Becket affair, notably in the confrontation between king and archbishop at Northampton in October 1164. The crisis in relations between the two men came after two years of rising tensions. The principal issue was the king's ambitions for legal reform, which included a demand from the Church hierarchy that clerks who committed offences against the crown should be tried in royal courts. This was not an issue that directly affected the magnates of the court, but it is striking how enthusiastically they embraced the king's side. The king intended them to be involved. They were the audience to witness his performance and to offer applause. Garnier de Pont-Sainte-Maxence, one of the archbishop's clerks, often comments on how the king demanded his master's appearance and submission 'in the sight of my barons'.[40] The climactic scene was played out at Northampton castle over five days, from Thursday, 8 October to the following Tuesday. The king was determined to humiliate and curb his archbishop and the magnates were there to support him. He may have been disappointed when the case for which Becket had been ostensibly summoned, his supposed denial of justice to John Marshal, was decided by the barons in favour of the archbishop. But a whole squadron of new charges was launched against Becket, notably that he had profiteered at the king's expense in his time as chancellor.[41]

The numerous accounts of these five days highlight the increasingly fraught atmosphere amongst the magnates present, caught between a defiant and emotional Becket and a glowering, aggressive king. The feverish atmosphere is captured by Garnier's report that the Monday before the crisis two great lords came to Becket secretly and 'assured him the report was true that if he appeared at court he would walk into a trap: he would be thrown in prison, where he would be put to death; it would be done promptly'.[42] Garnier clearly believed that they had been put up to it by the king to engender panic in the archbishop's following, but it might just as well have been the result of the king's goading of his magnates, as part of the isolation of the archbishop. Garnier says that Becket knew well that he would have very few friends when he came before Tuesday's assembly (*parlement*).[43] The king used the chief earls, Reginald of Cornwall and Robert of Leicester, as his mouthpieces on both the Monday and Tuesday. Their dignity and their position amongst their fellows gave an appearance of king and magnates united against Becket, and Becket's rejection of them was a demonstration of contempt likewise for their colleagues. The climax came when Becket finally confronted the court in the crowded hall of the castle on Tuesday, his own metropolitical cross in his hand. He found the king withdrawn into his chamber with a group Garnier variously describes as his 'intimate friends (*druz*): bishops, abbots, earls and barons' and as 'the most eminent of his councillors (*conseilz*)'.[44] When Becket proved intransigent despite close negotiations and messengers passing to and fro between him and the king, Henry eventually lost his temper. At this, the great lords of the court rallied to the king and agreed with him that Becket's intransigence needed to be punished, suggesting that should the archbishop appeal to the pope then he could be proceeded against. The earls of Cornwall and Leicester were sent to convey this to Becket, but he refused to listen. He stood and left the chamber, and as he did so the magnates of the court erupted in rage.

> When he turned his back on the king's chamber, the judges and barons, one of them – of such a high rank that I ought not to name him – shouted at Becket above the confused outcry and noise: 'There goes the traitor! There he is! There he is!' Earl Hamelin [of Surrey] could not contain

himself. When he saw Archbishop Thomas on his way out he abused him thoroughly, openly calling out: 'Wicked traitor, you're running off like a criminal!' Hugh Wake shouted at him till he was hoarse. Thomas got out of the chamber as fast as he could. When he reached the middle of the hall he tripped over some firewood and nearly fell. Then Ranulf Broc had his say, shouting: 'The traitor's off!' The holy man kept his mouth shut and continued on his way. In the hall he was called traitor and roundly abused on all sides. There could not have been more noise at the sack of a city. Some threw handfuls of filthy straw at him. He had no intention of justifying himself to them and went out. The Jews did the same when they judged Christ: they insulted him, struck him and slapped his face.[45]

This remarkable account catches a moment when the nobility found a joint voice, even though it was an abusive, hectoring one. Their choice of insult, that Becket was *traîtres*, was one particular to their group; for a nobleman and *preudomme* (a man of affairs) prized his reputation for loyalty above all else.[46] Some had been manipulated into this state of mind by the king, others – such as Hugh Wake and Ranulf Broc – were the archbishop's personal enemies, and others again, like Earl Hamelin, felt personally affronted by Becket's intransigence to the king, the earl's half-brother. The point is that the incident forcibly illustrates how Henry II's rule in the 1160s was founded on a conciliar base, and to attack the king was to attack the nobility. Becket himself registered this. One of his first letters after fleeing England was to the earl of Leicester as one amongst the leaders of the curial nobility. The letter singles out Earl Robert but is as much directed at those it calls 'your fellow magnates' (*comprincipes tui*), all of whom Becket says have wronged the church of Canterbury, and for which he requires penance and reparation. They have attacked the Church particularly on the matter of its liberties. Becket is therefore regarding king and nobility as having a common cause on legal reform. Earl Robert is required to intercede with the king to bring him to his senses on the matter; failing that, he and the rest will face 'divine vengeance', a threat directed as much at the entire curial nobility as at the earl.[47] From this, we could suggest that Becket's eventual assassination by men of baronial status was motivated not so much by the king's anger as by the hostility of an offended and articulate nobility.

The conciliar nature of Henry II's reign is particularly evident in the legislation the king made, the famous 'assizes' of his reign.[48] These key legal texts have much to say and are much studied, but what is generally overlooked is what they have to say about the way they were generated. However, Paul Brand has recently highlighted the process of discussion and consent before the magnates and bishops which can be distinguished behind their texts, and in particular in the legal text called *Glanvill*.[49] Here we find a world-view that sees law as declared *in consilio*, 'by the advice of the magnates and the supporting authority of the prince'.[50] The earliest surviving text of an assize, that of the Constitutions of Clarendon (1164), declares that the customs it records have been acknowledged 'by archbishops, bishops, earls, barons and the most noble and senior people of the realm'. It goes on to list fourteen prelates, ten men of comital rank, twenty-nine curial barons, 'and many other leaders and nobles, clerks and laymen'.[51] Something similar can be said of much of the rest of the legislation. So, in 1184, the minor Assize of Woodstock was reached 'by the counsel and assent of the archbishops, bishops, barons, earls and nobles of England'.[52] Rather than this being a simple form of words, Brand sees embedded in the text of *Glanvill* evidence that there was a real process of discussion and bargaining between king and nobility, particularly in the king's attempt at Windsor late in his reign to replace trial by duel with trial by jury, 'a royal benefit conferred by the king's goodness acting on the advice of the magnates', which was suspected and resisted by the beneficiaries.[53]

Henry II inherited a political situation where the English magnates had come together in a body and saw themselves as having a voice in the conduct of the realm. The Battle Abbey Chronicle, whose author was close to the family of the justiciar Richard de Lucy, makes the point forcefully in the speeches before Henry II that it puts in the mouths of Richard and his senior colleague, Earl Robert II of Leicester, asserting that the rule of the kingdom won at Hastings was their joint business, as it had been achieved by both King William and their forebears, the Conqueror's magnates.[54] Whatever he might have thought of this, it was in Henry's interest to make use of this perspective. The conciliar nature of his rule is a major expression of it. However, some qualifications need to be made. Henry II's kingship was personal, and it is evident that for whatever reason he could not abide certain of his magnates: notorious examples of this are Earl Richard fitz Gilbert of Striguil (died 1176) and Earl William of Gloucester (died 1183). Charter witness lists in fact demonstrate the rarity of the presence at court in England of over half a dozen of the great comital families, even those such as the Veres, Gloucesters and Redvers who had supported the Angevin cause in the time of King Stephen.[55] This was one limiting factor of the king's willingness to engage in dialogue with his nobility; the other was his itinerary. After his long initial stay in England, from 1154 to 1158, Henry was out of the country touring his continental dominions for years at a time. A few of the Anglo-Norman magnates became attached to his itinerant court, but most can have had little contact with it for long periods. The king relied principally for advice therefore on the intimates, household officers and captains who travelled with him.[56] This has been evident to historians for many years. To J.E.A. Jolliffe, it was a symptom of the gradual evolution of the institution of a privileged inner council that advised the king, a phenomenon already apparent to everyone at court in Henry's reign.[57] To more recent historians, it was simply a consequence of geography and logistics.[58] Did this narrowing of counsel have the effect of distancing the king from the magnates who thought themselves his natural advisers, stakeholders in the realm?

It is possible to suggest that the period after Becket's death in 1170 saw a change in the king's attitude to the rule of England. Having failed in his ambitions to assert control of the prosecution of clerics and faced a dangerous rebellion against his authority in both England and Normandy in 1173–4, it has been argued that Henry became more controlling and intrusive in his legal reforms, which naturally bore heavily on the jurisdiction of the Anglo-Norman magnates.[59] The Inquest on Sheriffs of 1170, put on foot as soon as the king returned to England that year, even before Becket's murder, is evidence of a new ambition of the king to monitor and curb authorities in the realm other than his own. Its third clause insisted that the the actions and impositions of ecclesiastical and lay magnates, their seneschals and bailiffs, should be open to scrutiny from the royal justices, particularly in the many hundred courts that had come under private control in England.[60] Did this and other such measures have a corrosive effect on the conciliar nature of Angevin government in England? Certainly the rebellion of 1173 included great magnates who played little part in the court of Henry II, and clearly had hopes of better treatment from his son, the Young King. Such were David II of Huntingdon (died 1219), the cousins Robert III of Leicester (died 1190) and Robert II of Meulan (died 1219) – who were particularly prominent – Hugh II of Chester (died 1181) and William de Ferrers of Derby (died 1191).[61] The king did not wait for other suspects to act, ordering at the outset the arrest and imprisonment of William of Gloucester and his wife and the seizure of his castles. However, the sources for the rebellion give little indication that it was inspired by particular dissatisfaction associated with the king's conduct of his court, though Ralph de Diceto said the increasing rigour of the king's pursuit of his rights and the intrusiveness of his government in matters of justice were major issues.[62] The rebel earls and counts were mostly young men with a generational sympathy for the Young King. They might have enlisted in the rebellion as a matter of personal loyalty to the Young King as much as in pursuit of political ambitions and grievances. If the rebellion shows anything about aristocratic views, it is that Henry II failed to appreciate the dangers of personal vendettas and indifference directed against various of his magnates.

The exclusion of magnates from counsel and policy becomes more evident as the century progresses. After 1174, the king's presence in England became increasingly rare. Henry II and Richard the Lionheart between them were absent from England for seventeen years out of the subsequent quarter-century. However, the general complaisance of the English magnates during this long period hardly seems to indicate much aristocratic discontent with the situation. Military success and opportunity on the continent may partly explain this. The king also took care to be inclusive when it was politic. The magnificent set-piece of Richard's coronation in 1189 toadied in its symbolism to the established place of the magnates in the polity of England.[63] The explosion of resentment against William de Longchamp as the absentee king's justiciar in 1190–1 might well be characterised as representing the English magnates' distaste at the behaviour of a curial parvenu set over them, but since Longchamp was replaced in 1191 by a committee of laymen and ecclesiastics of exactly the same type, this can hardly have been the principal motivation, which seems to have been the ambition of Count John of Mortain to control the realm in his brother's absence.[64]

The issue of the dialogue between king and magnates resurfaces in John's reign, though it has to be said that – as with the similar situation in Stephen's reign – it took a long while for the pressure within the aristocracy to reach critical point. Despite living on the knife edge of his displeasure, the magnates of the court still worked with John for years at a time. There were several reasons why they did so. The potential gains from John's generosity were enormous. He was renowned for being a spendthrift as well as greedy. The Béthune clerk talks of his gluttony and partying.[65] But a spendthrift king might direct a highly profitable stream of money to those he liked. The extent to which the curial knight and justice William Briwerre (died 1226) gained from his intimate friend King John's patronage between 1199 and 1215 is remarkable.[66] He was showered with lands, wardships and offices to the point that he grew wealthier than most earls. William Marshal in the same period acquired Pembrokeshire and the title of earl that went with it, together with offices, privileges and new lordships in Wales. Neither man was exactly a parvenu; both came from families identified with service to the king. Marshal was a nephew of the earl of Salisbury and Briwerre was closely connected with the family of Earl Reginald of Cornwall.

Huge potential profit was one reason certain barons continued to live on the edge of the volcano that was King John's volatile court. But there were other reasons. The magnates attached to the court were not a united group, and John knew it. He was renowned for playing one baron off against another. An example is the way John employed the Anglo-Welsh baron Meilyr fitz Henry as his auxiliary in Leinster and Meath against the disgraced William Marshal in 1207 and 1208 and his ally Walter de Lacy.[67] Meilyr seems to have despised Marshal as an intruder into the established community of Irish barons and an obstacle to his control over the region of Uí Fáeláin, which he was labouring to turn into his own fiefdom, but which was within Leinster, an ambition that the king's carelessness of others' claims in Ireland made possible.[68] Another of the king's expedients can only have added to the insecurity amongst the barons. The taking of hostages to ensure good behaviour was an ancient stratagem used against people thought to be untrustworthy. Although the word for hostage – 'obses' – started to be used chiefly in the twelfth century to mean a guarantor of a transaction, who would suffer a financial penalty in case of default, John revived the old sense. He took wives, children and relatives of his barons as hostages for their good behaviour, keeping them at the royal court if they were lucky, or in prison if not. He might also demand control of baronial castles as a way of neutering them politically. The chroniclers tell us that it was John's demand for Briouze's sons as hostages that was the immediate trigger for the family's defiance of the king.[69] The king asked for Marshal's two elder sons as hostages, and the trepidation the demands caused was intentional on the king's part. We are fortunate in that echoes of the household debates the demands gave rise to are to be found in the Marshal biography in the form of the reactions given to the biographer by men who were in the earl's council. John first took Marshal's eldest son, William, a boy of fifteen in 1205, and kept him at court until 1211. The biography says that Marshal 'surrendered him readily to the king, being as he was a man who would have nothing to do with evildoing or ever thought of it as such'.[70] However, when, in 1208, John demanded the second son, Richard, then around thirteen, Marshal's council was perturbed. It called the request a *felonie*, a disgrace. Nonetheless, Marshal handed Richard over, and when he was challenged by the king in Dublin in 1210 to hand over his vassals and castles, he summed up his compliance by saying: 'You have my sons as hostages and you hold all my castles in England. If here in this land of Ireland you wish to have my towns and castles I shall hand over plenty to you, and I shall also surrender to you many of the sons of my worthy followers. A man can afford to proceed boldly in this manner who has no intention of doing harm.'[71]

All these reasons and doubtless more besides kept the barons for years from combining as a group against the felon king with whom Fate had saddled them. However, they highlight the fact that John did not see the need for a conciliar approach to the rule of England. A very valuable passage in the *History of William Marshal* depicts the king in action at court. He had decided in June 1205 at Portchester that Marshal had betrayed his trust and made a treasonous private treaty with Philip II of France in order to keep his Norman lands. The king demanded that his barons, assembled in strength to embark for France, should immediately pass judgement on him. These men, Marshal's peers, refused to move on the matter, perhaps influenced by Marshal's appeal to their mutual interests and the common danger they faced from the king: 'My lords, look at me, for, by the faith I owe you, I am for you all this day an exemplar and a model. Be on your alert against the king: what he thinks to do with me he will do to each and every one of you, or even more, if he gets the upper hand over you.'[72] That refusal, however, was the limit of their solidarity. In an interesting parallel to Becket's isolation in the king's chamber at Northampton in 1164, the magnates withdrew from Marshal's vicinity, though on this occasion for fear of attracting the king's hostility, not because they shared the royal anger. The king for his part immediately looked for the support of his household familiars, his *bachilers*, meaning his knights and chamber officials, inciting them to condemn or even challenge Marshal. But he found them divided, and unwilling to confront the earl. The biographer put in the mouth of Baldwin de Béthune the opinion that landless household knights had no business judging great magnates such as Marshal.[73] The idea had become established by 1205 that the king did not want to talk to his magnates, and talked instead to lesser men who did not offer disinterested advice.

In John's reign we see the collapse of any conciliar role for the magnates at court. As a result, the political community whose consent had actually maintained Angevin rule in England disintegrated. The eventual civil war can be seen to have been inevitable in light of that. The final crisis began to unroll in August 1212 when John started to realise the extent of his isolation from his magnates and sensed a major threat to himself from the political community. The sources are united in their belief that rumours reached the king as he was preparing a campaign against Llywelyn ab Iorwerth of Gwynedd that there was a plot amongst the barons to do away with him when he was in the March of Wales. John would be apt to believe such a rumour. Plots to assassinate English kings were not unprecedented. King Henry I had broken one that involved his chamberlain, Herbert of Winchester, in 1118. Stephen survived an attempt in 1149 by assassin knights disguised as members of the royal household.[74] King John clearly knew what was energising the magnates: their agenda was not unfamiliar to him as he was not as deaf to the political community as he seemed. The Barnwell chronicler says that all of a sudden the king 'began to conduct himself more civilly to his people and the country subsided'. We are told he made a particular point of restraining his foresters and he pardoned the debts and fines incurred under forest law.[75] Hugh de Neville was certainly made a scapegoat over his management of the northern forests.[76] With the complaints over the forest, we are seeing the re-emergence of one of the principal items of the baronial agenda: one that had been evident in 1100. Significantly, the king went on in 1213 and 1214 to make rapprochements with magnates formerly in disgrace, making concessions over the debts and hostages by which he had controlled and dominated them.[77]

It was too late. The king's weakness meant that the new relationship would be formulated in the barons' favour, and there would be a legacy of alienation between king and magnates that would drastically modify the nature of their discourse. The brief civil war that preceded Magna Carta, and the much longer war of succession that followed it, forged a remarkable consensus within the political community of England, the magnates and their dependent knights. That consensus was summed up in the clauses of Magna Carta which from 1217 onwards became the basis of most of the discussions between king and magnates, and of the impulse to defy him. It made the thirteenth century a time of aristocratic self-confidence and strength, which caused serious difficulties even for a king like Edward I. John's reign has long had a reputation as a watershed in English politics. It clearly deserves it.

CHAPTER FIVE

✢

THE KING AND THE PEERS

A s has often been said, Magna Carta changed very little in 1215, but afterwards there was no doubt that the magnates of England had an agenda reached independently of the arena of the royal court and sometimes in opposition to it. Not only that, but Magna Carta established the baronial agenda in a written form to which there was continual recurrence and revision: a symptom, like chivalry, of the literacy of noble culture by the thirteenth century. It is evident in a number of ways that the world in general believed that the barons had a common agenda. Chroniclers talk of the 'magnates of England' meeting and discussing issues either together or with the king's agents. Most interestingly, we begin to find letters addressed by the magnates as a body to popes and foreign rulers, negotiating as a corporate power amongst powers. The end result was something new in England's social structure. The category of 'peers of England' appeared in the political consciousness, offering a novel way of characterising the social and political élite.

To return to the events of John's reign (1199–1216). The survey of corporatist behaviour amongst earlier generations of magnates I have already presented is a further argument against the belief stemming from Kate Norgate that what happened after 1212 was dependent largely on the intellectual organisation and inspiration of the archbishop, academic theologian and cardinal Stephen Langton (1207–28).[1] Given the right stimulus, the magnates of England had long been perfectly well able to organise themselves for political action and had long-term grievances and memories around which to unite. A London chronicle puts the situation succinctly: 'In that year [1215] a war erupted between the king and his barons around the Feast of the Invention of the Cross [3 May] because he denied them the liberties they had by the charters of the kings of England, his predecessors. These barons, though they came from all over England, were nonetheless generally called "Northerners".[2] To an onlooker at the heart of the kingdom, the struggle was between king and barons and it was over issues rooted in past relations between the two identifiable powers, whose customary relationship had collapsed. The barons themselves were projecting an image of an aristocracy united against a rogue monarch, which was perhaps why they themselves rejected the sectional label of 'Northerners'. In 1213 the pope regarded the barons and magnates of England as a group he could recruit in support of the penitent king. In 1214, the same body of magnates despatched three envoys to Rome carrying letters of authority issued in their name. From 1215, their meetings issued corporate letters to kings and to the pope, and even to shires, saluting them in the – rather presumptuous – name of the 'barons of England'. Likewise, letters of the pope recognised the 'barons of England' as a corporate body to be admonished and disciplined.[3] That the barons were not a united body is obvious. Several earls, notably Warwick, Derby and Pembroke, and a significant number of lesser barons, consistently took the king's part. John himself talked of the dissidents with more precision as 'the barons who are *against* us' (my emphasis).[4] For their part, the dissident barons stigmatised the minority of baronial loyalists as the king's 'evil advisers' or as 'foreigners' and therefore outside the category of proper English barons.

The fact that the barons focused on the coronation charter of Henry I as a basic discussion document for formulating their grievances is hardly surprising. The document was well known and freely available. We will never know precisely when it openly became the basis for discussion of the baronial agenda, though the story of its production by Stephen Langton at a meeting between barons and prelates in August 1213 is unlikely.[5] But, by 1214, it was certainly current as a discussion paper; indeed, there survives a brief from this time that assembles in Latin, with a French translation, the coronation charters of Henry I, Stephen and Henry II.[6] Clearly there was great interest amongst the political community as to what exactly were 'the liberties they had by the charters of the kings of England'. This was in the end translated into the terms of Magna Carta after John's defeat in the brief civil war of 1215. We know of the several meetings between January and June 1215 in which the barons – in consultation with the prelates and Londoners – hammered out their formal agenda for reform, even if we do not know the precise way it was done. Nonetheless, there exists a memorandum, usually called the 'Unknown Charter', which records a stage in the negotiations and is an annotation of a copy of the charter of Henry I. The memorandum is a baronial document. It only contains the things King John 'concedes' that were of pressing relevance to the aristocracy: the issues of reliefs for succession; wardship of heirs; marriage without disparagement; liberty to dispose of property in testaments; limits to military service outside England; the levying of scutage; forest abuses and Jewish debt.[7] All of these agenda items eventually made it into Magna Carta and the Charter of the Forest. They reveal the intellectual investment that the barons made in the reform process, and their energetic engagement explains why it was that the barons took to the battlefield to pursue their agenda. We can see from such passionate commitment why they decided to call themselves 'the Army of God and Holy Church in England'.

Magna Carta's most striking innovation is its attempt to formalise the baronial veto on, and monitoring of, the king's government. It tried to make the conciliar rule of England explicit rather than simply understood. It visualised a body of twenty-five barons, nominated by their fellows, whose duty was to supervise the way the king, his justiciar and officers administered the realm in the light of the terms of the settlement. Any four of the number could make representations over any perceived default, and if they were ignored they could take it to the rest. Then, if they wished to pursue the issue, the 'Twenty-Five' had liberty to take punitive action against the king's estates until their grievance was addressed. Its authority was to be affirmed by landowners' oaths to maintain it. The body was self-renewing and would fill any vacancies in its number. J.C. Holt saw the arrangement as applying to no more than the enforcement of the terms of Magna Carta,[8] but clearly the fact that it visualised the self-perpetuation of the Twenty-Five meant that it was intended to be a long-term consolidation of the barons' stake in how England was to be governed.

The importance of the Twenty-Five to future relations between king and aristocracy ought not to be underestimated. The overt idea behind the group – that the baronial agenda and the rights it claimed overrode the king's will – was unsettling to the political community. And it would take the best part of a century for the community to find ways to accommodate it. Though he was himself associated with the baronial party, the Béthune chronicler had little good to say about it, even while he recognised how pivotal its members were. The barons made a great point of choosing the Twenty-Five and, he said, 'by the disposition of these Twenty-Five the king consulted them on every issue'. But the writer called this arrangement several times a 'disgraceful peace'. He preserved stories of the misdeeds of the Twenty-Five, even though they operated for only a few months before war broke out again. They were so arrogant, he said, that the 'world in general' felt sorry for King John.

> One day the Twenty-Five barons came to court to make a judgement. The king at the time was off his feet, ill in bed, so that he couldn't come or go. So he asked the Twenty-Five to come into his chamber to give their judgement, because he was unable to go out to them. They replied that they would not budge as it would be against justice, but since the king couldn't move, he should be brought out. The king, who had no choice, had himself carried out before the Twenty-Five where they were, and they made no effort to accommodate him. . . . They committed any number of such outrages and acts of pride. The king was deeply angered and shamed by the arrogance he saw visited on him by his own men.[9]

This contemporary witness, even with his high contacts in the baronial party, saw it as no surprise that the political community should collapse in violence under such an objectionable power shift.

In the end, with John's death on campaign in October 1216 and the succession of a minor as king, the baronial preponderance in the rule of England was to continue in effect until Henry III finally engineered the downfall of Hubert de Burgh in 1231. The aristocratic council that ruled England did so with due reference to royal power, as it must, since it was the borrowed power of the sceptre that it ultimately wielded. One of the first acts of the new king's guardian, Earl William Marshal, revealed that the baronial party – defeated in alliance with Louis of France – had still achieved an intellectual victory. Even though the Marshal had supported King John in 1215, he put his seal to the reissue of Magna Carta in the council held in November 1216 immediately after the coronation of the boy king. This explicitly confirmed most of the agenda for reform that had been presented the previous year. Although it omitted some of the clauses that bore on raising revenue with the 'common consent' of the realm, and on the abuse of the forest, it made clear that those clauses were only on hold until 'a fuller council' should be able to consider them. The promise was honoured, and a further reissue of the chapter was made by the regency council, probably in November 1217, after the defeat of the French and the rebel barons, along with a charter specifically addressing grievances over the forest, a major irritation to the barons and the realm in general. In each case it was the seals of the legate and of Earl William Marshal that were placed on the documents.[10]

The corporate nature of the magnates ranged against the king and his council is expressed and reinforced in several ways in the reign of Henry III (1216–72), not least in the pronounced distaste that the magnates developed for the incompetence and erratic policy of the new king.[11] One of the least explored of these is the sudden currency in the 1230s of the term 'peers of England' to mean the barons who might expect a summons to a great council. The idea that the élite of a political community could be called *pares* or *compares* was an old one by the reign of Henry III. The leading men of honors in both England and northern France were being called 'peers' in the first half of the twelfth century.[12] The word simply meant 'fellows' and 'equals' in the corporate life of an honor. The idea is recognised as early as the compilation of the *Laws of Henry I* (*c*.1118), which talk of a plaintiff's *pares* in a baronial court as the men who judge him. The next decades see an extension of the idea. Geoffrey Gaimar in the late 1130s was already describing the barons of a royal court as its *parz*, which is a similar use of the term, though at a higher level.[13] The extension of the idea of the peers of a princely or royal court to that of the peers of a region or realm had certainly been accomplished by 1160. Wace of Bayeux talks in his *Roman de Brut* of the twelve *pers* of France 'who divided the territory into twelve each holding in chief and had himself called a king'.[14] The idea came out of the fictional Carolingian world of Charlemagne, Roland and Oliver, but it became translated into the real world of the twelfth century. The concept of the Twelve Peers of France (six bishops and six lay princes) was in existence in the 1170s when the archbishop of Reims and the count of Champagne were both reckoned to be of their number.[15]

There was never so formalised an idea of the peers of England as that which appeared in France, but the idea nonetheless had a clear impact across the Channel. Though there was never a fixed number of English peers, magnates in the thirteenth century claimed the status of 'peer' in ways that troubled Henry III's advisers. Magna Carta was another influence. Judgement by one's *pares* is referred to in several clauses, but clause 21 is most significant for our purpose as it said that earls and barons could not be subject to penal fines (amerced) except as imposed by *their* peers. The peers of magnates were clearly not the same as the peers of any free men, especially as clause 59 goes so far as to consider King Alexander of Scotland to be a man whose peers are to be found amongst the magnates of England. This lies behind the assertions on the part of successive earls of Pembroke between 1224 and 1233 that only their peers might sit in judgement upon

them, a position accepted by the regency, but which led an enraged Bishop
Peter des Roches to retort that there was no such thing as peers in England,
'as there were in France'.[16] The bishop was attempting to stigmatise the
barons as reading more into Magna Carta than was intended: the creation
of a privileged aristocratic caste.

The bishop may have been wrong in suggesting that this was the intended
result of the Marshal earls' ambitions, but was not wrong to see a 'peerage'
as the ultimate outcome of such an argument. In 1250, the baron William
de Beauchamp of Bedford was attempting to reclaim and assert his rights
as advocate of Newnham Priory, which his family had founded early in the
previous century. Alluding to Magna Carta's clause 46 (*c.* 33 in the 1225
reissue) which promised custody in vacancies to barons who had founded
abbeys with royal confirmation (the 1225 version in fact talked more generally of 'patrons of abbeys'), William claimed in the *curia regis* that he was
asking only for the rights of 'the earls and barons his *pares*, in England'.[17]
William de Beauchamp clearly believed that he was a member of a privileged caste, his privileges relying on Magna Carta and the individual
summons to councils that made him a baron. Only eight years later,
Henry of Germany, the king's nephew, son of Richard of Cornwall,
excused himself from swearing to the Provisions of Oxford, as he held no
land in his own right and so could not be regarded as a 'peer' of the assembled earls and barons.[18] The 1250s seems to have been the decade in which
the peerage of England became a commonly understood concept.[19]

A further aspect of the consolidation of this 'peerage' was the cultivation
amongst a section of the magnates of ideas of otherness. This was not
simply the well-known attempt to stigmatise objectionable Angevin royal
advisers, curial favourites and ministers as foreigners. It also had a broader
dimension in the period when the idea of a noble class was evolving. So the
biography of William Marshal, composed in the mid-1220s, stigmatised the
mercenary generals so favoured by Richard the Lionheart and John as
outsiders to the noble ethos of loyalty, service and liberal conduct of the
true aristocrat.[20] But in political terms the most effective means of consol-
idating a magnate identity was to claim for it a native English identity
against the objectionable foreignness of the king's circle.

English society in the later twelfth century was xenophobic, which
opened up a line of attack for envious courtiers against their enemies. The
first curial favourite to be sniped at because of his ethnic origins was
William de Longchamp. He was attacked for being of servile blood (which
he was not) and also because he was Norman. In fact, he was of the class and

background typical for members of the Angevin courts, and Henry II had furthered the careers of several Normans besides him in England during his reign.[21] However, being Richard the Lionheart's chancellor as count of Poitou, William de Longchamp was not of the circle of administrators and courtiers who had until then worked in England. So when he was imposed on England as justiciar in 1189, his foreign origins were a possible target by his rivals and their clerical auxiliaries for power. The attacks on him in the 1190s by the courtier-clerics Hugh de Nonant, bishop of Coventry (himself born and brought up in Normandy), and Gerald of Wales, archdeacon of Brecon (of a Norman lineage), were both illogical and remorseless. Gerald made a point of focusing on William's objectionable 'Norman' arrogance, boastfulness and inborn distaste for the English.[22] Exactly similar attacks were levelled against John's captain and administrator, Faulkes de Bréauté, a member of the lesser Norman nobility.[23] But more vulnerable to attack were the group of John's courtiers who were stigmatised as 'Poitevins'.

Henry II introduced few of his southern French subjects to England. The only major example was his half-brother Hamelin of Anjou, whom he married to the heiress of the Warenne earldom of Surrey in 1164.[24] John, on the other hand, enthusiastically recruited and imported southern French auxiliaries into England, despite being credited by Richard of Devizes in the political crisis of 1191 with the opportunistic view that only English-born constables should be appointed to keep royal castles. Richard portrayed John as at that point sharing the prejudices of his colleagues in the English nobility against intruders.[25] But two decades later it was a different story. John's foreign favourites were an issue by the time of Magna Carta, which contained a famously contemptuous clause (c. 50) banishing from office in England by name the king's foreign intimates whose activities had so offended the magnates. They were the more identifiable and contemptible members of the king's private *mesnie*, whose counsel he preferred to that of the barons and whom he used as agents against them. Most of these men were later identified as 'Poitevins', though they were rather more diverse in their origins. But the point was that they were neither Norman nor English, and so would have less sympathy with the subjects the king himself so distrusted. The ethnic characteristics attributed to natives of Poitou were that they were treacherous and naturally wicked. In fact, many of the men so stigmatised, notably their leader and patron Bishop Peter des Roches of Winchester – whom Roger of Wendover abused as introducing 'legions of Poitevins' to pillage England in his hatred of its natives – were from the Touraine, the eastern province of Greater Anjou.[26]

In this way, mutual suspicion between the great magnates and the king's curial henchmen reinforced the solidarity of England's social élite. It was a symptom of polarisation. Because of it, such a man as Simon de Montfort, whose family derived ultimately from the forest of Yvelines west of Paris and had held the county of Évreux in Normandy for most of the twelfth century, could come to England in 1230, assume his family's claim to the lordship and earldom of Leicester and be accepted as one of the anti-Poitevin party, simply because he was an English magnate amongst his fellows. Foreignness was merely a characteristic imposed on the king's objectionable familiar favourites.[27] A clerk writing around 1246 in south-east Wales stated as a fact that war broke out between King Henry and Earl Richard Marshal in 1233 'because of the foreigners whom Bishop Peter of Winchester and Peter de Orivall – his nephew or son – brought to England with the oppression of clergy and people in mind, just as in the days of King John'.[28]

Defence of the baronial agenda, a sense of shared status and a feeling of alienation from the king's intimate circles increasingly defined the magnate group as a peerage in the reign of Henry III. It was easy to rouse the magnates on those issues. A perfect instance is the first rebellion against the king, led by his brother Count Richard of Poitou, in the summer of 1227. As Wendover tells the story, the rebellion was sparked by a personal interview between the king and his brother over a disputed manor in the honor of Wallingford. The king lost his temper when Richard said he was prepared to undergo the judgement of the court of the king and the magnates of the realm. It was the use of the word 'magnates' that was objectionable to Henry. It is likely enough that 'trial by peers' was again at the heart of the political tension inspired by Richard, just as it was with the Marshals. Count Richard was associating himself with the agenda of Magna Carta while King Henry was attempting to resist its implications of conciliarism. The paranoia always evident amongst contemporary barons came out in rumours that Hubert de Burgh advised the king to have his brother arrested as he slept, which caused Count Richard to quit the court and take refuge with his brother-in-law, Earl William Marshal II, at Marlborough. Eight of the greatest earls and their baronial retinues rallied to Richard at Stamford in arms and made representations to the king over his treatment, but also about what Wendover calls the recent cancellation of the concessions in Magna Carta over forest jurisdiction (in fact, the records indicate something less dramatic: the king's officers had adopted the strategy of whittling away at the forest issue, county by county). The barons delicately suggested that the root of the problem was the bad advice the king was getting from the justiciar. The king – perhaps following Hubert de Burgh's canny advice – gave the appearance of backing down. He conceded the Wallingford issue to his brother, while temporising over the issue of the forests. When the fuss died down his officers continued to claw back forest jurisdiction.[29] In all this, the solidarity of the barons and their opposition to the king's curial advisers – even an Englishman like de Burgh – are as evident as the continued vitality of the spirit of 1215 amongst the new generation of earls.

A series of curious survivals more than hints at the intellectual turbulence amongst the politically aware community in the 1220s and 1230s as it came to terms with a nation polarised between a king and a self-defined peerage. Literary exercises of the time originating in the texts compiled for private schools in Oxford contain debates about the nature of royal power, and they continually resort to Magna Carta as the basis for political discussion. Take, for instance, the controversy kicked up by the marriage of Henry III's sister, Isabel, to the emperor Frederick II in 1235. The enormous sum of £20,000 offered as part of Isabel's marriage portion caused a financial crisis. It had to be answered by levying an aid on the king's feudal tenants, but there was no precedent for asking for assistance in marrying off the king's sister; custom only permitted it for an eldest daughter. When the barons had imposed their view of aids on King John in Magna Carta (*c.* 12), the king and barons stated the custom as follows: 'No scutage or aid is to be levied in our realm except by the common counsel of our realm, unless it is for the ransom of our person, the knighting of our eldest son *or the first marriage of our eldest daughter*, and for these only a reasonable aid is to be levied' (my italics). The charter laid the same terms for the levying of aids on any lord (*c.* 15).

A contemporary composition exercise from the Oxford of the late 1230s deals with this very question. It purports to be a letter of the king to his barons requesting an aid for his sister's marriage. In reality, the sum was granted early in the summer of 1235 by a council of barons and prelates, to be raised by a levy of two marks payable by a tenant-in-chief for every knight's fee, and a tax of a thirtieth on the goods of the English clergy.[30] The exceptional nature of the tax is noted by the king in the actual writ he sent to his sheriffs in July 1235 concerning its collection. He said that his barons 'conceded us a worthwhile aid to further our important business, *of their own free will and without creating any precedent*' (my italics).[31] The Oxford letter preserves a memory of the debate that had preceded the grant of the aid. It has a stark caricature of the royal position on aids in the observation ascribed to Henry III; 'We are justified in disposing of you and all your goods for our own honour and convenience, as follows from your oath of fealty.' That Henry was generally credited with so absolutist an outlook is evident from the king's own words on the influence of the disgraced Peter des Roches in 1234, denying he ever wanted to act towards his subjects 'as it suited me' (*pro velle nostro*).[32] Another Oxford letter provides the joint retort to that argument from 'the earls, barons and knights of England':

> Know that we acknowledge that we owe to you as our lord whatever and as much as we can, as due from our allegiance. Although you have lordship over us you have a duty not to harm us in the payments due to you. If the marriage of your sister uses up most of your wealth why then do you resort to us, when you have rents and farms with which you may be able to fill your treasury? Let it be far from the royal dignity to harass your free subjects in the customary payments due to you and to demand from them what they used never to do.[33]

It would seem from the writ of July 1235 that such representations actually were made, and the king was obliged to insert a clause in the writ for the tax's collection that affirmed that it created no precedent and, by implication, did not challenge Magna Carta.

It was the tragedy of Henry III's reign that the king was utterly unable to heal the widening breach of trust between himself and the magnates, despite being guiltless of the intentions imputed to him. The crises of 1227, 1233 and 1242 all involved baronial assumptions, first, that the king was out to thwart the agenda Magna Carta had enshrined and, second, that the party of advisers and foreign favourites around him was antagonistic to their established liberties. Nor was it just the barons who were nervous of the king's intentions. A formulary exercise of the late 1240s imagines a local knight agitating his neighbours because the king was attempting to get round the Magna Carta provisions on disparagement (unequal social marriages forced on heirs by their guardians; see below, pp. 60–1).[34] The imaginary knight took his stand on the principles of 1215. But real-life county knights also pored over the text of Magna Carta and presumably reflected on it. Sir Richard Hotot of Clapton, Northamptonshire (died 1250), included amongst his papers compiled in the 1240s copies of the 1217 Charter of the Forest and the 1225 reissue of Magna Carta, not to mention texts of King John's settlements with Pope Innocent III.[35]

But for all the suspicion of a royal agenda against Magna Carta, the reality was that the magnates were more powerful as a group in Henry III's reign than they had ever been and had more ability than their predecessors to thwart the king in his objectives. It is too easy to look at the huge and deeply impressive documentary output of the chancery and exchequer for the thirteenth century – the product of the national apparatus of justice and finance in England – and see it as a sign of enormous royal power. But this is a non sequitur. Bureaucratic expansion could as likely be a response to weakness as a sign of strength. The bankruptcy of the English monarchy in the face of the king's unrealistic ambitions from the 1230s onwards is a fact that hardly reflects well on the capacities of royal government. The bureaucratic machine was only as formidable as the king who operated it. For all his occasional petulance and high words, Henry III was conciliatory and unaggressive towards his magnates, a group that already had a rallying point around its own common agenda against the king. Indeed, the king's care to appear to be seen to be defending the provisions of Magna Carta is itself a sign of where the balance of power lay in his reign, even if he had a tendency to try to use clause 40 (about magnates' refusal of justice to their men) against them.[36] The diffidence of the king in using the power of his bureaucracy against his magnates is to be seen in the statement of Matthew Paris in 1256 that Henry forbade the issue by the chancery of writs that would affect the interests of his brother, the earl of Cornwall, his half-brothers, Aymer de Lusignan and William de Valence, Richard de Clare, earl of Gloucester and Hertford, and Peter of Savoy, his wife's uncle.[37] Though there is no surviving text of such a document as Paris describes, David Carpenter has found evidence that the king in 1255 did in fact personally intervene, at the instance of the earl of Gloucester, to frustrate the holding of an assize involving a member of the earl's affinity in Somerset.[38] This would tend to confirm that the king was lax in using his powers and that Paris's assertion had some basis in fact.

The definitive crisis of the reign in 1258 reveals the potential dominance of the magnates when they acted together. The king had bankrupted and overstretched himself in funding grandiose and unrealistic foreign ventures in Italy. This shifted further the balance of power between himself and the barons. As in 1235, the king had to go to a *parlement* of the magnates and face its demands. At Oxford he found them determined not merely to state their established grievances but also to demand a stake in government in return for their assistance. The magnates had clearly learned from the earlier financial crisis of 1235 that they could extract concessions. In 1258, they were demanding the fullest consummation of their grievances. The most objectionable aliens within the king's household were to be expelled, notably his Poitevin half-brothers, the Lusignans. The king was obliged to offer the concession that his council would henceforth only include native Englishmen. But the most sweeping demand was a reappearance of the sort of mechanism found in the original Magna Carta for formalising and perpetuating magnate influence in government. Twenty-four prelates, earls and barons were appointed as representatives of their peers, twelve from what was called the 'community' and twelve from the side of the king and his heir, the Lord Edward, with the purpose of 'the correction and reform both of their own affairs and the realm'. Four of the Twenty-Four (two king's men and two others) were to choose the king's council of fifteen. To make their voice the more effective, one of the baronial Twelve, Hugh, brother of Earl Roger Bigod III of Norfolk, was chosen to revive in himself the office of justiciar of England. The magnates were resurrecting a former instrument of royal control in their own interest. Unlike the barons of 1215, those of 1258 sought a permanent voice in the affairs of the realm, demanding 'parlemenz' of the Twenty-Four and others three times a year, to meet without the need for a royal summons. The Twenty-Four also had an assured say in the business of the kingdom and in matters of its reform.[39]

The baronial group in 1258 was no more cohesive than its predecessors had been in 1215, for there were English-born barons, such as Earl John I de Warenne of Surrey (died 1304), who appeared in the king's selected Twelve, even though the majority of the most powerful English earls and barons were in the other camp. But the agenda they embraced identified and defined a magnate group as surely as in 1214. Perhaps the principal difference in 1258 was the barons' description of themselves as the *commun de Engletere*, 'the whole community of England'. This was extending the principles of which they were the self-ordained guardians to the whole political community. They intended it to be taken seriously too, as the king notified the shires of his acceptance of the Provisions of Oxford in a writ composed in English, so that every estate and condition of his subjects should be included in the debate. This writ calls the magnates assembled at Oxford 'the people of the land of our kingdom'.[40] To outsiders also, the magnates appeared a distinct force pitted against the enemies of the realm. The evocative if fragmentary 'Song of the Barons' lists the barons involved in the political world of 1263 rather in the manner of a tournament roll, with verses describing each and his particular relationship to the court.[41]

The solidarity of this baronial group should not of course be taken for granted. Much can be and has been made of the appearance of a group in 1259 that embraced the same agenda but was called by the Burton annalist 'the community of the bachelers of England' (*communitas bachelarie Anglie*), who expressed at Westminster dissatisfaction with the implementation of the Provisions. This 'bachelery' has been interpreted variously as being a breakaway group of younger nobles or the ancestor of the commons.[42] In fact, the term *bacheleria/bachelerie* does not necessarily imply that. From its first appearance at the end of the twelfth century, *bachelerie* implies a body of knights gathered for a purpose, most usually a tournament.[43] Since tournaments were often the occasion and excuse for barons to assemble in arms for political purposes, the Burton annalist's *bacheleria* was almost certainly intended simply to mean an assembly of the aristocracy convened for a particular purpose, in this case as a pressure group. But, however we interpret it, the incident reveals that the baronial group contained both radicals and moderates. Tellingly their principles and agenda were the same, and the tumultuous and violent events of the subsequent five years amply demonstrate how a class might be defined and reinforced by a common social and political ideology.

PART THREE

IMPOSING HEGEMONY

CHAPTER SIX

✛

LOCAL VIOLENCE

THE threat of violence has long been recognised as a significant, and unhealthy, part of the armoury of social domination of one group over another (not least men over women). Norbert Elias, for instance, saw the princes' monopoly of violence as the fundamental cause of the appearance of restraint and civility as a characteristic of noble behaviour at court. To challenge the king openly was to call down vengeance. It was better to behave circumspectly around him (see below, p. 205). Medieval clerics saw unrestrained violence as a characteristic of the princes and knights of the eleventh century, and the means by which they imposed themselves on their inferiors. The French mutationist theory drew the conclusion from the writings of such men that a new level of violence was a consequence of a social revolution around the year 1000, when the king's grip on public order was usurped by the violence of princes and counts (see above, pp. xv–xvi). More recently, the historian Thomas Bisson in a broad study of medieval society perceives violence simply as a natural and generic consequence of medieval lordship.[1] The subject is inescapable in any treatment of medieval aristocracy, and this part of the book addresses the idea of social violence and domination from several directions.

PRIVATE WARFARE AND MAGNATE VIOLENCE

Roger the Poitevin, count of La Marche and lord of much of Lancashire and Suffolk in the 1090s, was a powerful figure in Anglo-Norman England, a younger son of the Conqueror's companion Roger de Montgomery. He had received large parts of north-west England in the aftermath of the Conquest, comprising the bulk of what was to become Lancashire as well as scattered estates across the Midlands and East Anglia. Roger obtained his surname and his county in Poitou from marriage to Almodis, heir after 1091 of her brother, Count Boso III of La Marche. In Domesday terms he was a very great magnate indeed, though at the time of the survey his fortunes were temporarily in decline. He was, however, close enough to William Rufus at the moment of the king's succession to retrieve his fortunes, and indeed increase his possessions, with a grant of the large East Anglian honor of Eye soon after 1088.[2] Count Roger was therefore a considerable figure in England in the 1090s, and we are privileged to have a glimpse of the way he exercised his power in the Midlands of England in that decade.

Amongst other lands Count Roger acquired from Rufus was the Staffordshire estate around Repton that had been held by Nigel of Stafford at the Domesday survey. This included the manor of Drakelow, which was adjacent to that of Stapenhill (at that time lying in Derbyshire), a posses-sion of the abbey of Burton. The abbey lay opposite both Drakelow and Stapenhill, across the river Trent in Staffordshire. In the early 1090s, a dispute broke out between count and abbot over two peasants who had fled the abbot's jurisdiction at Stapenhill and claimed that they were under Count Roger's lordship. We know of this because the incident formed the basis of one of the miracles of St Modwenna in an account of her life and wonders written in the later years of the next reign by Abbot Geoffrey of Burton (1114–50). The abbot's attempt to reassert his lordship over the recalcitrant pair by seizing their crops and possessions led to a complaint lodged by the peasants in the count's curia. Geoffrey's account continues:

> The count's anger was roused against the abbot, so much that he threat-ened to kill him wherever he might find him. Violently angry, he gathered a great troop of knights and peasants with weapons and carts and sent them in a great company to the monks' barns at Stapenhill and had them seize by force all the crops stored there.... Not content with this, Count Roger sent many men and knights to the abbey's fields near Blackpool, commanding them to lay waste the church's crops with all their might and encouraging them especially to lure into battle the ten knights of the abbot's own family whom he had in his company. The abbot heard about this and forbade his knights from going out.[3]

However, the knights of his household disobeyed the abbot's instructions, and, armed and mounted, sought out the count's men: 'few against many', Abbot Geoffrey said, quoting Caesar's *Gallic Wars*. They took on a force six times their number and, by knocking down the count's seneschal – probably the commander of his troops – and worsting a kinsman of the count amongst the knights, the abbey's small *mesnie* routed their opponents. Disturbed by this apparently supernatural intervention and by other tokens of the saint's anger, which much affected the fortunes of his own manor of Drakelow, Count Roger was so terrified by the power of Modwenna that he and his knights eventually came to seek pardon of the abbot and saint, backing up their submission with a formal written concord. So peace returned to the middle Trent valley.

Though this early twelfth-century account belongs to a generation after the events it describes, the basic details seem unlikely to have been invented: there had been a brief episode of private warfare in the middle Trent valley in the 1090s and a small body of Burton abbey's knights had defied expectations, routing the formidable household of the fierce and feared Count Roger the Poitevin. The cause of the violence had been a property dispute between count and abbot in which the abbot had antagonised the count by his use of what was later called 'distraint', a forcible seizure of goods to punish and discipline recalcitrant tenants.[4] Undoubtedly, the Burton account is partial and incomplete. The use of distraint implies that the defaulting peasants may well have been pursued through the abbey's court before more dramatic action was taken. There could have been a legal process of sorts. The count might have been angry because he believed the abbot had infringed his rights over the pair, and the authority of his own court had been defied. Nonetheless, the count had resorted to violence, and the confrontation had escalated to the extent that he had sent a detachment of his military household under his seneschal, with instructions to lay waste the abbey's lands across the river. It does not appear that anyone thought to resort to the king's court to settle the matter. Count Roger had assumed all power here, and he got away with that assumption.

Somehow, such an episode does not seem characteristic of Norman England, where the dominant narrative is all about an increase in civil peace and royal control of the legal process. However, it does seem in line with the following episode from contemporary South Wales. 'King Caradog of Glamorgan despatched his military household to St Maughans, an estate of Bishop Herwald [of Glamorgan] and Ss Dyrig, Teilo and Euddogwy. When they had seized the bishop's food-rents, Rhydderch ap Egwyd forcibly held and ate a feast there uninvited, and stayed overnight, drowned and intoxicated by strong drink. After such an imposition, the bishop sent messengers to the king demanding restitution and compensation for the damage done by his household.'[5] Another parallel might be made with the ensuing account from the contemporary Loire valley. 'In the time of Count Fulk, brother of Geoffrey the bearded, anger (*ira*) arose between this same count and Bartholomew, lord of L'Isle Bouchard. As that anger burned brighter, Count Fulk first gathered together an army against Bartholomew and then built a fortification (*castrum*) at Champigny-sur-Veude, which he gave to Robert de Blois to guard. But Bartholomew, after having gathered together his friends, burned down that *castrum* and seized those inside.'[6]

In these cases from three different realms, secular rulers and magnates employed naked violence in furtherance of their aims. This leads us into a wide historical debate. In France, the tendency to resort to violence by eleventh-century magnates has been seen by historians as symptomatic of a deep social transformation around the year 1000. The last relics of the Roman imperial ideal of public power, which had become vested in the post-Roman kingdoms, collapsed around the millennium as magnates, barons and even knights assumed the prerogative to exert their authority (the *ban*, as it is called by French historians) over regions great and small. The use of violence to establish rule went down the social scale over several generations so that anyone who had a castle and a military household became a petty prince, imposing his justice and financial exactions on less powerful or powerless neighbours.[7] Even though historians no longer subscribe to quite so catastrophic a view, aristocratic resort to violence is clearly something that happens a lot in French medieval sources, and is taken as the regrettable way of the world even in the comparatively ordered realm of Normandy. For one it colours the rhetoric of Orderic Vitalis. Dominique Barthélemy takes this state as characteristic of society from the ninth century onwards. He calls it 'la faide chevaleresque' to distance himself from the old 'feudal' explanations of violence. It was more to do with asserting rights than usurping lordship.[8]

What is described as happening between Count Roger and Burton abbey early in the 1090s is not too different from what Barthélemy sees in France: local violence sparked by a perceived affront to a lord and his rights. Such events are rare, though not unprecedented, in English sources. When such a level of violence occurred it was usually in times of general or local rebellion against the king. General rebellions, such as those against William Rufus in 1088 and 1095, Henry I in 1101, Stephen in 1139–47 and Henry II in 1173–4, are special cases because they were defined as a 'time of war'. They were fuelled (as we have already seen) by succession problems within the royal family as well as by a developing and recurring magnate discontent over a specific set of social problems. General rebellions are not useful comparisons to the Burton abbey incident, which happened in a time of general peace. Local rebellions by one or two magnates against the king are more readily comparable. An early instance is the rebellion in 1075 of Earl Roger de Breteuil of Hereford and Earl Ralph de Gael of East Anglia. The letter collection of Archbishop Lanfranc of Canterbury (1070–89), who had to deal with the crisis in the king's absence, reveals that what was at issue was Earl Roger's annoyance that he had not succeeded to his father's authority over the sheriffs of the southern March of Wales (Earl Ralph's particular grievances are not known). Earls Roger and Ralph recruited allies amongst their fellow magnates, the Danes and the Welsh kings. Knights were summoned and castles put in defence – to no good end, as it turned out.

However, we may be deceived as to what was really going on in 1075 by the words in which the events are described. Earl Roger would probably not have regarded his action as 'rebellion', but as 'defiance' – the repudiation of his allegiance to the king because William had not listened to his justified grievances. Such action represented a threat of violence within a process of negotiation, but how far the violence went depended on the king's response. The Conqueror and his agents in 1075 decided in the end to treat the defiance as insurrection.[9] Earl Roger was confronted, crushed and imprisoned for life. His allies were either executed (as was Earl Waltheof) or driven into exile (as was Earl Ralph). To use naked violence within England was dangerous for a magnate, and Earl Robert de Mowbray of Northumbria was subject to the same decisive treatment when he defied King William Rufus in 1095 over the intrusiveness of royal authority in his earldom, where his (reputedly excessive) taxation of Norwegian ships had led to complaints. He refused to answer the summons to court issued by the king, and by that act defied him as his lord.[10] Though Earl Robert's rising became the core of a more dangerous and more general rebellion, its origin was, as William of Malmesbury put it, 'a major difference of opinion between earl and king'.[11]

The use of violence in relations with the king was not always as fatal as it was to Roger de Breteuil and Robert de Mowbray, which may explain why certain magnates were willing to risk it. Violence could trigger the sort of negotiations for which the barons were hoping. When Earl Roger of Hereford fortified his castles and gathered his allies against Henry II in the spring of 1155, he got his way: negotiation produced a written settlement guaranteeing him the former royal assets he believed were threatened by the new king (see above, pp. 74–5). Conversely, similar action by Hugh de Mortemer in that same spring of 1155 was treated as rebellion and resulted in his being crushed and exiled. It depended on the king's assessment of the situation. Henry II could not afford to confront Earl Roger, so he negotiated, but Hugh was a much less dangerous opponent and his destruction served as a useful warning to his baronial colleagues. A precise parallel to these events in the first year of Henry II's reign (1155) can be found in the first year of Stephen's (1136). Baldwin de Redvers, lord of Okehampton, chose to assert his claim to the shrievalty of Devon by mobilising his knights and seizing Exeter. Stephen chose not to negotiate and went out of his way to stage a set-piece siege of the city to crush Baldwin, deliberately deploying the majority of his aristocracy in its execution in order to send out a message as to how isolated Baldwin was.[12] But the comparable action of Hugh Bigod in seizing Norwich that same year was let pass, and Hugh was treated with leniency, possibly because he had been one of the first barons to pledge allegiance to the new king.[13]

Violent defiance long remained a baronial strategy in relations with the king, though it was a always a dangerous one. When magnates contemplated defiance, they did well to be circumspect in their threat as the young Earl William Marshal showed himself to be in a letter to the justiciar in 1224, saying that he had absolutely no intention of withdrawing from the king's court 'unless justice is denied me'.[14] But violent defiance nonetheless happened, and we know of magnates like Earl Roger of Hereford and Count William of Aumale who challenged Henry II in 1155 and were lucky enough to get away with it. When Earl Robert III of Leicester attempted the same in 1173, however, the results were catastrophic. The 'rebellion' of William de Briouze against King John in the spring of 1208 is an instructive case. We are lucky to have an account of what happened from King John himself, who wanted to establish the facts for the benefit of the broader political community. Briouze was a man of good lineage, and a magnate in both England and Normandy. He had been high in the king's favour at the beginning of John's reign, and had acquired wide possessions in Ireland in return for very large rents which the king did not expect to be paid while Briouze was in favour. When the king and Briouze fell out in 1207, the money was demanded, but Briouze had no chance of paying his debt.[15] The Briouze estates were thus to be seized, the king making the point that what he was doing was entirely 'according to the custom of England and the law of the Exchequer'. But plainly, as far as Briouze was concerned, he was being victimised. There were attempts at negotiation through relatives and the surrender of hostages and Welsh castles as security and part-payment. In the end, however, Briouze could put up with no more. With his sons he gathered a military force in the March, and besieged his forfeited castles when their constables had gone off to collect their salaries from the king's agent, Gerard d'Athée. Since the castles disappointed him by resisting, Briouze moved on to the unfortified town of Leominster. There he sacked and burned the settlement, attacking a company of royal troops and inflicting casualties as he routed them. But since (according to another source) his tenants in the March refused to support his rebellion, he retreated across Wales and ultimately sought shelter with friends and relatives in Ireland.[16]

In the words of a sympathetic contemporary, the Briouze affair appeared thus: 'The king conceived such hatred for [William de Briouze] that he harassed him from every direction, so much so that he could not withstand him or endure his hostility. He remained for a time in Wales, but his men were so hostile towards him that he dare not put his faith in them and had to think of another course.'[17] Just as Robert de Mowbray thought himself hounded into resistance to oppressive royal action in 1095, so William de Briouze turned to violence in 1208, though probably with more justification. He had been reduced to such action by stress arising from fear of the king's intentions; humiliation at his inability to fulfil his role as lord and magnate; and probably the realisation that he had little left to lose. If he took to arms, he might make himself a sufficient nuisance to increase his negotiating position; or his fellow magnates might offer support and so unsettle the unrelenting king, as indeed did happen in Ireland when he got there. Perhaps most importantly, by taking to arms he might evade the stress caused by loss of honour and impending humiliation. The habitus of contemporary aristocratic mores *forced* Briouze into this hopeless act of violence.

A similar, well-documented instance is the incident that contemporaries called 'the Marshal war' of 1233–4. This is in many ways comparable to the Briouze insurrection, though since the king involved was Henry III, the outcome was not so decisively in the royal favour. The trigger was, as usual, a magnate's belief that his just claims were being denied by the king. In this case Earl Richard Marshal had been affronted by the way that his brother's young widow, the king's sister Eleanor, had taken so large a share of his inheritance in 1231, more indeed than the traditional third owed a widow.[18] There were other complicating factors, not least the dominance of the court by Bishop Peter des Roches, whose actions and prejudices were inflammatory to the English nobility. Nonetheless, the earl put up with the various annoyances plaguing him until he was presented with a situation that challenged his sense of honour: his inability to protect his affinity of local allies. Gilbert Basset of High Wycombe (died 1241) was a banneret associated with the households of Richard's predecessors as earl, and also a retained royal knight; he was therefore a central character in the Marshal interest group at court.[19] As a consequence of the dominance of des Roches, Gilbert was in February 1233 deprived of his manor of Upavon, Wiltshire, in favour of des Roches's ally Peter de Maulay. The gross injustice of this left Basset with no alternative but to defy the king formally. Earl Richard Marshal withdrew from court not long afterwards.[20] Basset and the long-time retained Marshal banneret Richard Siward (died 1248) opened a campaign of raids against the king's men in June 1233 which led to their outlawry. By the end of July, Richard Marshal had decided to throw in his lot with the Bassets and had summoned his supporters to assemble at Gilbert's chief manor of High Wycombe, Buckinghamshire. The assembly was no great success in terms of numbers, so the earl retired to the Marches, where he met a more positive response. The Marshal affinity and lordships responded to the raising of his banner and the crucial support of Prince Llywelyn of Gwynedd was secured. Though Earl Richard attracted few adherents amongst his fellow magnates, he was still able to mount some spectacular chevauchées across the Midlands and West Country, one of which liberated the captive Hubert de Burgh from imprisonment in Devizes. During the autumn and winter of 1233–4, he was committed to a full-scale war against the king. Though military victory eluded both sides, the Marshal's defiance destabilised the court and ultimately led to the fall of des Roches and his party in March 1234, which might be seen as the earl's chief objective.[21]

In England as much as France one can detect that individual aristocrats felt driven to draw swords to resolve arguments, to the point where they became what we would call lawless brigands. The case of Robert de Bellême, lord of Bellême and earl of Shrewsbury (fl. 1077–1112), is often mentioned as relevant in the context of Anglo-Norman England. He appears in the writings of Orderic Vitalis as a monster of violence. Orderic pictures him dominating southern Normandy by deploying squadrons of knights, intimidating churchmen and neighbours alike. He would imprison those who got on his wrong side and torture them hideously, laughing at their torments. To Orderic, Robert was a sadistic pervert and a butcher, at war with all the world, and secure from punishment while he had ducal favour.[22] This same man was also an English magnate, who held the earldom of Shrewsbury for four years after the death of his brother, Earl Hugh, in

1098. Even though there is good reason to set aside most of Orderic's verdict as mere rhetoric designed to exalt by comparison his moral hero, Henry I, Robert de Bellême's oppressive behaviour to his neighbours can hardly be disputed. It certainly corresponds to the way his brother, Roger the Poitevin, is alleged to have conducted himself towards Burton abbey. It is hardly surprising in England that Robert challenged Henry I militarily in 1102 under the growing weight of the royal prosecution of complaints against him. He allied himself with his powerful brothers, Counts Roger and Arnulf, Norse mercenaries from Ireland and the Welsh kings.[23] His defeat and exile by King Henry therefore completed a career trajectory parallel to that of his similarly violent contemporary Earl Robert de Mowbray of Northumbria.

In the course of Orderic's description of the unsuccessful rebellion of the Montgomery brothers against Henry I in 1102, he offers a reconstruction of a debate that supposedly occurred at a council held in the king's presence at Bridgnorth during the siege of the rebel castle. It is a debate that lifts some corners on the obscurity that mantles contemporary attitudes towards aristocratic violence. The way Orderic tells it, the magnates at court were troubled by the decisiveness of the king against the Montgomery brothers, seeing it as a challenge to their corporate autonomy. They therefore attempted to mediate a settlement that would bring peace but preserve Robert de Bellême's honour and position. But the assembly included a large group of *pagenses milites*, meaning the propertied knights from the shires who were with the army. They intervened robustly from the sidelines, hostile to the magnates' intentions. They urged the king to pursue Robert to the death, calling him a traitor (*traditor*) and identifying their own interests with the king and civil peace. Robert's tenants likewise seemed not to care to go to the scaffold for him, and willingly surrendered his castles. The only men ready to support him were his paid retainers (*stipendiarii*), who had to be neutralised by the locals once the retainers realised what was going on and took up arms to preserve themselves from the disgrace (*opprobrium*) that would attach to them and their sort from their forced surrender.[24] Orderic's intention is clearly to assert that it was the magnate – not the lesser local aristocrat – whose ambitions, military retinue and sense of personal honour principally led to local violence in both England and Normandy.

How much aristocratic brigandage went on in England in the eleventh and twelfth centuries? The sources do not help us much in attempting an assessment of this. Most records of disputes are the end result of a process that brought about a settlement, a written document. Such sources often mask any wilful, random and violent actions that might have preceded the documented conclusion. We know that Burton abbey suffered from the military aggression of Roger the Poitevin, and there may have been other such incidents. Between 1101 and 1107, the Norfolk abbey of St Benet of Holme drew up an account of the losses it had suffered at the hands of the neighbouring magnate, Roger Bigod, and his men. It cited fifteen cases of land and tenants abstracted from their estates. But it is clear here that in most cases the disputes were over small and long-contested items of property, and there is little implication that organised violence was part of the process.[25] Burton Abbey's records include formal agreements (*conventiones*) with other local landlords and magnates that might conceivably have been the culmination of similar unrecorded aggressions, such as the *conventio* reached between the abbey and Robert II de Ferrers (died 1138), the powerful lord of Tutbury and later earl of Derby, at some time between 1114 and 1126 after 'a dispute between them ... so vociferous that it got as far as King Henry'. That it may have involved some real violence is hinted by Robert piously renouncing his sins and taking on the future role of 'patron and protector' (*amicus et tutor*) of the abbey. It was reached in a baronial assembly that included a royal representative, the baron William Peverel.[26] Then there is the problem that contemporary legal process did accept that there could be forced dispossession (disseisin) as part of a dispute over land. So when the Domesday record for Lincolnshire documents seventy-one outstanding 'disputes' (*clamores*) over landholding within that large county, and says that claimants were 'disseised' or dispossessed 'by force' (which it does explicitly in six cases), this is not necessarily evidence of a level of intimidation and violence beyond what the courts would countenance.[27]

Unrelenting violent intimidation is hard to discern in the sources we have. However, even the text of Domesday occasionally records some deeds of the blacker sort. Robin Fleming points to incidents preserved in the 'encroachments' (*invasiones*) that Domesday Book says happened since the Conquest, encroachments carried out by one French aristocrat against another. The magnate Richard fitz Gilbert de Clare was apparently so notorious for his aggressions towards his Suffolk neighbours that Domesday calls him *malus vicinus* (a translation of the French *malveisin*, or 'bad neighbour'). Bertram de Verdun's long absence in France in the king's service tempted two neighbouring magnates to filch large pieces of land and plant an unlicensed mill on his detached property in Buckinghamshire.[28] Such

behaviour continued into the twelfth century, notwithstanding the reputation of Henry I and his ministers for enforcing civil peace, but we hear
of it only for the most part when contemporary writers notice it, which
they rarely do unless – like Geoffrey of Burton – they have a personal
interest in doing so.[29] Sometimes unusual sequences of documents can lift
a corner on violent power politics in the English shires. So a collection of
conveyances and grants relating to north-west Leicestershire in the 1120s
and 1130s, in the otherwise tranquil reign of Henry I, allowed Edmund
King and myself to reconstruct a violent conflict centred on the young
Earl Robert II of Leicester (died 1168). The latter apparently victimised
both Earl Ranulf II of Chester (died 1153) and the bishop of Lincoln in his
efforts to exert exclusive control over the town of Leicester, the lower Soar
valley and Charnwood. It was a conflict in which the earl of Leicester
forcibly seized the Chester-controlled manor of Garendon and the bishop's
manor of Knighton. King Henry I became involved in much the same
way he had in the conflict between Robert de Ferrers and Burton abbey. He
bribed Robert of Leicester to return Knighton to the bishop by offering
him the royal manor of Asfordby (see below, p. 138).[30] Similarly, the existence of a peace settlement between Earl Roger of Warwick (died 1153)
and his teenage neighbour and tenant Geoffrey II de Clinton of Kenilworth
(died 1176) reveals that the earl and the boy Clinton had a private war in
the valley of the Warwickshire Avon in 1136–7, which involved a siege of
Brandon castle. In this case, the fight was about the insertion of the Clinton
family into Warwickshire in the 1120s by King Henry at the expense of the
earl, who had probably fallen under suspicion during the Norman rebellion
of 1123–4.[31]

Despite the reputation for civil peace that England enjoyed under Henry
I between 1102 and 1135, which is broadcast alike by contemporary verdicts
from Paris, Rome and Peterborough, it nonetheless appears that English
magnates might on occasion, through hubris, slighted honour or sheer
aggression, deploy their military households to settle differences.[32] Of
course, the general warfare that frequently ravaged England between 1138
and 1147 complicates historical analysis. It made Henry I's England seem
all the more ordered and peaceful than the England of King Stephen which
succeeded it. But the very fact that Henry I's magnates had the military
resources, motivation and expertise in the next reign to carry on local
warfare during the war of succession with Empress Matilda hints that their
activities had always had the potential and inclination to tip over into
violence. Indeed, Pope Innocent's conviction that England had edged into

anarchy in the immediate aftermath of Henry I's death – a belief encouraged by Stephen's supporters – might be taken as an argument that contemporaries could readily conceive of an outbreak of private warfare within the realm Henry I had supposedly tamed.

The impact of Stephen's reign on subsequent magnate conduct might be argued to have been profound on several levels. As has been explained (see above, pp. 71–4), it gave the magnates a feeling of corporate responsibility for the civil peace of England, a feeling that is powerfully evident for decades after Henry II's succession. Furthermore, the settlement that was reached in 1153 enshrined new principles that had a clear and lasting impact on the behaviour of landowners. Since the settlement pronounced that 1 December 1135 ('the day on which King Henry was alive and dead') was the benchmark date for the establishment of possession of any estate, magnates had more incentive to seek a royal writ to fight out cases before the king's justices than to arm their knights and take matters into their own hands. It seems a worthwhile argument that aristocratic conflict found a new arena in the courts in the second half of the twelfth century, and litigiousness took the place of local confrontation, just as the tournament was their methodone for the drug of true warfare. The sources are not there fully to justify such an argument, but the comparative lack of evidence of private conflict in England after the 1150s – despite the huge increase in surviving documentation – is in contrast to what preceded it. Even when it occurs in the days of the early Angevin kings, local violence can turn out – as in the case of Roger the Poitevin and Burton abbey in Rufus's reign – to have some root in legal process. So when the Meaux chronicler depicts the Yorkshire knight Saer of Sutton as raiding the abbey's lands in the East Riding with an armed gang in John's reign, and carrying off cash and goods, he also has to admit that the monks were at law with Saer over his father's gifts to the abbey, and that Saer had disseised the abbey of a piece of contested moorland. Saer may have seen himself as acting within his rights by a forced distraint following a judgement for damages in his own court. The abbey, of course, saw it as an insult to civil peace.[33]

The outrage projected by contemporary writers at the serious dynastic disturbances of 1173–4 is noteworthy. The resort to arms by English earls and barons and the sieges of castles and recruitment of mercenaries were clearly thought to be something that belonged to the past and were indeed un-English. This rather echoes what Orderic had to say in the 1120s about the jaundiced way in which local landowners regarded the violent ambitions of the magnates from whom they held their land. It is also implied by words

imputed to the countess of Leicester by Jordan Fantosme in his history of
that rebellion, that English knights had little facility in arms, presumably
because it was perceived that they did not have much occasion to use
them.[34] Magnates might edge towards violence and then seek an advantageous compromise, as in the cases we have seen in Henry I's reign. But
with the ready availability of an authoritative central justiciar's court based
on the exchequer, the move into the legal arena was clearly attractive, more
so than awaiting local arbitration from touring royal justices. So in 1163 we
find that old warrior Earl William d'Aubigny of Arundel using his officers
violently to intimidate the peasants of Happisburgh in Norfolk, and then
deploying his men to resist the arrival of the abbot of St Albans. The abbot
had come to investigate the complaints of the peasants of the village
against his abbey's prior at Wymondham, who had begun the whole business
by calling in the earl to discipline Wymondham's tenants there. The earl's
temper was apparently notorious, and perhaps it had to be for him to get his
way in the neighbourhood. In fact, the earl seemed willing to meet and
discuss the problem both privately and before the justiciar, the earl of
Leicester, with no further physical violence, though his language to the
abbot is said to have been pretty rough.[35]

Even when there had been demonstrable violence and injustice, local
élites of the later twelfth century hoped that resort to the king might result
in justice, and neither were they necessarily disappointed. The tenure of
the lordship of Amunderness and shrievalty of Lancashire by Theobald
Walter (died 1205) between 1194 and 1199 was recalled over fifty years later
by a Lancashire jury as a time of violent depredation when neighbours had
their lands seized and occupied by force. Theobald was well connected. He
was a nephew, close friend and protégé of Henry II's justiciar, Ranulf de
Glanville. His brother Hubert was archbishop of Canterbury (1193–1205)
and justiciar of England (1193–8). Most importantly, Theobald was an
intimate of John of Mortain, lord of Ireland and Lancashire, with whom
he may have been educated in Glanville's household. Theobald's brigandage in Lancashire was so flagrant that on his accession John was faced
with a delegation of Lancashire worthies in France; in response he had no
choice but to have Theobald ousted from Lancashire and his lands there
seized, despite the long association of the two men.[36]

One of the most telling things about the descent of England into civil
war in John's reign is that it took so long for the aristocracy to get to the
point of contemplating violence against the king, despite the provocations
heaped on the curial earls and barons. When it finally did take action against

the king, the reluctant aristocracy was very anxious to identify itself with an agenda for reform that had prior royal acceptance. It also adopted an agenda for the defence of Church liberties, to the extent of calling its assembly 'the Army of God' (see above, p. 86).

Henry III may have long felt the consequences of the baronial rebellion of his father's reign in more militant behaviour amongst the magnates. Inquisitions taken after the fall of Faulkes de Bréauté in 1224 indicate that the violence of the years of rebellion continued to be a feature of English life long after the expulsion of Louis of France from England in 1217. Inquiries carried out into the activities of Faulkes de Bréauté's deputies, Richard Foliot and Vivian fitz Ralph, in Oxfordshire between 1216 and 1224 revealed a campaign of extortion, forgery, brazen theft, false imprisonment, intimidation and dispossession outside the law. Richard rode around the county with an armed retinue of several dozen armed serjeants, stealing and threatening at will, and victimising women, clergy and crusaders: all those, in short, whom knights were supposed to support and protect.[37] This persistent violence may also in part be a consequence of changes in the way that some magnates exerted themselves in the localities, disengaging from local tenurial networks of landowners – who had a vested interest in peace and civic order – and entering into flexible arrangements of retaining, which supported more aggressive local tactics (see below, p. 155).

The new magnate-dominated regency found that its fellows were more likely to take arms in pursuit of local ambitions than in previous reigns. Henry III's uncle, William Longespée, earl of Salisbury (died 1225), became notorious for this. The earl was a great pillar of King John's cause, and was not averse to using his loyalism as a cover for his own self-promotion, even against fellow loyalists. Earl William Marshal II wrote to Hubert de Burgh in 1221 complaining that his nephew Thomas of Berkeley had been obstructed in his inheritance of Berkeley castle and honor by Longespée's intervention.[38] In 1250, an even more revealing tale was told of him by a Berkshire jury. By their account, the earl had taken up the cause of one Henry Basset (died c.1241), a homicide outlawed and exiled for the death of a Hampshire knight, Henry Crok, at some time in John's reign. As a result of his outlawry, Basset was not allowed to succeed to his knight's fee in North Moreton, a component of the honor of Warwick, but was passed over by the earl of Warwick's judgement, with the inheritance being assigned to a younger brother. Longespée reconciled Henry Basset to the king after over a decade in exile, and to complete Henry's restoration Longespée made a parade of his power (*potestas*), marched into North

Moreton and forcibly reinstated his protégé in his estates, which Henry then enjoyed until his death.[39]

Examples of such decisive and violent behaviour in pursuit of local advantage can be found at the other end of Henry III's reign. Earl John de Warenne, lord of Conisbrough, fell out in 1269 with Henry de Lacy, lord of Pontefract, over a tract of pasture land in the West Riding of Yorkshire. The two magnates went so far as to muster military companies and prepare to march on each other, but hesitated to take the final step. So the dispute was settled by royal justices after a jury of local knights found in Henry de Lacy's favour. The chronicler who recorded this incident remarked that the same Earl John was embroiled soon after with the Leicestershire baron Alan la Zouche in a case at Westminster over (presumably) their inheritances from the co-heirs of the Marshal earldom. In July 1270, Earl John took the unsatisfactory progress of his lawsuit to heart and drew his sword on Alan and his son, badly wounding the father and also injuring the son as both fled through the palace to seek shelter with the king and queen. The earl, now guilty of *lèse majesté*, promptly retreated to his castle of Reigate in Surrey, to which he was pursued by the Lord Edward with a large party of soldiers. Panicking, the earl went to meet the royal army on foot to make submission, a settlement brokered by the archbishop of York and Henry of Germany. He had to return to London to make a humiliating and penitential walk on foot to Westminster, where he then had to purge himself and his retinue by an oath, offer compensation to the Zouches and accept a huge fine of 10,000 marks.[40] His submission and pledge of all his lands for his future good behaviour at court until judged by his peers survives and acknowledges both his violent offence (*trespas*) at Westminster against the Zouches and his insult (*despit*) to the king's peace. Perhaps the most revealing thing in this context is that such hair-trigger violence could be forgiven by the offended monarch.[41] Nor did Earl John's violent behaviour abate. Selby abbey had cause to complain of his armed depredations in Edward I's reign, and in 1286 or 1288, while the king was out of England, Earl John allied with the earl of Warwick in a private war with Reginald de Grey of Ruthin in the northern March of Wales.[42]

GENTRY VIOLENCE

There are certainly some other local and less high-profile parallels to the behaviour of Earl John de Warenne. Matthew Paris has the story of Robert de Candos, a household knight of John II, lord of Monmouth. In 1251, 'because of a grudge' Robert quit his lord's service and 'with many henchmen' conducted a campaign of fire, plunder and murder in the southern March. Eventually he was arrested by the earl of Gloucester's men and placed in prison, where he died.[43] Most intriguing, because it unveils the less accessible world of the gentry, is the longer-term behaviour focused on the infamous Leicestershire gentry family of Folleville in the thirteenth and fourteenth centuries. Instead of violence as a result of a flare of knightly anger, we see here a family in which violence and intimidation became a way of life. Historians of the fourteenth century have long been aware of a substratum of violent gentry behaviour in England in their period.[44] Though it is difficult to quantify, it certainly happened. Lionel Stones's reconstruction of the activities of the Follevilles from the 1320s to the 1340s is particularly evocative. Six Folleville brothers formed the core of a 'gang' (*societas*) based on the family manors of Ashby Folville and Teigh, Leicestershire, which was notorious for a campaign of murder, violent intimidation and kidnap across Leicestershire and southern Lincolnshire. Its accessories included members of other Leicestershire knightly families, the Hobys and Zouches, and the royal constable of Rockingham castle. The general turbulence of the time and the inefficiency of the law and support amongst the court aristocracy allowed such men to carry on their activities all but unhindered.[45]

However, this gentry criminality in fourteenth-century Leicestershire had deeper causes than political turmoil. In the case of the Follevilles, it might be suggested that the events of the 1320s were preceded by several generations of family brigandage. In the thirteenth century, the family was headed by Sir Eustace de Folleville (fl. 1247–74). Eustace was the grandfather of the Folleville brothers of Stones's study.[46] He was a knight of the shire, was associated with the Montfort affinity in the 1250s and fought for the baronial party in 1264–5. In the 1270s, he was engaged in a bloody feud with the Grimbaud family of North Witham, Lincolnshire, and was himself murdered at his home at Ashby Folville in 1274.[47] A namesake and cousin, Eustace de Folleville of Barsby, Leicestershire, was imprisoned for a murder in Warwickshire in 1248.[48] Another cousin and Montfortian, Ralph (II) de Folleville of Rearsby, was arrested and imprisoned at Leicester for committing homicide in 1272.[49] It is therefore a reasonable deduction that what we see in Leicestershire in the reign of Edward II was violent intimidation ingrained in at least one section of local society since the reign of Henry III, if no further back in time.

We lack equivalent sources for thirteenth-century gentry violence to the trailbaston and peace commissions that cast light on fourteenth-century disorder. The thirteenth-century eyre rolls would not seem at first sight to support in their presentments a view that county knights were as involved in gang violence as their fourteenth-century successors apparently were. But this negative evidence perhaps fails to take into account the way low-status thieves might be operating under the protection of gentry, especially in politically troubled times.[50] Nonetheless, a particularly revealing case is the famous robbery of foreign merchants in the pass of Alton, Hampshire, in the autumn of 1248, which was reported by Matthew Paris and features prominently on the Hampshire plea roll of 1249. It involved conspiracy amongst local knights, contacts at the royal court, planning, and an ambush on a highway as it passed through remote woodland. Since the robbers stole the large sum of 200 marks, the case was exceptional, as was the royal vengeance that followed, involving the round-up of sixty suspects, many of them men of substance, and the conviction of two young local knights, John de Bendinges and John Barkham, as ringleaders (though they were pardoned in 1254 through intercession by members of the king's family). The case throws out numerous relevant points. The gentry involved escaped capital punishment, though not some of the lesser robbers. There are hints that several of the accused were allowed to escape to sanctuary, and Bendinges himself temporarily evaded the sheriff. A jury of their peers was reluctant to accuse the ringleaders and many refused to co-operate with the royal officers. No wonder Matthew Paris, in his coloured account of the Alton conspiracy, concluded that 'the whole neighbourhood was infected with larceny'.[51]

When we go as far back as the twelfth century, the extent of armed brigandage and intimidation amongst local knights and their families is all but unknowable. We merely have tantalising hints. In 1221, for instance, a Warwickshire jury, asked to decide the right to a piece of land at Shuckburgh, had a long tale to tell. It involved the doings of a renowned stipendiary knight in Stephen's reign called Warin of Walcote, who had been denied the hand of Isabel, daughter of the lord of Shuckburgh. Following the death of Isabel's formidable brother, Warin came with a band of men, abducted and forcibly kept her as his lover. On the succession of King Henry II in 1154, Warin lost his livelihood and took to living as a brigand in wasteland near Grandborough on the eastern edge of Warwickshire. He was eventually arrested and taken to the king at Northampton, and there placed in the pillory as a discourage-ment to others. He did not survive the experience.[52] The story of Warin of Walcote has clearly entered the oral culture of eastern Warwickshire (where all the places mentioned are situated in Marton hundred) as a local romance.

But in some ways it parallels the gentry brigandage of the fourteenth century. Warin's base at Grandborough near Watling Street allowed him to prey on trade routes and cross into nearby Northamptonshire to evade local officers. He had enjoyed the patronage of local magnates, and was able to continue his depredations because of the aftermath of a long period of civil war. The main difference it hints at between the time of Henry II and Edward II is the greater will and ability of Henry II and his justices to put down local brigandage in times of peace.

Twelfth- and thirteenth-century English aristocrats were, according to these accounts, prone to use violence to get their way. There is some reason to believe that their violence was not unconstrained. The tenants of Earl Robert de Bellême and William de Briouze would not follow their lords in their confrontations with the king. Pragmatism could put a brake on the escalation of violent conflicts. We can also suggest a thought-world for these magnates in which they perceived armed confrontation as in fact a stage in a process ultimately aimed at a peaceful settlement of difficulties: a strategy to raise the stakes. Legal process itself anticipated violence in disputes, though at a low level. Nonetheless, private warfare outside times of general conflict was not unheard of in England between the Conquest and Edward I's reign. There is also good reason to believe that the dwindling importance of tenured knights in magnate followings in the late twelfth century (see below, pp. 152–9) released a brake on magnate violence in the localities, and that Henry III's England was therefore more violent than Henry II's. When magnates relied for support on retained knights of their *mesnie*, and not on their customary tenants, they were more capable of violent interventions and less tied to cautious local communities. This would explain the increasing evidence for localised violence and brigandage amongst the county élites in Henry III's reign, though it has to be admitted that we have no way of knowing whether the grandfathers of such men were doing the same in Henry II's reign, so it cannot be assumed that this was something new in the thirteenth century. This all has to be taken against a further impetus to violence: a willingness to draw a sword on an opponent was very much a component of magnate behaviour, and acceptable within certain limits. It was here that much of the problem began, and it is that habitus we will consider next.

✥

CHAPTER SEVEN

PERSONAL VIOLENCE

ARISTOCRATS were apt to fly off the handle, even with the king their lord, though it was a very dangerous thing to do. Every king of England between William Rufus and Edward I (with the exception of Richard) was subject to at least one plot on his life by an aristocratic malcontent. They were even more likely to fall out with each other when in close proximity. This can best be seen when the aristocracy came together in its periodic assemblies, notably at the royal court. Lords were hedged around by armed attendants, so that they themselves could not easily be directly challenged. But their satellites might sometimes come into contact and fight for their masters.[1] Not infrequently, the servants of barons, seeking the best quarters for their lord, ended up fighting for their lord's honour over lodgings, and the fighting sometimes became general and murderous, despite the dangers of committing an offence against the king's peace. This is an example of such an incident from John's reign, supposedly around the year 1210:

Once when the king was travelling to Marlborough, he was accompanied by a great number of the English nobility. Geoffrey de Mandeville [the eldest son of Geoffrey fitz Peter, earl of Essex] was there and sent his servants ahead to the town. When they came there, they found a very fine lodging and went inside. But the servants of William Briwerre also entered and expelled Geoffrey's servants. At that point Geoffrey entered Marlborough. When he came to the lodging, his servants approached saying, 'My lord, see here my lord William Briwerre's servants, who have chased us from the lodging which we had taken for your use.' Geoffrey went straight to the Briwerre servants and demanded that they quit the house. But they refused, upon which a fight broke out between them. Geoffrey killed the chief of William's servants. When he had done this, he feared the king, who hated him because he was loyal to his father, so Geoffrey and all his servants fled.[2]

This was by no means an isolated incident. The strict and onerous regulation that the marshals of Henry II's household exercised over lodgings in the vicinity of the court mentioned by Peter of Blois might well have been designed as much to prevent such outbreaks as to increase the marshals' income from bribery.[3] Clearly such regulation did not always work. At Christmas 1252, the courts of Henry III of England and Alexander III of Scotland were at York to celebrate the marriage of Alexander to Henry's daughter, Margaret. The queen mother of Scotland, Marie de Coucy, 'with a great crowd of French nobles', was present to add to the throng. In the circumstances, it is hardly surprising that the festive occasion was marred by violence. Indeed, it was probably expected, as the Scottish magnates were allotted a major street all to themselves 'to be on the safe side' (as Matthew Paris put it), in rather the same way that home and away football supporters are segregated nowadays. But non-Scottish magnates sent in their marshals to secure lodgings, nonetheless. The aggression of these men on behalf of their lords set off a street riot, 'at first with fists, then clubs and finally swords'. One man was reportedly killed and many others wounded, some maimed for life.[4]

Anticipation of casual violence when magnates and their households were in close proximity is evident much earlier. The famous conspiracy at Oxford in June 1139, when a court faction engineered the fall of Bishop Roger of Salisbury, was based on the assumption that armed retinues might very well fight over lodgings. In order to justify the bishop's arrest, a cabal of magnates headed by his rival, Waleran II of Meulan (died 1166), got Count Alan of Brittany to set his men on Bishop Roger's household on the pretext of a dispute over lodgings in the town. The count's men barged into the bishop's lodgings while his men were eating. After an exchange of insults, a general fight ensued, for which the bishop was blamed and arrested, along with his nephew, Bishop Alexander of Lincoln. The seizure of his family's castles and lands followed. When the case was later tried, according to William of Malmesbury it was alleged that the bishops' men had frequently picked fights with Count Alan and his Breton allies and relatives 'owing to an old hatred of Alan'. This was all put down to the undue power that Bishop Roger exerted and the consequent arrogance of his knights, who felt they could brawl with impunity. It betrays a general expectation that magnates and their knights would fight out their tensions if put into close proximity.[5]

Recent scholarship has tended to shy away from the idea that medieval people were emotionally uncontained and tended to resort to violence of speech and action more readily than modern people. In part, this is due to a recognition that such a view depended on the prejudices of historians of the Renaissance, beginning with Voltaire, that the humanists they studied represented a new, more admirable stage in human social development, different from the superstitious, dogmatic and violent personalities who had preceded them. It is a view that historians of Marc Bloch's generation still embraced. In part, the change is also owing to the fact that the investigations of legal historians tend to see much of what looks like aristocratic violence as simply an element in a recognised dispute structure. This in turn depends on cultural historians' ideas of ritualised anger and formalised behaviour in social relations.[6] The final challenge to the view was the collapse in the 1990s of the idea of a 'feudal mutation' in medieval society around 1000. This was a meta-narrative developed by French historians in the 1960s to account for the transition from Carolingian Francia to the politically fragmented Capetian kingdom of France, and depended on the idea of social disruption by the unconstrained violence of the Frankish magnates and their hired thugs, the knights.

Voices have been raised to remind us that if medieval society was not heedlessly violent, it was nonetheless still violent. Richard Kaeuper in particular has talked of the 'autonomy' of the medieval aristocrat, apt to set himself up as judge, jury and executioner in any situation he encountered.[7] Thomas Walsingham tells the story of Geoffrey of Childwick (died *c.*1271), a royal marshal, household knight and brother-in-law of John Mansel, a royal justice. Around 1250, he apprehended a servant of the abbot of St Albans whom he encountered on the Bedford road carrying a gift of venison to his master. Geoffrey – no friend to the abbot, his neighbour and the chief lord of his Hertfordshire estates – decided that the meat had been poached from the royal forest, and, as a royal officer, denounced the servant as a thief and traitor, knocked him from his horse and confiscated both horse and venison, for which deed he was excommunicated, a punishment about which Geoffrey often later joked.[8] The biographer of William Marshal tells a similar tale of how, in 1183, his hero encountered a runaway monk and his mistress in France. He stopped and questioned both, and, deciding the monk intended to use the money he had to set up as a usurer, deprived the couple of it, and used it to feast his friends.[9] Kaeuper also points to the uncompromising violence with which French vernacular literature of the twelfth and thirteenth centuries is saturated. Such a view can be answered with the argument that the violence of its literature is no certain indicator of the violence of the culture that produced it (twenty-first-century Western society being a very good case in point; Hollywood and TV drama alike depict, and rejoice in, levels of violence society itself rarely experiences). But medieval culture nonetheless unapologetically projected the acceptability of aristocratic aggression and resort to arms. The most characteristic and popular enter-tainment in those centuries was, after all, the mêlée tournament, a staged cavalry combat little different from real battle, except that violent deaths suffered in its course were thought regrettable.

The homicide rate in medieval society was certainly higher than in modern Britain, though comparative statistics are not easy to formulate convincingly, and indeed may be impossible. But as an indicator we can look at the plea rolls for Devon for the year 1238, where the jurors of the hundred of Axminster alone reported the murders of seven people in the past ten years, of whom five were unidentifiable vagabonds and strangers. In the entire county of Devon, the hundred juries reported 144 murdered people between 1228 and 1238 (a rate of just over fourteen murders a year), of whom twenty-two were unidentified travellers. Most of these were vagabonds, but the murdered also included two merchants and a pilgrim.[10] Such evidence indi-cates that travellers and the rootless were at much greater risk of homicide than settled citizens and gentry at this time. The conclusion is inescapable that homicide was all too common. A statistical study of thirteenth-century plea rolls concludes that 'there was a good possibility that there would have been a homicide in every settlement... once every twenty to forty years. Therefore it is possible that every person in England in the thirteenth century, if he did not personally witness a murder, knew or knew of someone who had been killed.' Homicide was therefore common, though not perhaps alarmingly so in comparison with our own day.[11]

In support of this deduction, the observation has commonly been made, based on any cursory survey of the *Complete Peerage*, that only a very small minority of medieval earls and barons came to violent ends. The over-whelming majority died in bed, and of those few who met violent deaths, the likes of Earl Geoffrey de Mandeville of Essex and Gloucester (died 1216) and Earl Gilbert Marshal of Pembroke (died 1241) perished in avoid-able tournament accidents. The much larger social group represented by the term 'knights' was clearly more afflicted by homicide, though any such assertion can be little more than impressionistic. We can point to quite a few instances of wilful murder in that group, though the circumstances are not always clear. For instance, in 1130, Ralph Butler, a substantial Warwickshire landowner and leading officer of Earl Robert II of Leicester, was paying instalments of a sum of forty pounds he owed as a pledge of one of his men who had killed a member of the household of the bishop of Winchester, the king's brother.[12] Was this the aftermath of one of those violent incidents at court or in town when the households of great men came together and clashed?

The society of this period certainly believed – as does our own – that there was too much violence on the streets. A certain paranoia surfaces about it. Roger of Howden, a royal clerk and justice, had a low opinion of the predilection of young English aristocrats for violence. He notes the murder in London in 1177 of a brother of Earl William I de Ferrers of Derby (died 1190), and traces it to the gangs of youths from the knightly patrician families of the city (he named the Buccuintes and Viels) who roamed the city at night looking for trouble and were ready to break into houses in pursuit of loot and excitement.[13] Around 1222, William de Ros, a knight of Earl William Marshal II (died 1231), sent word to his master that he was in daily fear of being assassinated by his enemies, whom the earl's rival and former friend, Faulkes de Bréauté, was stirring up against him in his neighbourhood.[14] In support of Roger's distaste and William's fears, there are some indications that casual aristocratic violence was readily accommodated within the habitus of their day. An outraged knight, for instance, would not be charged with homicide if he killed a man whom he had found in bed with his wife, providing it was done within a week of the event. The regulations for the holding of tournaments issued by King Richard in 1194 assume as a matter of course that knights were inclined to hold up travellers on the road, levy payments on them and otherwise do violence. Indeed, tournaments brought out the worst in some aristocrats. The accidental death of the knight Ernald de Montigny at the hands of the royal knight Roger of Leybourn, in a Round Table at Walden in 1252, eventually – as a result of the investigations of Richard de Clare, earl of Gloucester and Hertford – come to be suspected of being a disguised assassination as a consequence of a grudge Roger had conceived against Ernald, who had been responsible for breaking Roger's leg in a previous encounter on the field.[15]

The biography of the elder William Marshal (died 1219) is the nearest we can get to the place of violence in the outlook of an English knight, and its message is oddly mixed. The work can sometimes surprise. For instance, despite its subject having an active military career of over fifty years, full of skirmishes, sieges, tournaments and one major battle, the biography fails to confirm that Marshal ever actually killed anyone. Indeed, it can be unhappy about the subject of homicide. William was a member of the military household of his uncle, Earl Patrick of Salisbury, when it was ambushed by a party of soldiers of the Lusignan family in Poitou in 1168. The unarmed earl was struck down and killed in front of William's eyes, a deed the biography calls assassination rather than a show of prowess. William's reaction was to fight, first, to preserve his uncle's life by riding into the midst of the attackers; after Patrick had fallen, he tried to preserve himself, taking station with his back to a hedge and holding off the Lusignan soldiers until he was brought down by a stab in his thigh from a lance thrust through the branches behind. William was not killed but, as was usual for that time, was taken prisoner by the Lusignans for ransom. After his release, William apparently took every opportunity to deplore the disgraceful nature of his uncle's death, yet took no violent action against the Lusignans; his biography claims, however, that he forced a shamefaced admission from them that it had all been very regrettable. In 1183, indeed, Geoffrey de Lusignan was characterised as interceding with the Young King for William when he was in disgrace, despite the acknowledged antagonism between the two men. The biography on more than one occasion regards the death of a warrior as tragic, even when it occurred in fair and open battle. At the other end of William's career, in 1217, in the fighting at the Exchequer Gate of Lincoln, his young cousin Count Thomas of Perche was killed by a sword thrust penetrating the eye slit of his helmet: 'the sorrow there was intense . . . it was a great pity that he died in this manner'.[16]

The Marshal biography is a product of the mid-1220s. Its young author is recalling and reflecting on the attitudes of an older generation of aristocrats in the person of its hero, who was born as early as 1146. If any source can tell us how autonomously violent and heedless a medieval knight was in the high middle ages, it should be the *History of William Marshal*. The encounter between the Poitevin and Capetian army threatening Le Mans and Marshal at the head of Henry II's guards on 12 June 1189 is revealing. Marshal rallied a group of friends to defend the southern entry to the city while the enemy army attempted to force entry. The latter were driven back on the gate in a fierce and hard-fought *meslee*. We are told this was no game (*gieus*), but a deadly business. There were none of the cheerful insults (*rampones*) that the two sides in a tournament would exchange. It was a mounted combat with swords and lances, in which the Marshal succeeded in routing the invaders. He adopted the strategies he would have used on the tournament field, snatching bridles out of the hands of at least three riders and dragging them back to the gate as captives. Knights had to cut their bridles to escape him as best they might. This famous skirmish seemed to result in no deaths amongst the knights. Andrew de Chauvigny, a cousin of the Plantagenets, had his arm broken by a rock from the walls. Hugh de Malannoy, of the royal guard, was tumbled in a ditch. The Marshal had his horse maimed by a discarded lance. The Marshal biography tells us nothing about any collateral damage to foot soldiers in the encounter, if indeed there was any. What it does tell us is that the city was set on fire on Henry II's order to cover his company's retreat, devastating the lives of the citizens: the Marshal even dismounted to assist an old lady in retrieving her possessions from her burning home.[17]

Knightly violence might thus flare up, but it was not unconstrained or conscienceless. A knight's entire behaviour was monitored by a social habitus that awarded him honour or recognised his prowess according to his actions. 'What is *chevalerie*?' asks the author of the Marshal biography, rhetorically. 'Such a difficult, tough and very costly thing to learn that no coward ventures to take it on. Is every knight really such? Not at all, for there are many who do nothing with their arms, but that does not prevent them from boasting. Any man seeking to achieve *haute enor* must first see to it that he has been well-schooled.'[18] 'Chivalry' here is the skill of a warrior, his 'knightliness'. The possibility of recognition and honour is entirely tied up with military success. Non-practising knights are by definition unworthy men. Therefore, the aristocrat must seek out opportunities to display his prowess in arms. But *display* is the point. The tournament was so popular because it allowed for military display without risk, other than that of disgrace and accidental injury. In a tournament a dangerous fall could cause the watching crowd to shriek: 'They're dead! They're dead! Lord God, what a tragedy!'[19] In warfare we see the same sentiment, at least when applied to the military aristocracy.

There were, however, exceptions, especially in wartime. It may be true that some accounts of medieval pitched battles remark on the few fatalities amongst the knights. In the Anglo-Norman victory over the French at Brémule in 1119, three knights are said to have died out of around nine hundred engaged: 'they were all clad in mail and spared each other on both sides out of fear of God and fellowship in arms; they were more concerned to capture than to kill the fugitives.'[20] Furthermore, savage acts that did occur are often explained, as in the sources for the wars in England between 1138 and 1147, as being the work of mercenary outlanders, Welsh or Flemish, semi-barbarians who did not respect the ethos of the Anglo-French knight, as the Marcher baron William de Briouze (died 1211) once explained to the royal clerk Walter Map.[21] The Ramsey chronicle preserves the apologetic demeanour and embarrassment of Earl Geoffrey II de Mandeville (died 1144), driven by political dispossession to garrison monasteries and prey on the countryside for his survival like a brigand.[22]

There are thirteenth-century examples of how political expediency could nonetheless encourage deliberate savagery amongst the aristocracy. The death of Earl Richard Marshal is a case in point. He had withdrawn to his estates in Ireland after the collapse of the rebellion he had sponsored in England and the Marches. On 1 April 1234, he went to the relief of his castle of Kildare, then being besieged by the justiciar, assisted by Marshal's political enemy Walter de Lacy, 'a notorious traitor to his many lords'. The earl meant business and his first onset killed a number of knights, but he was surrounded, his bodyguard was slaughtered and he himself was brought down, being dealt a serious wound in the back which eventually – assisted by a physician – killed him. Opinion at the time believed his death had been an assassination contrived by his enemies.[23] In the civil warfare of 1264–5, the battle of Lewes seems to have incurred very few aristocratic casualties, but in the royalist revenge at Evesham the next year there was perpetrated a political execution of unparalleled savagery. Simon de Montfort's defeat left him isolated with his retinue on the field. No one was spared, including Montfort's son Henry. Montfort's own death was particularly violent. He was felled and probably killed by a lance thrust to the neck, but, once he was down, soldiers entrusted with the task before the battle mutilated his body, cutting off head, hands and feet. The trunk of his body was stripped and slashed, and his genitalia were hacked off. The battle remained notorious thereafter as one in which aristocratic norms were transgressed: Robert of Gloucester described it as 'the murder of Evesham, for battle it was not'.[24] Significantly, its egregious brutality was avenged in due course by the assassination in an Italian cathedral of Henry III's nephew by Montfort's surviving sons. Such a transgression of the habitus could only be answered by equal horrors, provoking enmity, desire for vengeance and sometimes a long-term feud.

Mortal Enmity

Medieval magnates did not want to be challenged and defied. Should it ever happen, there had to be a response, perhaps a disproportionate one, or the magnate's standing in society would be damaged and with it his honour and his ability to protect his own. The line in the sand might be summed up by the fictional Guivret, who in Chrétien de Troyes's *Erec et Enide* – a work of the 1170s – says of himself: 'I'm very rich and powerful, for in this land there's no lord whose lands border mine who goes against my authority and does not do everything I wish. I have no neighbour who doesn't fear me, however proud and confident he may be.'[25] In 1174, Jordan Fantosme wrote similarly of Earl Robert III of Leicester (died 1190), whom he depicts boasting that in his part of England there was hardly a knight whom he could not overthrow if he refused him aid.[26] But what if such lords were challenged? In flattering a lord, people employed the sort of phrases used by Geoffrey of Monmouth when he dedicated editions of his *History of the Kings of Britain* indifferently in 1136 to Robert, earl of Gloucester (died 1147) and Waleran, count of Meulan (died 1166), saying to both magnates: 'You have learned through your father's precedent, to be a terror to your enemies and a protection to your own people. Faithful defender as you are of those dependent on you, accept under your patronage this book which is published for your pleasure.'[27]

Such a man could not let his prestige and reputation be challenged without fighting back. The challenge could call forth a retaliatory threat of 'mortal enmity' against the offender. An epistolary composition exercise from Oxford around 1230 imagines how an offended lord would respond towards the offender by a formal defiance.

> I marvel and am completely astonished at what sort of brass nerve might motivate you to do harm to my men, since you know that I am a man in full possession of my powers and perfectly secure in my position. I want you to know that you will have me for a mortal enemy unless you make me satisfaction for that injury as soon as possible. If you are wise you should arrange it that you come to a settlement so that the punishment the sin warrants may not follow.[28]

The phrase 'mortal enemy' does not necessarily mean that the speaker would seek to harry his enemy to death, just that he would maintain animosity against him for the rest of his life: the lord here says he will be 'an enemy until I die' (*inimicum quam diu vixero*). The prevalence of mortal enmity in society is hinted at further in the tournament regulations propagated for England by Richard I in 1194, which provides that 'if any tourneyer is at odds with another man, or any servant, or whoever he may be, he is to be under a binding truce (*legalem treugam*) with him during the tournament and on the road there and back. If he refuses to give truce then he should be forced to do it, or not be allowed to tourney.'[29] Similarly, a roughly contemporary Norman legal collection pronounces: 'No one should presume to conduct hostilities (*guerra*) against another but should complain of any injury done him to the duke or his justiciar, so that evil doing or injury should be put right by fine on goods in a civil case or by loss of limbs in a criminal case.'[30] The message is the same: mortal enmity occurred but its social inconvenience meant it had to be contained and deplored.

'Mortal enmity' is a social sanction met with universally in medieval Europe. It was the custom to inaugurate such a state of enmity by a formal defiance of the enemy, and the text cited above may be interpreted as just such a defiance.[31] The idea – which owes something to Roman law – occurs in England in a Canterbury document as early as 1091, where St Augustine's influence was praised for curing human hearts and reconciling enemies thought to be irreconcilable.[32] The equivalent French phrase occurs in the Anglo-Norman history of the conquest of Ireland (*c.*1190), where King McDonnchadh of Osraige is described as Earl Richard of Striguil's *enemi mortel*, owing to the fact that he had attacked the earl's father-in-law.[33] The idea features prominently in French literature composed in England in the twelfth century. Thomas of Kent in his *Roman de Toute Chevalerie* (composed in the last decade of Henry II's reign) referred to Alexander and Porrus of India as *mortels enemis*.[34] When the wicked Duke Otto of Pavia, the anti-hero of the romance *Gui de Warewic* (*c.*1199), captured Guy of Warwick and his friend Harold of Arden, he gloated: 'they are my *mortels enemis*, never will we be friends!'[35] Mortal enmity might very well – as here – embrace families and friends as much as specific individuals. In 1215, according to the writer called the Anonymous of Béthune, a Flemish knight, Walter Bertaut, was on a boat from England that had been driven ashore in the county of Holland, and was very fearful. Walter was the first cousin of the count of Loos, who had challenged Count William of Holland for his lands, and so Count William 'hated Walter to the death'.[36] The same impulse and the same trivial nastiness are to be found in England. In 1247, one Walter of Lange was cleared by a Somerset jury of harbouring thieves, the charge having been 'inspired by the hatred which Henry of Earley felt towards him for his – that is, Henry's – brother's sake by reason of a certain pasture'.[37]

Mortal enmity did not by any means necessarily erupt in violence and murder, the phenomenon loosely called by some 'feud' or 'blood-feud'. William Marshal may well have considered that he was the mortal enemy of the Lusignans after 1168 and their murder of his uncle. However, he seems not to have contemplated actually killing a Lusignan, but contented himself with broadcasting his ill-will and low opinion of their treachery. Another man might have reacted differently, though that must have been unusual when things came to the point of extreme violence. We can see this because the blood-spattered results of mortal enmity turning murderous tended to become notorious, and were recalled with horror by later generations. There is a concentration of evidence about 'blood-feud' in the earlier period, which leads to difficult and probably unanswerable questions as to whether pre-Conquest English society was feud-ridden, whether that mind-set survived the Conquest, and how feud-prone were the French incomers. A case has been made that eleventh-century French society was radically different in its basic approach to the more extreme part of human relations; more forgiving and forbearing than the murderous 'Iron Age' mentality that still prevailed outside the Francophone area.[38] John Gillingham has made the interesting argument that the change in French attitudes as to what to do with defeated opponents can be linked to the tenth-century spread of castle lordship and a more monetarised economy. Negotiation and compensation became part of the French way of conflict.[39]

Much might be made along those lines of sources from Henry I's reign (1100–35). The legal treatise called after him, and compiled in the middle of his reign, harks back to earlier English lawcodes (and their acceptance of blood-feud), though it claims to describe current procedures in shire courts. 'Feud', or something like it, is not mentioned in the tract as such (the label has more to do with modern anthropology than medieval perceptions); in fact, it stresses peace-making as a royal and lordly function.[40] But it contains an awareness of the way that a violent response, associated with a vocabulary of vengeance (*vindicta*), might be expected in retaliation for certain offences. Vengeance is the responsibility of kin, and weighs heaviest on children and close relations. The treatise states that those who kill in self-defence are not legitimate subjects for the penalties of vengeance killing. It also excuses cuckolded husbands who kill their wife's lover, or men who catch lovers in the act with their daughters or sisters.[41] In effect, the *Leges Henrici Primi* accepts that an impulse to vengeance is the way of the world, but nonetheless should not be regarded as acceptable. An associated legal tract, the *Quadripartitus*, was even firmer in stating what the *Leges* had said, that crimes of violence were offensive to the king's majesty, and that in this world it was the king and his justices who had the chief responsibility for doing justice to the malefactor.[42] Mortal enmity was no excuse for murder in such a world. Self-defence and crimes of passion remained excusable, but not murders planned in cold blood. Vengeance killing was an offence against the king's majesty, and ultimately against the idea that was growing up behind that majesty: the civic order of the commonwealth. Even the recognised right to punish adulterous wives and their lovers was restricted. Around 1215, Thomas of Chobham, a canon lawyer and subdean of Salisbury, summarised the position as he understood it, moderating the situation of a century earlier: 'It is worth noting that secular law once allowed a man to kill an adulterer found with his wife. This is no longer permitted, but only for him to cut off the man's genitals so that he will never spawn another who will follow him in his vileness.'[43] That Thomas was reflecting on actual practice is evidenced by the castration of the unfortunate William Wake for his adultery with the wife of Robert Butler of Candover, Hampshire, in 1212, a case noted in the close rolls of the English chancery. Robert and the men who helped him take vengeance had their possessions seized, but if their account of the offence proved true, they were to be restored and taken back into the king's peace.[44]

Particularly revealing in the context of the post-Conquest period is the murder of an English landowner called Osulf in Cornwall in the second half of the reign of King Henry I. Osulf's death was blamed on a man called Toki, and was in turn avenged on Toki's six French-born sons who were trapped and murdered near St Michael's Mount by a gang of Anglo-Normans led by the native sheriff of Cornwall, Frewin. This caused a national scandal and the king pursued the assassins. The fines levied on the young men's murderers were noted on the pipe roll of 1130 as still being paid, and reveal that Frewin lost his lands (and perhaps office) for his offence. The affair was recalled three decades later by the theologian John of Cornwall in his commentary – probably composed in France – on Geoffrey of Monmouth's prophecies of Merlin. And it was recalled again in Westminster a century after that in an exchequer memorandum in the Book of Fees.[45] Such deeds might seep into the folk memory, which hardly indicates that they were common. It is tempting to see the massacre of the *Tokenses*, the 'sons of Toki', as an extension beyond the Conquest of an Anglo-Saxon legacy of blood-feud, like the bloodbath that ensued from the murder of Earl Uthred of Northumbria in 1016, which led to sixty years of bloodshed; vengeance was still being pursued in Yorkshire in the early 1070s, when Earl Waltheof avenged his grandfather by massacre his murderers' kin at a banquet at Settrington.[46] Furthermore, the perpetrators were English, so far as we can tell, while Toki's sons were said to have been 'French-born', so was it a racially motivated killing? In fact, it is not even absolutely certain that Toki was French, though his children were born in France, so it is difficult to conclude decisively either that the avenging of Osulf on his sons was anti-Norman or that it was a continuation of pre-Conquest mores.

Wilful murder continued to occur amongst the aristocracy, though I believe it was rare. In December 1135 – between the news of the death of Henry I reaching England and the consecration of King Stephen – the tenants of the honor of Pontefract rose against William Maltravers, the lord the old king had imposed upon them, and murdered him, forcibly rein-stating Ilbert de Lacy, a scion of its original family. The new king pursued the offenders briskly, outlawing them all. But when the homicide came to trial, Ilbert and his accomplices were pardoned, apparently because there had been no king at the time with a peace to be broken.[47] The process of royal justice nonetheless occurred, the king assuming to himself the prime responsibility for investigation and punishment and thus deflecting the tendency towards blood-feud. A similar case in 1200 called forth a similar response. Meurig, son of Roger of Powys, a knight of a prominent Marcher Anglo-Welsh family, managed to secure for himself from the new king, John, the castle and lordship of Whittington in Shropshire, which his father had enjoyed at the pleasure of King Richard. The rival claimant to the lord-ship was Fulk III fitz Warin of Alberbury (died *c.*1254), who some months after the royal grant encountered Meurig and killed him. Fulk was outlawed in the county court of Shropshire and spent nearly three years as an exile until he was pardoned by the king (whose boyhood friend he had apparently been) and was given the castle soon afterwards. The killing provoked no feud with Meurig's powerful and well-connected family, though it may have left Fulk with an unsavoury reputation. As with the case of Frewin and the sons of Toki, the notorious incident passed into local legend. As far as the later fitz Warins were concerned, the killing had happened in a fair and equal fight after much provocation. Others may have regarded it differently, however. In 1255, a year or two after his death, Fulk III was publicly called a 'traitor' to his son's face by a local rival at a meeting where the Welsh magnates of Powys were present. It may have been the type of odium that called forth a justificatory romance a generation later. In the late thirteenth-century *Fouke le fitz Waryn*, the historical Fulk's homicide of Meurig is characterised as occurring during a short campaign fought between the two lords in western Shropshire, when Meurig's knights encountered Fulk's on the road to Shrewsbury.[48] (See also below, p. 131.)

ACCEPTABLE VIOLENCE: DEFIANCE, RENUNCIATION AND DISPOSSESSION

There is a red thread of violent aristocratic confrontation in England that runs from the Conquest to the reign of Henry III. The examples given above allow us to see why it happened. The impulse to arms in many cases stemmed from offended honour. This might have been because a lord found his ability to protect his men compromised, or what he regarded as his rights challenged and eroded. In the instances of Briouze and of Richard Marshal, the king was the offender and the violence was directed against him. Society in general was not necessarily offended by the aristocratic resort to action, and recognised the inevitable results of such impasses. So an irate magnate or knight could resort to a formal *diffidatio* ('defiance') to terminate any obligations he had to a king or lord before retaliating. Explicit reference to formal defiance features in literary and historical sources of the time. Perhaps the earliest comes from Normandy in 1119, when Reginald de Bailleul went personally to King Henry I at Falaise and 'returned his faith to the king (*fidelitatem regi reliquit*)'. According to Orderic's account, the king chose not to arrest him, even when he refused to return the lands for which he had sworn faith to the king. Reginald's defiance was apparently politically inspired: he was choosing to join the insurgent party of William Clito in Normandy. The king promptly punished Reginald by seizing his castle and reducing him to abject pleas for forgiveness.[49]

Rather more famous is the formal defiance of King Stephen by Earl Robert of Gloucester in May 1138. The circumstances were broadly the same as in 1119. The earl had decided to withdraw his support from Stephen and transfer it to his rival, the empress Matilda, his own half-sister. The defiance in 1138 was managed by emissaries and (probably) a letter. William of Malmesbury, the earl's apologist, states that it was done 'according to custom'. He also gives as part of the earl's reason that the king had taken no account of the earl's 'faith', which is difficult to interpret, but might refer to the king's repeated failure to listen to the earl's advice; in that way Stephen had demeaned his vassal. For good measure – and just to emphasise that his patron had no choice but defiance – William of Malmesbury asserted that the king had conspired to have Earl Robert assassinated the previous year in Normandy. The message was that Stephen was no true lord, and therefore deserved no faith.[50]

The process of dishonour and defiance can be glimpsed again in the account of a plea concerning two bannerets from Shropshire in 1256. An assize met to ascertain whether Thomas Corbet (died 1274) had unjustly

deprived Fulk IV fitz Warin (died 1264) of 120 acres and a castle at
Alberbury on the borders of Wales in the Corbet lordship of Caus. It was
part of a long-running dispute between Thomas and Fulk's family that had
begun at least five years before over other lands in Caus. A very public and
acrimonious dispute at an assembly of magnates in the summer of 1255
sparked a revealing legal case. When it reached the justices in eyre at
Shrewsbury, Thomas was happy enough to appear and justify himself,
saying the land in question was part of his honor and that Fulk had publicly
returned both his homage and his land to him. For that reason Thomas
had taken possession of Alberbury, as was his right; Fulk had in any case
renounced it (*wayvavit*). When the justices consulted the jurors of the
county, however, the latter had an interesting tale to tell:

> A peace conference (*dies amoris*) was held between Thomas and Gruffudd
> ap Gwenwynwyn [i.e., prince of Powys] over a number of disputes, at
> which many magnates were present, Fulk amongst them. Thomas and
> Fulk had a severe difference of opinion, because of which Thomas called
> Fulk's father [i.e., the legendary Fulk III] a traitor (*proditor*). Fulk was
> enraged at this and told Thomas that because of imputing so terrible a
> crime to his father and himself he would return his homage to him and
> would never more hold land of him. When asked if Fulk had returned his
> homage in person, the jurors said he had not, but employed an interme-
> diary, one Hamo le Strange. When asked if Fulk, after he had instructed
> this to be done, resumed his possession of Alberbury, the jurors said yes,
> and that Fulk was in possession of Alberbury castle, the chief place of
> that estate. They said that he caused the estate to be farmed and works
> carried out for over a week before Thomas expelled him from Alberbury.[51]

The essential cause of the defiance was in this case an insult to the honour
of Fulk's father (the killer of Meurig of Powys: see above, p. 129) and thus
to Fulk himself, though there was clearly a longer-term background of
tension caused by Thomas's aggression over land disputes. The knight
jurors of the Shropshire county court had a view on the propriety of Fulk's
defiance. They clearly believed he had defended his honour according
to expectations, and that the offence of Thomas was real enough. The fact
that Thomas had failed to repossess the land at Alberbury for eight days
after the defiance, and that Fulk had been able to continue to manage his
estate, was taken as justification for their recommendation that Fulk should
continue in possession of it, as his 'seisin' had not been challenged.

There seems no reason to doubt that the world of the twelfth- and thirteenth-century aristocrat was one where postures were struck and violence could ensue, but that a settlement would nonetheless follow on from that. As has been said, one of the chief engines of violence seems to have been the individual aristocrat's sense that his honour was being compromised, which diminished him in the public theatre that was medieval conduct. This could trigger menace and a threat of mortal enmity. Less commonly, it might precipitate personal violence and ultimately murder. How frequently serious violence followed on from offended honour is an open question, but the indications here are that it was not too common, however saturated medieval life was in the rhetoric of menace. It was more likely to happen in certain times and places. The infringement of a magnate's space certainly seemed to be one occasion where it might happen, and the royal court, being one of the aristocracy's principal theatres, was a likely place for the performance of threat and violence to be staged, despite the established (and obviously necessary) concept of the king's peace within the precincts of the court. Magnates could feel crowded and threatened in the countryside too, where the rivalry and ambitions of local rivals could likewise trigger violence and conflict, even outside a *tempus guerre*, as we have already seen in the previous chapter. So local acts of autonomous violence might happen, as an aristocrat, knight or magnate sought to demonstrate that he could protect his own. Honour and habitus were in this case viruses in the social body. And if we pursue the metaphor, the king and his advisers came to see themselves as physicians to the realm, with aristocratic violence a disease to be fought.

✦

CHAPTER EIGHT

DOMINATING LOCALITIES

HISTORICAL tradition assumes, usually correctly, that the ambition of a medieval magnate was to express his sense of his own power by exerting exclusive influence over a discrete area of the realm. That impulse did not just express his need to demonstrate his power and importance, it also gave the magnate some defence from his enemies. His self-defined patch of lordship gave borders to his own little political world. He could then easily tell if a rival was moving in on him, and indeed he could plot to extend his sphere beyond those borders himself, if he were aggressively inclined. Castles, dependants, judicial privilege, borough plantation and ecclesiastical patronage were all ways in which a magnate could put down markers on his lordship and warn off others. This chapter will examine this reflex, and test out its universality, for, on analysis, it seems to me that magnate behaviour was not necessarily as deterministic as is sometimes assumed.

The French who came to England in 1066 for the most part had all experienced magnate control over well-defined localities as the norm in their home regions. There was a impulse in France towards the localisation of power on magnate lordships in the tenth century, as the spread of castles and decay of royal influence on local office and communities removed the dampeners on magnate ambition. The early eleventh-century construction of the Coucy lordship in the Rémois at the expense of the king of the Franks and the archbishop of Reims by its aggressive lineage, as illustrated by Dominique Barthélemy, is a classic example of this. Coucy was a lordship with no Carolingian predecessor, but a construction of its lords based on castles they had acquired, or simply chosen to build.[1] Tenth-century Normandy experienced something of the same process, and was probably still experiencing it in the reign of the Conqueror's father. The formation of exclusive, territorial, castle-based lordships in the Pays de Caux was well under way before

1000, and can also be seen in central Normandy south of the Seine. The appearance of such lordships is by no means a symptom of ducal weakness.[2] It took place during the time of the powerful Norman rulers Richard I (942–96) and Richard II (996–1026), both of whom promoted their male relatives to be dependent counts. Such new lordships might arise out of a collaboration as much as competition between princes and their magnates, as acts of patronage cemented bonds between prince and dependant. We will see much the same process at work throughout the twelfth century in England.

However, exclusive territorial lordships did not become typical of England after the Conquest. The reason for this is that royal acts of patronage in England created a different political structure over most of the country than that which the Normans experienced at home. Between 1066 and 1086, King William and his advisers did not choose entirely to dispense with the former structure of landholding of the kingdom they had conquered. There are a number of reasons that can be suggested for this restraint. William claimed his kingdom by right of inheritance, and to ignore the rights of surviving English landowners would be implicitly to deny his own claims and even his authority as king. So a former courtier of Edward the Confessor was adjudged in 1086 by a Berkshire hundred to have been illegally reduced to being a tenant of Robert d'Oilly, since the Conqueror had restored him to his lands as his own tenant and had issued a writ to that effect.[3] There was also the matter of convenience. A simple way of allotting estates to an incoming Frenchman was to designate one or more dispossessed Englishmen, who had backed the wrong side and been killed or exiled, as the *antecessores* (predecessors) of the lucky beneficiary.[4] Sometimes the grant would be *in toto*, or sometimes comprise selected estates within a certain county. Thus Geoffrey de Mandeville had as *antecessor* in Essex the pre-Conquest court official Ansgar the Staller, but did not get the bulk of Ansgar's lands in Hertfordshire or Buckinghamshire.[5] The Frenchman would then make what he could of the grant, and sometimes he could be very free in his interpretation of what the king's grant had given him.[6] He might find that the grant had given him a ready-made following of surviving English subtenants, and also the scope to make grants to his own foreign dependants at the expense of the natives, by grant of demesne, by force or by subinfeudation. Domesday Book, with its concern as to who held estates in King Edward's time, who held them after the Conquest and who held them in 1086, is a testament to William's anxiety to tidy up the structure his ad hoc decisions had created. But an unintended consequence of the Conqueror's land grants was to perpetuate in many parts of England the diffuse pre-Conquest structure of aristocratic landholding.

England had great magnates before 1066 – ducal figures with huge influence over entire regions of the realm. But these great men focused their power on securing control over shire, hundred and wapentake courts, and on assuming profitable jurisdictions or 'sokes' that were the prerogative of earls within their regions. What they did not have for the most part were the mechanisms French magnates used to establish their local domination, particularly the castle and the authority of their private, seigneurial court. Pre-Conquest English magnates could secure local domination through control of existing local institutions and communities, and had a social mechanism of 'commendation' by which lesser landowners might seek the personal protection of a greater man.[7] Such power may have been only passing and contingent, but it was nevertheless formidable in its day. Contemporary French magnates had mostly to build theirs from scratch, even where – as in Normandy – there were still local offices such as the *vicomté* that could be part of their armoury of dominance. But power built on French lines was more permanent in the political landscape, because it created something hereditary.

There was the further question of control over localities. As far as pre-Conquest English magnates and their lands were concerned, their estates were usually scattered over several shires and lacked any obvious centre. The lands of Earl Harold of Wessex were distributed across almost all of the shires of England, though there was a concentration of them in the Severn valley around Bristol.[8] The need to concentrate possessions was unnecessary where power lay in communal courts and shire administrations. When incoming Frenchmen inherited such complexes of estates they found themselves in a new and possibly confusing world, where jurisdiction was not clear-cut and ambition had less scope for play, as the existing structure of landownership – still dependent on strong royal and communal courts – could not easily be modified to suit them.

The honors created by the land patronage of William the Conqueror and his sons could therefore be as dispersed as the estates of their Anglo-Saxon predecessors, becoming further dispersed as the tide of conquest moved north in the 1070s, as initial arrangements were adjusted and as more patronage was offered.[9] So William I de Warenne (died 1088) initially gained the lordship of Lewes in Sussex (probably as early as 1067) and another based on Castle Acre in Norfolk, which he seems to have acquired through his wife in succession to his brother-in-law after 1075, with other lands scattered across many counties. At some time after 1071, he was given extensive lands in the West Riding of Yorkshire centred on the existing soke of Conisbrough.[10] By 1086, the process of estate formation left William one of the ten wealthiest lay magnates in England. It also presented him with a big administrative headache and no obvious centre around which to construct a castle-lordship such as he had in his native Normandy at Bellencombre. In fact, there was to be no Warenne castle in Norfolk – where most of his estates were concentrated – until his grandson built one in Stephen's reign, probably around 1140.[11]

However, the Conqueror's acts of landed patronage could be more focused and geopolitical. There are a number of instances of his deliberately awarding all the estates within certain areas to the same lord, with no regard to *antecessores*, and thus creating a castellanry on the French model. This has been evident to historians for some time, and the explanation they have generally agreed on is that the Conqueror had defensive purposes in mind.[12] Where such exclusive lordships appeared, a military logic can often be found: thus the earldoms and honors of Cheshire and Shropshire controlled the Welsh March. The rebelliousness of Devon and Cornwall in the 1060s and 1070s accounts for castle-lordships centred on Launceston, Trematon, Okehampton and Totnes. The lordship of Holderness, centred on a huge coastal castle at Skipsea, protected the exposed Yorkshire coast and Humber estuary, where Scandinavian invasion forces had landed in 1066 and 1069.[13] Richmond outflanked any drive south from hostile Scotland towards York. Others were less obviously defensive. The castle-lordships along the Sussex coast at Arundel, Bramber, Lewes, Pevensey and Hastings – constructed between 1067 and 1075 – had no obvious military imperative to them, despite suggestions that they guarded ports towards Normandy and protected the land from Viking raids.[14] In fact, Dover, Wareham and Southampton were the ports most used by Normans for continental crossings. There was no naval threat to that part of the Channel coast, and a 'beach-head' logic for them did not survive the fall of London and the coronation of Christmas 1066. The four oldest of the five, Arundel, Lewes, Pevensey and Hastings, had in common that they were bestowed on some of the Conqueror's closest Norman supporters. Likewise, the most well-defined, artificial castle-lordship in the Midlands, that of Dudley – which is actually called a *castellaria* in 1086 – cannot easily be accounted for as a response to any obvious domestic or external threat, though the aftermath of Earl Edwin's rebellion in 1071 has been suggested as a cause. But that ineffectual rising had ended with Edwin's murder in Northumberland by one of his own household and may barely have troubled the region.[15] The equally unaccountable Midland castellanries at Tutbury and Stafford were constructed for the king's close adherents Henry de Ferrers and Robert son of Roger de Tosny the elder. So it may be that such lordships reflected as much particular acts of royal favour as defensive logic.

GEOPOLITICAL AMBITION IN ENGLAND

Thus the honorial geography of England in 1100 did not have the coherence of that of contemporary northern France. Estates of a variety of magnates intermingled in large areas of the realm. In France, magnates knew what territory was theirs and were alert to defend it, if need be. They also knew that trespassing on another's land would lead to conflict. A good example of this is Lambert of Ardres's account of what happened when, in the 1140s, the lord of Beaubourg attempted to extend his power into an area claimed by the count of Guînes. He sent troops to occupy a former fortification and had a prefabricated keep erected on it. This led to retaliation and a brief war, which chased Henry de Beaubourg out of Guînes.[16] Borders were far less coherent in English honorial geography, and conflict was thus paradoxically more likely, since it was difficult to say where one lord's influence began and another's ended. In Leicestershire, for instance, the earldom created in 1107 on the back of the former Grandmesnil lordship (organised in the early 1070s to serve the castle at Leicester built in 1069 by the Conqueror) had a large castle, with the earldom's manors surrounding the town and castle to south and west, principally in Guthlaxton wapentake. But the wapentake was not exclusive of other lordships, for the Leicester manors there were interpenetrated with the manors of the earls of Warwick, Northampton and Chester, as well as those of barons such as the lords of Stafford and Tutbury.[17] The earl of Leicester could not in 1107 ascend the keep of his castle and be lord of all he surveyed; even the suburban estate of Knighton and land next to his castle belonged to the bishop of Lincoln. Leicester is a particularly important example for us, as the accidents of historical survival allow us to reconstruct successive earls' resentment at this situation, and the evolution of a long-term policy to counter it.

Orderic Vitalis in the 1120s had heard that Robert of Meulan had successfully brought the entire town of Leicester under his control with royal help before 1118, swallowing up the shares of the king, the Grandmesnil honor and that of Earl Simon de Senlis. He believed that he had taken over the bishop's share too, though some late evidence tends to indicate that this was not the case when he endowed his collegiate church of St Mary de Castro in Leicester castle.[18] Earl Robert II (died 1168) may have been challenged in this appropriation of his lands by the bishop in the 1120s, for the king intervened in a dispute between the two. Before 1130, he gave the earl one of his royal manors in return for the restoration to the bishop of his suburban and urban estate in Leicester.[19] In the meantime, the earl of Chester's isolated estate based on the soke of Barrow in the lower Soar valley north of Leicester had come under pressure from the earl. He is alleged some years before 1133 to have deprived the Chester honor of a considerable amount of land in the Charnwood forest area and to have taken it for himself. Once again the king was involved in the transfer, taking the contested land from the earldom of Chester (perhaps in 1129 on the succession of Ranulf II) and granting it on to Robert II. The triumphant earl arbitrarily disseised at least one Chester tenant, and used some of the land to found monastic houses that would look to Leicester and not Chester for their allegiance.[20] The conditions of Stephen's reign, particularly those of 1139 when the bishop of Lincoln was in disgrace, allowed Earl Robert free rein to pursue his local ambitions. The Lincoln fee was once again seized, and the Chester estate came under further pressure, leading ultimately to Earl Ranulf's surrender of control over the castle of Mountsorrel which gave Earl Robert command of the Soar valley down to the Trent. This was done in a famous treaty the most probable date of which is the autumn of 1149.[21]

The treaty, the last of several arrangements concluded with the earl of Chester by Robert II, is remarkable for many things, but most interesting for us is the fact that Robert II incorporated in it his view of geopolitics looking out from Leicester castle. The earl projected an arc of influence which the earl of Chester would not contest, which included north-eastern Warwickshire, all but the very fringe of Leicestershire and most of Rutland. His vision was based on territory defined by castles. The arc was projected as beginning at Rockingham in Northamptonshire, stretching north to Oakham and Belvoir on the Lincolnshire border, north-west to Kinoulton and Gotham, then west to Hinckley and Donington and thence south-west to Hartshill and Coventry. Within that area the earl had or had acquired allies, such as Simon II, earl of Northampton, his son-in-law, Roger, earl of Warwick, his cousin, and William d'Aubigny Brito, royalist castellan of Belvoir, himself a long-term enemy of the earl of Chester, who had ambitions to seize Belvoir. Earl Robert had also identified enemies within the area, such as a rogue tenant, William de Launay, a Charnwood knight who had allied with the earl of Chester and whom Earl Robert had either crushed or was planning to crush.[22]

It might be thought that the earl of Leicester's local ambitions would have subsided on the succession of Henry II in 1154, but far from it. The earl's victory at Mountsorrel in 1149 was not irreversible. The castle did not stay with the earls of Leicester, for during the war of 1173–4 Earl Robert III of Leicester (died 1190) lost it to a royal confiscation since his title to Mountsorrel was regarded as poor. During 1215, the husband of Robert III's daughter and heir, Earl Saher de Quincy, took advantage of King John's weakness in the Midlands to secure a restoration, only to lose Mountsorrel once again in 1217 to a siege by Henry III's chief supporter, Ranulf II's grandson, Earl Ranulf III. Once conceded control of Mountsorrel by the regency, Ranulf III grandly solved the problem and shame that it represented to his family by razing it to the ground.[23]

Meanwhile, Robert II's victory over the bishop of Lincoln also continued to cause problems, though ultimately his family maintained themselves against episcopal counterattacks. Before his death in 1168, Robert had attempted to deflect a claim on Knighton and the episcopal urban properties by offering compensation elsewhere and shifting possession of Knighton to the Augustinian abbey he had founded in Leicester around 1139. His grandson, Earl Robert IV (died 1204), entered into two conflicts with the bishops over his possession of the suburban estates. In the later 1190s, he defended himself from a suit by Bishop Hugh of Avalon, and in 1203–4 he unleashed a suit in the *curia regis* that routed Bishop William de Blois and even reclaimed the compensation his grandfather had offered before 1168. The claim continued to be argued between the earl's heirs, the abbey of Leicester and the see of Lincoln until the 1230s: a whole century of dispute all kicked up by a magnate who decided he should be sole lord of his town, an ambition maintained with stubbornness by his successors.[24] The accidents of survival allow us in the case of the twelfth-century earls of Leicester and their successors to see how magnates evolved ideas of a sphere of influence that could have long-term consequences and a life of their own. There are other examples that can be offered, though they generally concern particular places that magnates set their heart on possessing and pursued down the generations. Two particular ones are the earls of Warenne and their long-term ambition to control Thetford in Norfolk, and the castle-hunger of the Marshal family of Hamstead, which focused on the royal fortresses of Marlborough and Ludgershall.

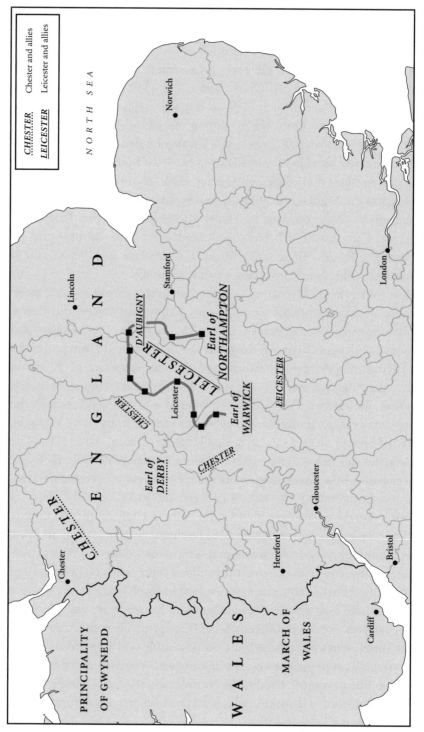

2. Map showing Robert of Leicester's View of his Sphere of Authority, c.autumn 1149

The Norfolk estates of the Warenne family in 1086 were the second largest block of lay estates in the county after those of the Bigod family, the sheriffs of Norfolk and Suffolk. Some at least had belonged to William de Warenne's brother-in-law, Frederick, and the original grant had been augmented by royal favour when William had given up part of his lordship of Lewes in Sussex to construct an honor there for the Briouze family.[25] The Warenne estates in Norfolk occupied a diffuse arc across the north and west of the county, and their miscellaneous nature meant they had no obvious centre – either a fortification or urban centre – though a principal residence was established at the large estate of Castle Acre (not a castle until after Henry I's reign), between Swaffham and Lynn, where there was already a substantial pre-Conquest residential complex.[26] As with the Leicester example, the crisis of Stephen's reign triggered acquisitive behaviour in the Warennes, assisted by the predominance at court of Earl William III's half-brother Waleran of Meulan from 1137 to 1141. The earl set his sights on control of the two large urban centres of Norwich and Thetford. A grant of the very substantial royal assets in Thetford had been secured by Earl William III from King Stephen in 1139 or 1140, when the earl promptly founded an Augustinian priory in the town to celebrate the fact and commemorate his recently departed father.[27] The vital importance of Thetford to the Warennes is evident, in that it provided a natural strategic centre to their estates in Norfolk and Suffolk. If they could also secure Norwich, their control over Norfolk would be complete. When, in 1148, the heiress of the earldom was married to King Stephen's younger son, William, the king gave the couple all his rights in Norwich and Norfolk, saving only the third penny of the earl, which went to Hugh Bigod. A guarantee of this grant was written into the settlement of 1153 between the king and Duke Henry.[28]

The conflict between the Bigod and Warenne spheres of interest is implicit in the text, and we have confirmation of it from evidence that Earl Hugh Bigod in 1140 moved simultaneously with the Warenne acquisition of Thetford forcibly to secure the town of Bungay on the Norfolk/Suffolk border from William III de Warenne's other half-brother, Earl Robert II of Leicester.[29] This dispossession was eventually conceded to Earl Hugh by a family arrangement involving a marriage between Earl Hugh and Earl William III's infant niece, Gundreda, the daughter of Earl Roger of Warwick.[30] We can see a source of the conflict in the fact that the Bigods had fifty-five tenants in and around Thetford in 1086, and in 1106 Roger Bigod I founded and endowed the priory of St Mary in the former cathedral church in the town. Earl Hugh and his successors continued to claim rights as advocate of the priory, which became their burial church.[31] We can see the lavish foundation of Holy Sepulchre by the Warennes in c.1139 as a challenge to the Bigod priory it faced on the Suffolk bank of the Ouse. The 1153 treaty seemed to consolidate what William III de Warenne had manoeuvred to gain in Norfolk, but it was not a sustainable victory. Norwich was lost as early as 1156, though it appears that William, King Stephen's son, may have held on to Thetford somewhat longer, finally losing it before his death in 1159.[32] Nonetheless, the subsequent earls of Warenne or their councils did not forget the ambition. The second husband of Countess Isabel, Hamelin of Anjou (died 1202), half-brother of Henry II, acquired the ambition with his new wife. In 1191, King Richard, Hamelin's nephew, granted Thetford to his uncle in return for Hamelin's lands in the Touraine, at which Hamelin triumphantly issued a confirmation of its lands and goods to Holy Sepulchre priory, Thetford, 'as well and freely as King Richard of England ever held it and gave it to me'.[33] Thus, after the best part of a century, three generations of magnate ambition and manoeuvring led – as with Leicester – to a permanent expansion of an honor, driven by the inexorable imperatives of tenurial coherence, defensibility and maybe also in this case commercial ambition.

The story of Marlborough and the Marshal family is not dissimilar to that of Thetford and the Warennes. John Marshal I (died 1165), son of Gilbert Marshal I (died before 1129) and grandson of Gilbert Giffard, a Domesday tenant in Wiltshire, possessed in 1130 a scattered assemblage of estates principally in Herefordshire, Somerset, Berkshire and Wiltshire.[34] His chief residence was Hamstead Marshall in Berkshire, which he held by right of his court office of royal marshal. Much of what he had was held of several lords, and he fits the pattern of a minor curial baron who had put together his estates from a variety of sources as opportunity allowed.[35] When Stephen came to the throne in 1135, John Marshal was able to acquire custody of the two royal castles of Marlborough and Ludgershall, which, with a castle at Hamstead, nicely consolidated the Marshal holding in Berkshire and northern Wiltshire into a coherent block and much enhanced John's power, turning him into a major player in the subsequent wars of the period 1138 to 1147. The identification of John with this new lordship can be seen in the name 'John of Marlborough' then applied to him. John's strength was in the end his undoing. In the mid-1140s, the neighbouring earl of Salisbury took him on and defeated him, forcing him into the role of auxiliary. However, this was not the end of John's ambition to consolidate his power. In or just before 1150, he built a castle near Newbury to strengthen his position towards the royalist garrisons of Berkshire and Oxfordshire.[36] He was eventually ousted from Newbury by Stephen, but nonetheless continued to enjoy his gains in Wiltshire under Henry II until 1158, when the king abruptly repossessed Marlborough (and Ludgershall too, judging by retrospective evidence). At John's death in 1165, the king resumed the last of his gains in Wiltshire, the manor and hundred of Wexcombe.[37]

We can assume that the Marshal family resented these substantial losses, because Marlborough and Wexcombe became a constant bone of contention for them. When the reign of Richard the Lionheart began in 1189, and the next generation of Marshals were in high favour, John Marshal II (died 1194) received back Wexcombe, though on stiffer terms than his father had held it.[38] The brief ascendancy in England of the king's brother, Count John, between 1192 and 1194, found John Marshal II as the count's seneschal, well placed to regain Marlborough, and it was in defending the castle against King Richard's justiciar that John Marshal died in March 1194.[39] John's brother, William, inherited Wexcombe and did not forget Marlborough. It was not, however, until the civil war of 1215–17 that the family was able to do something about it, and it was not the elder William, but his son and namesake who accomplished the recovery. He had joined the rebel party against John early in the spring of 1215, partly in hopes of regaining Marlborough for the family. But when Louis of France arrived in England and took Marlborough, he bitterly disappointed the younger William Marshal by offering the castle to a rival.[40] It was this snub that caused William Marshal II to rejoin his father on the royalist side in the spring of 1217. The recovery of Marlborough led to its grant – along with Ludgershall – to the younger William by his father, then protector of the child king Henry III. William Marshal II remained in control of the castles when he succeeded his father as earl in 1219, and his tenure of them caused considerable anxiety to the regency council. In the winter of 1223–4, a memorandum drawn up by the teenage king himself recalled that his regents had been so concerned that, in 1219, they offered the earl the marriage of the king's infant sister, Eleanor, in return for the castles, which he eventually delivered up in April 1221.[41]

The three examples of magnate territorial ambition we have examined here are instructive. They could easily be multiplied. David Carpenter has recently examined the efforts made by the Ferrers earls of Derby over three generations to extend their power up from the lowlands of the Dove valley and into the Peak, a struggle with some resemblances to the Marshal bid for

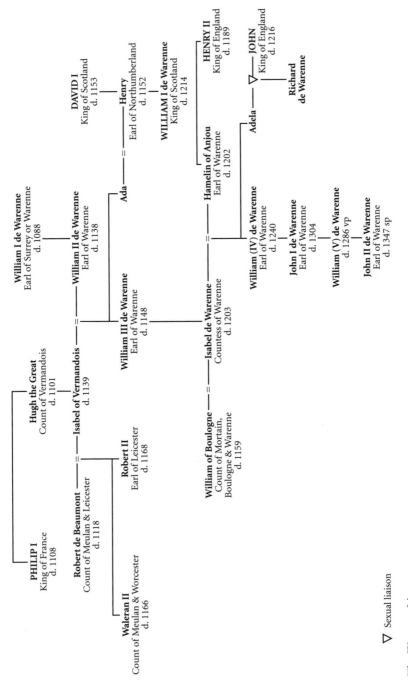

The Warenne Lineage

∇ Sexual liaison

Marlborough.[42] Paul Dalton has looked at the ambitions of the Roumare earls of Lincoln in Lincolnshire and the counts of Aumale in both Lincolnshire and Yorkshire.[43] The earls of Norfolk troubled the peace of East Anglia over possession of the town and castle of Bungay. All these struggles reflect long-term, and sometimes cross-generational, policies, probably embedded in the memory of magnate councils down the decades. Since the objects of magnate desire were hundreds, boroughs and castles in the hands of the king or others, their pursuit was easiest in the times when war offered leverage and the freedom to disseise and negotiate. Hence we see most movement in the civil war of Stephen's reign, the war of 1173–4 or the rebellion of 1215–17. But magnates might secure their aims though exceptional periods of royal favour in times of peace, as Robert of Leicester did in the 1120s and Earl Hamelin and John Marshal II did on King Richard's succession. Magnates' ambitions likewise offered avenues by which the king could achieve his own aims, as Henry III's council was able to do against the younger Marshal in 1221.

It should be noted that purposeful territorial acquisitiveness also occurred at a much lower level in society. A local landowner who had accumulated a major estate from one lord might well extend his lands by acquiring other, contiguous properties from another, despite the dangers of mixed allegiances. So, under Earl Henry I of Warwick (1088–1119), the Warwickshire Montfort family acquired a major barony in Warwickshire and Rutland from the earl. Having secured a concentration of estates in western Warwickshire in the Alne valley, the Montfort of Henry I's days acquired a neighbouring isolated fee from the Tosny lord of Stafford at Ullenhall, on which in the 1130s he erected a borough, called Henley-in-Arden, dominated by a large castle called Beaudesert ('fine retreat') that he had built across the river on his Warwick fee. Thus, by a strategic extra-honorial acquisition, he was able to enhance his local influence and construct a formidable lordship centre which was the family's power base in Warwickshire for three centuries.[44]

Concentrated study of the tenantry of great honors throws up an abundance of evidence as to how widespread was the practice of tenants taking estates from other lords. We rarely know how, when or why individual examples occurred, though it is a fair assumption that friendships, patronage and local ambitions had a lot to do with the process, as with the Montfort case already cited. Richard Mortimer's pioneering study of the tenantry of the honor of Clare in Suffolk made the point. Those substantially endowed families that held lands several generations after 1086 tended to acquire more and expand their interests, at the expense of their lord's demesne, through advantageous marriage or, finally, by grants from other lords. Thus, already in 1086, William Pecche held lands of other Suffolk magnates: the Veres and Bigods. One Enguerrand d'Abenon, was so well connected that he was brought up in Henry I's household, a perfect place to acquire wider lands and patronage. In the same way, substantial tenants from honors outside Clare acquired lands within it. Beyond the surveys of tenure and knight service – which give a misleadingly static picture of the pattern of landholding – we can see an active, indeed a volatile, land market being played to their advantage by ambitious knightly families. The practicalities of the provision of knight service to multiple lords for their diverse possessions seems not to have concerned such men. Indeed, that in itself is an argument against the real expectation of military service from the twelfth-century English honor.[45]

THE EXERCISE OF MAGNATE POWER: THE COMMUNITY OF THE HONOR

The mobility of allegiance observable in landholding is the key to the pursuit of an understanding of how magnate politics worked in England in the twelfth and thirteenth centuries. In 1995, I published a study that analysed the various and complex ways in which it happened, and I want now to return to the mechanisms identified then.[46] To begin with, there is the nexus of lordship created by the Conquest and its aftermath, the network of magnate honors whose origins we have already looked at. The recognition of how central the honor was to eleventh- and twelfth-century society was the achievement of Sir Frank Stenton (1880–1967) in his Ford Lectures for 1929. Nearly a century later, social historians of England are still accommodating his insight. Stenton, of course, wrote in the Maitlandish thought-world which saw society organised 'feudally', as if tenure by knight service could define and link a society together. Later historians have generally rejected this model of society, but it is a testament to the solidity of Stenton's own reconstruction of twelfth-century society that his ideas have nonetheless survived the repudiation of the feudal construct.[47] The honor was at one level an assemblage of estates, sometimes concentrated and sometimes geographically diffuse, as we have seen. It had its centres: physical ones in the sense of great honorial castles, such as Richmond, Arundel, Lewes or Chester, which might initially have a dimension of community to them in the communal performance of castle guard (see above pp. 24–5). But it also had a political centre in the *curia* (court) of its lord. In one of its aspects, this assembly was a law court. Depending on the prestige and wealth of the lord of the honor, his court might be a very powerful and respected one (see below, pp. 166–7). But the dimension we will be looking at here is the honor court as the focus of the political life and local domination of a magnate connection.

The lord enthroned and at ease amongst his men is a pervasive image in twelfth-century literature. The lord's hall was the stage for the hospitality he would offer at his board, and the lord's honour was measured by the quality of his welcome and table, as Thomas Becket, chancellor of England, knew in the 1150s. As well as feeding his men and guests hand-somely, he made sure his servants kept his hall fragrant and clean, glittering with a display of gold and silver vessels and plate. Other lords offered games, songs and stories to divert their guests before the meal, while some dined to the music of viols and singers.[48] Lords were warned very seriously about the importance of not shutting themselves away in private chambers, and to make sure to dine publicly with their men in an enactment through commensality of the bonds of loyalty between them and their people So, in the 1170s, Arnault-Guilhem de Marsan, a magnate of the court of Richard, duke of Aquitaine, the future king of England, lectured his fellows thus:

> When you are holding court (*en cort*), don't be deaf to what I say. If you take my advice, be generous in your expenses and keep an open house with neither closed door nor key. Don't believe tale-bearers nor employ porters who lash out with their staves at squires, pages, hangers-on or musicians who want to get inside the doors. Don't imitate those rich misers who take themselves off on the quiet as soon as they enter court. It doesn't please the Lord God that the court should be broken up for your sake just because you're the first to leave. Instead be the last to do it. Be an even-handed host to all your people.[49]

This human side of the magnate's *curia* is unfortunately the least well docu-mented. Such sources as there are talk almost exclusively of the legal activ-ities of the honorial court. However, it was in social interaction that the *curia* would have been at its most dynamic, affirming and creating bonds between the lord and his dependants, the *compares* of his honor. We do get a few glimpses of this. Around 1140, Earl Roger of Warwick (died 1153) heard that Robert de Montfort of Beaudesert, a leading tenant of his honor, was ill at Thorney abbey in Cambridgeshire, to which Robert had retired.

So the earl crossed England to visit his sick dependant and, while at the abbey, helped with the arrangements for Robert's reception as a monk.[50] There is occasional evidence of a lord's feeling of responsibility for his men that even went beyond death. In 1199, the Marcher baron Roger de Mortemer made a grant to the Welsh Cistercians of Cymhir, not just for the souls of his family but for those of his men 'who died in the conquest of Maelienydd'.[51]

However, not all was quite so positive within honorial communities. Some could be poisonous places. As we have just seen, Arnault-Guilhem de Marsan made a point of warning lords against 'tale-bearers' (*lozengiers*), generally regarded in twelfth- and thirteenth-century literature as the curse of the court.[52] William Marshal in his days as a courtier suffered considerably from the hostile gossip and whispered plotting that buzzed around the pillared aisles of noble halls. A party of hostile Norman knights in the household of the Young King Henry engineered his downfall by a programme of innuendo and accusations of profiteering at his young master's expense.[53] Lords too might find that their courts were not eirenic places. It is notorious how, in December 1135, the tenants of the honor of Pontefract, West Riding, Yorkshire, combined to murder the intruding lord Henry I had forced on them, and to restore their former Lacy overlords.[54] In the later 1160s, Count John of Eu (died 1170), lord of Hastings in England, complained miserably to the archbishop of Rouen that his men were out of control. They were making a victim of him, abstracting his demesne estates and pillaging monasteries under his advocacy. The count was a magnate of great lineage and power, but he seems to give an example of how an honorial community might be alienated from its rightful lord, as much as an intruding one.[55]

The honorial geography of England had been established by the second decade of the reign of Henry I (1100–35). As we have seen with Leicester, scattered or not, honors usually had some sort of regional core by means of which a magnate could attempt to exert a local dominance over lesser families. It is with this mechanism that the process of emotional entropy might begin to affect the honor's communal strength. As son succeeded father in his estates within an honor, he might find himself out of sympathy with his ancestral lord and averse to spending time at his court, as did the tenants of the count of Eu. There were centripetal forces that acted against such entropy. One was locality itself: a tenant would find it difficult to ignore the magnate whose castle was his neighbour. Studies have stressed that, in the case of the compact and exclusive honors found in the Welsh Marches and the Midlands of England, there could be a good turn-out of tenants in support of lords at times of crisis until quite late in our period. So, in 1173–4 Gervase Paganel, lord of the compact castellanry of Dudley, was well supported by his tenants when he took the field in support of the rebels, chief amongst whom was his brother-in-law, Earl Robert III of Leicester.[56] Professor Holt found that the majority of the tenants of the Isle of Axholme in Yorkshire followed their lord, William de Mowbray, into rebellion in 1215.[57] Across the Welsh border, the semi-autonomous Marcher lordships had a capacity to command the allegiance of their tenantry well after the period of this study. In this case, the external threat of Welsh princes must have compounded the effect of the force of hereditary loyalty and concentrated lordship.[58] Similarly, the right of wardship of heirs could bring younger members of tenant families into the households of their lords, and in the right circumstances, if they perceived themselves to be well treated, their residence might well perpetuate and strengthen emotional links to the honorial community. They might even be offered marriages within the lord's family, adding kinship to the bonds that connected them. The early years of knightly heraldry sometimes reinforce this impression of solidarity. Groups of early thirteenth-century shields of arms – such as those of knights of the honors of Clare, Leicester and Chester – show a family resemblance to those of their honorial lords. The resemblances may derive from the earlier use of badge devices on equipment issued by lords to their households, from kinship of some degree, or might simply reflect honorial sentiment and loyalty.[59]

The gradual distancing of tenants of honors from the court of their lords is nonetheless a theme in current scholarship on magnate power.[60] How an honor's major tenants disappear over time from their lord's court can be demonstrated from a discriminating analysis of magnate acts. Sometimes this was due to the extinction of a family, but more often it is simply because the new head of a dependant family chose not to attend on his lord. In the case of the honor of Warwick, this point of crisis occurred before the close of the twelfth century, on the death of Earl William (1153–84). Nearly three-quarters of the service owed to him by his tenants was represented in his charter witness lists. In the case of his brother and heir, Earl Waleran (1184–1204), it was only just over a third. It declined to a fifth with Waleran's son, Earl Henry II (1204–29).[61]

There may have been several reasons why tenants chose not to attend on their lord, but 'emotional entropy' must have been a major one. The Bloets of Silchester illustrate this. The family in its various generations was the principal tenant of the honor of Striguil in both England and the Welsh March from the 1080s onwards, and a stalwart example of how generational loyalty might be perpetuated. Bloets fought with the successive Clare and Marshal lords of Striguil against the Welsh in Stephen's, Henry II's and John's reigns. Members of the family took part in Earl Richard fitz Gilbert's expedition to Ireland, and had the keeping of the honor of Striguil after his death. A Bloet carried the banner of the younger William Marshal at the battle of Lincoln in 1217. Another died fighting for Richard Marshal in his war against Henry III in 1233. However, for all these long-standing links, Earl Walter Marshal chose not to take the under-age William Bloet into his own wardship when Ralph Bloet IV died around 1242. Instead, in 1243, he sold the wardship to Simon de Montfort, and took the option of making a profit out of the boy and his inheritance. Sir William Bloet of Silchester (viv. 1287) thereafter does not appear in connection with a lord of Striguil in his long and active career; indeed, he found the resources and connections to make an independent way in political life as a curial banneret.[62]

The Exercise of Magnate Power: The Locality and Affinity

For all the honor's undoubted importance, there are grounds therefore to differ from Sir Frank Stenton's placing of the honor at the centre of the English aristocratic social structure. There are glimpses of realities beyond it, other social imperatives to which magnates were responding. So we can see that control of the neighbourhood and local community *outside* the tenantry bound to a magnate by customary tenure could be of particular importance to him. As has been said, domination of the local community was the principal means of expressing magnate power before 1066, and the continuing importance of shire and hundred courts after 1066 meant that exploiting pre-Conquest power structures remained an option for the incoming French magnates. There were instances of magnates securing nominees to the office of sheriff in the reigns of the two Williams; indeed, Earl Roger de Breteuil rebelled in 1075 because he was not allowed to control the office of local sheriff as his father, William fitz Osbern, had done (see above p. 103). Control of the shire remained an object of desire for certain ambitious magnates. So when William fitz Corbezun, principal follower of Earl Henry I of Warwick (died 1119), was sheriff of Warwickshire in the 1090s, it is unlikely that he exercised his office with scrupulous disregard for his homage and service to the earl.[63] Furthermore, local magnates who were themselves sheriffs had a major base for their power beyond their own estates. Norman sheriffs such as Roger Bigod, Ivo Taillebois and Urse d'Abetot were men of enormous local influence because they combined sizeable estates in, respectively, East Anglia, Lincolnshire and Worcestershire with the presidency of the shire courts, the keeping of royal castles and the receipt of the king's writs. Taillebois and Bigod were in addition royal stewards.[64] The shrieval families of Gloucester and Salisbury had built on their position to attain earldoms by the 1140s. In the case of the Gloucesters, we even find that female members of such a family in the 1120s were called *vicecomitissa*, in the same way that the wife of an earl was a *comitissa*.[65]

Norman kings were alert to the potential power of the sheriff, and on occasion showed hostility both to subordination of the shrievalty to magnates and magnate occupation of the office. Henry I made two known clean sweeps of his sheriffs, in 1110 and 1129, temporarily combining large numbers of shires in the hands of a few trusted *curiales*. This may have been as much to do with distrust of the occupiers of the office as with a concern to monitor efficiency.[66] The results of King Stephen's widespread abandonment of the control of the office to his earls must have persuaded Henry II of the wisdom of his grandfather's frequent substitution of curial appointees. Nonetheless, on occasion magnates such as Earl William Marshal (died 1219) were allowed to gain control of the office of sheriff, as Marshal did in Gloucestershire and Sussex in John's reign, appointing nominees to do the real work. However, despite his apparent generosity, the king was able in such a case to use deprivation of office to signal that Marshal had fallen into disgrace.[67] Under the Angevin monarchy, such gifts to magnates were as precarious as they were rare. But by then the shire court was in any case in gradual decline, its meetings poorly attended, dominated by an inward-looking group of lesser landowners with an interest in administration. The social standing of sheriffs progressively declined from 1194 to match that of the shire court, and from the 1230s sheriffs were functioning as little more than the local nominees of the exchequer bench in the shires.[68] This development paradoxically brought the domination of the shire court back within the range of a magnate's ambition. When, in the 1220s, Earl Henry II of Warwick (died 1229) looked to find a power base to enhance the failing local influence of his family, he deliberately retained a significant number of the knights active in the county court of Warwickshire, offering amongst other inducements the office of seneschal of his estates, a perquisite that would appeal to such semi-professionals. Some of those knights held parcels of land of him by knight service, but others did not. It was the imperatives of locality, not of loyalty to his ancestral honor, that led to their recruitment. We find a similar strategy with Earl Roger Bigod III of Norfolk (died 1258), who constructed a local affinity of Suffolk knights in the 1220s and 1230s, only a third of them having tenurial links to his honor and many of them being active in the county court and local office. One of them, Sir Herbert d'Alençon (viv. 1255), was sheriff of Suffolk between 1227 and 1232.[69]

At the end of the twelfth century, English society once again developed the same sort of association between magnates and neighbouring land-owners that had been characteristic of pre-Conquest society. In itself, this is testimony to the abiding predominance of localism over tenure in England. In 1990, I demonstrated how William Marshal, newly come to magnate status in 1189, developed a political connection or 'affinity' designed to dominate a particular area of England: Wiltshire, Berkshire and Gloucestershire. This was the area where he had spent his boyhood and from which he drew many of his friends, as well as being the place where his small paternal honor was located. But his ambitions to control it were much wider than such initial ties can entirely explain. Eighteen bannerets and knights are associated with William Marshal's retinue on a long-term basis between 1189 and 1219. Of these, just half can be demonstrated to have derived from families with a link either to the Marshal patrimony or the honor of Striguil he had acquired by marriage (the same proportion, coincidentally, as in his grandson Earl Roger Bigod III's affinity in the next generation). Some of the more significant of them, such as John II of Earley, Henry fitz Gerold, Roger d'Abenon and Stephen d'Évreux, had no initial tenurial connection with him at all, and were either tenants-in-chief (like Earley) or tenants of other honors (like Évreux and Abenon). The lands of these men were predominantly situated in Berkshire, Wiltshire, Gloucestershire and the southern March of Wales. In addition to these, there were other minor magnates of the area who were drawn into Marshal's orbit. The Gloucestershire castle-holding bannerets Ralph Musard of Miserden and Thomas of Berkeley allied with him in John's reign. Musard became his sheriff and castellan of Gloucester; Berkeley was an acknowledged member of the Marshal council before 1219, which would indicate that he swore fealty to Earl William.[70]

The Marshal example is the earliest documented example of a political connection resembling the later medieval 'affinity', and just like the later affinity it already had a focus in the *concilium* which was composed of lay and clerical members and advised its lord. It should be stressed that the connection also included Hugh le Rous, bishop of Ossory, and the abbots of Notley and Bristol, all clerics within Marshal's political sphere of influence, the abbot of Bristol being a man we know undertook business for the earl.[71] It has to be said that it would be going too far to assume that Marshal's was the first known magnate affinity: it is possible to find regional political connections in earlier generations, for all they may seem to be more defined by their honorial dimension. The political affinity of Earl Roger of Hereford (died 1155) that increasingly dominated the southern March and south-east Wales between 1143 and 1155 included several minor magnates and a Welsh king who had no tenurial connection with the earl. It was also sufficiently powerful to cause the young King Henry II to retreat from an attempted confrontation with Earl Roger in the first months of his reign.[72] Just as with the affinities analysed by K.B. McFarlane in his classic study of fourteenth-century aristocratic society, Marshal knights were recruited with a particular purpose in mind, in this case to express and further regional domination. But they had some additional uses. Four of them – John of Earley, Hugh of Sandford, Henry fitz Gerold and Geoffrey fitz Robert – were men with court connections, holding hereditary offices there or deriving from families that did. Marshal himself came from such a background, and one of his closest associates at the courts of Richard I and John was Geoffrey fitz Peter, the justiciar, son of a Wiltshire royal forester. Just as with McFarlane's affinities, this late twelfth-century example was recruited in part by offers of office, such as the Marshal seneschalcies held by William Jardin, John of Earley (and his son) and Jordan de Sauqueville. Others of his knights held royal offices controlled by Marshal, such as the under-shrievalties and constableships held by Ralph Musard, Thomas of Rochford and Nicholas Avenel. The Marshal affinity under William Marshal I was therefore a product of connections both at court and in the country.

Subsequent work has tended to reinforce the idea that thirteenth-century magnate affinities could be recruited for a variety of purposes. As we have seen, the affinities of Earl Henry II of Warwick and Earl Roger Bigod III were both detached to a greater or lesser degree from their lords' honorial communities, and the logic of the recruitment of both was firmly tied to their lords' local interests. Henry II of Warwick's affinity was recruited with a view to dominating the shire court and providing experienced local seneschals for the earl. Earl Roger Bigod's was recruited in part with the shire court in mind, and in part also to express its lord's territorial domination of northern Suffolk. With an earl such as Roger de Quincy of Winchester (died 1264), slightly different imperatives came into play, as the earl's interests were more diffuse territorially, even including substantial estates in Fife in Scotland. The Quincy family's patrimonial interests were concentrated in Cambridgeshire and Northamptonshire, but their greatest possessions were derived from the marriage between Saher de Quincy and Margaret, co-heir of the earldom of Leicester, Earl Roger's parents. These were centred on the castle of Brackley, Northamptonshire, and the town (though not castle) of Leicester. The knights associated with Earl Roger's affinity predominantly reflect his interests in Northamptonshire and Leicestershire. They included substantial tenants of the former earldom of Leicester, the bannerets Richard de Harcourt and Arnold VI du Bois (died 1255). Earl Roger, indeed, intensified the connection by marrying Sir Richard to his sister Orabile; he also retained Arnold's younger brother, William du Bois. But as with the Warwick and Bigod retinues, the affinity included a majority of knights with no tenurial connection to Earl Roger.[73] In this case, the earl was choosing to recruit an affinity that reinforced a connection with a particular area associated with his one great castle, but where his family had no historical dominance to defend.

The same is true of Earl Roger de Quincy's contemporary and co-heir in the ancient earldom of Leicester, Simon de Montfort (died 1265), whose affinity has been scrutinised by several historians. In this case again, the earl's developing recruitment of his affinity after 1240 reflected a desire to dominate the region around a great Warwickshire castle, that of Kenilworth, which he had by gift from the king, and which had no historical connection with his family. He was active both in Warwickshire and in Leicestershire across Watling Street, where he had a castle, priory and borough at Hinckley, and control of Leicester Forest. As with the other magnates we have discussed, the earl recruited from outside his tenantry, including tenants of the Quincys (who lost the Du Bois, the leading banneret of their affinity, to him), the extinct Neubourg earldom of Warwick (whose last earl died in 1242) and the defunct earldom of Chester (whose last earl died in 1237). In some ways, therefore, Montfort had the advantage of being able to exploit a political vacuum in the Midlands, being the only magnate who could offer the opportunity to local bannerets and knights to further themselves. Some of his leading bannerets were minor magnates in their own right: the Du Bois of Thorpe Arnold, Seagraves, Despensers and Montforts of Beaudesert. John Maddicott's analysis of Montfort's affinity was able to illustrate not just its construction and purpose, but also the interlinking marriages that reinforced the solidarity of its personnel, its world of legal and family friendships being 'more akin to that of Jane Austen than to that of the romances'.[74]

The key point about the affinity is that, unlike the honorial community, it had no stabilising bonds based on hereditary tenure, attendance at seigneurial courts and customary military obligations. Nor – unfortunately – did it have the honor's vested property interests to provoke tenants into restraining the lord from risky political ventures and forsaking him if he went too far (see above p. 107). The affinity was a creature of its day. The first generation of an honor would have perhaps been not unlike an affinity: a community structured around one magnate's ambitions and recruited with men of his choice. It would have been vital and dynamic, but, as we have seen, it necessarily fossilised over the generations, unless a magnate continually invested new resources in maintaining old bonds. Some did, which is why there is generally an element in thirteenth-century affinities that maps on to the older honorial structure.[75] But for the most part retainers recruited into affinities made links with their lord for their own lifetimes, and the affinity did not survive a magnate's death as a political grouping. The affinity of the second Earl William Marshal was already forming before his father died. In 1216–17, he was making an effort to recruit young and notorious soldiers with somewhat shady backgrounds, men such as Franco le Tyes (*Teutonicus*), Richard and William Siward, Fulk III fitz Warin and Faulkes de Bréauté. The younger William recruited very few of his father's retainers into his affinity after 1219.

Thirteenth-century knights were well aware of the impermanence of the structures they lived in, and it is not unsurprising that some wanted the link recorded in much the same way that it became usual for grants of lands by knight's service to be committed to parchment after 1100. We call these records 'indentures' (from the resemblance of the serrated edge of each copy to bite marks). They might also be called 'cirographs', from the word 'CIROGRAPHVM' written across the indented edge before it was cut. The two (or three) copies with their indented edges could be put back together to validate the authenticity of the separate parts if any question arose. The form of such documents had its origins in the multiple copies of fines reached in the royal courts of King Henry II.[76]

Something resembling indentures of service can be found in England as early as the reign of Henry II, but it is apparent that such arrangements were not just an insular phenomenon. They are to be found more broadly within French-speaking lands when the link between lord and dependant was principally cash – which tended to be rents drawn on a designated estate or resource, such as mills or markets. The serenely wealthy twelfth- and thirteenth-century counts of Champagne were given to issuing such documents, and since their registers survive we can see that counts as early as Theobald (died 1152) and his son Henry (died 1181) made links with their kinsman Archambaud, lord de Sully, by means of a rent of 120 *li*, which Count Henry renewed on his father's death, but which expired when Archambaud put it up as security for a loan.[77] The indenture may have been a lot more widespread in twelfth- and thirteenth-century society than we know, for there was no logic in a man's heir retaining a copy if the relationship recorded was an ephemeral one limited to his father's day. An early English example survives. It is the record of a grant of a rent of £10 on his English demesne estates by Robert III, earl of Leicester (died 1190), to the Norman knight William de Cierrey (viv. 1189), his long-time seneschal, which is described as money William was owed annually. The reason it survives is that Earl Robert opened the possibility that he might exchange the rent for escheated land, if it suited him, in which case the rent charge would expire.[78] Earl Aubrey III de Vere of Oxford (died 1194) gives another example from Henry II's reign, which indicates that these arrangements went a long way down the social scale. He recorded that the prior of Earl's Colne retained the earl's forester, Peter, by a rent charge of two shillings on land at *Acstede*, 'not holding it by hereditary right but only for his lifetime ... and take note that Peter received a cirograph to that effect from the prior of Colne in my presence'.[79]

The brief career of Earl Gilbert Marshal of Pembroke (1234–41) provides some examples of how a great earl might attempt to forge links with curial figures and other allies by means of strategic gifts. So the royal charter rolls contain records of his grants of lands and rents to three royal household knights, two of them seneschals. The land grants required only the nominal service of the return gifts of gloves and spurs.[80] But the most intriguing surviving document the earl issued is a cirograph by which he allied with the Wiltshire and Gwentian knight Sir William de St Maur, promising to assist William by any means that might be lawful to gain the manor of Undy, Gwent, occupied by the Welsh lord Morgan ap Hywel (died 1246).[81] None of these documents is an indenture of service, but all are records of temporary alliances for the sake of furthering a great magnate connection. Notices of indentures of service from the first half of the thirteenth century are, however, in evidence in suits laid before the royal justices by parties aggrieved that their rights had been abused. In 1247, a knight, Peter Saracen, sued Earl Simon de Montfort (died 1265) over the arrears of 240 marks from a large annual fee of £20 he was owed; the latter was therefore unpaid since at least 1238. Earl Roger de Quincy (died 1264) was in 1242 likewise sued over the arrears of a five-mark annual rent he owed one Alan of Swinford, 'which was owed him out of his chamber'. The earl settled the debt and offered compensation.[82]

These arrangements must have been backed up by written cirographs which would have given us more detail had they survived. Scott Waugh has pointed to the most detailed instance of such a lawsuit that does survive. In 1250, the minor baron Gerard de Oddingseles was summoned to answer the plea of a knight, Robert of Mapledurham, over twenty-nine marks and ten shillings' arrears from an annual rent of five marks, which sets the initial agreement well before 1246. Robert in this case produced the actual indenture (*scriptum*) that recorded the terms by which he had entered Gerard's 'service'. Though the precise terms are not preserved, it seems that Robert was supposed to act as Gerard's financial agent or seneschal, in which duty he had been found sadly wanting. The court, however, ruled in Robert's favour.[83] When we do begin to find actual copies of indentures for military and civil service between lords and dependants at the end of our period, in the 1270s, all such cases tend to indicate that they arose out of long-established practice. They begin to appear not because they present a new phenomenon but because of more retentive archiving of such documents by Edward I's reign.[84]

Much less easy to penetrate is the military dimension of the thirteenth-century affinity. Simon de Montfort's retinue for war did not much resemble his civil affinity, though some of its members did accompany him when he assumed the lieutenancy of Gascony in 1248. Recruitment to a retinue was only partly undertaken for civil reasons, and some affinities were more purely military and curial. The retinue of William de Valence, lord of Pembroke (died 1296), has been demonstrated by Huw Ridgeway to have had little regional orientation, unlike the others we have examined. William retained fellow courtiers and men who can be identified as sharing his tourneying enthusiasm. The Valence affinity demonstrates how flexible and multifaceted a magnate retinue might be.[85] The size and permanence of an affinity are easiest to demonstrate with the case of William Marshal I, which is also our earliest instance. It was by no means large or regular in size. When Marshal was summoned to the side of King Henry II for service in Berry, he was asked to bring 'as many knights as you can get'.[86] Analysis of his biography and his charters produces a total number of eighteen knights associated with him for long periods of his career, but this was just a pool of potential companions. The Marshal biography talks of ten knights crossing to Ireland with Marshal in 1207, and the witness lists of his eighty surviving charters indicate that it was usual for him to have seven knights around him at any time. By comparison, we are told in 1219 that his two sons, William and Richard, expected to take five knights and their servants with them when they travelled from England to France.[87] A 'riding retinue' recruited from amongst a magnate's affinity might therefore total between five and ten knights.

Of course, the *mesnie* or retinue would be expanded further for war or recreation, particularly the tournament, where temporary adherents would latch on to a lord's following to acquire status and perhaps get help with equipment and expenses. William de Tancarville, an exceptional tourneying enthusiast of the 1160s, rode out with over forty knights, though our source, the Marshal biography, says that he was quite happy to discharge them abruptly – including his cousin William Marshal – in quiet times.[88] This matches information in a model letter of around 1249 which mentions the tourneying retinue of young Edmund de Lacy (died 1258), a lesser magnate than any Tancarville or Marshal earl, on its way from Pontefract. A knight writes: 'we shall meet you with Lord E. de Lacy, constable of Chester, who is travelling across those parts with twenty knights to the tournament at Blyth'.[89] In 1309, we have a list of the tourneying *retenaunces* of fourteen magnates at a meeting at Dunstable. Their companies range in size between five and twenty-five knights, with the earls of Gloucester and Lancaster having companies in the twenties. Nine of them had companies of between five and eleven knights, which tallies well with the figures from earlier in the century.[90]

***

The question of aristocratic hegemony in medieval England is bound up with the identification of the affinity as a vehicle for magnate power as early as the twelfth century. It is an essential complement to Stenton's discovery of the honor. Stenton visualised England's medieval power structures as unique to the country, as a peculiarly national form of 'feudalism'. In fact, what his discovery tells us is that what was unique about England was not its 'feudalism', but its ability to frame magnate hegemony through control of communities. This had been true before 1066. The great earls of the pre-Conquest period had expressed their power through their control of communal courts. The new aristocracy of the post-Conquest period continued to look for control of localities. Influencing the old shire and hundred communities was part of the way they did it. But they also created their own supplementary communities of lord and honorial tenantry. Sometimes these were long-lasting and concentrated communities, and sometimes they were not, but by the end of the twelfth century, the mechanism of power in England had settled back into what it had been before 1066: the control of localities by lords forging links with lesser landowners – tenantry or not – in an area that a magnate chose to dominate. This was to be the future for the aristocratic power structure of England until at least the fifteenth century. Affinities were in general individual to the magnate who formed them, but ephemeral structures need not be weak simply because the man at the centre of them was mortal. They made the English social structure remarkably dynamic at the magnate and gentry level; they also encouraged violence and further tipped the balance of power away from the monarch and towards the magnate class.

PART FOUR

DELIVERING JUSTICE

CHAPTER NINE

✦

THE SEIGNEURIAL COURT

O NE of the more intriguing noble prerogatives during the period this book covers was that of doing justice. It was both a consequence of raw power, and an expression of it. Magnates did justice because lesser people went to them for it. They also benefited from it financially and in their personal authority. But there was an ideological dimension to private justice. Magnates, as much as kings and princes, justified their power by declaring it was righteous, rooted in an ethic derived from biblical Wisdom literature (as found in the Books of Ecclesiasticus and Psalms). They were men who were called on to protect the weak and overbear the proud, and they could do so by imposing justice. This was part of the rationale for chivalry, as it appeared in the thirteenth century. Doing justice was by no means an aristocratic monopoly, but it was a way that aristocrats imposed their hegemony and expressed their status.

The 'seigneurial' court is by no means easy to define, other than in reductionist terms: it is a court held in the name of a lord for his dependants. Such a court might operate at a number of levels: it might be the central court of the honor of a great magnate such as the earl of Leicester or Warenne. It might be the court of a 'soke', a distinct grouping of settlements linked historically under the lordship of a man of any status. It might also be the court of a single manor, which could be a large village or only part of a village. It might even be the court of a man holding a few tenements in a town and its surrounding countryside (for examples of all of which, see below). There is little evidence that people in the twelfth century had any hierarchy of private jurisdictions in their minds, or even that they distinguished 'public' from 'private' justice. To contemporaries, there was simply a category of 'lords' courts', *curiae dominorum*. As well as these, there were communal, public courts which had come under the control of an individual. Though not strictly speaking 'seigneurial', such courts – and they included between a third and a half of England's hundred courts – have to be fitted into this study.

It is difficult to say much about whatever analogous seigneurial justice pre-Conquest English society may have had. Maitland, who saw pre-Conquest England as in its way 'feudal', was sure that it must have existed before 1066. Even Maitland's greatest admirer, the late Patrick Wormald, was not convinced that this was the case, or even that manorial courts could be found before 1066.[1] For that matter, there is very little to say about their existence in England in the reigns of the two Williams, but seigneurial courts were certainly a highly visible feature of English social life by the reign of Henry I (1100–35). The legal tract that bears that king's name, composed around 1110, dedicates several chapters to problems between lords over pleas in their respective courts. The *Leges Henrici Primi* treats a lord's court as an expression of his authority. There he could begin pleas against his vassals, or his vassals could argue pleas between themselves before him. Tenants might also use it against a lord, proceeding against him and his officers in his own court. The seigneurial court was perceived as the centre of a community bound together and to its lord by tenure and homage, in the same way that a hundred court was a community bound by locality and its allegiance to the king. The *Leges* gives some insight into the legal process apparently then common to these courts. Litigants were summoned to the proceedings and might be expected to give pledges and oaths in pursuit of claims, not unlike in the royal court. As with royal courts, a plea in a seigneurial court might concern a murder or theft, so it dealt with what we would call criminal pleas as much as civil.[2]

The *Leges* highlight a particular problem in English seigneurial justice, one that would ultimately subvert its effectiveness. The difficulty – as we have already seen – was essentially geopolitical. English noble honors were rarely concentrated geographically, but intermingled across several shires. The *Leges* admit this difficulty but assert nonetheless that the dispersed tenants of an honor must attend on their lord's court. Furthermore, it was not uncommon for English tenants to hold land in several honors, taking lands where they could and as opportunity allowed (see above, pp. 145–6). So a rather confused Norman monk who was sent to administer his abbey's lands in Oxfordshire around 1160 complained to his colleagues back in Fécamp that 'this place has as many lords as it has neighbours'.[3] The *Leges* are aware of the consequences of this state of affairs. The author describes situations in which the holders of fees might be held liable for justice in the courts of several lords. So we find: 'If his lord holds several fees, a person who is the vassal of one honor is not lawfully obliged to go to court in another, unless the matter concerns a case in the other honor court to which his lord has summoned him' (*c.* 55.1b). Likewise there is this: 'If a man holds of several lords and honors, then however much he may hold of others, he owes more to – and shall be subject to the judgement of – the lord whose liege man he is' (*c.* 55.2). Elsewhere we find a clause that hints at a broader jurisdiction over men who are not tenants of an honor, but live within an area where justice is in private hands: 'If a plea arises between the men of two different lords *who have soke*, the accused shall answer the accusation in the court of his own lord for the whole affair' (*c.* 25.2).[4] All three represent pragmatic solutions to the problems caused by multiple allegiances, and indicate a society where those problems were well understood. The situation was obvious to all. Henry I himself acknowledged it. In a well-known writ issued around 1108, he addressed himself generally in this way to the assemblies of the shires and hundreds of England: 'if there is a plea between landholders of the honor of any of my barons, it should be argued in the court of their lord. If it is between landholders of two different lords it should be argued in the shire court. Let there be a trial by combat on this unless the tenants defer on these matters.'[5]

These statements from the first half of the reign of Henry I reveal a sensibility both of the importance of the honor or seigneurial courts, and of the complexities they could cause. But they also show that the problems were by no means insuperable if reference could be made to a dominant lord or to an external forum, such as the shire court. The tendency towards resolving difficulties by sending cases to a neutral tribunal continued to develop. The most satisfactory such tribunal, of course, would be one of the established communal courts, especially if a royal justice was sitting in it. This is reflected by other observations on the process of law that come from the 1130s, in the so-called 'Laws of Edward the Confessor' (*Leges Edwardi*). They depict a world in which jurisdiction is split between royal justices and honor courts. The *Leges Edwardi* are more aggressively royalist in expression than the *Leges Henrici Primi*. They insist that if a case between men of two different lords is heard in an honor court, then a royal justice should be present as a member of the court. The *Leges Edwardi* assume that the king has power to oversee the practices and decisions of England's seigneurial courts.[6] This was the reality of the matter. In the 1160s, a Yorkshire land plea in the honor court of Roger of Mowbray was brought to a conclusion before three groups of men, as the concord stated: the first group was made up of five men 'sent by the sheriff' to witness it, including the king's larderer; the other groups were eight 'of our neighbours' and eleven men 'from my court', including two of Roger's brothers.[7]

The continuing importance of seigneurial courts can be seen in the next major legal treatise, a work called *Glanvill*, which was composed in the 1180s. Its anonymous author was probably a justice in the courts of Henry II. *Glanvill* has a fair amount to say about the honor courts of England. But by the time it was written seigneurial courts had come to be portrayed in a different way, as part of a network of tribunals. Private and public courts were interlinked, for a royal writ could take a plea from an honor court and transfer it to a royal one. In *Glanvill*, it was the king's sheriff who arbitrated when two lords were in dispute over jurisdiction and when a lord pretended to a jurisdiction he did not possess. The use of the specialised 'writ of right' in *Glanvill* attested to a situation in which the crown's authority might penetrate honor courts. It directed lords to do justice in their own court; should they fail to do so, the king's officers would take over responsibility for the case.[8]

The evidence of twelfth-century legal commentaries and statements is that private courts remained important through to the end of the century and beyond, and that lords considered them worth resisting the king to preserve. But the evidence is also clear that the king consistently tried to exert some control over them, even if he apparently had little interest in suppressing them. Other than that, we are not well placed to know exactly how important these seigneurial courts were in their society. We only know that the king saw their jurisdiction as subsidiary to his own.[9] Sources generated by lay seigneurial courts themselves are not easy to come by for the period of this book. For the twelfth century, we have the evidence of magnate charters. When charters begin to appear in some numbers, the lists of witnesses written down at the ends of the act often reveal that they were transacted in a seigneurial court. For example, close on a hundred acts of Robert II, earl of Leicester (died 1168), have survived. Besides these, there also survive a score of acts that were transacted in his court, as we can tell since their witnesses include the earl, his officers and his tenants. Sometimes such an act is sealed by Earl Robert's own seal, as is the case with a charter of one Robert of Croft in favour of Nuneaton priory, Warwickshire, one of the earl's foundations, a Fontevraldine house. The seal imposed the earl's own authority on the transaction.[10]

It is perfectly possible that twelfth-century honor courts were a frequent recourse for tenants who wanted to confirm a deed recording a conveyance of any sort of property. To that extent they formed a 'court of record'.

Robert of Leicester, being justiciar of England from 1155 to 1168, was a particularly powerful and influential individual and his court may well have reflected that fact. It may even have attracted business from the realm in general, not just his own tenants: the degree of his power may have blurred distinctions. It is a reasonable assumption that the courts of lesser nobles would have been less attractive. However, even lesser honor courts produced some evidence that they were used in the same way as the earl of Leicester's, and were the places in which agreements or settlements (*concordiae, conventiones*) between competing litigants were reached and drawn up. Furthermore, such a function continued throughout the period of this study. A settlement survives from 1242 that was drawn up in the court of the honor of Wallingford, before the honor's seneschal. The texts of two final concords, one dated 1269 and the other 1272, survive that were drawn up in the court of Bramber in Sussex, before the seneschal, constable and knights of the honor.[11]

An informative example is a settlement drawn up in the court of William de Montecanesi, a lesser baron of the Midlands and Essex. The head of his barony was the town of Towcester in Northamptonshire. Here, in 1197, two parties – the prior of Luffield and a certain John, son of Roger Lengineur – reached an agreement composed in the form of a cirogaph concerning the priory's lands in the manor of Silverstone. The circumstances of the agreement are very revealing. The case had been commenced in the court of a knight of the honor of Towcester by royal writ. The verbal agreement ironed out in this lesser court was taken thence to the higher court of Towcester, where it was accepted and drafted into a cirograph by a clerk. That was not the end of it. The same agreement was taken for ratification in the Northampton shire court before the sheriff, and put in the form of another cirograph.[12] The Towcester settlement accords rather well with the situation described in *Glanvill*. It shows the honor court to be part of a network of jurisdictions arranged in something of a hierarchy, with the king's authority reaching down through it as far as the petty court of the knight of Silverstone. Royal influence is just as evident in the shape of the concord recorded in the Towcester cirograph. Its diplomatic structure matches those reached before the justices of the royal courts.[13]

There are a number of other such accords reached in seigneurial courts, sufficient to suggest that they might have been relatively popular forums for dispute settlement in twelfth-century England. It is less easy to reconstruct what the actual processes of such courts were. We have already seen some hints provided by legal tracts. One of the best sources, however, is a charter drafted in the court of Roger II de Nonant, a Devonshire baron. Between 1169 and 1184, Roger had a report written for the benefit of Bishop Bartholomew of Exeter describing the proceedings over a case heard in his honor court of Totnes in the fifteenth year of Henry II's reign (October 1168–October 1169). According to this text, a knight of the honor of Totnes, Walter de Meroi, moved a case concerning a small piece of land, ownership of which he was disputing with the canons of Plympton. Walter chose to transfer the case to the royal justices sitting at Exeter, but they sent it back to the honor court of Totnes for trial. The honor court asked Walter for proof of his right to the land in question. He could produce neither witness nor document to establish that he had ever possessed it. The canons then provided evidence that Roger de Nonant's mother had given the land to the priory as far back as the reign of Henry I, and that the priory had held the land the year the king died and for some years afterwards. Roger himself informed his court he had issued a charter of confirmation to that effect. He ended by offering a trial by combat to establish the truth of the matter, either in person or by one of his knights. William Bozun, a leading knight of the honor, delivered the court's judgement in favour of the priory based on the evidence that they had heard from Walter, Roger and the canons.[14]

The Totnes concord gives several indications about the nature of proceedings in twelfth-century English honor courts. They resemble those of the royal courts: right was established by reference to possession on the day Henry I was alive and dead; there was the evidence of witnesses, the production of relevant documents,[15] and the offer of combat to prove the truth of a point.[16] There are other scattered indications of honorial legal process from a variety of contemporary sources. There is an account of proceedings in the honor court of Richmond around the year 1194 concerning a dispute over land in Lincolnshire. In this case, the honor court employed the same procedures as other courts, especially the use of summons and the procedure of essoin (excuse) for non-attendance. When the tenant failed to appear or send an excuse, the land in dispute was confiscated.[17] Other documents show that honor courts were using a jury of recognition to establish facts. In the 1170s, Earl Simon III of Northampton recorded an inquisition carried out 'by the older members of my court' as to the truth of claims contested between the Cluniacs of Northampton and the canons of Huntingdon.[18] In the 1190s, Robert IV, earl of Leicester (died 1204), mentioned a piece of land 'which was recognised in my court by oath of law-worthy men as belonging to the monks of St-Evroult'.[19] The lord of the honor of Eye, Count John, issued a writ of darrein presentment at some time in the early 1190s so that his court would establish the right to an ecclesiastical benefice, just as the king might.[20] This resemblance in procedures is natural enough. The procedures and customs of a seigneurial court would be likely to follow the model offered by hundred and shire courts, and the *curia regis* itself. Moreover, since well over half of the more than six hundred courts in England were in the hands of monasteries and private individuals by the end of the thirteenth century, it would hardly be surprising to find a broad similarity between the customs of seigneurial courts and hundred courts in seigneurial hands.[21] Thus the idea that private courts fitted naturally into a twelfth-century network of jurisdictions is all the more compelling.

The Totnes case provides some evidence to account for the suggested decline of the honor court, which had come about by the thirteenth century. At the beginning of proceedings, Walter de Meroi insisted that it should be shifted to the justices hearing cases at Exeter, and indeed he seems to have succeeded in having this idea adopted. Why this should be so pressing a concern for him was revealed when the justices refused the case and sent it back to Totnes. Walter wished to avoid a confrontation with his lord, Roger de Nonant, whom he knew would favour the canons of Plympton. At Totnes, his case would inevitably fail, and it did. The lord and his own interests would always dominate the business of his court. Whether or not Roger de Nonant was in fact serving the cause of justice here, his decisive intervention illustrates how lords might distort and so corrupt their own justice. The foundation chronicle of Wigmore abbey gives a colourful account of the argument Oliver de Merlimont, seneschal of Hugh de Mortemer, had with his lord in the 1140s. Because of it, Oliver was harassed by a number of cases begun against him by Hugh in his own court. Oliver refused to answer the summonses or offer excuses, fearing the malice and cruelty of his lord, as it was said, so the lands in dispute were confiscated.[22]

This suspicion is one possible explanation for the decline of honor courts in the thirteenth century. Tenants might think their chances of success would increase in a more neutral and distant court, especially if they were uncertain of their lord's favour. It was necessary therefore for magnates and barons to be vigilant for tenants trying to escape their jurisdiction, and indeed they were. In 1200, the attorneys of Earl Robert IV of Leicester argued in the *curia regis* that a Buckinghamshire case between his tenant William de Tourville and Herbert de Bolbec belonged in his court, and it was consequently transferred to him.[23] A Lincolnshire knight, Peter de Lekeburn, attempted to avoid the jurisdiction of Gilbert de Gant's honor court of Folkingham over a plea that he had seized stock from a neighbour by alleging that he held no land of Gilbert and therefore did not have to answer to him. It later transpired that he held some property of the honor through his wife.[24] The problem of distortions of justice in seigneurial courts was not resolved during the period of this study. In 1261, Simon of Pateshill went before the *curia regis* and complained of his treatment by Ida de Beauchamp and her court. He had been summoned to answer a plea of trespass at her court at 'Rouhal'. He came to dispute the charge, armed with the names of two Bedfordshire knights who would act as pledges for his innocence, only to be taken aback when the Lady Ida refused to accept those names, as she said they were not suitors of her honor court. She went on to make it clear she would only accept such suitors as pledges. Simon was at a loss to find anyone present who would stand surety for him, so Ida instructed her court to find him in default and fine him the large sum of twenty marks. As he complained to the royal justices, she had been able to do this because some members of the court were his personal enemies. She and nineteen members of her court were summoned to justify themselves.[25] Unfortunately, the record does not preserve her side of the case.

THE DECLINE OF HONORIAL COURTS

There are other considerations that need to be registered at this point. It is a long-standing tradition in legal historiography that the honor court was stronger at the beginning of the twelfth century than at its end, and that its story was one of decline. The fortunes of honor courts supposedly sank as the Common Law of England rose. This idea was developed in F.W. Maitland's great work, *The History of English Law*. In Maitland's view, Henry II encouraged the centralisation of justice on the royal court, by which he might also mean local courts where the justices in eyre were sitting. In these forums, Henry II and his justices developed and administered a truly national system of law.[26] This assumption lies behind a lot of the work of the school of medievalists, who believe that the study of law is key to understanding medieval society. A natural corollary is that if the law of the royal courts was in the ascendant and the *curia regis* established a supremacy in England, then other courts must have sunk into insignificance as litigants spurned them. One view that developed amongst the historians of the twentieth century was that the reforms of Henry II came out of an attempt to increase the efficiency of the honor courts in administering justice. The king and his councillors intended to enhance the system of writs so as to oblige the earls and barons of England to deal out justice more rapidly in their courts.[27]

Another argument is that Henry II intended decisively to subordinate private courts to royal authority, seeing them as an obstacle to his power. His reforms have been viewed as an attempt to eliminate private jurisdictions in England, his assizes and writs being regarded as an attempt to neuter the power of the honor court. By this interpretation, it is suggested that the *breve de recto*, the 'writ of right', which obliged the recipient to do justice at the king's command, was a stratagem devised to weaken the authority of the private court, since the writs subordinated them to royal authority.[28] But, as we have seen, what evidence there is shows no sign of any hostility to private jurisdiction from the royal court in the twelfth century; rather, it seems that private courts were integrated into the wider system of justice. The increasing alienation of hundreds into private hands in the twelfth century would in any case argue against royal hostility to courts in the possession of individuals. The king saw all the courts of England as doing justice under his supervision, interlinked in procedures, even if they varied a little in customs; and if any of those courts failed in giving justice, then it was his business to deal with the default.[29]

King Henry II's animosity in legal affairs was directed at quite a different target: the ecclesiastical courts, which he believed were attempting, with some success, to evade the control that seigneurial courts could not. Barons may have come to believe in King John's reign that there was an anti-seigneurial agenda in the king's mind. There existed from 1176 a writ called *praecipe*, which removed a land plea from seigneurial jurisdiction into a royal court.[30] It was always a temptation to use *praecipe* indiscriminately, and indeed it became increasingly so used by John's courts.[31] Magna Carta preserves a baronial concern that John was using *praecipe* to remove business from their courts and so undermining them. When the Béthune writer around 1220 reflected on the reasons for the baronial rebellion in 1214, he said it was because – amongst other things – the barons feared the king wanted to remove their right to do 'high justice' in their lands.[32] The usual meaning of 'high justice' is the power to inflict capital penalties in criminal cases (see below, p. 180), but this was never an issue in John's reign. What the Béthune writer might be reflecting, however, is a widespread baronial feeling that the king had ambitions to diminish their prerogative to do justice wherever he could, and at a time when their honor courts were becoming less attractive to their tenants.

Setting aside the historiographical baggage around the question of the decline of seigneurial courts in the face of rising royal ambition, was there nonetheless a decline in the honor court's importance after 1200? It should first be said that such courts did not by any means disappear during the thirteenth century. Right at the end of our period, the honor court of Bramber in Sussex, which met in a churchyard, was a court of record in which substantial landowners still sought to make fines.[33] But, in assessing their importance, we are as much plagued in the thirteenth as in the twelfth century by a lack of evidence. Royal records only notice seigneurial courts when their activities overlap, for whatever reason. So, in 1232, we hear of a plea concerning property in Southwark, begun in the earl of Warenne's Surrey honor court at his castle of Reigate, only because the defending party had to pursue his guarantor through the *curia regis*.[34]

It is the earl of Warenne and his estates in Sussex that provide us at the very end of our period with our best evidence for the surviving level of honorial justice. Four plea rolls survive for the honor court of Lewes for 1265–6. They reveal for once how a great earl's court might function in the last years of the reign of Henry III. To begin with, it should be said that Lewes was very much a top-of-the-range honor court, and its lord in the later 1260s was one of the very greatest men of the realm. It could never be considered to be representative. Lewes was one of the concentrated castle-lordships created in the Conqueror's reign. The lordship (or 'rape') of Lewes consisted of nine Sussex hundreds subordinated to the earl's authority. From the rolls we find that the honor court was presided over in the 1260s by the earl's seneschal, one Richard de la Vache (he is found presiding over it also in the 1270s).[35] The rolls reveal that its business was – it has to be said – overwhelmingly small-scale. It usually only dealt with 'trespasses' or minor disputes concerning land and dues of various sorts. What criminal pleas feature are mostly assaults, and when a rape (that is, a sexual assault) case was mentioned, it was referred on to the sheriff and his bailiffs. However, the court of Lewes was nonetheless clearly still an important forum. Pleas came to it from the hundred courts in the rape of Lewes, which were treated as subordinate to it, not to the sheriff and shire court. It was used in a disciplinary way by the earl. In 1265–6, he launched two pleas of *quo warranto* (justifying a right) against his tenants to force them to justify their claims, just as the king might against one of his tenants-in-chief: one had cleared land in one of his forest chaces and another claimed assize of bread and ale on his own manor. The court had a very decided concern to enforce the earl's control over his own forest, both in hunting rights and timber.[36]

However, the court of the earl of Warenne should not necessarily be seen as simply an instrument of oppression, even if it was a source of discipline to tenants and of income to their lord. Numbers of Earl John's tenants were perfectly capable of pursuing pleas against him and his officers in his own court. This would not have been so had the honor court been believed to be irredeemably corrupt and biased in favour of the earl's interests. The fact that the summons to his court included offences against 'the peace' was cheekily interpreted by one defendant as an offence against the *earl's* peace, and so he refused to answer it, as the summons was not specific as to whom he was supposed to be answering.[37] But the idea of an 'earl's peace' might be taken as evidence that the honorial officers had some ideal of seigneurial justice they were pursuing on their master's behalf, just as royal attorneys and justices had their own brand of idealism.

Valuable though the Lewes evidence is for honorial justice, its lord and the scope of its authority were not representative. I would argue that there was a decline in such courts in the thirteenth century, purely from the evidence that courts no longer attracted major tenants of the honors. We have already seen that the private court could be a very small operation indeed. The lord of Silverstone, Northamptonshire, in the honor of Towcester, who held a land plea in his own court in the 1190s, seemed unsure of his ability to conclude an authoritative settlement between the parties, and allowed it to go elsewhere. Every lord who held land in fee might consider he had a right to hold a court. So when, in Stephen's reign, Earl Roger of Warwick (died 1153) granted property in his town and land in fee in its suburbs at Longbridge to a local cleric, Master John, he was asked to confirm 'that [the tenants there] should in no way be impleaded over any case concerning myself or my men except in Master John's court'.[38] Both examples indicate that the seigneurial court at the manorial level in the twelfth century was already a limited operation, aware that its authority was easily compromised by higher lords and their courts, as much as the king's courts. On the other hand, such courts did not simply fade away. They might certainly be regarded as effective in small local cases, as was the seigneurial (soke) court of Ralph de Rodes at Langar, Nottinghamshire, in the first half of the reign of Henry III, where the prior of Thurgarton made a concord with the parishioners of Langar and Barnston over tithes 'before the whole soke, being present the knights and free tenants of Sir Ralph, who are witnesses to this *conventio*'.[39] Furthermore, the manorial court exercising jurisdiction over the villeins and free tenants dependent on it continued to attract a whole range of business on a small and very local scale, to which the increasing survival of manorial and leet court rolls after the mid-thirteenth century gives us free access.[40]

The authority of a medieval court depended to a large extent on the authority of those who gathered to ponder and deliver its judgements. In those circumstances, any court that contained justices sent out from the royal court was going to have the greatest authority, as they had direct access to the king's mind. But it also followed from this that the court of a great magnate might well have a similar authority as he too had access to the king. Moreover, the suitors (or customary attendees) of his court would be substantial men in their own right, and their joint verdicts would have as much weight as perhaps any other tribunal. It is worth noting again here the attraction of the honor court of the earl of Leicester for his tenants. Other courts must have been equally attractive at a quite late date. Hamelin, earl of Warenne (died 1202), as uncle of King Richard I and one of the greatest magnates in England, is a case in point. His courts were particularly notable as two of his lordships – the rape of Lewes in Sussex and the soke of Wakefield in Yorkshire – served sufficiently concentrated lordships to have judicial officers called *vicecomites* (sheriffs) appointed to oversee them.[41] In 1198, the prior of Lewes and one of the tenants of the earl's soke of Wakefield came before Earl Hamelin himself to record a settlement over the church of Kirkburton, West Riding, Yorkshire. The plea had already been settled before royal justices, but nonetheless the tenant still came before 'the court of my lord Earl Hamelin of Warenne at Wakefield, being there present my lord the earl, William de Warenne, his son, and his free men, and there in their presence with my hand laid on the holy gospels I swore and gave faith for my part and on the part of my heirs never to start a claim or dispute over the presentation to the church of Kirkburton'.[42]

Personal authority counted for a lot, but it is demonstrable that honor courts were not as attractive to a lord's tenants in 1220 as they had been a century earlier. I have presented elsewhere an analysis of the acts of the earls of Warwick across that century, where it can be seen that the suitors present in his court represented a radically smaller proportion of the tenured service of his honor by the thirteenth century. The *curia* of Earl Roger (1119–53) included men who commanded three-quarters of the knight service of his honor; the *curia* of his grandson, Earl Henry II (1204–29), only a fifth. The most serious decline occurred at the end of the twelfth century, under Earl Waleran (1184–1204). None of the major tenant families became extinct during this period, though the fortunes of two of them declined to the extent that Earl Waleran actually negotiated back the $10\frac{1}{4}$ fees of the Corbezun barony within his honor.[43] The decline can only be due to a form of emotional entropy, where an originally vibrant

1 An early thirteenth-century psalter intended for a lay household. Reciting the 150 psalms of the psalter was in itself an act of devotion and could be offered as a form of intercession for the dead. Since the psalms were a major part of the daily office said by the clergy, a psalter was desirable for those lay people with ambitions to follow the office. Earl Robert II of Leicester (died 1168) and his wife are known to have owned copies. Hubert de Burgh took great comfort in his psalter in his times of tribulation and imprisonment in the 1230s, and this page would have been the one he would have meditated on, for it features Psalm 27, David's great psalm of consolation. See p. 235. (Bodleian Library, Douce ms 293, fo. 33r.)

2 The tombstone of Gundrada wife of William I de Warenne. She died in childbirth on 27 May 1085 at Castle Acre, Norfolk. Her tomb was one of at least seven tombs of Warenne earls and their wives, once in the chapter house of St Pancras priory, Lewes, Sussex. The inscription claims her as the spiritual mother of the monks of Lewes priory, as she was the physical origin of the Warenne lineage. The stone itself now lies in the church of St John Baptist, Southover, near Lewes. The fragmentary inscription is eager to associate the Warenne lineage with the fortunes of the priory, probably as it dates to the period immediately after the extinction of its male line. It can be translated as follows: '*Gundrada, the ornament of her age, noble in origin and progenitor of dukes, brought to the churches of England the balm of her good conduct. Martha ... to the poor she was like Mary in her piety. The part that was Martha died, but the great part of Mary lives on. O Holy Pancras ... and she makes you heir, do you clement receive (your) mother. On 27 May, the light of greeting broke the urn of her flesh ...*' (with thanks to Richard Sharpe). See p. 227.

3 Obverse of the seal of Margaret de Quincy, countess of Winchester (died 1236). The countess was the daughter of Petronilla de Grandmesnil, countess of Leicester, and the five-petal flower on the arch alludes to her Norman lineage, as well as to Margaret's status as joint heir to the great Leicester earldom, whose last earl (Robert IV) died in 1204. Her elegant seal depicts her as dressed in a 'jupe', or long, sleeveless gown, embroidered with the heraldry of her husband, Earl Saher de Quincy of Winchester (died 1219). She holds a lily in her hand, a symbol of chastity. She contemplates her husband's shield of arms (made up of seven 'mascles', or voided lozenges). Lower down is the shield of her husband's brother-in-arms and tournament partner, Robert fitz Walter of Dunmow. The seal evokes an aristocratic world saturated with the symbols of lineage and alliance, emerging as the system we now call heraldry. See p. 222.

4 Obverse of the seal of Ela Longespée, countess of Warwick (died 1297). She continued to use this after the death of her first husband, Earl Thomas of Warwick, in 1242, but combined it with a reverse counter-seal bearing the arms of her second husband, the leading courtier, Philip Basset. Here she stands between the arms of Warwick (left) and Longespée (right), asserting her status as the daughter and husband of an earl. Her hand however grasps the Longespée shield, and Longespée lioncels (little lions) adorn the counter-seal. It was clearly her royal lineage, through her father, Earl William Longespée of Salisbury (died 1225), the illegitimate son of King Henry II, which she most prized, and that she emphasised heraldically. See p. 222.

5 The castle gate of Striguil (Chepstow), whose timber, dendrochronology establishes, was felled around 1189. It proves that one of the first acts of William Marshal on his marriage to Isabel countess of Striguil in August 1189 was to order a major rebuilding and extension of the castle which was the centre of his new lands. He can only have financed it from the huge profits of his tournament career. (R. Avent and D. Miles 'The Main Gatehouse' in, *Chepstow Castle: its History and Buildings*, ed. R. Turner and A. Johnson (Logaston, 2006) pl. 39, p. 52.)

6 Silver penny minted for Earl Robert of Gloucester (died 1147) at Bristol in the early 1140s, found at Box, Wiltshire, in 1994. The earl took to minting coins during the civil war of Stephen's reign, when he led the party favouring the king's rival, the Empress Mathilda, between 1139 and his death. The lion device may refer to his own personal heraldry, but more probably to the heraldry of the Angevin dynasty whose cause he espoused, and which we see also in plate 4.

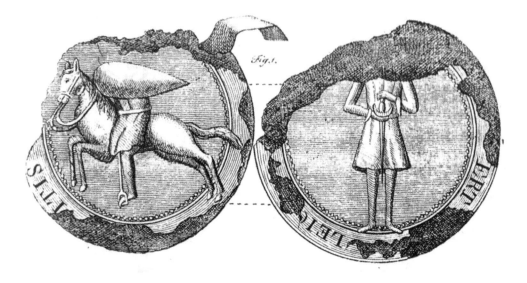

7 Eighteenth-century sketch of the seal of Count Robert of Meulan and Leicester (died 1118). His double-sided seal, adopted c.1107, gives several messages. Its double face alludes to the grandeur of the king's seal. On one side Robert appears as count of Meulan in the guise of a mounted warrior; on the observe, he is earl of Leicester in civil robes, his sword displayed as a symbol of his office of earl and his right to do justice. The original of this seal survives (Keele University Library, Robert Richards Collection 72/56/1(1)) verifying the accuracy of this sketch.

8 Impression of intaglio gem counterseal of Earl Robert II of Leicester (died 1168). The gem, showing an antique image of Victory and an eagle, was enclosed in the earl's ring. The surrounding legend reads: SECRETVM R(OBERTI) COMITIS LEGRECESTRE ('Personal to Earl Robert of Leicester'). The earl applied it to the back of his great seal probably to signify that he had himself approved the transaction. The earl was a cultured, literate and learned man. The Roman gem in his ring connects him with the classical world his contemporaries were rediscovering. Use of such stones became fashionable amongst clerics and aristocats in the 1140s. (British Library Additional charter 48299.)

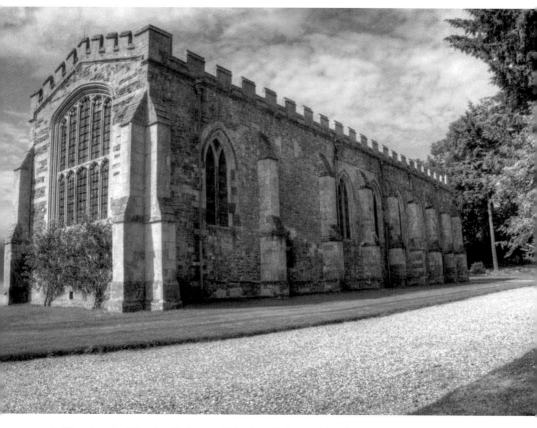

9 The chapel of Noseley Hall, near Billesdon, Leicestershire, home to the senior line of the
Martinwasts, a Norman family that arrived in England early in the twelfth century and was absorbed
into the county gentry. Noseley retains a thirteenth-century private chapel in what was once its
manor house circuit. It was founded by Sir William Martinwast, sheriff of Northamptonshire (died
1246), for the saying of his private devotions and for masses to be said for his soul. It eventually
became home to a large collegiate chantry of priests saying mass for the family, and founded by the
last of them, Bishop Roger Martinwast of Salisbury (1315–30). See p. 17.

community of earl and tenants, linked by political interest as much as customary knight service, became a different sort of institution, where the earl was no longer a friend and father but merely a landholder collecting his dues (see above pp. 149–50). Attendance at his court would become a duty that had to be enforced or compounded for; courts could impose fines on those who failed to turn up despite their customary duty to do so. The magnates of King Henry III's reign were particularly aware of this financial opportunity, and some of them exploited it ruthlessly.[44]

This exploitation would account for the prominence of prosecutions for 'suit of court' in the early thirteenth century, and the angry resistance to them in the Provisions of Westminster (1259). The first three clauses of the Provisions propose severe limitations to the efforts by magnates and knights to impose suit at their courts and place obstacles in the way of the distraints they tried to make on alleged defaulters.[45] For it was not just magnates who had made the most of such opportunities. An Oxfordshire fine of 1247 demonstrates that county knights were as apt to exploit the possibilities as were magnates, as well as giving details about why the victims might get so annoyed. A prominent Oxfordshire county knight, Guy fitz Robert, established that one William Basset of Williamscot owed him service for two-thirds of a knight's fee, which included suit at Guy's manor of Shotteswell across the Warwickshire border every three weeks, a burden that William had refused (though the distance between the places, north of Banbury, was actually not that considerable). William also had to make suit four times a year at Guy's court of Wardington, Oxfordshire, on or after the feasts of St John the Baptist, Michaelmas, Christmas and Easter, and he also had to turn up whenever a plea was heard there by a royal writ of right. William at least managed to negotiate away the regular and objectionable trips into Warwickshire.[46]

There is in fact an early awareness that it was unreasonable to expect tenants of a certain degree to attend seigneurial courts. When, between 1154 and 1166, Maurice of Berkeley (died 1190), the son of the Gloucestershire baron Robert fitz Harding, was granted several estates in that county by one Richard Foliot, it was 'by service that Maurice should go to Richard's councils (colloquia) and pleas twice a year at Tytherington, if he can get there with no inconvenience and trouble, either himself or someone on his behalf'.[47] There was clearly little expectation that such a man would actually do the service he was required to do, and, as with the suit owed by barons to the shire or hundred court, a reeve or seneschal could do it in his place.[48] Nonetheless, honor courts continued to meet, even though evidence of their meetings and activities is very limited. That of Earl Henry II of Warwick is particularly interesting. David Carpenter has drawn attention to a meeting of his court *c.*1217, which we hear about because of its dispossession of a widowed tenant who had refused to hand over her son, to whose wardship the earl believed he had a claim.[49] When the widow appealed to the king, a report of the honor court's proceedings was duly sent to the king's justices in 1221 and the members of the court who had been present at the objectionable verdict were listed.[50] Six knights were named, all but one of whom were tenants of the honor; the exception was Henry of Tubney, a tenant of Abingdon abbey and a former seneschal of the earl's father-in-law, Thomas Basset.[51] The five tenants present answered between them for only a tiny fraction of the earldom's service. The largest service owed amongst them was the two fees of Ralph Butler, but Ralph was a newcomer to the Warwick honor and his principal possession was the extensive barony of Oversley, Warwickshire, in the honor of Leicester.[52] If this record suggests that magnate's honor courts were alive and indeed kicking in the early thirteenth century, it also indicates that they were no longer necessarily the focus of tenurial communities, any more than was Earl John of Warenne's court of Lewes. Earl Henry II's court may indeed have been more visible than most as a consequence of its decisiveness. A Berkshire jury of the 1240s recorded that, some thirty years before, one Henry Basset (died *c.*1241), an outlawed murderer, had not been allowed to succeed to his knight's fee in North Moreton, a component of the honor of Warwick, the inheritance being assigned by Earl Henry II's judgement to a younger brother.[53]

The evidence marshalled by David Carpenter, and added to here, tells us that it would be unwise to write off the honor court as a functioning tribunal in the thirteenth century. In the context I have been sketching, it can in any case be seen as an established part of a network of national justice, which would preserve its importance. I have, of course, already firmly stated that it was rarely by then a principal focus for a magnate's *political* activity. That one of its purposes was by the mid-thirteenth century to provide and safeguard a source of income for a magnate is clear from the Lewes example. But that is not the whole story. It is possible to say that the honor court was more than just a sterile tribunal chasing customary dues. Courts were arenas for the *display* of lordship as much as the assertion of it. A document for the Cluniac priory of St Augustine, Daventry, issued by Earl Simon I of Northampton, depicts the earl's tenant, Robert fitz Vitalis, seeking him out in 1109, coming before the earl and his countess and asking him to concede the grants made to the priory some years previously. The earl recalls Robert 'beseeching' him for this, and uniting with the earl's other barons in his prayer for his graciousness in the matter. Here we have a picture not unlike the one that we have fashioned of the dynamics of the royal court: a place of debate, alliances and public theatre.[54]

The earldom of Warwick indicates that the court of its earl had an important ceremonial function linked with his high dignity and lineage. His household officers still performed ceremonial functions before him in the reign of Henry III. A glimpse of the courtly aspect of the lives of the earls is provided by the earliest version of the romance *Gui de Warewic*, composed for the court of Earl Waleran around 1200 to celebrate the alliance between the earl's young son and the heiress of the barony of Hook Norton. It was not just a courtly entertainment. It included a description of a great earl – like Earl Waleran – holding an assembly of his dependants and allies in state at Warwick on the high feast of Pentecost, with a mass at a nearby minster and a subsequent banquet in his great hall.[55] Coincidentally, there is confirmatory evidence that the earl of Warwick did just that at high feasts in the thirteenth century. In 1316, it was recorded that one John Durvassal held his land at Spernall, Warwickshire, by service of being chief butler of the earl of Warwick at the high feasts of Christmas, Easter and Pentecost, whether the earl was at his castle of Warwick or at his halls at Claverdon, Tanworth-in-Arden and Sutton Coldfield.[56] This was John Durvassal III, the (probable) great-grandson of the knight John Durvassal II of Spernall (died *c.*1256), who had been seneschal of both Earls Henry II and Thomas of Warwick in the 1220s and 1230s. The grant of the honorific office must date back at least to his day and probably before.[57] We also hear of Alan of Woodloes, the hereditary master cook of Earl Henry II, who laid claim in the 1230s to the status of a body squire of the earl's chamber, with the same robes and horses as other body squires.[58] State and ceremony were part of the court of even a minor earl, as was the case with Warwick for most of the thirteenth century. Therefore its judicial aspects must be regarded as one of the ways in which noble status was expressed and defined. This would be even more the case when the power of life and death over convicted criminals was at issue, as we will now go on to see.

CHAPTER TEN

✥

CAPITAL JUSTICE AND THE RISE
OF LIBERTIES

As we have seen, the barons of the reign of John, according to the Béthune chronicler, saw the ability to exercise 'high justice' as their right, which was not to be interfered with by the king. 'High' justice in this instance was the right to do capital and corporal justice, justice of 'life and limbs' as it was called throughout our period.[1] Historians talk broadly of the 'liberties' enjoyed by magnates and some knights in the thirteenth century, by which they generally mean the right of magnates to hold courts and do criminal justice unimpeded by the king's officers. Sometimes the word 'franchise' is used as a synonym (though a franchise is technically a delegated royal privilege).[2] In fact, liberties were claimed by most boroughs and many ecclesiastics, as well as by certain magnates, and broadly speaking liberties might include other rights, such as the right to hunt over particular areas, monitor the quality of bread and ale within a manor, and round up stray animals.[3] 'Liberties' were not therefore the exclusive prerogative of magnates by any means.

But there is some evidence that King John was dissatisfied with the right to do capital justice claimed in particular by magnates, if it was exercised unsupervised. In 1192, before he was king, John is said to have dispossessed Roger de Lacy for hanging two of his own household knights who had failed him by surrendering the castle of Tickhill to John, and then executing a squire who had tried to drive crows from his master's gibbeted body.[4] The tendency of the king's exchequer to question such privileges grew throughout Henry III's reign, when those who claimed liberties were increasingly pressed by touring royal justices to show some 'warrant' for what they claimed. The king's advisers clearly believed that royal rights were being usurped by some of his subjects, for a liberty could divert a considerable income for its possessor which might otherwise have gone to the exchequer. The royal challenge to liberties grew through the 1240s and 1250s, but on the king's part it has been argued that it was neither a consistent programme, nor for that matter was it directed principally at magnates: the main targets were the ecclesiastical holders of liberties.[5]

A baronial preoccupation with defending liberties is nonetheless visible throughout the thirteenth century. How the word 'liberties' became attached to this variety of privileges is not difficult to work out. When, early in Henry II's reign, his uncle Earl Reginald of Cornwall confirmed to Launceston priory its judicial privileges of sake, soke, tol, team and infangentheof (the right to apprehend thieves), the earl referred to them as the priory's *libertates*.[6] So when baronial officers were challenged in exercising their lord's accustomed rights, they would reply, as did Simon de Montfort's Buckinghamshire bailiffs in 1246, that their land was 'in the liberty of the earl of Leicester'. The same earl's Warwickshire bailiffs in 1250 simply refused the sheriff's officers permission to enter Wilmcote, as it was their lord's 'liberty'. In 1250, royal officers in Berkshire would not even attempt it, refusing to enter the town of Hungerford because 'it is of the liberty of the earl of Leicester'.[7] Using significant language, in 1258 the attorney of Earl Simon de Montfort claimed frankpledge (the right to monitor public order) in his lord's manor of Hidden, Berkshire, as the *dignitas* and *libertas* of the honor of Leicester, reclaiming for his lord a right that his bailiffs had let slip during a period of royal wardship. Jurisdiction was clearly seen as a matter of high status, not just profit, and its breach was to be pursued relentlessly as a matter of a lord's honour.[8] A nice example of the way liberty was linked to status is in the reaction of the noble Earl Robert II de Vere of Oxford when he found himself liable to pay four pence annually in frankpledge to the manorial lord of *Wlfmaneston'* and in 1269 put up the money to terminate the objectionable imposition.[9]

One of the more significant developments of the thirteenth century was the way the higher aristocracy in England in effect pursued something not dissimilar to the *ban* that eleventh-century French magnates are alleged to have usurped from their king: that is, the right of exclusive jurisdiction.[10] For all that there was a decline in the drawing power of honorial courts, there was a parallel insistence by magnates on their liberty to do justice, particularly capital and corporal justice, as a measure of their status, the *dignitas* of which Simon de Montfort's men spoke. In this development we can see another symptom of the rise in aristocratic power relative to that of the king in the thirteenth century. The machinery of royal justice was geared to recognise it. By John's reign, it was already established that holders of liberties had a right to receive from the sheriff at least a copy of the royal writ ordering action to amend abuses or injustices within their bounds. In some cases, the baronial officers themselves received the writ and 'returned' or acted on it, thus displacing the sheriff and his subordinates. Michael Clanchy suggests that the right was generated – or at least reinforced – as a result of clashes in East Anglia in John's reign, a place where powerful earls (notably those of Arundel, Warenne and Norfolk) and privileged abbeys (such as Bury St Edmunds) could kick back hard against the unwelcome intrusion of royal officers into their hundreds and manors.[11]

Capital jurisdiction was in fact widespread in thirteenth-century English seigneurial courts, though it is important to note that by no means all lords of such courts claimed it. It seems to have been an expression of status as early as John's reign, when William Marshal the elder, earl of Pembroke, was willing to concede all jurisdiction to the Cistercians of Duiske, 'except alone justice of life and limbs', which he reserved to himself and his heirs.[12] In 1243, Earl Hugh de Vere of Oxford extorted a recognition from the abbot of Bury St Edmunds that he should have a gallows in his manor of Lavenham, Suffolk, even though it was in the abbot's liberty, and that he could hang bond or free men there, provided it was under the supervision of the abbot's bailiff.[13] The grandeur of the magnate concerned was the main issue. In the Buckinghamshire *quo warranto* inquisition of 1286, twenty-four lay lords had their rights to hold their courts challenged. But, of those, most when questioned admitted they had no gallows 'nor any other *judicialia*'. They just laid claim to view of frankpledge and in some cases the right to take stray animals. These were clearly not inconsiderable rights, as Ralph Pipard of Linford was willing to fine with the king for his view of frankpledge to the amount of forty shillings a year and a palfrey worth five pounds. Ralph certainly expected to make a profit from his court at Linford even after paying out the annual sum. However, only three lords in Buckinghamshire claimed rights to a gallows, a pillory and a tumbrel (probably a form of ducking stool). All three were of baronial status: William de Montecaniso at Duddington, Richard fitz John (grandson of Earl Geoffrey fitz Peter of Essex) at Aylesbury, and Roger de Somery, who claimed them at Newport Pagnell and its dependencies as part of his *baronia* of Dudley in Warwickshire.[14] The status of these lords and their courts, and the privileges they claimed, were clearly linked. Lords of single manors were not usually so ambitious.

THE INFLUENCE OF THE EARLDOM OF CHESTER

The fact that there were within England exceptional areas where a subject held *exclusive* rights to justice (other than the widespread *delegated* rights in private hundred and wapentake courts) may well have led magnates to be more ambitious in excluding royal officers from their lands. Chief of these areas was the county of Cheshire, which was exempted from royal jurisdiction as early as the Conquest period. The reason for this privilege is assumed to be the county's special position facing the March and the powerful Welsh kingdom of Gwynedd. In the time of William the Conqueror, Herefordshire and Shropshire were likewise exempt. But the dispossession of the grantees of these earldoms ended the privilege, so their sheriffs once again became royal appointees. The fact that Earl Roger de Breteuil of Hereford rebelled because he had lost control of the sheriffs his father had commanded shows that the right had been prized as a measure of status.[15] In Cheshire, however, the earl remained in control after the Conqueror's reign and his position was reinforced by his being the lord of the entire shire (apart from the few estates of the bishop of Lichfield within it). The earl's seneschal, constable and justiciar presided over the county's judicial structure, administered by his own sheriff; no royal officers participated in their judgements and no appeals could be made to the *curia regis* from Cheshire. By the 1150s, it was accepted that Cheshire had become a quasi-principality within England, in a position analogous to Normandy within France. We can tell this because its lord – just like the duke of Normandy – held 'pleas of the sword' in a parallel to the 'pleas of the crown' held by the king. Royal assizes (statements of law) did not apply in Cheshire.[16] So although the tournament was banned in England between 1154 and 1194, the count of Mortain could legally hold one at Chester in 1185.[17] Its exceptionality produced some peculiar manifestations, such as the office of 'master of the buskers (*leccatori*) and whores (*meretrices*) of all of Cheshire' held by the constable of Chester in the later twelfth century.[18] In 1215, the earl of Chester issued his own Magna Carta to his barons and tenants, presumably in part because the king's charter did not apply in his county and his barons wanted the same protection as their fellows in the rest of England. The document talks of his 'pleas of the sword', his officers, forests and the dominance of his court. It makes no mention of any superior jurisdiction in Cheshire to his.[19] Cheshire was alone in its position of privilege within twelfth-century England.[20] Its incorporation within the royal estates after the extinction of its line of earls in 1237 resolved any problems it might later have posed to the Plantagenet kings and removed the necessity to define exactly what sort of political entity Cheshire had become.[21]

The special position of Cheshire must, however, have had a broader impact on magnates' perceptions of their power. Nor was it just Cheshire that affected their views of themselves, for magnates knew very well that their jurisdictions in Normandy were of a different order from what they were in England. Magnates such as the earls of Richmond, Pembroke, Buckingham, Warenne, Chester and Leicester, or lords from the Briouze, Lacy, L'Aigle and Vernon families, enjoyed exclusive and concentrated lordships in the duchy. This alone might have provided the impulse for lords to attempt to maximise their authority within their English lordships. But there was also the fact that several English barons enjoyed independent lordships within the March of Wales, where a magnate such as the earl of Gloucester could take possession of the temporalities of the bishopric of Llandaff in a vacancy, and where lords could go to war with their neighbours, Welsh and English, as it suited them.[22]

There is some indication that Cheshire's exemptions had an effect on the ideas of contemporary kings and magnates before 1237. During Stephen's reign (1135–54), the king himself transferred control of the judicial and administrative structure of shires and the appointment of sheriffs to his earls, a reform that he began to implement in 1138 and that did not entirely disappear after his death. Royal demesne and forest within shires, as well as sheriffs, shire courts and certain tenants-in-chief, all came temporarily within magnate control.[23] After the reclamation of royal rights elsewhere, Cheshire's exemption nonetheless continued, as did something like it in Cornwall. Earl Reginald, the king's uncle (died 1176), maintained a degree of exemption in his shire that remained effective until his death. On one occasion in Henry II's reign he claimed the shire court operated under his supervision.[24] His sheriffs did not account at the exchequer and he controlled the shire's forests and stannaries. But, on the other hand, Cornwall was not closed to the king's inquisitions (there was a return for Cornwall in the 1166 *Cartae Baronum*) or justices (though in 1233 the earl had a grant of the eyre's profits). The king's writ still moved pleas there, as when Henry II issued a writ in Poitiers to order an inquest to be made in a hundred jury in the shire, with Earl Reginald the officer responsible for ensuring it was done.[25] But the memory of the privileges of the earl of Cornwall did survive 1176. Henry III's brother, Richard, was granted the earldom on much the same terms as Earl Reginald.[26] Moreover, a similar state of affairs was transferred to the county of Rutland when Earl Richard acquired it, for he was given control of the sheriff there, as well as in Cornwall.[27] Such privileges had a way of extending themselves, as would be more apparent in the construction of 'palatinates' in the next century.

Cheshire and Cornwall, not to mention the Marcher lordships across the Welsh frontier, gave English magnates a model of exclusive jurisdiction that plainly attracted them.[28] We can see this in the earl of Chester's bailiffs' claim in 1218, when the earl enjoyed control of the honor of Richmond, that they, rather than the royal sheriff of Yorkshire, had the right to execute royal writs in his three private wapentakes in the North Riding. The earl's men were in effect declaring that they regarded Richmond as an exclusive liberty. It is very likely that their lord's ownership of a genuinely exclusive shire in Chester made them believe just that. By 1252, the bailiffs and sheriff of the honor of Richmondshire had secured exactly that right, and the honor had become a franchise from which the royal sheriff of Yorkshire was excluded.[29] The existence of hundreds and wapentakes in private hands was therefore a further stimulus to magnate ambitions. Where private wapentakes and honors were close to coterminous, as at Richmond and Holderness, the consolidation of power was likely to occur first, as indeed it did. The fact that both honors had private *vicecomites* also helped the process on its way, as it provided an alternative administrative and judicial figure to set against the royal sheriff.

We get glimpses of the process of building up private liberties elsewhere in the thirteenth century. The hundred of Rothwell, Northamptonshire, came to the earls of Hertford early in John's reign, and their subsequent tenure of it saw continual pressure to expand their jurisdiction. We learn from a later inquisition that Earl Gilbert (died 1230) was already forcibly obstructing tenants in the hundred from attending the sheriff of Northamptonshire's customary biannual visits (tourns) to the hundred to view frankpledge – which by then meant collecting 'aids' or fees and hearing 'presentments' or alleged breaches of the peace. They were obliged to attend the earl's own tourns instead. Around 1256, Earl Richard de Clare of Gloucester and Hertford (died 1262) began excluding the sheriff entirely from his hundred. The sheriff used to collect the substantial sum of £5 12s. 4d. for the year, but the earl compelled the landowners of the hundred to pay suit to him, and his officers collected the fees on his behalf, as we find from other sources.[30] The earl's tightening grip on jurisdiction caused Pipewell abbey – which held a small estate at Desborough in the hundred – to seek a composition with him. He was induced to grant the abbey an exemption from suit of his courts, the mandatory attendance at the hundred's regular 'lawedayes' and 'our great tourn of view of frankpledge', by which *his* officers, rather than the sheriff, enforced his control over capital and corporal cases and took their own aids.[31] Earl Richard took advantage of his position in other ways. Within his hundred was a manorial court of the honor of Peverel, then in the king's hands. Just before he died, the earl obliged the tenants to perform their suit at his hundred court with no explanation given. Perhaps he justified himself that, as he had the hundred, he had acquired the king's rights within it. He certainly behaved as if he believed it.

The example of the Clares at Rothwell is by no means an isolated one. Earl John I de Warenne (died 1304) controlled nine adjacent hundreds in his lordship of Lewes in Sussex. An inquisition into his exercise of his jurisdiction in 1276 alleged that the earl's officers had long been excluding royal officers from his lands in the matter of jurisdiction over certain pleas in his hundred courts in Sussex. These hundreds formed his judicial liberty, within which he had rights of capital justice, represented by a gallows. As we have seen, in the 1260s Earl John I de Warenne exerted a very effective lordship through his honor court in Sussex, which heard pleas and imposed his peace on the honor of Lewes. Since the pleas of the hundred courts of Lewes moved to the honor, not to the shire court, the sheriff's influence was decisively diminished by the earl. The court's rolls show some sign of the earl exerting jurisdiction over criminal pleas; assault was one of the commoner trespasses his bailiffs prosecuted. The earl's armed bailiffs and archers were everywhere. They were perfectly capable of using force to exclude royal bailiffs, and in one case attempted to arrest a clergyman for entertaining suspicious characters at night in Rottingdean but he scared them off with a crossbow.[32]

Earl John, like his father before him, was enthusiastic about hunting his parks and forests in Sussex, an amusement that he sometimes conducted at his neighbours' expense. The inquisition of 1276 records their complaints that he incorporated their lands within his forests and chased deer across their lands with his dogs and an armed retinue. His foresters were so successful at stocking his parks that the beasts of the chase were making depredations on neighbouring fields. The Lewes honor court rolls fully confirm this. His bailiffs can be seen there as assiduous in prosecuting any trespass against his hunting and timber in his Sussex chaces. As with Earl Richard de Clare, Earl John forbade his tenants from attending the sheriff's 'tourn' or sessions in Sussex, something that again the honor court records confirm.[33] Earl John had the means to be an uncomfortable neighbour, and the tenant who most suffered his harassment was Robert Aguillon, who was a prominent knight of the retinue of the earl's colleague and in-law, the king's half-brother, William de Valence, and a royal seneschal, as well as a tenant of the honor of Lewes for the manor of Perching.[34] Robert's loud complaints to the inquisition of 1276 show that some of the earl's tenants perceived that he was high-handed within his liberty. Robert alleged that the earl was hunting over his lands in Sussex where the earl had no rights other than those his father had usurped, riding across them with armed men and dogs, and exerting a forest law of his own over Aguillon and his tenants. The earl's seneschal of Lewes, Richard de la Vache, simply defied a royal writ to restore a large herd of oxen confiscated from woods the earl claimed to be within his forest. It was not until the sheriff came in person to confront the earl that Aguillon had justice. Robert also brought the commissioners' attention to what seems to have been an incident associated with his earlier complaint of 1274, that the earl's bailiffs and soldiers hunted down a party of Aguillon's men, arrested them and held them without charge in Lewes castle until they were freed by the king's writ.[35]

Language gives some clue to the growth in aristocratic claims. The process went deep into society's perception of what jurisdiction was. The growing tendency in the later twelfth century for landowners to identify themselves as *dominus/domina* of this or that village demonstrates that it was power over others as much as land that was important in defining status. In the early 1240s, the Midlands knight Thomas II of Astley (died 1265) referred to a road running 'on land of his jurisdiction' (*in terra potestatis sue*) at Broughton Astley and Sutton-le-Elms, Leicestershire, rather than just *in terra sua*. His father, Thomas I (died *c*.1236), had appeared in his acts as *dominus de Estlega*.[36] The impulse to claim *potestas* or *ditio* (jurisdiction) as a matter of status was clearly as characteristic of county knights as it was of magnates.[37] But the jurisdiction of a liberty was limited territorially. The earl of Arundel's attorneys argued as much in 1214, when the bishop of Ely claimed the right of wreck on his lands by reason of the holdings in Norfolk of a couple of his men. They asserted that the bishop had his liberty only within his own lands in Cambridgeshire.[38]

JURISDICTION AND ITS EXTENT

What exactly was being claimed by magnates and manorial lords in the twelfth and thirteenth centuries? It was the case that seigneurial courts had the right to do justice 'over loss of life and limbs' throughout the period of this study, which meant they might impose capital or corporal punishments on those their courts convicted of criminal actions. Such justice is explicit in the *Leges Henrici Primi* of *c.*1116 (see above, p. 164). It is also implicit in the key phrase we encounter frequently in twelfth-century grants of lands from the king or greater lords to lesser men, that they will hold it with 'sake and soke, tol and team, infangentheof and outfangentheof'. This curious formula emerged out of the pre-Conquest past. Its meaning is generally taken to be that lords holding 'sake and soke' might exercise an undefined jurisdiction over pleas and offences on their lands, and in the more explicit case of 'infangentheof and outfangentheof' might take criminals caught red-handed on their lands (infangentheof), and – more rarely – pursue them beyond their bounds (outfangentheof).[39] Following Maitland, Sir Frank Stenton believed that the parcel of rights the phrase represented was a relic of pre-Conquest thegnly privilege, and was of the opinion that the pre-Conquest thegns therefore had courts analogous to post-Conquest seigneurial ones. Some modern opinion still favours this interpretation.[40] As Stenton pointed out, such privileges were widespread. They were attached both to land grants in favour of men of high degree and to those of only local significance. Earl Ranulf II of Chester (died 1153) granted them to, amongst other more considerable men, his cook, along with a parcel of land in Lincolnshire.[41] The corollary of this point is that rights of capital justice permeated the landholding group in society in the first half of the twelfth century, right down to the manorial lord. Although grants of soke, sake, tol, team and infangentheof become less common as the twelfth century closed, the Yorkshire baron Nigel de Mowbray (died 1191) was still routinely doling them out to recipients of quite small parcels of land in the 1180s, though perhaps by then the grants were formulaic and a matter of custom.[42]

We know that in the thirteenth century the possession of 'soke, sake, tol, team and infangentheof' was interpreted as including the right to take and hang thieves. In 1223, Ralph le Moine of Shipton Moyne, Gloucestershire, went before the *curia regis* to claim that he had a right to raise a gallows and tumbrel on his manor, because his predecessor Geoffrey le Moine had a charter of Henry II granting him Shipton with soke and sake, tol, team and infangentheof. Indeed, Ralph claimed that his forebear Geoffrey had raised a gallows at Shipton as soon as he had the charter. It was when Ralph 'renewed' the gallows and cut off the ear of a female thief brought before his court that the abbot of Cirencester disputed his right to hold a court at Shipton, as it was within the jurisdiction of the abbot's private hundredal court. Further investigation through local juries indicated that Ralph's predecessors had not in fact exercised any such rights, the charter of Henry II notwithstanding, and that he was intruding his own authority where he had previously claimed none. The point for us, however, is the way that a local knight could in the 1220s seize on such a phrase from an earlier age and exploit it to the limit.[43] Just such a grant by Henry I to his ancestor was brought forward by the Berkshire knight Peter Achard of Finchampstead in 1260 as his warrant for hanging a female thief arrested in possession of a stolen horse and fabrics. He was nonetheless judged to be at the king's mercy for doing so without a royal officer present to supervise the sentence.[44] Likewise, the court of the noble lady Rohese de Verdun in Belton, Leicestershire, ordered a captured cattle thief to be hanged. She was subsequently challenged in 1247 in front of the royal justices in eyre as to her right to do so. She could cite only 'ancient tenure' as her warrant, which was regarded as insufficient.[45] Grants of criminal jurisdiction after 1220 tended to be more specific than in the previous century, perhaps to accommodate the literal-mindedness of inquisitive royal justices. So when Earl William Marshal II of Pembroke (died 1231) confirmed the foundation by the Hospitallers of their borough of Baldock in Hertfordshire, it was 'with judgement of fire and water, of duel, and gallows'.[46] The same earl made a grant of the manor of Wantage, Berkshire, to Fulk III fitz Warin in a mixture of phrases apparently designed to cover all jurisdictional eventualities, uniting old and new definitions: 'with gallows, pillory, judgement of fire and water, with sake and soke, tol, team, infangentheof and outfangentheof'. Unfortunately for later fitz Warins, the king's attorney was to argue that their control of the double hundred court long believed to be attached to Wantage was not covered by the phrase.[47]

There is scattered evidence that magnate bailiffs were active in the pursuit of criminals within their jurisdictions, despite the close interest of royal officers in their actions. We have already observed the intrusive energy of the Warenne officers at Lewes in Henry III's reign. Earl Simon de Montfort's bailiffs get particular notice in the record. In 1247, their separate hangings of a murderer and a thief in the town of Leicester were challenged: the execution of the homicide because his two victims were buried before their bodies had been viewed by the coroners. The same year they handed over to the prioress of Nuneaton a thief they had apprehended at Hinckley, Leicestershire, and allowed her to take the man illegally into Warwickshire to be hanged.[48] In 1262, a pair of housebreakers were peremptorily hanged by the earl's bailiffs in his court at Long Crendon, Buckinghamshire.[49] The earl's bailiffs were particularly noted for their resistance to the authority of local sheriffs when it clashed with their master's liberties, as at Wilmecote in Warwickshire in 1250.[50]

Magnates' officers were frequently blamed for excesses in the administration of their lords' justice. A particularly ugly case recorded in 1232 concerned the officers of the then under-age Warwickshire baron Peter de Montfort of Beaudesert. A teenage boy, Robert Palmer, was apprehended by a gang of men, including the constable of the castle of Beaudesert, on suspicion of the theft of the purse of a servant of Studley priory. The boy was stripped naked, suspended by his genitals, and sadistically tortured to death. His body was thrown into a well and the shaft part-filled with earth to conceal it. Robert's bereaved and determined father eventually motivated the justices to take action, but it is notable that their investigations were obstructed by an unco-operative hundred jury and that four local knights were willing to stand pledges for three of the more well-heeled murderers, which may be a sign of noble influence at work. Only a lowly castle door-keeper and his associate, a reaper-reeve, were outlawed over the murder. Since the castle was occupied at the time by men who can be identified as retainers of William de Cantilupe, who held Peter in wardship, it may be that this case arose because predatory seigneurial officers were acting unsupervised.[51]

As the thirteenth century progressed, so complaints about the high-handedness of baronial bailiffs multiplied. None was more notorious in his day than William de Bussey, a member of a family of Sussex county knights who gravitated around 1247 into the service of William de Valence, the king's half-brother and lord of Pembroke. As Valence's bailiff, Bussey was alleged to have conducted a campaign of extortion on his lord's lands, and he was also ruthless in his criminal jurisdiction. At some time in the 1250s, he is said to have arrested a husband and wife as sheep stealers in his own manor of Trumpington, Cambridgeshire. They were not brought to trial; instead, Bussey had them confined in a mill-house in such harsh conditions that the husband died. He had the body gibbeted and displayed to the neighbourhood. Bussey was taken by Matthew Paris as a representative of the class of aggressive baronial bailiffs that was troubling the shires of England under protection of their masters and sometimes by the king's indulgence.[52] Likewise, William of Rishanger tells the story of Bussey at Trumpington exhuming and gibbeting the rotting body of a boy who had died in custody after throwing a stone that accidentally killed a cockerel. Rishanger believed Bussey avoided proper legal processes to prevent his outrageous cruelties coming to notice. He also says that Bussey intimidated anyone who made a complaint to him with this little homily: 'If I do you an injury who will put it right? The king wants what my lord wants, but my lord cares nothing for what the king wants or commands.'[53]

It is clear from this that there was a connection in England between noble status and an ability to impose capital or corporal justice at the end of the thirteenth century. The latter defined high nobility in part, in much the same way as possession of the *ban* is held by French historians to define noble status in France. But whereas French historians make it the key to nobility and noble rule in an aristocratic order, we can see in England that it was one of several ways that nobility could be demonstrated by the magnate and (to a much lesser extent) knightly groups. This must necessarily have been so in a realm where the king's authority and presence were so universal, and noble power therefore had to be circumspect.[54] Only in Cheshire in the period of this book was there a substantial area of England where the crown was entirely supplanted by the sword of magnate authority, and even there only until 1237. Nonetheless, the fact that English nobles asserted such rights so vigorously, even in a realm where royal justice and its machinery were so intrusive and pervasive, tells us that English magnates were aware of how their French relatives and fellow magnates exerted their own status. The fact that they got away with it tells us that the king quite understood their outlook. The success of the barons by the 1280s in resisting desultory royal challenges to the exercise of their judicial liberties is evidence enough of where the balance of power lay between king and aristocracy in the thirteenth century. Walter of Guisborough's famous series of anecdotes advertising baronial anxiety about the intentions of Edward I in his *quo warranto* legislation demonstrates the same alertness in defending their noble privilege as we encounter at the beginning of the century in John's reign.[55] This sets the scene for the erection of 'palatinates' for particularly favoured magnates in the next century.

PART FIVE

LIVING NOBLY

CHAPTER ELEVEN

✥

CONDUCT

I SUBSCRIBE to the view that the most sustainable definition of a medieval nobleman is of a man who acted in a noble manner and was not laughed at by his neighbours. Wealth and birth were not everything; looking the part counted for at least as much. Medieval aristocracy defined itself by its military culture, to embrace which by the end of the twelfth century was to embrace nobility. The medieval aristocracy did, of course, depend for its dominance on political and economic weight, as aristocracies always have done. The coalescing of a 'noble' rationale for such eminence made the aristocracy more identifiable at court and in the country, through its members' summonses to royal councils, its own political agenda and claims to jurisdiction in its own courts. But the most visible way of staking a claim to be noble was to live nobly. It is possible to see this mechanism in pre-Conquest society, where conspicuous consumption, the display of status objects and the pursuit of activities such as hunting one's forests were already characteristics of the aristocracy of Edward the Confessor's England, as much as William's Normandy.[1] But these indicators of a noble lifestyle became much more sophisticated, exclusive and self-conscious during the twelfth century.

A great English lord or Norman count in 1000 would have sat surrounded by followers in a wooden hall set within an enclosure. He would have had a household and military retinue. He would have sat in an elevated chair and may have been marked out by his use of a ceremonial sword or staff. In those days it would chiefly have been the ostentation and weight of his riches that marked a man out as great amongst his fellows. In 1300, an English lord would have likewise sat in a hall on a chair of state, but the hall would have been in Gothic stone and like as not set in the bailey of a masonry castle. His household would have had departments and offices, and each would have accounted for its expenses in parchment rolls. His hall would have been glazed and painted; the heraldry of his family and his parage (family connections) would have gleamed and glittered everywhere in his home. His heraldry would also have prominently adorned the abbeys and priories under his advocacy, and the robes of his retainers as they rode the countryside. Etiquette would have attended the appearance of the lord and his wife. Retirement to his private apartments would have limited access to him, and he would make his devotions in his private chapel, furnished with his collection of vestments, books and relics. Society had learned a new material and behavioural language to express social distinction by the end of the fourteenth century, and it was possible for a landowner to make his claim to nobility by lifestyle and conduct.

I have already explored the development of the material aspects of noble culture in my 1992 book, *The Image of Aristocracy in Britain*, and given the mechanism behind it a historiographical context in chapter 7 of *The Birth of Nobility* (2005). I take advantage of that to turn my attention here to the less well-known behavioural aspects. Conduct and nobility is a subject that has to be included in this study, though it has by no means been ignored by historians. Conduct was central to what it meant to make a claim to nobility in the later middle ages. Other subjects looked at here are less familiar. Noble forms of piety have rarely been engaged with, other than through the material aspect of monastic religious patronage. Yet in a society where most intellectual activity and almost all art were religious, piety was clearly going to be a major expression of social distinction, however contradictory that might seem to basic Christian principles. Finally, and this is by no means an afterthought, the place of gendered behaviour in expressions of nobility has to be close to the core of what noble behaviour was.

CHIVALRY

It was through personal conduct that nobility could best and most easily be claimed by the aspirational medieval man or woman. Historians have long been aware of this. The scholarly debate as to what chivalric conduct was goes back almost to the days of chivalry itself. But, as Maurice Keen demonstrated in 1984, what we call chivalry is a later manifestation of noble conduct, different because it was intellectualised and prescriptive. Chivalry was the crystallisation of conduct defined as noble; a self-conscious way of erecting an additional barrier to those who would claim nobility in a time when other social barriers were being put up in the increasingly stratified society of around the year 1200. There was, however, conduct before chivalry that was regarded as characteristic of a great man. As I have suggested elsewhere, what we had before the codification of chivalry, and indeed after it, was behaviour that was generally understood to be appropriate for an aristocrat, a habitus, generated within society itself. The noble habitus of the eleventh and twelfth centuries was as useful to contemporaries as chivalry was in the thirteenth in defining conduct that could be considered noble; it just lacked the spiritual, prescriptive and intellectualised dimension of chivalry. The habitus was taught to the young aristocrat principally through expectations of him if he ever wished to be respected as a man of affairs, a *preudomme*. To conform to the habitus brought a ration of honour to an aristocrat, and to transgress it brought disgrace. To be judged by all one's contemporaries as having breached the habitus was what every aspirant to nobility wished to avoid. It was a potent social sanction.[2]

Twelfth-century England, and the courts of the English kings, produced some of the key literature that helped generate ideas of chivalry, not least the tales of that noble king, Arthur of the Britons, first given its classic form by the bishop of St Asaph and canon of St George's, Oxford, Master Geoffrey of Monmouth (died 1155), who in 1136 published his fictional *History of the Kings of Britain* and dedicated it to the two principal courtiers of the day, Count Waleran II of Meulan and Worcester (died 1166) and Earl Robert of Gloucester (died 1147). It was on the foundation of his Latin work that the great vernacular cycle of Arthurian tales began, first with the Norman canon Wace's *Roman de Brut* (*c*.1160), and then with the retelling and expansion of the legend by Chrétien de Troyes (*c*.1170–80), in whose work we find the French word *chevalerie* used for the first time to describe noble conduct.[3]

Characters close to the twelfth-century English court produced some of the first attempts to define in writing what noble conduct might be. One of the most notable of these was the vernacular *Livre des manières*, composed late in the 1150s or early in the 1160s by a royal chaplain, Master Stephen de Fougères (died 1178), before his promotion to the see of Rennes in 1168. It is a prolonged lecture to each and every order of society about what was right conduct for them. Its strictures on knights and magnates are particularly significant in understanding expectations of their behaviour. Finally, in Henry II's reign, and in his dominions, appeared the influential genre of southern French and Catalan *ensenhamen* (instruction) literature. One of the earliest examples directed at nobles was the work of the southern aristocrat

Arnaut-Guilhem de Marsan, a Gascon subject of Henry II of England, indeed, a man who had attended the court of Richard the Lionheart while he was duke of Aquitaine. The significance of his *ensenhamen*, a poem of 629 lines is that it was written around 1170 by a lay aristocrat for his fellows. It was an insider's view of noble conduct.[4] When it appeared a boundary was crossed. Now writers were self-consciously describing the conduct a nobleman should display. The fact that this occurs in the same generation where the recognition that knighthood was *itself* a sign of nobility is found simply adds force to the argument of this book.

However, even before this literary efflorescence we find work that unconsciously defines conduct by praising laymen whose conduct was judged entirely noble. As has been said, the *preudomme* was the first manifestation of the chivalrous man; he was a man whose conduct was assumed to be admirable and courtly. One of the finest illustrations of this comes from the pen of a canon of Merton priory who decided around 1130 to immortalise his house's founder, Gilbert of Surrey (died 1125), a royal sheriff and household knight. He sought to project the image of a man who was an ideal soldier, courtier and nobleman. Thus his portrait of Gilbert was of a man who displayed accomplishment in all areas: military, devotional and administrative. He was a man who was an active *miles* (indeed 'Gilbert the Knight' was one of his names) and an *illustrissimus vir* (a very noble man), *generose nobilitatis linea procreatus* (born to a family of great nobility). He displayed *liberalitas* (largesse) and worked to earn the *dilectio* (affection) of everyone he met. He spurned tale-bearers and blasphemers, loved and honoured his mother, supported the clergy and the poor, and invested in intercessory prayer for his dead ancestors. He was listened to respectfully by counts and barons, and was perfectly at ease (*intrepidus et hillaris*) at court, where the servants of the king were happy to serve him. He was a man of honour (*honorabilius*), distinction (*elegancius*) and courtliness (*curialius*).[5]

It is possible to attempt to depict Gilbert as a forerunner of the chivalrous knight, but he was not, and would not have recognised the distinction. The point is that he was flattered in Latin by the Merton source as *probissimus virorum*, a *preudomme*.[6] He was depicted as possessing and cultivating the qualities the habitus told his biographer he needed to possess to succeed at court and amongst his fellows. Gilbert's biography tells us, indeed, a lot about the *origins* of the code of chivalry, even though Gilbert was not himself an exemplar of self-conscious chivalry. He may have been a courtly man, but he was not a practitioner of a 'code' of courtliness. The reason why the *preudomme* himself did not generate a code to which his name is attached is clear enough from early twelfth-century literature. Kings, counts, barons, knights, popes, bishops, saints and God himself could all be *preudommes*. When a code of lay conduct emerged it was called *chevalerie*, because all laymen of birth and note were trained as *chivalers: chevalerie* was what they had in common. *Preudommie* (a word that appears late) did exist, but it was far too wide a concept on which to found a code of noble conduct. So *chevalerie* and *courtoisie* (courtliness) were both constructed out of it.

The instruction of young English aristocrats in appropriate conduct for the *preudomme* in the pre-chivalric twelfth century did not come out of a book but from a variety of sources. It had a lot to do with the use of oral examples and of proverbial literature, whether by means of vernacular proverbs relating to the *preudomme*, the maxims of the biblical books of Proverbs and Ecclesiasticus, or though their own Latin education. There is even some possibility that the world of Classical conduct impinged on the teaching of conduct to medieval youths. Latin was taught to medieval boys and girls by means of a set course of basic texts. One of these was a Christianised collection of third-century moral maxims called Cato's *Distichs*.[7] Literally everyone who learned Latin in a school learned it from the *Distichs*. Many of the youths concerned did not go into the Church – and were never intended to do so. So, from Cato they would be warned in a rather pertinent little tag: 'Learn from the examples of many what deeds you should emulate and which to avoid; another's life is a teacher to us.' (3.13). Another such that bears heavily on noble conduct is: 'At feasts make sure to be modest in speech, so that you won't be called loud-mouth when you want to be considered urbane' (3.19). The existence of the *Distichs*, as much as the Book of Proverbs in the Bible, reinforced the tendency of early conduct literature towards the snappy and memorable punch line. We find just such devices in Marsan's *Ensenhamen*. Marsan tells us: 'you can tell the lord by his household' and 'the greater the risk the greater the honour' and 'Be first in the pursuit and last in fleeing.' But he also uses avatars of good conduct from history and literature, a common and well-understood medieval teaching aid for conduct.[8] The knight should bear in mind the heroes of the past. He should be as courtly in his behaviour as Yvain, and as well dressed, for Yvain was the first to wear sable fur on his cloak and gloves on his hands. Paris, Tristan, Aeneas, Apollonius of Tyre and Arthur are all cited as avatars of bravery, but Tristan, Yvain and Paris especially for their attractiveness to women. One of his avatars is not so well known to scholars, but this man, Ignaura, was apparently notorious as a lover. In the mind of

Marsan, correct conduct was of use in acquiring honour, but that in turn could be traded in the marketplace of seduction. The pursuit of women by young men is also a matter of no great trouble to the writer of the popular mid-twelfth-century tract on the education of the aristocratic young, called *Facetus* or the *Urbanus Minor*, though this writer, unlike Marsan, thought that it was bad form for a young man to boast of his conquests.[9]

The instructional literature of their contemporary Master Stephen de Fougères (died 1178) is, unsurprisingly, very different in content. Its intention is entirely located in moral education. This is what it has to say about knights:

> A knight must draw his sword to do justice and to defend those who cannot implead others for themselves: he should suppress violence and theft. But most knights forget their duty. . . . When the starving surrender to their lordship, these knights rob and tax them, they impose on them and work them hard – there is no shortage of heavy corvées to lay on them. They take their lawful rents from the poor, and then they feast and drink on the profit; they deceive and cheat them – they do not protect them as they rightfully should. . . .
>
> The knight does not shrink from doing ill: he despoils and pillages all his people; he has no thought for his own final hours. May *he* then find the sort of protection he offers *now*! We ought to cherish our tenants, for the peasant carries the burden of maintaining us all our lives, knights, clerks and lords. Peasants, yes! But they are Christian folk, not pagans or Saracens. We should not pillage them nor ought we to put them in chains. Knighthood was once a high order, but it is now no more than debauchery. Knights love dancing and pirouetting rather too much and know nothing of responsibility. Born of a free father and a free mother, a man is invested as a knight to pursue a strenuous life, so he should be sensible, and should not be corrupt and full of vice. He should be sensibly prudent and tough and of honest conduct. He should bear himself gracefully towards the Church and all folk.[10]

This is a very significant statement about knightly conduct from a man at the centre of affairs, a chaplain of King Henry II of England and an associate of the great noblemen around whom the idea of chivalry coalesced. What was the message? Knights had an obligation to protect the weak and use their power to do justice. If they taxed the poor, they had to offer protection in return. That was the justification for their power. But in reality knights plundered and tyrannised over the poor. All they did with the money they extracted was party, drink and dance; as, indeed, a superficial reading of Marsan's *Ensenhamen* would also lead us to believe: 'Knighthood was once a high order, but it is now no more than debauchery.' Like all medieval social reformers, Stephen harks back to a time when things were better. His message is that knights have to get back to a golden age. And Stephen knows how they should do it: by honouring the Church's view of rightful authority, protecting the defenceless, the poor, the peasants and, of course, the Church itself.

Stephen was not the only clerical subject of Henry II of England who was keen to define noble conduct and find it in his master's lands. His contemporary Master Andrew de Coutances, a well-connected clergyman of the Cotentin in Normandy, wrote a satire on the French in the 1180s. As a way of denigrating his subject, and praising the Anglo-Normans to whom he addressed his work, Andrew projected on to the hateful French all the bad characteristics he did not want to see in the aristocracy of his own lands. So he depicts King Frollo, the indolent and cowardly leader of the French, lounging in his bed and lecturing his knights: 'Accept no one who fears God or keeps faith with man. Be cruel beyond measure, capricious, faithless and perjured; use every chance to look after your own interests, take from everyone else as your right. ... Be good gamesters of dice and happy perjurers before God, be haughty in any court, doing little and boasting much. Promise but don't deliver, despise those who do you good, live more vilely than a dog and be in every way an Armenian!'[11] By reversal, therefore, Andrew proclaims that the good Anglo-Norman aristocrat should fear God, help the poor and religious, keep faith, be mild and reasonable, generous and modest, honour benefactors and live respectably.

These were all compelling and powerful moral messages about noble conduct, and the Church had been broadcasting them for centuries before Stephen and Andrew. But it had not been broadcasting them to what we call knights. The protection of the poor and the dispensation of justice had long been part of the Church's preaching to the violent kings of western Europe, and the characteristic formula by which this was expressed was drawn from the Book of Psalms (notably 145: 8b–9) 'the Lord loves the righteous and protects the stranger in the land; the Lord gives support to the fatherless and the widow, but thwarts the course of the wicked.' This was the way God ruled the world, and any king who wanted to be considered as righteous and his power valid should rule in that way.[12] Its application as a job specification for the good knight was, however, obvious, and we find it used in an approving epitaph of the Norman warrior Robert of Rhuddlan in 1102. It was carved on his tomb that 'all priests, monks, orphans and homeless men, held in honour by him, received his gifts'.[13] The writers who report Pope Urban's contemporary preaching of the First Crusade (1085) say that he offered knights as well as magnates the chance of reform. If they had until then oppressed orphans, robbed widows, killed, robbed and dese-crated churches, they could now leave their bad ways and go and fight for the Church in the East.[14] This preaching went home, as can be seen in the prologue of a diploma, or solemn act, issued in 1146 in the name of the great nobleman Count Ralph I of Vermandois (a first cousin of the English earls of Warwick, Leicester and Surrey). The count's clerk began by stating on his master's behalf that 'those in priestly or *knightly* orders' (my italics) should attend to scripture, because it was their particular responsibility to govern others in the light of it. Knights were particularly bound to attend to past writings, because it was by their swords that peace and peaceful possession of goods were maintained.[15]

When we finally get tracts that consciously set out to define noble conduct – that is, chivalric texts – it is notable that the writers seize on just this Judaeo-Christian Davidic ethic to offer reasons why barons and knights have a status superior to others in society. The message is: behave ethically and God will sanction your authority. So we find that on occasion historical knights do behave in just that way, perhaps a little ostentatiously, but never-theless sincerely, and so demonstrate that one aspect of chivalry at least was derived directly from the Church's teaching. The first formulations of self-conscious chivalry in the 1220s, notably the influential text the *Ordene de chevalerie* and the *Ensenhamen* of Raimon Vidal de Besalú, integrate this sentiment into their vernacular instruction of the nobleman in ways that Marsan's earlier tract did not, though, indeed, Vidal de Besalú quotes Marsan liberally and was strongly influenced by him. Vidal de Besalú's hero is not offering instruction in seduction, but is more interested in teaching moral qualities: nobility of heart, good judgement and intelligence. These, with loyalty, make the knight useful and respectable. He is much more concerned with the importance of lineage in determining a man or woman's conduct, and warns against bad qualities: arrogance, greed, poor judgement and even excessive love of violence. These, he says, are not pleasing to God.[16] Vidal de Besalú is offering what his predecessors did not: moral instruction. He is perfectly willing to accept that men can be noble without high birth, because for him honour and nobility are attained by moral excellence; this is what makes him a writer on codified chivalry. Such men (and he cites as examples King Richard the Lionheart's routier captain Mercadier and Magarit, admiral of Sicily) have nobility of heart. As he says: 'Honourable deeds and outstanding fame come from the heart and from intelligence, not from family and power.'[17] Vidal de Besalú is self-consciously codifying conduct in his tract, which he significantly calls a *guitz* or 'guide', an instructional booklet for those aspiring to nobility through acquiring noble conduct.[18]

By the second decade of the twelfth century, his *Ensenhamen* reveals a shift in perception of conduct within the aristocracy itself, for Raimon Vidal de Besalú was a nobleman as much as a poet. Much of the literature that allows us to chart these perceptions derives from Occitania and the north-east of France. But thirteenth-century England does offer some material to assess how conduct literature and the self-conscious formulation of chivalry made its impact on the real-life insular aristocrat who wished to be seen to be noble. It produced the text that has most to say on the proper conduct of a model nobleman: the biography of Earl William Marshal of Pembroke (died 1219), commissioned by his son and executors from a Tourangeau poet around 1224 and completed by the end of 1226.[19] It was composed and written in South Wales and England, and drew on the reminiscences and memoirs of the Marshal circle. There can be no more immediate evocation of the conduct acceptable in a nobleman as it was generated within the lay world of Marsan and Vidal de Besalú, not urged on contemporary aristo-crats from the clerical world of Stephen de Fougères as an external biblical hermeneutic.

The message of the *History of William Marshal* is rather different from the ethical norms urged by the clerical and clericalised writers of the same decade of the 1220s. By contrast it highlights two particular noble qualities: loyalty and liberality. One abiding purpose behind the work was to prove to the world what a loyal man Marshal had been. The reason can be found in its painstaking efforts to discredit allegations that he had feathered his own nest on the tourney fields of the 1170s at the expense of his duty to protect his lord, the Young King Henry, and committed *lèse majesté* both by appropriating the royal war-cry to his own use and allowing his retinue to praise him above the king. There was also the matter of the odium he incurred at John's court in 1205 by swearing homage to King Philip Augustus in order to retain his Norman lands, despite King John's opposition. This had led to his downfall at court in 1207–8 and long exile in Ireland.[20] The Marshal biography also focuses on its hero's liberality or largesse. In some contemporary writers' hands, largesse became a spiritualised virtue, showing a contempt for the material world which would one day pass away. The liberal man gave away his goods, seeing them as nothing compared to the spiritual riches stored up for the world to come.[21] The Marshal biographer was less reflective on the moral aspects of largesse, but still very decided about it. Largesse, he said, was the parent of nobility (*gentilesse*) and the result of a good heart (*boen cuer*). For him, as for his contemporary Raimon Vidal de Besalú, nobility arose out of a man's disposition. There was no more noble a man, therefore, than the Young King, not because of his lineage but because he gave freely and borrowed money without limit simply to employ and pay lavishly as big a company of knights as he might. But the greatest man of all was the Marshal, who uniquely combined accomplishment (*proëce*), good nature (*bonté*), largesse and intelligence (*sens*).[22] The Marshal's chivalry was to his biographer still the pragmatic conduct of the *preudomme* and not the spiritualised warrior virtues of the tracts. The word *chevalerie* does appear in the work, but not as signifying a code of conduct.[23]

Was England therefore a little behind the times in its perception of conduct in the 1220s? The great writers on chivalry in the thirteenth century do not come from there, but from Occitania, Cyprus and Picardy, where Raimon Vidal de Besalú, Ramon Llull, Philip de Novara, Raoul de Houdenc and Baldwin de Condé worked. No tract describing idealised chivalric conduct comes from an English writer, which is more than a little surprising.[24] The best England can show is a work such as Walter of Bibbesworth's *Tretiz*, a practical school book for instructing a noble youth in French dating from the 1240s.[25] Historians of an earlier generation might well have nodded and observed that the 'English character' would have resisted such high-flown continental effusions. Earl Roger Bigod III of Norfolk would not have agreed with any idea of French superiority in manners, however. When crossing Guînes on a diplomatic mission in 1249, he found reason to complain of the lack of politeness, respect and reassurance (*civilitas, honor et consolatio*) he encountered at the hands of the count and his officers, though he was as noble as any Frenchman was.[26] The French themselves, however, had a different view. Around 1240, the French tourneyer and *bailli*, Philip de Remy, a man who had been to Scotland, and possibly England too, composed his popular romance *Jehan et Blonde*. The central character is Jehan, a charming and noble squire from the Île-de-France, who goes to England and makes a living as an au pair teaching manners and the proper way to speak French to English noble households. He ends up in the employ of a voluble and uncouth earl of Oxford, but finds at least that the earl's daughter, Blonde – his future wife and countess of Dammartin – had a natural good demeanour. He says of her, in feigned surprise, that 'it could hardly be guessed from her manner of speech that she had not been born in Pontoise'.[27]

There is reason to believe therefore that in the matter of chivalry, as with the idea of noble squirehood (see above pp. 55–9), French and English noble societies had diverged in the thirteenth century, or at least were perceived to have done so. The French liked to consider that the English were not fully aware of what civil conduct was, and the English were themselves uncomfortably aware of this. It is worth recalling again here the testimony in the 1220s of the biographer of William Marshal, who the writer says was hated by his French enemies at the court of the Young King Henry, as he was an Englishman set over them and more applauded in the world of the tournament for his *chevalerie* (meaning his deeds of arms).[28] There was, therefore, something of the defensive 'cultural cringe' evident in English interaction with the French. The biography itself justifies this belief, for it betrays a pragmatic but dated ideal of noble conduct current in the Marshal circles in the 1220s which was essentially that of the *preudomme*. The contrast with the elevated views on noble conduct we find in Jean de Joinville's biography of Louis IX is very striking in that regard, in that Joinville was a young knight in the 1240s and would have acquired his ideas of chivalry while the Marshals were a major force in English life.

This idea of English chivalric inferiority lasted through the century. There was a not inconsiderable literature composed in thirteenth-century France on the subject of the English, and some of it relates to the fact that the French kings had closed down the tournament circuit in their domain and thus imperilled their own nation's chivalry. The anonymous poem called *La Paix aux Anglais*, composed during the period of the baronial ascendancy, 1258–64, imagines Henry III, his son and the English earls gathered in council in London and plotting the taking of Paris. In passing, it ridicules the king of France because the comically truculent English were willing to take the field, whereas no one in France could remember when he last put spurs on his heels. Nonetheless, it portrays the English as inferior knights, and has the French-born earl of Leicester trying to knock some sense into Henry III's court: 'A Frenchman is no lamb! If you attack a wolf, it will fight back! He will burn your tents to ashes. No man is so brave that he will await their onset. The man the French are able to capture will rue the day!'[29] In his diatribe against King Philip III's tournament prohibition in 1278, the French herald Sarrazin pointedly commented on the contrasting chivalric excellence of King

Edward of England. Philip's indifference had put France at a disadvantage
against an inferior nation in chivalric terms.[30] Nonetheless, for all the French
condescension and absence of English literature on the subject, advanced
ideas of chivalry were current in England, and English chivalric heroes more
recent than King Arthur and King Richard the Lionheart were being found.[31]
This might be seen to best effect in the developing legend of Sir William
Longespée II, son of the earl of Salisbury, who died in battle with the
Mamelukes at Mansurah in 1250 during Louis IX's disastrous Egyptian
crusade. The treatment of his death by Matthew Paris held up William's
supposed selfless, Christian heroism against the arrogance, incompetence and
cowardice of the French, which were said to have betrayed the Englishman
to his death. By the 1270s, William's bravery and sacrifice were legendary in
England, and it is as a noble martyr that he appears in the *Flores Historiarum*
in the reign of King Edward I, himself a crusader.[32]

COURTLINESS

A distinction needs to be made at this point between chivalry (which was
codified and self-conscious) and idealised conduct appropriate to a court.
Courtliness was essentially career-orientated behaviour. It was the property
of the *preudomme* and thus not necessarily confined to noblemen (clerks,
women and even peasants are called 'courtly'). When it appeared, it was
'chivalry' that established a man's nobility of heart. To practise it was to
lay claim to noble status. Nonetheless, courtliness was important for a
nobleman to possess. The idea that there was a set of behavioural skills and
expectations laid on aristocrats at the court in the presence of the king (or
knights before their lord) is implicit in most historical writing on the middle
ages. 'Courteous conduct' and 'courtly love' were part of the social
discourse of French nineteenth-century literary scholars, particularly the
great Gaston Paris (1839–1903).[33] When these men talked of courteous
conduct it was because they saw the court as the arbiter in what C.S. Lewis
(1898–1963) called 'polite' behaviour, and the court was the source of the
romances they analysed. Paris influenced in his turn the seminal works of
two Anglophone scholars: the literary critic Lewis and his famous *The
Allegory of Love* (1936) and – through the intermediaries of Léon Gautier
(1832–97) and Gustav Cohen (1879–1958) – the American medievalist
Sidney Painter's *French Chivalry* (1940). Both Lewis and Painter in their
different ways introduced the French courtly construct to Anglophone
scholarship. With it, they also introduced the French ambiguity regarding

the relationship of courtliness to chivalry. Since the 1830s, there has always been a tendency amongst literary scholars to use the words 'courtly' and 'courtesy' in contexts where others might say 'chivalrous' and 'chivalry'.[34] For the most part, the word 'courtly' has been used exclusively and carefully by such scholars, even if military and moral behaviour is at issue.[35]

The key work in understanding what lay behind courtly behaviour is Stephen Jaeger's *The Origins of Courtliness*, launched on the world of medieval studies in 1985. It was a work that for the first time historicised *courtoisie, curialitas* or 'courtliness'. Jaeger set it in a timeframe that began with the rediscovery of Roman civil conduct amongst the clerics of the tenth-century German imperial court and ended with the conscious teaching of *curialitas* by twelfth-century French clerics to the aristocrats of their day.[36] Whether one follows this model or not, courtliness is an important social construct because it describes something evidently going on in medieval society, but like all such constructs it has its problems. As one mid-twelfth-century writer said (in Occitan): 'it is easier to speak about *cortesia* than actually possess it, for it differs in so many ways and has so many guises.' He concluded that no one ever entirely mastered it.[37] Courtliness mostly belonged to the habitus and as such was neither fixed nor prescriptive. It simply described how a *preudomme* operated amongst his superiors.[38] It was behaviour acquired by good example and through tried-and-tested maxims. There was no handbook on it in the thirteenth century.

A useful text here is – once again – the canon of Merton's discussion of the qualities of his priory's patron, Gilbert the Knight (died 1125), a royal sheriff in the reign of Henry I of England (see above, p. 196). Gilbert was himself the son of a sheriff of Cambridge and Huntingdon, and in his younger days was also an active knight in Normandy, perhaps in William Rufus's campaigns of the 1090s. He is described by his biographer as a *preudomme* (*probissimus vir*), an accomplished man of affairs. As a *preudomme* he was capable, upright and therefore able to gain the favour of his superiors. He charmed Queen Matilda II of England (1100–18), acquiring her pious enthusiasm for the poor and for confessional discipline. In return, she furthered his career. Her husband may not have trusted most of his sheriffs, but he is said to have made an exception for Gilbert. The picture of Gilbert at court portrays the definitive courtly man:

> Counts and barons held him in the highest regard and they recognised his nobility of mind with great gifts. He also had the respect of the lesser attendants of the royal household to the extent that he was treated by

them all as if they were his own servants. He was served by them all as if
he were the king. You might frequently see many bishops and other people
of the highest distinction hanging around the door of the royal chamber
for long periods, begging to go in, but quite unable to get a hearing. But if
Gilbert happened to appear the doors were flung wide as soon as the
ushers knew who it was. He was admitted to the royal presence as often as
he wanted. When the sheriffs of England assembled at the exchequer and
were all agitated and apprehensive, Gilbert was the only man who turned
up unperturbed and cheerful. As soon as he was summoned by the
receivers of money, he sent the cash in and he promptly sat among them,
quite at his ease, as if he were one of them himself. As everyone who
knew him would confirm, it is impossible to underestimate the respect in
which he was held, so much was he loved, esteemed and praised.[39]

Gilbert was a *preudomme* and, as such, his biographer also described him as
curialius (most courtly). The two qualities went together. A successful man
of affairs knew how to conduct himself with advantage to his superiors. On
the other hand, an unsuccessful one was ill at ease with his betters and had
no idea how to talk to them to get his way. So Gilbert's contemporary Guy
of Merton, a scholarly but socially inept Augustinian canon, did not go
down well when promoted to be prior of Taunton around 1110, 'because he
did not know how to entertain guests, men of influence by whom the
Church's work was furthered, and he didn't honour them as was proper'. So
important were courtly skills that Guy was removed from office by the
priory's patron.[40]

Courtliness was not chivalry; it was a much broader behavioural trait.
Like *preudommie*, both knights such as Gilbert and clerics such as Guy were
supposed to possess courtly skills, as indeed were women (for which see
below). But only a layman could possess *chevalerie*. When chivalry became a
code at the turn of the twelfth century, it exhibited elements that were of
benefit to the careerist at court. The Plantagenet courts of the second half
of the twelfth century gave rise to many of the texts that describe courtly
conduct. It was the courts of Henry II, and of his sons the Young King
Henry and Richard the Lionheart, that provided the setting for the courtly
activities of William Marshal, and the satires of Peter of Blois, Nigel
Wireker and Walter Map.[41] It would be profitable to suggest that it was the
Plantagenet courts that were the most likely Petri dish in which chivalry
mutated out of a fusion of the courtly and military skills of its inhabitants,
and of clerical preaching and pragmatic statesmanship. Though primacy in

such a development is often given to the courts of Champagne and Picardy, such a view may attribute far too much to the contribution of Chrétien de Troyes. For it was at the courts of Henry II of England and his sons that knightly conduct, Arthurian cultic development, tourneying excesses and clerical courtly culture were brought closest together in the 1170s and 1180s.[42] Although it may be that chivalry thrived intellectually thereafter more in France than England, the skills of courtliness continued necessarily to be cultivated and to flourish in the latter.

CHAPTER TWELVE

❖

EXPECTATIONS AND DEMANDS

NOBILITY made demands on its possessors. Some were open, mostly those relating to power and position. Noblemen and noblewomen both had to offer patronage and protection to their followers. They had to live and dress in a way recognised as noble. Noblemen had to embrace a military career and maintain or join a military household. Other demands were less open, and indeed were not necessarily even consciously articulated or appreciated by medieval nobles. Chief of these were the expectations that their gender and sexuality placed on individuals. Sometimes, however, they do surface into the conscious thought-world of the medieval person. We have a rather rueful twelfth-century meditation on the subject from an Anglo-Norman dramatist, the author of the *Jeu d'Adam*. He has God describing Paradise to Adam and Eve as a place 'where women need not experience the rage of men, or men experience shame and unease before women'. It is an astonishing precursor to Lévi-Strauss's final, sad reflection in his great study of gender, family and society, dwelling on humanity's unfulfillable longing to escape its own gendered hell and live 'entre soi'.[1]

The efforts of British medieval historians have not to date been equal to the wistful humanity of such a characterisation of the expectations of gender. Part of the explanation is the socio-legal dominance of historical writing on medieval English society. Since he thought in terms of law and tenure, Maitland's reading of history reduced the position of women in the middle ages to that of an animated title deed. As the debate on medieval aristocracy from the nineteenth century onwards centred on land, law and power, much of the literature on women within it therefore relates to female power or powerlessness, and how it was expressed and accommodated. Likewise, the status of women in particular historical periods has been reckoned according to the extent of their control over property and their own lives.[2] A notable example is Kimberley LoPrete's accomplished biography of the Conqueror's daughter, Adela of Blois (died 1137), subtitled 'Countess and Lord', which is framed as a dialectical study of female lordship.[3]

However, there is a lot more to say. The status of women was not wholly decided in society by their control of land, their marriageability or even their degree of legal subjection to men. Power, as Foucault and Lévi-Strauss both suggest, may lie elsewhere in society than property, whether in the enforcing of normative behaviour (such as compulsory heterosexuality), or in making women and their sexuality objects to be controlled and deployed. I would myself argue that gendered behaviour – like courtly conduct – was pre-eminently a creature of the habitus, from which it did not escape until the nineteenth century. The habitus is particularly suitable as a vehicle to explain gender relations, because (unlike feminist characterisations of patriarchy) it was not necessarily a harsh mechanism; it could be flexible and forgiving within its limits, as we will see below. It demonstrably acted on men and women alike, through the formation and teaching of ideal types. And if there was a *preudomme* constructed to encapsulate the best in male conduct, there was also (though she is a character almost entirely neglected by historians) a *preudefemme*, who, as a writer associated with King Richard's court around 1190 said, 'should be especially cherished, held in esteem, loved and rejoiced in'.[4] The self-conscious codified conduct of chivalry, of course, applied only to men, though no one thought of actually saying so in the middle ages. Though society produced no parallel explicit code for females, there was conduct that helped define the noble female, though it never acquired a name. This is what I principally want to analyse here.

The earliest surviving *ensenhamen*, written before 1160 in Occitan by the Tolosan *trouvère* Garin le Brun, is in fact addressed to women, not men. It comes from the southern realms of Henry II of England and a poet patronised in the circles of Eleanor of Aquitaine.[5] Its 649 lines laid out (non-clerical) male expectations of aristocratic women, and, in the terms of the modern debate on gender, it offers an 'ideal type' of femininity. It urges women to take good advice so as to avoid committing acts of folly, which was a great concern of such writers. It has a surprising amount to say on the great care women should expend on their manner of dress. It also discusses the type of servants they should employ (preferably well-trained and modest), and the manner of speech they should use to all sorts of men, 'it being better to be silent than speak like a fool', advice deriving ultimately from the Book of Proverbs and addressed elsewhere by contemporaries to the courtly man.[6] Speech and its dangers are a major theme of biblical Wisdom literature and by the twelfth century that concern had clearly filtered down to the educated layperson, if he or she had not already worked out the problem pragmatically.

A woman must guard her tongue. She should speak sweetly and calmly, not too high or too low, but without hesitancy. She should be careful of the company she keeps, and whom she is alone with. Her jewellery and adornments should be new and rich, and also tasteful. She should learn songs and *novas* (political poems of the day) and patronise *trouvères* who amuse and elevate company. The feminine dangers of *follage* (silliness) and *putage* (acting like a tart) were to be avoided. The more specifically courtly danger of being too hilarious was also to be avoided, for it made you look a fool; the writer emphasises that *cortesia* (courtliness) was at all times to be pursued. Love from a valiant knight would follow for the woman who took Garin's advice.[7] The best of women were therefore wise, poised and collected. It should be emphasised here that some parts of a woman's conduct were not gendered: those relating to the skills of *cortesia*, the 'courtliness' we have already analysed, which related to how she should operate in a public forum, for it was assumed by Garin that she would be able to operate therein. Such a woman would care for her appearance and make herself agreeable to sensible men. She should have opinions and be able to express herself becomingly. She should choose both her servants and male friends with care, and make her home welcoming and cheerful.

We have an exactly contemporary clerical male's opinion on the same subject, for Master Stephen de Fougères preached at noblewomen as much as at any other condition of society. His *Livre des manières* is in fact dedicated to Cecilia, the widowed countess of Hereford, a woman by then on her second or possibly third husband. Stephen clearly thought her a paragon, especially for her patronage of religious orders and efforts to build churches. She herself worked up ecclesiastical vestments and lavishly supported the poor. In terms of lay expectations, we hear only that the countess was a loyal and supportive wife to her husband.[8] Elsewhere Stephen talks generally and at length in highly coloured terms of noble females. He expresses himself violently against the wealthy and idle women who flirt, paint themselves with cosmetics and whine at their husbands. He stands appalled at women who plot and scheme against innocent men, and counteract the consequences of sexual promiscuity by procuring or offering abortions. As with Garin, women's tendency to silliness and sexual misconduct is one of

Stephen's concerns, but at a cruder level. He pictures the dissolute noble-woman, careless of her lineage, arranging liaisons with lovers under the guise of attending vespers and, when she cannot get a social equal, indulging in orgies with servant lads. Then there are the women who enjoy lesbian intercourse, which he describes with the help of lavish and baroque sexual imagery.[9] Stephen seems to have thought about female sexuality rather more than was good for him, sufficient for him to want to define what was 'normal' in it and thus control it. But though unease about women's sexuality made a Foucaultian out of him, he was not a misogynist. He was quite explicit about women's high place in God's scheme. Pondering on the salvation that came by means of Mary, and the ultimate fate of Eve, he echoed Anselm of Canterbury's sympathetic conclusion: 'God raised woman above man, even indeed over St Peter in Rome; the lady is now with the angels who let evil into the world with an apple.'[10] If one ignores his fixation on sexuality (for the moment) and reverses his strictures, he, like Garin, makes the sober points that the ideal noblewoman is sensible of her birth, attentive to her husband and a devoted mother, and, in terms of courtliness, is modest and controlled in speech. Stephen differs from Garin in the place that the Occitan poet gives to love in a woman's own expectations, and in Garin's open rejoicing in female beauty and adornment.

Other contemporary clerical writers, seeking patronage, were more flat-tering in their depiction of noblewomen, and more than willing to credit them with an active role in noble society. Stephen de Rouen provided a pen sketch of Countess Agnes of Meulan (died 1181), a woman of the Montfort family, counts of Évreux and (later) earls of Gloucester and Leicester, when he wrote a lament on her husband, who died in 1166:

> His widow is a great beauty, his equal in nobility, in deportment, intellect, birth, character and faith. The countess is accounted equal to the count. She very much resembles the father to whom she was born. She is like him in mind and wealth, in good will and eagerness, in feelings, speech, generosity, understanding and enterprise. Alike to Waleran in all things may she indeed be, apart from length of life, which Nature will bestow, so may the Fates hold their hand from her a while![11]

As was not uncommon at the time, Agnes (then in her early twenties) had ruled her husband's French, English and Norman lands while he was on crusade in 1146–8, and after his death she went on to rule her own lordship of Gournay-sur-Marne, east of Paris, for fifteen years. Here, in 1169, she talked of her own court, foresters and knights when she sponsored the building of a bridge over the Marne.[12] The fact that her husband addressed administrative writs to her on several occasions in the 1140s and 1150s and included her in a list of the members of his council indicates that she was involved in the governance of his lands, spread as they were across three realms, from the Welsh March to the borders of Champagne.[13] The willingness of Stephen de Rouen to describe her as the equal of her formidable husband would seem to be more than flattery. It was recognition of a respected woman whose place was in her husband's council as much as in his bed. The biography of William Marshal features his countess, Isabel (died 1220), in much the same terms: mother, counsellor, lieutenant and, by her birth, a source of high nobility and claims.

It would not be too difficult to multiply such studies of influential countesses, married or widowed, and likewise influential wives of barons. Susan Johns has amply explored the way that such women entered into a discourse with secular power in Anglo-Norman England. Noblewomen were heirs or acquired lands by gift at marriage, a fact that brought them necessarily within the male world of conveyancing and legal process, and some were quite at home there.[14] Even clerical writers were happy to acknowledge that a woman could be more than equal to the task of governing her late husband's lands and bringing up his heirs, as did Orderic Vitalis of Countess Agnes of Buckingham in the 1120s, though he could not resist reporting the gossip that she had simultaneously carried on an affair with Duke Robert II of Normandy in the early 1100s.[15] Women could also end up in the thick of political events. When, in 1207, William de Briouze fell into political disgrace, his wife, Matilda, sometimes called Matilda of Hay, was at the centre of the action. According to the account of the business dictated by King John himself in September 1210, Matilda had led a delegation of Briouze's family to him at Gloucester in 1208, proposing to arrange an interview between the king and her husband over the debts for which John was pursuing him. The failure of the conference led to a brief outbreak of violence in the March and the flight to Ireland of Briouze, Matilda and those of their children not yet held hostage by the king. When the king finally pursued the Briouzes to Ireland in 1210, he found Matilda in charge of their interests, and on his arrival she fled by boat to Galloway with her children and followers, but she was arrested and delivered to the king at Carrickfergus. Unabashed, she negotiated and stalled in her husband's interests, while William tried to carry on a campaign against the king in the March of Wales. The king was persuaded to release her from custody in Bristol to meet her husband and ratify a peace deal, but William carried on regardless and eventually fled England. When the king tried to get her to pay up and argued her into a corner, she rounded on him: 'she curtly told me that she would pay me nothing and she had no more money to pay toward the fine than 24 silver marks 20 gold coins and 15 ounces of gold. So neither then nor subsequently did she, her husband or anyone else on their behalf, pay me anything of the debt.'[16] Her contemporary reputation was formidable. A Flemish historian of King John's England says of her: 'She was a fair lady, very wise and accomplished and particularly energetic. She was never absent from any of her husband's councils. She carried on warfare against the Welsh in which she conquered a good deal.' Her service to the king and gifts to the queen were handsome, and her commercial enterprise in cattle ranching and dairy farming was renowned in her day.[17] It was believed by some that she owed her subsequent sad end in Windsor Castle to her failure to restrain her tongue on the subject of their master to King John's messengers, a freedom Roger of Wendover called the 'sauciness of a woman', echoing the strictures of both Garin le Brun and Stephen de Fougères.[18]

Condemnation of inappropriate conduct betrays the borders of habitus, and the equanimity over Matilda of Hay's activities in our sources is instructive in that regard. Even her enemy the king does not question her right to negotiate and act, or her capacity to offer proposals as her husband's representative. She and her like contradict any simplistic ideas of a hierarchical understanding of female–male relations in the middle ages, the one gender defined by its subjection to the other. Matilda was only criticised in the sources for talking out of turn, and when she did so, she was implicitly admired for confronting a king who was a capricious tyrant. As with all the other examples we have looked at, Matilda was a public person and a social actor. Her husband's willingness to use her talents to the full is not turned into an accusation against him; rather, it is commended. William Marshal was likewise not condemned for leaving his wife to govern Leinster in his absence, knowing that to do so would put her at the head of a military campaign. Even when a manifest breach of the habitus as regards women is registered, the reaction is often equivocal. The Hotot family of the mid-thirteenth century rather cherished the tale of a sister of one of their predecessors in the manor of Clapton, Northamptonshire. As a young woman in Stephen's reign, she supposedly armed herself with shield, helmet, mail coat and lance – all the symbols of male chivalry – and took a horse to ride out against a raiding party from a local garrison. She rode down one of the knights, unhorsed him and took his mount, riding back proudly with it to Clapton.[19] On the other hand, the outspoken militancy of Countess Petronilla of Leicester in her husband's council in 1173, as reported by Jordan Fantosme, and her husband's subsequent equipping of Petronilla in knightly gear so she could ride in his army, is called *folie*. When the king's troops defeated her husband at Fornham, she rode off in a panic and ended up unhorsed, distraught and in a ditch; thus the habitus was avenged on her, in Jordan's opinion at least.[20] It certainly seems that clerical writers were more unforgiving of apparent breaches of expectations than lay writers. The negative theological stereotype of the woman as intellectually and morally inferior to the man was well established amongst clerics and in schools by the end of the eleventh century.[21] Orderic Vitalis, who can be approving of women he regards as responsible, and who even seems to accept Isabel of Conches' riding armed as a knight in her husband's retinue, gives a crude and unforgiving portrait of the militancy and treachery of Mabel of Bellême, who rode with a retinue of a hundred knights and was murdered in her bath, another appropriate end for such a grotesque transgressor of female and moral norms.[22]

As Sharon Farmer commented when analysing the expectations of women in Thomas of Chobham's English confessional manual of *c*.1215, 'the position of women was more complex than historians have thus far implied.'[23] Clerics, especially pastorally inclined ones, had to compromise and find a hermeneutic between cold theology and living habitus. It is in such a hermeneutic that we are more likely to find the true expectations made of the noblewoman. Chobham particularly brought forward the capacity women have to exert themselves in persuasion of their menfolk to moral behaviour.[24] It is the same phenomenon as the inclusion in counsel that we have already seen above, both with specific noblewomen and in Garin le Brun's belief in the informed judgement of a *preudefemme*. This has been observed by other historians in relation to queenship and the queen's capacity to intercede with her lord, soften his inexorable will and change his mind. Pauline Stafford has gone so far as to call this an 'exercise of power', although to do this is to give in to the bankrupt discourse of Maitland and Duby.[25] Intercession may have been an accepted and expected female function, but it was certainly not 'power', for it neither enabled nor was it routinely exercised. It is better seen as part of the more general role of the *preudefemme* to stand outside masculine counsel and offer her own distinct, broad and independent view, and thus give her husband an escape route in an otherwise impossible situation.

A good example of a contemporary imagining of this comes from *c.*1190 and the Anglo-French epic the *Chanson d'Aspremont*. An aged and domi-neering duke of Burgundy is planning in council to seize power in France while the king he hates is fighting Saracens in Italy. The duchess – hitherto silent at her husband's abuses of his power – then takes the floor, ahead of his sons, grandsons and vassals, and gives a forceful (and perhaps unrealisti-cally forthright) critique of the worst possibilities of medieval lordship:

> Emmeline, his wife, she of the proud demeanour, said: 'Lord Gerard, what on earth are you saying? The king of France has authority over all; he has the protection of God by law and according to scripture. What are you talking about, you unfortunate and wretched man? Have you not heard that Agolant of Persia and his son Amon are murdering Christians? They have crossed the sea in force and disembarked. They are destroying Christendom, as I see it. You, who have committed such wicked sins, burned churches, killed and disgraced men, you who are stained with such great sins, what will happen to you, unless you do penance?'

The Lady Emmeline does not let her husband continue. 'Gerard,' she says, 'give up your evil plans! Assemble your men and go to Rome to serve Our Lord. Help Christendom in its need. March with Charles against the pagans.' When the duke then proclaims his intention of overthrowing the king, she continues in the same vein, and urges him instead to unite with the king against the Saracens:

> Gerard listened to her, and became less grim. When he heard his wife's rebuke he said, 'Lady, what can I conceal from you? Yes, I would gladly go to Italy, but I would get no praise or honour there. [King] Charles will be there, and that's the truth.'
>
> 'Indeed,' she said, 'that should not hold you back. I would gather all my troops. I would follow Charles to Aspremont. I would fight for God with everything at my disposal and travel down to St Peter's in Rome. I would make amends for all my sins. You're an old man and you are getting weaker.'
>
> Gerard paid attention and his heart softened. With patience he conceded her point and agreed.[26]

This vignette reflects both the secular idea of women's ability to give seasoned and practical counsel and the capacity clerics credited them with to motivate men to religious conversion. It claims no power for women to coerce, only a recognition of their moral authority and sense. Duke Gerard still has a choice to accept or deny what his wife says. But he loves and respects her, and there is no loss of status in admitting the force of her special claims on him, claims that his male followers and relatives do not have. He can listen to her – unlike to his male followers – without being diminished, and so escape the runaway and remorseless logic of his fatal feud with King Charles.

The expectations on men in the situation in which Duke Gerard found himself trapped were an unfortunate consequence of their gender. Masculinity is no more a simple construct than femininity, but the demands on a man made by expectations of his gender might be a harsher imperative to deal with.[27] Some of the components of noble behaviour as it was formulated at the end of the twelfth century articulated what these demands were. So the quality of 'hardihood' (*hardiz*) in chivalric treatises encapsulated the endless, edgy competitiveness of male behaviour, though thirteenth-century reflections on it try to warn against the 'rashness' that makes it less admirable.[28] This danger was already being signalled by the *Song of Roland* at the beginning of the twelfth century, which tellingly contrasts the prudence (*mesure*) of Oliver with the fatal recklessness of the more dominant male, Roland.[29] Twelfth-century literature is nonetheless saturated with praise of male competitive striving and the courage and enterprise with which it should be pursued.[30] The fact that this expectation sanctioned violent personal behaviour hardly needs pointing out, and, as has already been said, the behaviour of the English aristocrat in our period sometimes slid into a violence that could be uncontrolled and murderous (see above, pp. 117–32).

William Marshal unapologetically takes centre stage here. He was superbly fitted by nature for his roles as soldier and tourney champion, and his behaviour in these capacities was unrelentingly competitive, though the financial rewards for his tourneying success were perhaps as compelling a motive as his chromosomes. His story of his capture and captivity in Poitou following his uncle's assassination in 1168 is instructive. Disabled by a lance blow to his thigh while defying the assassins, he was hauled off by them in the hope that he might survive and be ransomable. His wound was not tended other than what he himself could manage as he was taken from place to place in the assassins' retreat. Luckily, a woman took pity on him and smuggled food and bandages to him so that he could treat himself. Then he reopened the healing wound by joining in a game of weightlifting with his captors. The story dwells on this episode. A Poitevin knight made a mighty throw, and his discomfited competitors, seeing the impressiveness of the Marshal's physique, asked him to try. He demurred, indicating his incapacity, but they renewed their request. So, making no promises, he picked up the stone and amazed all by throwing it half a metre further than the Poitevin.[31] The story sets out the physical and moral expectations of a man in a military culture: defiance of death in the face of overwhelming odds (the author says Marshal was up against sixty knights before his capture); the mastering of pain and refusal to complain; modesty in conduct combined with achievement in the face of overwhelming difficulty. It should be particularly noted that this anecdote survives because it was used as a teaching aid to male youth. The Marshal told it to the squires of his household and his sons as a way of instructing them in those self-same expectations, and they repeated it to his biographer.

What were the consequences of failing to measure up to expectations? One of the Marshal's younger sons, Gilbert, had been intended for the Church. But on his brother Richard's untimely death in 1234, Gilbert Marshal renounced his orders by the simple mechanism of receiving knighthood. He inherited the earldom but found it very difficult to live up to his father's and brothers' reputations. As a result he entered a tournament near Hertford in June 1241. Matthew Paris explains it in this way: 'The earl was eager to earn the admiration of his fellow knights at Hertford by the manful and energetic pursuit of military skills, so that everyone would be deservedly united in admiration for the undaunted prowess of himself, a man who was lacking in physical stamina compared to the rest. Earl Gilbert was all the more eager to earn this praise because his first vocation was as a clergyman, and common gossip had it that he was inexperienced and useless as a knight.'[32] The earl's poor choice of a mount, his inexperience as a rider and the poor discipline of his *mesnie* led to his accidental death, but he had been driven to taking risks by his sense of what was expected of a nobleman, and in particular of a son of the great Marshal. There is likewise evident here a feeling that celibate male clergy, such as Gilbert had once been, had dissociated themselves from the rest of their gender, and were all but a third sex: excluded from the proper pursuits of the élite male. Contempt for the clerk as a defective male is very much evident in certain forms of twelfth-century epic literature.[33] The fact that clerical males might nonetheless try to emulate their secular peers in sexual and military matters was registered by contemporary aristocrats. William Marshal, on the road in France in 1183, dealt severely with a young cleric whom he discovered eloping with a noblewoman, staring the man down when he drew a sword, despite himself being unarmed at the time. The young cleric was riding armed, with his telltale tonsure covered. The biographer has him asserting defiantly when challenged as to who he might be: 'uns hom sui' ('I am a man'). The poignancy of that choice of phrase is no doubt unintentional, but it illustrates how he, like many other clergy, found it difficult to escape the masculine habitus of his day.[34]

But, by way of return, the clergy could be equally or even more acidic on the subject of the masculinity of laymen. The poisonous rhetoric of Orderic Vitalis in the cause of his hero, Henry I of England, led him to stigmatise the culture of the court of Henry's predecessor as openly homosexual. King William Rufus (1087–1100) plainly associated with a homosocial set of young, hard-living knights and indulged in their lifestyle of gambling, tourneying and risky jokes, especially on the subject of religion. Orderic found that evidence enough to condemn Rufus's court as dominated by outlandishly dressed *effeminati*, indulging unashamedly in same-sex relationships, associating with male prostitutes and heedlessly courting perdition. Piously standing up for contemporary expectations on the lay male allowed Orderic both to score political points and take some personal revenge on a world of gender expectations that was inimical to him. Nor was it just Orderic. His contemporary and fellow Benedictine Eadmer was as vociferous, and subsequent twelfth-century moralists Bernard of Cluny and Alan of Lille were fixated on the subject of homosexuality as a way of attacking contemporary male culture.[35] It was as a result of this that in the generation after Orderic and Eadmer the author of the tract on aspirational conduct for go-ahead young men, the *Facetus*, urgently warned youths against any fashionable dress or habits that might be interpreted as effeminate. They were career-killers.[36]

Simply being female incurred a personal cost, but failure to live up to gender expectations carried greater penalties for a man than a woman, both in personal terms and, for the aristocrat, in political terms. The *Gesta Stephani* in around 1147 singles out two magnates who in 1141 first embraced the cause of the empress Matilda and then, when her fortunes took a downturn, repudiated it. The author talks of Earl Roger of Warwick (died 1153) and Robert d'Oilly (died 1142) as *viri molles* (weak men) and sybarites.[37] To be judged a coward (*coärt*) – which might cover any treasonous, underhand act as much as baulking at danger – was about the most shaming act of which a man might be accused by his peers. When Henry of Essex, the influential household officer of both King Stephen and King

Henry II, was convicted of abandoning the royal standard in battle in 1163, his disgrace could only be expiated by retreat to a monastery, which in itself was symbolic of abandoning his gender as much as secular life and its expectations.[38]

WOMEN, STATUS AND FAMILY

One gender concern in relation to women was liminal: their place as a bridge between lineages and a source of honour through their descent and connections. This is very much linked to Lévi-Strauss's contribution to the understanding of women's place in human societies, in the way they are exchanged between families, and so help define both them and society beyond the family. Lévi-Strauss's model invalidated the nineteenth-century theory of the narrowing of medieval society into patriarchal lineages, which produced a theory of the inexorable decline of women's positions in the period 1000–1200, a redundant hypothesis that unfortunately still clogs up a lot of writing on medieval aristocracy. Historians now suggest a greater continuity in structures and a cyclical model of family linked to child-birth.[39] The place of a woman as a bridge between families is indicated not so much by a worry over the property she might bring to her husband as by a frequent concern over the suitability of a potential bride in terms of her family and connections (*parage*), which often comes out in our sources. Geoffrey Gaimar in around 1139 depicts King Edgar debating with his council as to whether he should take the beautiful Æthelfryth as queen, for she was merely the daughter of a baron. He takes into consideration that she is the granddaughter of an earl and that her mother was of royal blood, therefore that 'ele est asez de halt parage'. However, it was the question of quite *how* beautiful she was that eventually swung the decision against her in Gaimar's retelling of the Anglo-Saxon Chronicle's account.[40]

The issue of 'disparagement' (*disparagacio*) is prominent in complaints of English and French barons against their king for much of the twelfth century. This is significant in the understanding of women's position as a bridge between families, for there were some families where it was feared that the bridge was more of a ladder. Disparagement is when the heir of a noble family was married to someone of socially inferior standing. The word itself first appears in Latin at the end of the century, in 1194, but appears in a French form maybe a dozen or so years earlier than that.[41] The problem at the root of disparagement was the ability of a king to use the wardship of noble girls and boys and the disposal of their marriages to reward his servants. When the servant was a man of comparatively low birth and connections, the 'parage' of the woman might very well become irate at the ward's treatment. The classic statement of this is in clause 6 of Magna Carta (1215): 'Heirs shall be given in marriage without disparagement (*disparaga-cione*) and so that before the marriage is contracted it shall be made known to the closest relatives of the heir.' Disparagement could occur when there was a mismatch in the social status of a ward in an arranged marriage, whether male or female. But the outcry was loudest when the injured party was female.[42] The issue would seem already to have been a heated one when King Henry I came to the throne of England in 1100. In his coronation charter he felt obliged to assure his subjects: 'if when one of my barons or other men die leaving a daughter as heir, I will not give her in marriage except according to the advice of my barons.'[43] The intention here seems to have been to reassure his magnates that noble heirs would be treated responsibly by making their marriage conditional on baronial advice. It was this level of monitoring that the barons wanted over King John when they were negotiating Magna Carta, although the eventual settlement drew back from that position. The potential for revenue and patronage implicit in the control of marriage was too much for the king to resist.

Sir James Holt reminds us that in fact the disparagement was not necessarily committed by the king, but by the person who obtained a wardship from him, and that the king himself seems to have imposed 'no disparagement' clauses on people who bought wardships. He also points out that Richard I and John married off noble heiresses to relatively humble royal servants without incurring any known condemnation.[44] This does not, however, explain why it was that the barons brought the issue forward in 1215. Indeed, in 1218, the Anonymous of Béthune singled out the clause on disparagement as one of the major issues between the king and barons when he described the negotiation of Magna Carta, and disparagement was an issue with which Earl Ranulf III of Chester had to deal in 1215 when his tenants demanded a charter of liberties.[45] Nor did the insecurity over disparagement end in 1215, despite the fact that, as the canon law of marriage developed in the late twelfth and thirteenth centuries, it became impossible for any ward to be forced to marry someone to whom he or she objected.[46]

Magna Carta was seen as a bastion against the king's inclination to disparage girls in marriage. Why was this? One explanation is that social levels were becoming more self-conscious and structured in the first decades of the thirteenth century. As this happened, the possibility of disparagement became more of a challenge to an emerging social order. As a result, the king was demonised, especially by the social group that was in its first generation of securing recognition as being noble: the knights. Other, later thirteenth-century attacks on the king's alleged misuse of grants of marriages focus on the grants to 'aliens', unworthy foreign favourites. Matthew Paris was particularly exercised by this issue.[47] A case in point is that of Margery du Neubourg, countess of Warwick (died 1253). She knew that, as the last of her great lineage and chatelaine of Warwick, she was likely to be used as a pawn in the king's game of patronage. On coming into her inheritance in 1242, she was married within a month without royal licence to John Marshal of Hingham, a Norfolk cadet of the great Marshal family, the man of her choice. Unfortunately for her, he died not long afterwards. She resisted for nearly a year the king's demands that she now marry one of his foreign favourites, John du Plessis, even after he had put pressure on her by seizing Warwick castle as security for her conduct. There is good reason to believe that she had already by then formed a clandestine marriage with another man of her choice. In the end, under enormous pressure, she capitulated and married Plessis, who survived her and enjoyed her inheritance for ten years after her death.[48]

Once suitably married, the woman brought with her a dowry of honour and lineage, which was as much or even more important than any land she brought from her family. As we have seen with Isabel de Warenne, countess of Surrey (died 1203), her impressive lineage and inheritance were adopted wholesale by her second husband, although he was a grandson of one king and half-brother to another (see above, p. 142). Their sons were given baptismal names from the Warenne line, and indeed took the Warenne surname and heraldry. This was by no means unusual elsewhere. When Amice, daughter of Ralph de Gael, brought her Breteuil lineage into the family of the earls of Leicester, Earl Robert II (died 1168) chose to adopt the Breteuil surname for his children (rather than his own father's distinguished toponym of Beaumont). It was in use until the 1190s by the Leicester family. It must have assisted them in getting their Norman tenants to identify with their lordship.[49] A similar instance is provided by Isabel de Tosny, sister of Roger I de Tosny, lord of Flamstead and Conches, a Norman whose lineage stretched back to the tenth century. She married Walter fitz Richard fitz Pons (viv. 1155) and brought with her on her marriage the lordship of Clifford in Herefordshire. It was as Isabel 'de Tony' that she made a grant out of her marriage portion for her late husband's soul to a Wiltshire church, though her husband's family had adopted the toponym of Clifford.[50] Other women of great families simply

alluded to their fathers to establish their claims to lineage. The example of
Countess Matilda of Clare 'daughter of James de St-Hilaire' indicates that
women from exotic foreign families might make a point of it.[51] It was not
general in our period for women to take their husband's name on marriage,
though it happened. Margaret (died 1235), wife of Saher de Quincy, earl
of Winchester, though a sister of the great Earl Robert IV of Leicester,
appears as '*Margareta de Quency comitissa Winton*' in a charter of 1225, even
though she says she is *in mea ligia potestate et viduitate*, so she could suit
herself, while the Quincy lineage was not originally all that notable despite
having a descent from the Anglo-Saxon earls of Northumbria and the
sainted Waltheof.[52] She takes the same style on her magnificent seal (see
plate 3), though here there were heraldic motifs which widened the
message. Though an armorial shield and indeed her gown are adorned with
the mascles (voided lozenges) that were her late husband's armorial bearings, the seal also prominently displays the cinquefoil (five-leaved flower)
which – as with her brother's arms – alluded to their mother, the heiress of
Grandmesnil.[53]

The seals of Countess Ela Longespée of Warwick (died 1297) show a
constant renegotiation of identity as a woman used her lineage to establish
a relationship within two successive marriages (see plate 4). The seal she
used during her second marriage, to Sir Philip Basset (died 1271), preserves
on its obverse what must have been her original seal as countess, where she
stands between representations of the arms of Earl Thomas of Warwick
(died 1242) and of her father, Earl William Longespée I of Salisbury (died
1225). Interestingly, her effigy clasps her father's, not her husband's, shield
and she uses the Longespée surname on it as well as her father's heraldry.
Ela was the granddaughter of King Henry II from his affair with a woman
called Ida, probably of the Tosny family, who later became countess of
Norfolk.[54] It was a royal kinship acknowledged by Henry III, Ela's second
cousin.[55] Her baptismal name reinforced the message of lineage. It alluded
to her descent from the ducal house of Burgundy through Ela, daughter of
Count William Talvas of Ponthieu (died 1172), her grandmother. The
reverse side of that same seal, however, must have been made after her
marriage to Philip Basset, for it shows his shield of arms, though it contains
it between two Longespée lioncels, as if to make the same point in a new
context.[56] After her second husband's death, Ela took a third seal, elimi-
nating the heraldry of both her former husbands, though still claiming the
title of countess of Warwick. The Longespée arms and ornamental lioncels
dominate the reverse and advertise quite how much value this lady placed

on the lineage she had brought to her marital families. It was how she dealt with her liminality.[57]

The reverse side of this equation occurred when a wife's family fell into disgrace. Agnes, daughter of the curial baron Henry of Essex (see above, p. 218), was married as a child to Aubrey III de Vere, earl of Oxford (died 1194). Within a year, the public disgrace of her father, after being charged with and convicted of cowardice in battle, caused the earl to attempt to divorce her, as the value of the alliance collapsed, on the grounds that his younger brother had first been betrothed to the girl. Gerald of Wales says Earl Aubrey's motive was 'ignominy': the nature of the disgrace she had brought into their marriage through her father. Interestingly, the divorce was being pursued in 1166 by the kin (*parentes*) of the earl on his behalf, as if the whole family had been dishonoured by Agnes's father's disgrace.[58] The young countess fought on, however, and appealed to Rome. Despite being placed under house arrest by her husband and being badly treated, Agnes was able to secure a bull of Pope Alexander III in 1172 commanding the earl to take her back as his wife. The pair remained married for another twenty-two years and produced several children.[59]

Gender and its expectations were issues that shaped perceptions of nobility and the means of being noble. They were part of the same habitus that dictated whether conduct was noble or not. As a result, gender was not necessarily a straitjacket to behaviour. Noblewomen could exercise a public role and assert themselves and, in one case, even aspire to the throne, without incurring condemnation. Male clergy could follow the same sexually charged behaviour as male aristocrats, despite their ordination committing them to celibacy. Notwithstanding the competitiveness of male behaviour and its frequent manifestation in both permissible and illicit violence, the idea of peace-making and compromise was deeply embedded in aristocratic society, as it attempted to limit the damage that male confrontationalism caused.[60] Gendered expectations of behaviour did not add to the happiness or peacefulness of medieval society, and its unhappiness is visible enough in its literature, but at least there was sufficient tolerance in the habitus to mitigate the worst of the potential damage. The sources can sometimes ambush modern expectations of medieval attitudes. Despite the hysterical ecclesiastical condemnation of sodomy, it is a little reassuring to find the Anglo-Norman cleric Wace saying of an openly homosexual king of Britain, Malgo, that he was an attractive man, affectionate and generous, and that his liking for other men was the only fault others found in him.[61]

CHAPTER THIRTEEN

✦

PIETY

I T may not be easy to reconstruct noble piety in the central middle ages,
but it is important to try. Most studies in the past have taken the route of
analysing religious patronage and burial practices. Since these aspects can
be approached through surviving property deeds and some scattered material
remains, the advantages of this approach are obvious.[1] But these are only
facets of a much greater whole and, as far as medieval aristocrats were
concerned, not necessarily the most important facets. Individual aristocrats
doubtless reacted to the demands and enticements of faith individually: some
were devout, others less so. But they all lived within a religious culture quite
as well defined and pervasive as their noble habitus, and they could not escape
the necessity of relating to either. Beyond this, there is the point where
habitus and religious practice met: there were patterns of religious behaviour
that were distinctively noble, and it is these that this chapter will examine.

THE NOBILITY AND THE MASS

Christian practice, theology and witness all focused on the mass in the
middle ages, so it is the natural place to begin our investigation. For the
layperson, the mass was essentially an act of witness, with a minimum of
participation on his part, though there was more than some studies suggest.[2]
By the early thirteenth century, a layman was expected to take communion
once a year, though some aspired to receive it weekly.[3] Communion and
attendance are two different things, of course. We do not know how often
an Anglo-French nobleman might hear mass sung or said. What we do know
from contemporary literature are the expectations of what he should do.
William of Malmesbury around 1126 makes some comment on the defi-
ciencies of pre-Conquest English religious practice as compared with the
exemplary behaviour of the contemporary Norman court, whose supposed

excellences we could interpret as his idea of what a layperson of his day should aspire to. He condemns the Anglo-Saxon nobles who failed to go to church in the morning 'in the Christian way' but would impatiently and inattentively hear a hastily garbled mass in their chambers instead. William the Conqueror, by contrast, devoutly attended daily mass and for good measure heard mattins and vespers sung by his chapel clerks.[4] These passages may well reflect Malmesbury's ideas as to what was bad and what was good practice amongst the laity of his own day. It should be noted that he thought the pre-Conquest nobility, however inattentive, at least viewed hearing a daily mass as a duty. In reality daily attendance at mass was probably more desired than practised amongst the well-off. Very close to the time when William of Malmesbury was writing, Sigar, priest of Newbold in the East Riding of Yorkshire, reflected on the practices of a pious young man, Orm of Howden. Orm, a boy of fourteen in 1126, brought up in a comfortably-off English family, practised fasting, ostentatiously embraced chastity and gave what alms he could, but attended mass only on Sundays and high feasts.[5] His family apparently found his austerities excessive.

Where households contained priests as chaplains, daily attendance at mass was more likely to occur, as the priest was obliged to say mass daily and would doubtless hope for more of a congregation than just an acolyte. So, in the 1170s, Arnaut-Guilhem de Marsan, a Gascon subject of Henry II of England, noted that the ideal noble household would be daily called at dawn by its priest to hear mass, after which it would break its fast.[6] The idea that the aristocratic day should commence with mass was widespread. Recalling the 1090s, the later twelfth-century historian William of Newburgh believed the future Henry I of England heard mass at the beginning of the day, and had taken Roger of Salisbury into his service because he ran through the rite swiftly and efficiently.[7] Twelfth- and thirteenth-century literature is in fact full of instances of aristocratic characters rising at dawn to go first to hear mattins and mass; nor are the ones who do so always the heroes of the story.[8]

Aristocratic piety would seem in this case to have been emulating the religious observance magnates encountered at the royal court. The court of William the Conqueror had a particular reputation for observance. In the late 1070s, his former chaplain, William of Poitiers, wrote of his master's religious practice as follows:

He was accustomed to lend an eager ear to readings from Holy Writ and to savour their sweetness; he found in them a feast for the soul, for he wished to be delighted, corrected and edified by them. He received and honoured with seemly reverence the Host of salvation, the blood of the Lord, holding in strong faith to that which true doctrine has ordained, that the bread and wine which are placed on the altar and consecrated by the word and hand of the priest according to the holy canon, are the true flesh and blood of the Redeemer. It is certainly not unknown with what zeal he pursued and endeavoured to drive out of his land the wicked error of those who thought otherwise. From a tender age he took part devoutly in religious services, often joining in the celebration of them in the company of a religious community of monks and nuns. To old men this youth shone as a fine example for the daily assiduity with which he attended the sacred mysteries. Likewise his children learnt Christian piety from infancy, thanks to careful provision he made for them.[9]

William of Poitiers explicitly says that the Conqueror's court challenged contemporaries by its level of religious observance, and that the Conqueror communicated his piety to his children and magnates alike. The sketch does not seem to have been an exercise in flattery, for there is supporting evidence for what it depicts. Domesday Book gives us examples of how King William instituted a daily mass in royal churches for his soul. Furthermore, in the *Life* of Count Simon of the Vexin, who was brought up at the Conqueror's court, we find described a similar level of devout piety before Simon left the world for the professed religious life in 1077.[10] Royal practice in this as in other cases had a powerful effect on society's ideas. We will see other and later instances where royal piety had a major impact on the dependent aristocracy. In the twelfth century, it was to provide an impulse towards a culture of individual confession and penitence, and would inspire the spread of the institutional chantry mass to commemorate the dead. It would not therefore be going too far to suggest that it was the royal court that made attendance at daily mass fashionable and respectable for aristocrats in the centuries after the Conquest.

Social distinction is the theme of this book, so it is necessary to note how it could be affirmed within the mass. At great feasts of the Church, magnates and knights would attend dressed in their finest robes 'to exalt the high feast'.[11] When, around 1160, Wace of Bayeux imagined the Norman ducal court of Duke Robert I at mass, he portrayed the offertory being made in due social order, with the duke giving his handsome donation first, and the rest of the court and congregation following.[12] Social order also asserted itself at the peace. Once the clergy had finished with the pax tablet it was presented to the laity. Daniel of Beccles says, in Henry II's reign, that it should be offered in order of precedence, beginning with the 'most noble' in the congregation.[13] The mass united the Christian people in a perpetual banquet, but it seemed that some people wanted place settings.

The efficacy of the mass as a means of intercession for the dead appealed particularly to the aristocracy. Aristocrats had the resources with which to finance the multiplication of masses when it became noble practice to do so. The movement that led to the perpetual institutional chantry is a complex one to disentangle, but Sir Howard Colvin made the point that in the mid-twelfth century monasteries were beginning to find it difficult to supply the necessary liturgical resources – priests and altars – to cope with the great demand for intercessory masses for their founders and benefactors. This must have been a result of such masses being demanded not just annually (the mass and associated offices called the 'obit', or 'anniversary'), but daily. Colvin argued that it was because of this crisis that the wealthy laity looked to found alternative institutions outside monasteries, in freestanding chapels and within parish churches, where dedicated altars and priests were funded in perpetuity.[14]

The crisis point in the demand for masses for the dead had clearly been looming for some time. Magnates had begun the ambitious foundation of Benedictine monasteries in Normandy in the 1020s, in direct imitation of the duke, according to Orderic Vitalis.[15] One of the principal purposes of such abbeys and priories was to pray for the souls of the founder and his kin and offer a magnificent *anniversarium* mass on the death days of the members of the lineage.[16] Cluniac Lewes, founded by the first Earl William de Warenne (died 1088) to be the repository of the bodies of himself and his descendants (or so the priory later claimed), is a fine example of the intertwining of dynastic pride, community and perpetual prayer. An anxiety to link the Warenne dynasty, the priory and its patron, Pancras, is advertised heavily in the priory's restoration (in the later 1140s, or perhaps subsequently) of the tombstone of Gundreda de Warenne (died 1085), wife of the first Earl William, which lay in the priory's chapterhouse (see plate 2). Its remarkable epitaph reflects on Gundreda's place as root of the Warenne dynasty's nobility and the line of earls (called here *duces*) sprung from her. The priory itself calls her its mother, having inherited her upright conduct (*mores*), as the earls had inherited her lineage. It is as if the monks too were descended from her, and in this way had become the spiritual kin of the Warenne family. Gundreda lies safe in the priory under the protection of its holy patron, the Roman martyr Pancras.[17]

A second wave of foundations occurred in the first half of the twelfth century with the adoption and multiplication of new orders: Cistercians, Augustinians and Premonstratensians.[18] There is some evidence that the magnates who founded these monasteries were beginning to be more particular and demanding about the provision of masses of intercession. Around 1100, we find Count Roger the Poitevin asking from Shrewsbury abbey a daily mass for himself, his wife and son, and father and mother.[19] Early in Henry I's reign, Count Stephen of Brittany requested from St Mary's abbey, York, 'two monks bound in the abbey for ever to say a mass for him, alive or dead, and to celebrate his anniversary each year'. Before the 1160s, there are examples of similar magnate claims on the services of (presumably) priest-monks, at Norwich cathedral priory, Bordesley abbey in Worcestershire, Dunmow priory in Essex and Kenilworth priory in Warwickshire.[20] The royal family did no less. King Henry II also solicited this type of perpetual intercessory mass within a community. Probably in the later 1150s, he secured the services of four priest-monks at Dore abbey in Herefordshire to say mass for himself, and his predecessors and successors as king.[21]

The first decided move towards detaching such masses from cloisters into new institutional masses in large churches occurred in Henry II's reign, amongst his children. The death of the Young King Henry in 1183 moved his brother Geoffrey of Brittany and his wife, Queen Margaret, to endow altars in Rouen cathedral where daily mass would be said in perpetuity for his soul.[22] It was another of Henry II's sons, John of Mortain, who in 1192 endowed Lichfield cathedral with the church of Bakewell, to provide for an annual daily mass for his soul.[23] In both cases we see the move to endow daily masses in collegiate churches where there was a community of priests available and in need of a regular income. The contemporary aristocracy must already have been moving in the same direction in its desire for intercessory masses. A suggestive example as early as 1138 comes from the Île-de-France, when Enguerrand II de Coucy conceded the collegiate church of his castle of Coucy to the abbey of Notre-Dame de Nogent in return for the construction of a chapel under the church's tower in which mass would be said daily for the soul of his father, Thomas de Marle (a man in need of every prayer he could get, according to Suger of St-Denis).[24] This makes explicit what has been suggested elsewhere, that magnates perceived the collegiate churches under their control as having a perpetual intercessory function for their souls. The castle-church of Coucy may have been granted away, but Enguerrand made sure its intercessory function for his family would continue, just as John of Mortain did when he gave away the collegiate church at Bakewell to Lichfield in 1192. Secular colleges under magnate patronage had proliferated in Normandy before 1066, and the pattern was duplicated in England after the Conquest. It is highly likely that when collegiate churches were founded or came under magnate patronage at Arundel, Hastings, Leicester, Waltham, Wareham and Warwick, one of their principal and most valued functions was – like regular monasteries – prayer for their lords' souls.[25]

From the end of the twelfth century, there was an aristocratic movement to institutionalise the perpetual mass, rather than solicit the mass from an institution. Not long after the sons of Henry II were endowing chantries in Rouen, the magnate Amaury II de Montfort (died 1213), count of Évreux (1181) and later (1200) earl of Gloucester, endowed two priests in the cathedral of Évreux for masses for his parents and himself. The act contains a good deal of detail as to how the endowment should be administered and the priests conduct themselves.[26] In some danger in Ireland in the winter of 1207–8, Countess Isabel of Pembroke (died 1220) lavishly endowed the cathedral priory of Dublin with a major church at Kilcullen, co. Kildare, where a canon was to say mass perpetually for herself, her forebears, her husband and her children. Since her two eldest sons were being held hostage by King John at the time, and she was threatened with a rebellion in Leinster in her husband's enforced absence, the gesture was more than perfunctory piety.[27] The concern to endow appropriate daily masses had spilled down the social scale by John's reign. Not long after 1200 we find knights endowing chapels and altars, where priests would say perpetual daily masses for their souls. Before 1221, Roger Rustein, a Norfolk knight and seneschal of Earl William III of Arundel (died 1221), endowed the altar of St James at the parish church of St Mary Snettisham, Norfolk, to finance a priest saying a daily mass for his soul. Roger made a compensatory grant to Wymondham priory, which was to take responsibility for the appointment and payment of the priest. Roger, like a good businessman, also laid down regulations about the conduct and replacement of chaplains. The Rustein chantry seems to be the earliest clear example of an institutionalised perpetual chantry altar in England, though not by much. Henry III's reign saw a rapid multiplication of examples of the privatisation of the mass.[28]

The irony is that the mass – an expression of the Christian people united – became a private devotion for the nobility.[29] This movement was helped by the increasing localisation of pastoral care in England after 1100, as the ancient network of large minster jurisdictions broke down. Instead, smaller parishes based on villages emerged.[30] But localisation went further, as lords built chapels in their own manor houses. Private chapels were convenient for a lord, but they antagonised parish priests for a variety of reasons, particularly because they drew income away from the parish church. We see the process at work in July 1236, when the well-connected Berkshire knight Henry of Earley reached a final settlement with Wallingford priory over tithes contested between the priory and 'the knight's chaplain at the time who will say mass in his chapel at Earley'.[31] Manorial chapels could easily host chantry masses. Around 1200, Earl Ranulf III of Chester (died 1232) allowed his seneschal, William Marshal of Coventry (died c.1209), to have a chaplain at his manorial chapel at Asthill, Warwickshire, giving tithes in return for the chaplain's saying mass for the earl's father as well as William's own forebears.[32] The mass at Asthill was not stipulated as being daily, but the transfer of the chantry mass down the ecclesiastical and social scale, from magnates to local landowners, is plain to see.[33] Such was the extremity to which the privatisation of the mass had come before the end of Henry III's reign. Institutions like these further hedged off the local knight from his neighbours and dependants, and affirmed social boundaries.

Patronage

A good deal has been written about the piety of the aristocracy in relation to its patronage of monastic movements. The aristocracy's engagement with the foundation of abbeys and priories was focused on the first half of the twelfth century, the time of the proliferation of new monastic rules – principally, as stated above, Cistercian, Augustinian and Premonstratensian. The capital investment in these ventures was enormous, though that impression has to be qualified by noting that much of it was funded by the refoundation of former secular collegiate churches. It is not often easy to tell what the precise motivation behind the movement to increase regular monasteries at such evident expense was. We have already considered the major discernible motive: the securing of intercessory prayer and masses for the salvation of the souls of the founder, his patrons and his family. Orderic Vitalis, a monk from his boyhood profession and perhaps therefore prejudiced in favour of his way of life, believed that some aristocrats simply despaired at the state of the world and saw monasteries as their only safe place of retreat. Such men would not so much found monasteries, perhaps, as seek refuge in them.[34] Gerald of Wales gives us what he imagines to be the thoughts of

Henry II's chief justiciar, Ranulf de Glanville, when he was pondering which monastic order to patronise in founding a proposed new monastery.[35] But this was not much more than a vehicle for expressing Gerald's own prejudices about the varieties of monasticism of his day. The nearest we will get to the core of self-conscious aristocratic motivation may be the remark by Waleran of Meulan in 1139 when refounding a college of secular canons as a regular priory of Bec, which he did 'in all good will and to improve the standing of the church of Holy Trinity of Beaumont, aiming for the future increase of religious feeling amongst the souls in the same church'.[36] If nothing else, it gives some idea that a great nobleman might think it incumbent on him to take responsibility for the worship in churches under his patronage, rather than leave it to the clergy.

The total monastic patronage of a great Anglo-Norman family could be quite staggering, not to say eclectic. The Anglo-Norman counts of Eu and lords of Hastings are instructive in this regard in a surviving fourteenth-century treatise and seigneurial cartulary detail the extent of their patronage in England and Normandy. The six generations of the family from the Conquest to the thirteenth century between them brought into being five abbeys (Eu, Le Tréport, Foucarmont, Robertsbridge and Sèry), two priories (St-Martin-au-Bois and Criel) and a major secular college (Hastings). The most active period of patronage was the time of Count Henry I (died 1140). Count Henry refounded the ancient secular college of Eu as an Augustinian abbey, founded another at Sèry, took over the Bec priory at St-Martin-au-Bois and commenced the large Cistercian abbey at Foucarmont, where he was buried. Not surprisingly, he ended his days as a monk, as did his son, Count John (died 1170). The family patronised secular chapters, Benedictines, Cistercians, Augustinians and Cluniacs. The final resting places of the several generations of the comital family were liberally distributed amongst these foundations, principally Eu, Foucarmont and Hastings.[37]

There is little comparison between this rising wave of religious patronage in the twelfth century and what followed in the thirteenth. The impulse to find burial places and liturgical commemoration in the mass was diverted from monasteries into the movement to found perpetual chantries in secular churches. Such foundations as were made after 1180 were most frequently funded by 'arriviste' magnates (such as Ranulf de Glanville, William Briwerre and William Marshal) who needed to make a statement about their new position in the world. A perfect example is Geoffrey fitz Peter (died 1213), the justiciar, created earl of Essex in 1199. As he rose socially, Geoffrey founded a new Gilbertine monastery at Shouldham, Norfolk, in the 1190s in which he had his late wife reinterred. Geoffrey is also notable in his attitude to existing monasteries. He conducted a vigorous and remorseless campaign to get the monks of Walden to acknowledge his advocacy. Walden was the principal house of the Mandeville earls of Essex, whose honor Geoffrey had acquired. The recognition of Geoffrey's place as its advocate was material to his recognition as earl, which explains why he was so energetic in pursuing it.[38]

The religious movements that arose after 1200 found little aristocratic patronage compared to the bonanza of land grants made towards the regular monks in the twelfth century. But this material comparison may underestimate their spiritual influence within the aristocracy. At first sight, the friars seem to have been far more important in the universities and towns of thirteenth-century England than in aristocratic households. However, there is a good deal of evidence that the greatest of thirteenth-century aristocrats valued their intellectual and spiritual resources. The Franciscans honoured Loretta de Briouze, countess of Leicester – who lived after her husband's death in 1204 as a recluse at Hackington, north of Canterbury – for her support on their arrival in England, 'like a mother for her sons'.[39] Similarly, Ela Longespée, widow of Thomas, earl of Warwick (died 1242), was in 1267 and again in 1282 one of those who endowed the Franciscans with property to expand their house in St Nicholas Shambles in London.[40] Women were certainly attracted to the ministry of the friars. Henry III's aunt, Princess Joan of Gwynedd, was buried in 1237 in the Franciscan friary of Llanfaes, founded by her husband, perhaps at her deathbed request.[41] In 1251, Cecilia of Sandford, a member of a family of prominent thirteenth-century *curiales*, had a Dominican as confessor, a man of some spiritual austerity, according to Matthew Paris.[42] The popularity of friars as aristocratic confessors explains this influence. In the 1230s, Solomon, the warden of the London Franciscans, had such a powerful clientele of penitents, 'as much amongst the Londoners as the court', that he was able to ignore the bishop of London's attempts to control his activities. The Franciscans later celebrated the distinction of their confessors in the first half of the thirteenth century in the provincial towns of Gloucester, Lynn and York. Around 1235, Geoffrey of Salisbury, a Franciscan at Lynn, was credited with inspiring the leading courtier Sir Alexander of Bassingbourn to quit the world and join his order.[43] Henry III's half-brother, William de Valence (died 1296), brought with him from Poitou a friar, Peter de la Roch, as his chaplain and confessor.[44] The

Dominicans were no less popular amongst the aristocracy, and indeed had the edge over the Franciscans in royal patronage.[45]

As the thirteenth century progressed, the highest circles in the land sought out the acquaintance of the great Franciscan teachers of the day. Simon de Montfort, earl of Leicester (died 1265), had a particularly close relationship with the Franciscan scholar Adam Marsh (died 1259), and also with two other Oxford Franciscans, Geoffrey de Bosellis and Thomas of York, as well as the influential Franciscan archbishop of Rouen, Eudes Rigaud, King Louis IX's closest friend and spiritual adviser.[46] Marsh's correspondence reveals connections to the highest in the land. Montfort's wife, Eleanor, was the king's sister, and Marsh's letters embraced the circle of royal women about the king; not just Eleanor but Sanchia, wife of Richard of Cornwall, Eleanor's other brother, and Henry III's queen herself.[47] Marsh had a further connection with William de Beauchamp III of Elmley, sheriff of Worcestershire (died 1269), and his appearance in Marsh's correspondence is symptomatic of Beauchamp's wider attachment to the Franciscans. In his will, dated 1268, Beauchamp requested burial in the house of the Franciscans of Worcester, and set up a lavish chantry for his and his family's souls in a chapel he had specially constructed adjacent to the Franciscan precinct.[48] Some seemed to have felt that the influence of the friars went too far. Marsh's boyhood friend and patron Bishop Robert Grosseteste of Lincoln (not himself a friar) developed an agenda during his episcopate for the purification of lay life. Matthew Paris reports in 1246 an inquisition staged across his large diocese, inspired, it was said, by the Franciscans and Dominicans. His archdeacons and deans were urged to undertake a large-scale witch-hunt into morals and behaviour. The bishop went too far by including the aristocracy in his inquiries and exposing a dangerous level of scandal amongst the powerful. The king was persuaded to intervene and forbid the use of sworn inquisitions into lay conduct by church officials.[49]

Aristocratic Devotional Practice

There was a range of distinctly aristocratic devotional practices apart from those centred on the mass. The first was an engagement with the daily office, the daily round of prayer laid down for clergy and marked by the canonical hours of the day (prime, tierce, sext and nones, vespers and compline). The daily office was not supposed to be for the laity, but nonetheless some at least of the nobility became caught up with it as a vehicle for the expression of their own devotions. In the 1220s, Sir William de Martinwast expected to be in the chapel of his manor house in Leicestershire at the time of certain at least of the canonical hours. Here he would have heard the set psalms, responses and readings read, or possibly sung, by his chaplain. It is hard to know how prevalent this practice of attending the offices was amongst aristocrats, and only a noble household could provide the clerical manpower to offer it. However, there are several hints. The same period saw the compilation of the 'Ancrene Riwle', a rule of life intended for a group of aristocratic English ladies living in an informal religious community under guidance, rather like beguines and certainly not as professed nuns. The women it addressed undertook to follow the daily office said for them by a clerk, though they were not supposed to join in saying it.[50] Though these ladies were perhaps exceptional, it is a defensible argument to say that they represent the visible peak of a submerged island of lay aspirations to engage with the canonical hours.

Did this enthusiasm have a starting point? There has been a temptation to see lay spirituality taking a leap forward following the publication of the canons of the Fourth Lateran Council (1215), principally because they are the first source with much to say on the subject of lay devotion.[51] But the idea that devout lay aristocrats followed the clerical daily office can plausibly be traced back well before 1200. The possession of a psalter (the book of psalms) is one indicator, for the recitation of a course of the psalms was one of the principal components of the canonical hours. Sir William de Martinwast's grandfather's lord, Earl Robert II of Leicester (died 1168), might by that indication have had some aspirations to follow the hours of the office. He and his wife left their own personal copies of the psalter to Leicester abbey at their deaths; the psalters were still to be seen in the abbey's library in the fifteenth century.[52] Since Earl Robert is known to have been literate and to have employed a large clerical household, he would certainly have been capable of following the hours. We might recall here William of Poitiers' testimony in the 1070s that King William the Conqueror from his youth would hear mass daily and join in the 'celebrations' of the religious communities he visited. William of Malmesbury believed the Conqueror had regularly attended at least mattins and vespers. And this level of royal piety may have been as much English as Norman. When talking of that exemplary queen, Margaret of Scotland, Malmesbury said she would hear triple mattins in Lent – hearing offices of the Trinity, the Cross and the Virgin, and reciting the psalter.[53] Did she read a text, or had she memorised the 150 psalms like any choir monk or nun? We have the account of the devotions of her son, David, given by his sometime house-hold officer, Ailred of Rievaulx, who says that the king, on his deathbed, followed the recitation of the office being said by the clerks of his chapel. He restrained them if they went too fast, so that he could hear every word and respond appropriately to each versicle.[54] Around 1188 Peter of Blois indicates that Henry II aspired to hear daily mass and the offices in church and might hear them said by his clerks in his own chamber.[55] Royal servants would have been wise to follow the spiritual discipline of the court. Hubert de Burgh, chamberlain of King John and justiciar of Henry III, possessed a psalter and found such comfort in its use while in sanctuary at Brentwood chapel in 1232 that the king ordered the sheriff of Essex to take it from him. He seems to have found a similar consolation during his later impris-onment at Devizes.[56] The survival of books of hours from the 1240s onwards is testimony to the fact that many amongst the laity were by then pursuing a regime of prayer in their homes, and reading in Latin a stripped-down version of the daily office. Around sixty such books are still extant from before 1300, which is no mean total in view of the accidents of survival.[57] Books of hours encouraged meditation on the office of the dead, the penitential psalms, and they particularly focus on the figure, joys and sufferings of the Virgin Mary.

It is more than likely that the users of such books were undergoing regular auricular confession, which was a feature of lay spirituality throughout our period. The ladies to whom the 'Ancrene Riwle' was addressed were supposed to undergo directed confession 'each week'.[58] This was not new. A concern for private confession and subsequent penance can be glimpsed as far back as the time of Henry I, and it is unlikely to have been a new feature even then, either in England or France. The English queen of Scotland, Margaret, daughter of Edward the Exile, was apparently, before 1095, given to making frequent confession to the senior cleric who wrote her *Life*.[59] The same anxiety to make frequent confession is evident in the mother of Guibert de Nogent in the 1090s.[60] The Conqueror's half-brother, Count Robert of Mortain, apparently confessed to Vitalis of Savigny in the 1080s, and on one occasion stripped to receive a flogging from the abbot as a token of his penance for sins that otherwise could not be amended.[61] The practice of confession was certainly a prevalent form of spiritual discipline and educa-tion at the court of Henry I, with Queen Matilda (died 1118) taking the prior of her Augustinian foundation of Holy Trinity, Aldgate, as her *pater confessionum*.[62] He is said to have turned her towards the relief of the poor as part of her penitential regime. Matilda's wider influence on the court can be seen in Gilbert of Surrey, who we are told was a particular friend and follower of hers, and was likewise devoted to confession and poor relief. Henry I himself undertook a confessional regime. Robert of Torigny tells us that Æthelwold, Augustinian prior of Nostell and bishop of Carlisle in 1133, was 'the man to whom he was accustomed to confess his sins'.[63]

Royal confessional practice was constant throughout the twelfth century. Stephen, while count of Mortain in the 1120s, absorbed the atmosphere of his uncle's court. He and his wife, Matilda of Boulogne, both patronised Aldgate priory, whence they sought their confessors from the 1120s until their respective deaths in 1152 and 1154.[64] It is no coincidence that the first English aristocrat whose personal confessor is named, Euphemia, countess of Oxford, in the 1150s, was a close friend of Queen Matilda of Boulogne.[65] In his day King Henry II took at least one confessor in England, Paulinus of Leeds, master of what was then St Peter's (later St Leonard's) hospital, York, whom he nominated as bishop of Carlisle around 1186.[66] The conversation Peter of Blois imagined in 1188 or 1189 between Henry II and the abbot of Bonneval is in fact a depiction of the king being counselled by a confessor, with his penance being earnestly discussed. Since Peter was the author of more than one work on confession and penance, and was one of the royal chaplains, we can assume that he knew his master was accustomed to seek auricular confession and undertook a penitential regime.[67] The thirteenth century saw a shift from Augustinian confessors to the friars. Henry III's confessor was a Dominican, John of Darlington.[68]

Other than their participation in the daily office and regular confession, we have a few pen sketches that extend our view of the range of piety of Anglo-Norman aristocrats. One of the fullest is that given around 1160 by Master Stephen de Fougères, later bishop of Rennes, when talking of the devotional life of Cecilia, countess of Hereford (fl. 1137–1205), the widow of Earl Roger (died 1155). The countess was the daughter and heir of the sheriff Payn fitz John (died 1137). She had married Roger early in the reign of Stephen, but they produced no surviving children. She was subsequently married to the barons William of Poitou and Walter de Mayenne, but retained the title she derived from her first husband.[69] Master Stephen – not surprisingly – praised her principally for her gifts to the Church. She built chapels and endowed altars; she made and distributed ecclesiastical vestments cut from expensive cloth. Her main act of piety was in her cheerful devotion to the poor, whom she fed, housed and even washed; her ready hospitality to clergy might be put in the same class of charity.[70] These are paralleled in the sketch of the godly conduct of Gilbert, sheriff of Surrey (died 1125), given by a canon of Merton priory. Gilbert was distinguished by his generosity to Merton, naturally. But there is the same emphasis on his charity to the poor, especially in time of famine. This was so marked that he kept little account of his hospitality, which was occasionally abused by the undeserving. Knowing his weakness and his route, young servants of his household would run ahead of him as he rode and pretend to be beggars, then, having got a coin, would dodge around and encounter him again further along his road. One of the rascals apparently got four or five coins out of him in this way in a single day. He also appears to have adopted advanced practices associated with Henry I's court, notably regular confession ('when in health and prosperity') and penance, in his case the wearing of a heavy iron chain around his hips as a sign of his identification with Christ's passion.[71]

To see the Anglo-Norman court as an advanced school in spiritual discipline would, of course, be going far too far. It is notorious how Henry I's courtiers became desperate at the consequences of their heedless misdeeds when they found themselves on their deathbeds. For all his reputation for personal piety, King Stephen had, as a young member of the English court, taken a concubine by whom he had several children and so in the view of the Church would have been a flagrant fornicator.[72] Nonetheless, there was clearly a sensibility of the importance of, as much as a fashion for, an introspective and informed spirituality amongst the twelfth-century court nobility. Amice, countess of Leicester, who ended her days in the Fontevraldine community at Nuneaton, and her husband, Robert II, who became an Augustinian canon of Leicester on his deathbed, in the 1160s received letters of spiritual counsel from Bishop Gilbert Foliot of Hereford, who referred to the countess's household as containing learned and reverend fathers with whom she was given to discussion of the state of her soul. In the case of this noble husband and wife, the bishop was very keen to emphasise by scripture and exhortation the place of charity to the poor in their spiritual life.[73] We have already seen how this was the same prescription Stephen de Fougères wrote out for the soul of Countess Cecilia of Hereford. It was part of a package of godly qualities that had been urged on the aristocracies of western Europe for at least two centuries (see above, pp. 199–200).[74] The openness of the Anglo-Norman court to spiritual introspection and a culture of penance might be taken as ways by which that particular ethic became embedded in the noble habitus. The parable of Dives and Lazarus seems to have been a particular worry. Bishop Wulfstan of Worcester (died 1087) is said to have forced the noble youths fostered into his household to serve the poor he fed at his alms table on their bended knees, and reproved them if they showed distaste for the task.[75] Gilbert Foliot harped on his duty to the poor to Earl Robert of Leicester. To deflect the consequences for their souls of their own wealth, aristocrats such as Gilbert of Surrey (died 1125) and Robert II, count of Meulan (died 1207), fed the poor at their gates when they dined, while others gave a tithe of their table to monastic houses. The almoner (*elemosinarius*) was an officer found in many great aristocratic households.[76]

The culture of the camp, where the military aristocracy spent a lot of its time, would have been even less conducive to spiritual meditation than the royal court. It is worth noting how little spirituality or open piety is found in the biography of Earl William Marshal I of Pembroke (died 1219). This work exalts its subject as a practised tourneyer, a loyal servant of the Angevin kings and a good lord to his men. It does not much praise his religious feeling. The dispute on his deathbed with a household knight Henry fitz Gerold about penance for his tourneying prowess has been brought forward as an example of aristocratic anticlericalism, though in fact it is a knight who is making the case for penance.[77] The biography fails to mention the several monastic houses the earl founded in England and Ireland, though it does note the hospital for the poor he founded at Sandwich with the spoils of his naval victory over the French in 1217. However, the Marshal was not a man without a spiritual dimension, and indeed had close relations with the clergy. He maintained a large clerical household after 1190, including a Templar almoner. He was particular friends with the Augustinians Hugh, bishop of Ossory, and David, abbot of Bristol. His family provided aristocratic clergy. His brother Henry Marshal and nephew Anselm le Gros became bishops, while his son Gilbert was ordained deacon before returning to lay life. We do hear something in the biography about the Marshal's one recorded moment of spiritual crisis, when he was in his late thirties. He appears to have been profoundly moved by the death in 1183 of his lord, the Young King Henry, and his subsequent experiences during his extended stay in Palestine in the last years of the Latin kingdom of Jerusalem. Marshal resolved in the 1180s to end his days as a Templar and purchased silk palls in the East to cover his bier and his tomb. On his extended deathbed he made daily confession, perhaps to make up for the lack of practice earlier in his career.[78] The Marshal biography is not unique in this respect. It has been pointed out that the evidence of secular literature paints a generally similar picture of insensibility to spirituality except at times of crises such as the prelude to battle or at the point of death.[79] If his biography was the only evidence we had about Marshal's spirituality we would conclude that he was a secular-minded man, who took religion on his own terms. But other evidence – particularly his charters – indicates that he was by no means alienated from the clerical world, especially the Templars and Augustinian canons he favoured. Indeed, as we will see (below, p. 243), he or his circle appear to have been influenced by a rather advanced Marian spirituality.

If William Marshal represents one pole of aristocratic spirituality, can we offer a contrast? Alan of Lille's handbook on penance, written when Marshal was a rising figure at the Angevin court, contains rather more positive ideas about the spiritual thirst that laymen might suffer and the ways it might be satisfied. Alan had encountered laypeople whose spiritual striving included not just the giving of alms (pressed on the laity by other writers), but fasting, prayerful vigil through the night, disciplined meditative prayer and biblical instruction.[80] Simon de Montfort, earl of Leicester (died 1265), is perhaps the thirteenth-century aristocrat whose spirituality we can approach most nearly, though it is clear he had an individual outlook on devotional practice that did not necessarily match those of his peers and contemporaries. He was literate in Latin and the vernacular. He may also be exceptional in that his devotional practices would have been developed in his youth in France, in a family closely engaged with crusade and the defence of orthodoxy from Cathar heresy. He did not arrive in England until he was in his twenties. Yet he was in sympathy with the religious expression he found in England, and struck up close friendships with English churchmen, notably Walter de Cantilupe, bishop of Worcester (1237–66), and the pair of West Country friends Robert Grosseteste and Adam Marsh. It was these two whom Simon made co-supervisors of his will in 1259 in so far as it concerned dispositions for the poor on his estates, 'and particularly the *gaaneours* whose goods I have many times acquired, and whom I suspect that in some people's eyes I have wronged'.[81] Montfort was deeply involved in the debt market, and it clearly preyed on his conscience: the *gaaneours* would seem to be those whose goods he took in pledge for money, for which there is independent evidence of his rapacity in a surviving Leicester bond.[82]

There is some insight into Simon's acute introspection on the subject of his sins and obligation to the poor, the same as we see amongst English magnates in the previous century. Since his friend Grosseteste was a noted writer on confession and penance, it would seem likely that Montfort's introspection was due to a confessional regime, and his correspondence with Marsh hints as much, as well as his possession of a copy of a confessional handbook, which his son passed on to a Dominican convent near Paris.[83] Later tradition at St Albans and amongst the Franciscans had it that Montfort undertook mortification, wore a hair shirt, and appeared in plain and unassuming dress.[84] In this he was not unlike the twelfth-century aristocrat Gilbert of Surrey, who had subscribed to Augustinian teachings on the contempt for vanities, and on confession and penance. Montfort showed apparently less interest than his contemporaries in the spirituality and use of the mass. Apart from his conscience, his other religious fixation – not surprisingly in view of his family background – was the crusade.

King Henry III's love of ecclesiastical pomp and external acts of devotion is well known: for instance, his habit of fasting on the eve of high feasts of the Church and wearing penitential dress.[85] We do not know whether his magnates shared his enthusiasm, though they were obliged to join him in it. But it is clear from contemporary evidence that Louis IX of France (1226–70) did inspire the magnates of his court by his open devotional practice, as Jean de Joinville and Philip de Remy both witness.[86] Alexander Neckam's attack on the hypocrisy of devotional forms around 1200 rather indicates that ostentatious devotion had already got to the point of odium by the time of King John. Echoing the gospel parable of the widow and her mite, Neckam decried the indulgence by laity in fasts, vigils, genuflection and prayer that had only public praise as their object.[87] The flip side of an identifiable noble culture of piety is that many pursued it for no other reason than public distinction and conformity.

Aristocratic Focuses of Devotion

The wealth of the aristocracy allowed it to promote particular forms of worship and devotion. One of the earliest ways we can trace this is in its accumulation and display of devotional objects such as relics. The adoption and use of ecclesiastical banners is one of the earliest and most potent ways the aristocracy matched status to the sacred. The banner appears in eleventh-century France as the symbol of the advocacy of a magnate of a particular great church, by which time it was probably already an ancient practice. The best-known example is the banner of St Denis which was the symbol by which the ancient counts of the Vexin showed themselves as the abbey's protector, a symbol famously transferred to the kings of France in

1125. Less well known are the banners of St Mary borne by the twelfth-century earls of Gloucester and counts of Aumale as respective protectors of the cathedrals of Bayeux and Rouen. The twelfth-century tradition at the abbey of Mont St-Michel was that the count of Mortain was the banner-bearer of St Michael since at least 1070.[88] Banners and ecclesiastical military service were being linked very early in England. When the Yorkshire military contingents of St Mary's abbey, St Peter's cathedral and St John of Beverley were summoned for service by writ of Henry I, they were led by men carrying the banners of each saint.[89] In the 1170s, three magnates – the earls of Arundel, Hertford and Norfolk – contested the right to bear the banner of St Edmund of Bury and thus to be distinguished by a special relationship with the great East Anglian martyr saint.[90] The banner was a symbol of such power that it was to give its name to the superior grade of knighthood, the 'banneret', by the thirteenth century, which might be interpreted as another instance of devotional practice lending its weight to lay status.

Lay society was avid to possess relics of sanctity. The aristocracy was distinguished by the greater number it could afford, and the greater range it could find. This was as true of the pre-Conquest period as after 1066. The collegiate church of Waltham founded by Earl Harold of Wessex received a prodigious collection of relics from its patron, many apparently deriving from Rome, Flanders and the Rhineland. Earl Leofwin of Kent seems to have been another pre-Conquest contributor.[91] Norman aristocrats were also collectors. Some hint as to the richness of English relic collections in the twelfth century is given by the list of 242 relics accumulated by Reading abbey between 1121 and 1193, many deriving from as far afield as Rome and Constantinople, which in some cases had travelled to England well before the abbey's foundation.[92] In the 1120s, William d'Aubigny, a royal butler and leading magnate of Norfolk, 'grieving and in tears' on the day of his wife's funeral, gave to his priory of Wymondham a silver cross inlaid with splinters of wood from the True Cross and Christ's manger, as well as fragments of the tomb of the Virgin Mary at Ephesus. This very precious relic had claims to having been put together from materials collected all over the eastern Mediterranean, and must have been commissioned some time before its use, with this purpose in mind. It had mementos of the birth and death of Christ as well as his mother, who had been assumed into heaven immediately after death. What more suitable relic to reassure a bereaved man, 'looking to the salvation of the departed and her prospect of endless punishment'?[93] Twelfth-century aristocratic chapels seem to have been stacked with such objects, and they had uses beyond the devotional. Around 1141, the Winchester merchant Ralph fitz Picard acquitted himself by an oath at Gloucester on Earl Milo of Hereford's gospel book and the relics of his chapel.[94] There are few inventories of such things, but there are some indications of what might have been collected in a list made by Tewkesbury abbey in 1239 of the furnishings of the chapel of Countess Isabel of Gloucester, which she left the abbey in her will. It included ecclesiastical furnishings: a silver chalice, gospel book and thurible, silk copes, chasubles, dalmatics and tunicles for a high mass with priest, deacon and subdeacon. But she also had a large collection of relics, including ones sent to her from Rome in a silver phial by the pope, including relics of Ss Cornelius and Damasus, popes, and a horde of Roman martyrs.[95]

We have already seen from the surviving thirteenth-century books of hours how the person of the Virgin Mary was a powerful focus of lay devotion by the 1240s. The writer Philip de Remy is another witness to the intensity of Marian spirituality amongst the aristocracy by the thirteenth century. The heroine of one of his novels addresses prayers to images of the Virgin in church and at home: 'she was devoted to the service of the Virgin Mary ... this sort of devotion (*mestiers*) seemed very comforting to her.'[96] It was the intercession of the Virgin, 'the star and jewel by whom all good folk are saved', that she most counted on in her various personal crises. Her husband, the king of Scotland, likewise appealed to the Virgin, 'the one who can lead home those who are lost'. Philip's tour de force is an extended meditation in 105 lines of French verse on Luke 1: 28–33 (the Angelus), Latin versicle by Latin versicle, his hero putting his faith in the Virgin because 'the holy annunciation' saved all sinners and would save him. The meditation further reveals that Philip had read one of the texts of the *miracula* of the Virgin Mary, because he quotes the example of her saving Theophilus of Adana from the consequences of an ill-advised bargain with the Devil written in his own blood.[97]

It is not easy otherwise to trace the penetration of Marian spirituality into lay aristocratic life. Recent work by Nicholas Vincent has proved with authority and some style that the cult of the Virgin was a major feature of the devotions of the court of Henry III of England as much as it was of that of Louis IX of France.[98] Professor Vincent also draws attention to instances of aristocratic adoption of the cult. A Margam chronicler tells us that, trapped in sanctuary in the church of St John at Devizes in 1233, Hubert de Burgh, earl of Kent, like Remy's king and princess, 'devotedly prayed for the help of the Blessed Virgin'. As he was escaping with the help of Earl Richard Marshal's military household, this time temporarily trapped in a wood on the Gloucestershire shore of the Severn estuary while loyalist troops from Bristol closed in on them, Hubert again prayed to the Virgin and heard a voice saying repeatedly, 'Fear not, the Lord will deliver you!'[99] Professor Vincent also points to another egregious aristocratic manifestation of Marian devotion in the chapel of the Virgin at Caversham, whose relics and statue were much patronised by Henry III. Caversham was a manor and residence of the Marshal earls of Pembroke, and indeed William Marshal I died there in May 1219.[100] The 'gloriose e bele' chapel of the Virgin at Caversham had been built on a lavish scale by Marshal and his countess in the 1190s and was endowed to be served by a cell of canons from his Augustinian abbey of Notley.[101] That the chapel was conceived as a particular Marian cult centre is evident from the Marshal's stipulations that the canons must find wax candles to burn in it on Saturdays, the weekday devoted to a celebration of the Virgin, the Lady Mass.[102] Though his reputation for devotion may not be high, William Marshal, or at least his circle, clearly honoured the Virgin Mary. That his family went on to promote Caversham as a cult centre is certain. Henry III's attraction to Caversham might have been the result of his sister Eleanor marrying William Marshal II. Successive Marshal earls were commemorated there in lights at the altar. At some time in the 1240s, Sir Walter de la Hyde, a Marshal household knight and seneschal, endowed the chapel with nine acres so that a wax candle would burn at all the masses of the Virgin and also at vespers on her feast days for the soul of his lord, Earl Gilbert Marshal (died 1241).[103]

Apart from the chapel at Caversham, there are some other and earlier twelfth-century instances which indicate that aristocratic devotion to the Virgin was not new in the 1190s. The canons of Laon cathedral brought their outstanding collection of relics of the Virgin to England in 1118 and toured the south of the kingdom, meeting devotion from laypeople of all stations in the process, and collecting a large sum of money for the rebuilding of their cathedral. William III de Warenne, earl of Surrey (died 1148), granted Durford priory an annual rent of two marks 'for lights at the celebration of the mass of St Mary'.[104] Robert III, earl of Leicester (died 1190), and his countess Petronilla (died 1212), made particular gifts of bucks from their forest and fish from their ponds so the canons of Leicester could celebrate the principal feasts of the Virgin appropriately in their refectory.[105] England has a reputation for its precocious devotion to the Virgin, and the evidence from the aristocracy's religious practices indicates that it was merited. Particular devotion to other saints is not easy to demonstrate, especially as dedications of aristocratic foundations do not usually help. The earls of Arundel or Sussex, for instance, were the founders and patrons of Wymondham priory in Norfolk, dedicated to St Mary. But there is no hint in their charters, even the ones to Wymondham, of any particular devotion to the Mother of God. In fact, Earl William II of Arundel (died 1193) is noted in the sources as a devotee of St Thomas the Martyr, to whom he raised and endowed a chapel in the marketplace of Wymondham, funding perpetual lights in honour of the saint there, and also before St Thomas's altar in the Norman abbey of St-Sauveur-le-Vicomte.[106]

Aristocrats were the part of lay society most able to undertake pilgrimage as an expression of their piety, and collections of *miracula* depict a remarkably mobile population in search of shrines, indulgences and cures. Philip, prior of St Frideswide, Oxford, around 1190 records a blind, deaf and partially paralysed knight called Hamo de St-Ciry, who rode to Canterbury in his nineties looking for a cure for some of his ills at Becket's tomb, before travelling on to Oxfordshire to find relief at St Frideswide's intercession.[107] But the definitive aristocratic enthusiasm was for the crusade. Richard Kaeuper's recent study of knightly piety through romance literature concludes that the perils and trials of undertaking crusade were the fullest expression of the knightly impulse to express faith through self-imposed privation, struggle and, indeed, ecclesiastically sanctioned violence.[108]

Though the level of English participation in the First Crusade was very low, the subsequent attraction of the pursuit drew many English magnates and knights to the East. The Second Crusade (1146–8) for all its disastrous results, attracted a large Anglo-Norman contingent led by the brothers Waleran, count of Meulan and Worcester, and William III, earl of Warenne. William did not return. He was caught and killed with many other nobles in an ambush of the crusading army in the rocky passes of Cappadocia while riding with Louis VII of France's rearguard.[109] William was by no means the last high-profile English casualty of the crusade; a large number of English nobles fell at Acre in 1191. His fate prefigures that of William Longespée II, King Henry III's first cousin, cut down at Mansurah in 1250 in the army of Louis IX (see above, p. 204). Other crusaders died en route, such as Earl Robert III of Leicester at Durazzo in 1190, or the baron Henry Hose, who was travelling to or from Jerusalem with Joscelin of Louvain, lord of the Yorkshire Percy honor, in around 1174.[110] The Lord Edward's joining of

Louis IX's crusade in 1270, which ended up in Tunis, was therefore fully in line with English noble tradition. And just like the previous crusades, it responded to movements that were as much French as papally inspired.

***

We can therefore distinguish a form of noble piety evident throughout this period and intensifying as it progressed. From the beginning of our period, it appears to have been imitating the devotion of the royal court, which was able to stage the hours and elaborate liturgy on the scale of a great church by means of its well-staffed mobile chapel. Magnates could and did enjoy the same possibility with their own large chapels. It was not beyond the means of kings, queens or magnates to hear and follow the daily office, and even manorial lords could imitate something of it. Some magnates clearly did follow the office, and were doing so in the eleventh as much as the thirteenth century. We do not know how widespread such a practice was at any period, and there are certainly instances of magnates – William Marshal, for instance – who might not much care for it. There must always have been noblewomen of the sort stigmatised by Stephen de Fougères for attending vespers just to make illicit sexual liaisons.[111] Then there were knights like those described by Joinville, who laughed and joked through a colleague's funeral mass as they worked out who was to get the remarriage of the widow.[112] But other aristocrats were intellectually engaged with the Church in ways rather more deeply than the Church itself requested. Bishops and sermons asked only of the aristocrat that he should remember the poor and the downtrodden, and not be such a man as Dives in Luke's gospel had been.[113] But some took up their psalters, employed confessors, accumulated relics, went on pilgrimage or crusade, read and even wrote devotional works.

The dominant spirituality of the books of Wisdom, the ostentatious and austere *contemptus mundi*, moved some knights to the hermitage, the preceptory and the cloister. Asceticism in religious practice was a by-product of an outlook that regarded the world and all its joys as mere distracting vanity; Richard Kaeuper suggests that this inspired and was paralleled by a knightly cult of embracing egregious self-denial and suffering, particularly in the practice of crusade. But even if such a limited approach tends to ignore the great range of options that defined aristocratic spirituality, *contemptus mundi* had its undeniable impact. It may not have lured aristocrats to the regular religious life or the heroic self-denial of the religious orders of knighthood, but it still coloured a distinctly aristocratic form of spiritual life and devotion, where denial of the world was an especial virtue in those to whom the world had given most in material terms. So Stephen de Rouen meditated gloomily in his lament for that most fashionable and elegant of aristocrats, Waleran II, count of Meulan and Worcester (died 1166), a literate man and indeed a writer of Latin verse: 'Wealth melts away, honour is trodden down and the world's glory is one day remembered, the next forgotten, and once forgotten is gone forever. Count Waleran himself saw that he would be earth, worms and dust: he dreaded eternal punishment and he strove to enter heaven. He gave away, dispersed and thought little of his goods and he took the easy yoke of Christ upon his body with a pious heart.'[114]

CONCLUSION: A SOCIAL TRANSFORMATION

THE end of the reign of Henry II in England and France in 1189 saw the forming of a new social world. When contemporaries were in a reflective mood, they recognised as much. The elder Marshal, reminiscing late in life on his younger days, startled his sons when he recalled how few servants and horses a knight of the 1160s needed. Richard de Lucy grew irascible in his court when a Sussex 'petty knight' boasted of a seal he possessed, for that had been a prerogative of rather greater men in Lucy's youth in the 1130s. Other magnates of the 1170s in both England and France, feeling jostled by the pretensions of common knights, began proclaiming a superior form of knighthood: conferred by a banner, not merely a sword and spurs. At the same time, the oddity of the citizens of London calling themselves 'barons' was drawing so much attention that it needed to be explained that they made no claim to parity with the magnates of the royal court. And, in Louis VII's last decade in France, Chrétien de Troyes composed magnificent romances in which noble conduct was described as 'chivalry'. All were registering what had become increasingly evident: that the quality of nobility was being publicly defined by ideology and by material means. Since knights comprised a social group that included men who perceived they were noble, all knights could claim to be noble; this had the natural corollary that barons, who were already manifestly noble, wanted their greater nobility acknowledged. They had invented an élite, self-conscious and exclusive social class that demanded deference from outsiders.

As I said at the beginning of this book, this was not a process confined to England, though England gives us a lot of evidence as to how it played out. As is also evident, the process of forming a social hierarchy of groups defined by possession of 'nobility' was not uniform in England and France. The inevitable 'cascade effect' moved faster in France, where the social hierarchy was better defined in the 1230s than it was in England, where the noble status of the squire was not readily accepted. Likewise, the status of the knight might be seen to have been higher in England than in France. In England, there were fewer, more privileged knights than across the Channel. Nonetheless, ideas were shared within the Francophone world, where there were no impediments to literary and intellectual exchange. *Facetus* and other literature of conduct circulated widely; aspects of the *ensenhamen* of Occitan France were being imitated within a generation by the northern French authors of the *Roman de la rose* and *Ordene de chevalerie*. Where magnates and knights gathered in supra-national courts and entertainments – such as the tourneying venues of Picardy and Flanders – noble fashion and customs crossed national boundaries with ease. This was so much the case that French writers felt moved to assert that *their* chivalry must be seen as the true and authoritative type. Anyone else was inferior in their achievements and aspirations. It was for this reason that Andrew de Coutances in the 1180s stigmatised the French as a race of peasants. The claim of the French to nobility as being *their* particular sphere made its pretensions a point on which they could be attacked.

This observation reinforces the point that social transformations in medieval western Europe were not confined to one nation, but were generated supranationally – a point already evident to the early nineteenth-century British students of chivalry, who were deeply irritated by the French tendency to regard chivalry and the crusade as part of their particular national heritage. Of course, *twentieth*-century French historians, and those influenced by them, were less parochial than their predecessors, and made some sporadic attempts to fit England into their schemes of social transformation. Generally, they came up short against the absence of the sort of political breakdown that had supposedly happened in France in 1000. They therefore came to the conclusion, as did Marc Bloch, that England's strong monarchy gave it a unique form of feudalism adapted to Norman energy and dynastic drive. Only when that faltered, as it did in Stephen's reign, did symptoms of a 'feudal transformation' appear in Outre-Manche. English historians' own admiration for the precocity of the eleventh- and twelfth-century English nation state has simply reinforced the idea of England's specialness in social structure. This historical particularism – even, at times, narcissism – belongs in the nineteenth century, and has muddied the streams of historical analysis. It is for this reason that the idea analysed here of a universal transition in north-western Europe from an undifferentiated aristocracy to a stratified noble society in the twelfth century is so very powerful. It is not just that such a social tsunami works as an explanation for what we see happening, it also puts a stake through the heart of Rankean national determinism, an undead creature that still preys on innocent historical minds.

'Tsunami' is not an unsuitable metaphor for what happened to the twelfth-century social world: a great swelling wave of changes that was barely noticeable until it was upon people, turning their world into a tumbled and unfamiliar place. What had previously been left to the habitus of contemporary mores was now a matter of conscious definition and clear boundaries. We see the reaction in the intellectual turmoil of late twelfth-century literature. It was a time of major shifts in the habitus, large enough to be obvious to contemporaries. And since the idea of 'nobility' was the engine of the process, much of the new literature dwelt in many different ways on what nobility actually was. Laypeople as much as clerics participated in the discussion, whether through romances, poetry or tracts. The literature addressed a wide range of social issues, some completely new in Western thought, including those of gender and expectations. If society became more self-conscious, so men and women became more conscious of themselves, and of their relationship to each other and to the God they worshipped. In all these areas, superior conduct was advocated and described.

It might be suggested that behind all this social change was the increasing intellectual power of the schools and the skills of literacy, analysing and categorising. But it would be too easy to account for the process as the side effect of a more lettered society. Clerics might have an impact on social thinking, as the invention of chivalry reveals, but the engine was always lay expectations and ideals, and laypeople could think and analyse for themselves. Literacy was a quality the ideal aristocrat possessed, and had done well before the period of this book. An unregarded element of the work of Stephen Jaeger is his commentary on French noble education. He points to Marbod of Rennes's comment in the late eleventh century, when talking of the Angevin nobility, that it was the custom of nobles to hand over their children to masters to learn their letters.[1] The historical writings of Count Fulk IV Rechin of Anjou (died 1109), as well as Orderic's comments on educated eleventh-century Norman aristocrats, provide some justification for believing that Marbod was referring to a widespread custom in northern France. It might be noted that an eyewitness account of the consecration of the seven-year-old King Philip I of France in 1059 tells us that the boy *read* out his coronation oath in Latin.[2] Such an intellectually curious laity did not need the clerks of the schools and scholars of the universities to articulate a changing society.

The brightest Western aristocrats of the eleventh and early twelfth centuries already belonged to a wider world than was to be found in castle halls and tournament fields. The late twelfth century has more to say on the subject. Walter of Arras advocated that noble children should be put to learn their letters at the age of five.[3] Philip of Harvengt states in his correspondence that knightliness (*militia*) does not preclude learning (*scientia*) and that it was knowledge that 'ennobled' (*nobilaverat*) the mind of a magnate. He also observed in another work that in his day and province the knights were better educated in letters than the clergy, and were superior in both reading and the composition of Latin verse.[4] Across the Channel, Gerald of Wales echoed Philip in his handbook for princes: the greater the learning, he said, the greater the warrior, recalling the historical examples of the Julio-Claudians and Carolingians.[5] Magnates and knights did not look to a clerical, intellectual élite for their ideas of nobility; they found them themselves. Thus it was through the introspection of great aristocrats, the increase of wealth and means of display and the focus on the knightly ethos as a defining characteristic of the social élite that aristocracy became nobility. And in this manner, it may be said, the society of western Europe's *ancien régime* evolved.

NOTES

INTRODUCTION

1. This is seen in extreme form in G. Garnett, *Conquered England: Kingship, Succession and Tenure 1066–1166* (Oxford, 2007), a work written entirely within the Maitland tradition, as if no other interpretation had entered academic debate since 1906, and as if England (and by extension Normandy) were the only realms in the middle ages.

2. D. Crouch, *The Birth of Nobility: Constructing Aristocracy in England and France, 900–1300* (Harlow, 2005), 174–7, 184–7, 265–73. See particularly P.R. Coss, 'From Feudalism to Bastard Feudalism' in *Die Gegenwart des Feudalismusets* eds N. Fryde, P. Monnet and O.G. Oexle (Veröffentlichung des Max-Planck-Instituts für Geschichte, 173, 2002), 91–9.

3. Crouch, *Birth of Nobility*, 191–8. The standard text for the mutationist model of social change is J. P. Poly and E. Bournazel, *La Mutation féodale, x^e–xiiie siècles* (Paris, 1980), trans. C. Higgitt as *The Feudal Transformation, 900–1200* (New York, 1991).

4. D. Crouch, *The Image of Aristocracy in Britain, 1000–1300* (London, 1992), 123.

5. J.C.D. Clark, *English Society, 1660–1832* (2nd edn, Cambridge, 2000), 200–32, on the élite hegemony, which treats it as a European, not an insular, phenomenon, as also do I here. Dr Clark eschewed the internationalist term '*ancien régime*' in the revised edition of his work, which is a pity. The continuing and conscious enforcement of social deference to innate nobility by English society's upper ranks in the eighteenth and early nineteenth centuries is now commonplace in scholarship: see P. Langford, *Englishness Identified: Manners and Character, 1650–1850* (Oxford, 2000), 258–66.

6. See now the summary view of the transition of imperial to royal modes of authority in the early West in the landmark study by C. Wickham, *The Inheritance of Rome: A History of Europe from 400 to 1000* (Harmondsworth, 2009), especially 104–8.

CHAPTER ONE: THE KNIGHT IN ENGLAND

1. For a broader summary of these views in English, see D. Crouch, *The Birth of Nobility: Constructing Aristocracy in England and France, 900–1300* (Harlow, 2005), 243–8. A judicious digest of current French scholarship on these topics can be found in J. Morsel, *L'Aristocratie médiévale, v^e–xve siècle* (Paris, 2004), 88–128. For a new and coherent view of castle origins in France, see A. Debord, *Aristocratie et pouvoir: le rôle du château dans la France médiévale* (Paris, 2000), 19–48 (though written within the obsolete paradigm of the feudal mutation). For the origin and development of the knight, a current French view is to be found in D. Barthélemy, *La Chevalerie: de la Germanie antique à la France du xiie siècle* (Paris, 2007), 117–66.

2. *Vita Herluini*, in *The Works of Gilbert Crispin, Abbot of Westminster*, eds A.S. Abulafia and G.R. Evans (Auctores Britannici Medii Aevi, viii, British Academy, London, 1986),

xxi–xxv, xl–xli, 185–212; trans. P. Fisher in S.N. Vaughn, *The Abbey of Bec and the Anglo-Norman State, 1034–1136* (Woodbridge, 1981), 67–86. For Gilbert Crispin, see generally W.A. Robinson, *Gilbert Crispin, Abbot of Westminster* (Cambridge, 1911), 1–27. For Herluin and Gilbert, see the study by C. Harper-Bill, 'Herluin, Abbot of Bec, and his Biographer', in *Studies in Church History*, xv, ed. D. Baker (Ecclesiastical History Society, Oxford, 1978), 15–25.

3. WP, 102. This is confirmed by the penitential ordinance promulgated in 1070 in relation to the conquering army. Heavier penances were placed on those who fought 'for personal gain' as opposed to those who were discharging an obligation to their lord. Though the canon does not specify these were knights, the implication is clear enough that the Conqueror's army did contain many stipendiaries: H.E.J. Cowdrey, 'Bishop Ermenfrid of Sion and the Penitential Ordinance Following the Battle of Hastings', *Journal of Ecclesiastical History*, 20 (1969), 242.

4. Archives départementales de Maine-et-Loire, H3710.

5. *Cartulaire de l'abbaye de St-Martin de Pontoise*, ed. J. Depoin (Pontoise, 1895), 51.

6. See examples in D. Crouch, *The Image of Aristocracy in Britain, 1000–1300* (London, 1992), 137 and n.

7. WP, 130.

8. *Vita sancti Waldevi*, in *Chroniques Anglo-Normandes*, ed. F. Michel (3 vols, Paris, 1831–40), i, 124.

9. The horseback mobility of pre-Conquest English soldiers has been evident since the publication of J.H. Clapham, 'The Horsing of the Danes', *EHR*, 25 (1910), 287–93. S. Baxter, 'The Earls of Mercia and their Commended Men in the Mid Eleventh Century', *ANS*, xxiii, ed. J. Gillingham (Woodbridge, 2001), 29, points to a tenth-century source describing an ealdorman riding out with a mounted retinue 'as is the custom among the Angles and Saxons': *Frithegodi Monachi Breuiloquium Vitae Beati Wilfredi et Wulfstani Cantoris Narratio Metrica de Sancto Swithuno*, ed. A. Campbell (Zurich, 1950), 165. See also A. Williams, *The World before Domesday: The English Aristocracy, 900–1066* (London, 2008), 110–12, for the evidence of horsebreeding and the equipment of mounted pre-Conquest English warriors. For pre-Conquest Anglo-Scandinavian military life, see N. Hooper, 'Anglo-Saxon Warfare on the Eve of the Conquest: A Brief Survey', *ANS*, i, ed. R.A. Brown (Woodbridge, 1978), 84–93, 211–14; *idem*, 'The Housecarls in England in the Eleventh Century', *ANS*, vii, ed. R.A. Brown (Woodbridge, 1985), 161–76; R. Abels, *Lordship and Military Obligation in Anglo-Saxon England* (Berkeley, CA, 1988), 146–84. See also in general C.W. Hollister, *Anglo-Saxon Military Institutions on the Eve of the Norman Conquest* (Oxford, 1962). The presence of a French count, Ralph of Mantes, as a pre-Conquest earl in the West Midlands in the 1050s, and evidence of his French military household there, does, however, remind us that French aristocratic influence did cross the Channel well before the Conquest: A. Williams, 'The King's Nephew: Ralph, Earl of Hereford', in *Studies in Medieval History Presented to R. Allen Brown*, eds C. Harper-Bill, C. Holdsworth and J.L. Nelson (Woodbridge, 1989), 327–43.

10. See surveys in J. Bumke, *The Concept of Knighthood in the Middle Ages*, trans. W.T.H. and E. Jackson (New York, 1982), 10–21; R. Mortimer, 'Knights and Knighthood in Germany in the Central Middle Ages', in *The Ideals and Practice of Medieval Knighthood*, i, eds C. Harper-Bill and R. Harvey (Woodbridge, 1986), 86–103, especially 96–7.

11. *ASC s.a.* 1067, 1086. But note the horse and foot of William's army as 'mycclan here ridendra manna ond gangendra', *ASC s.a.* 1085, and Rufus's garrisoning of Norman castles with 'rideras', *ASC s.a.* 1090. An early twelfth-century administrator in Cumbria is known variously as Richard 'ridere' and Richard *miles*, showing how the equation of knight and 'rider' was current in English for a couple of generations after the Conquest: see R. Sharpe, *Norman Rule in Cumbria, 1092–1136* (Cumberland and Westmorland Antiquarian and Archaeological Society, Tract Series, xxi, 2006), 13–14.

12. *ASC s.a.* 1088. It is interesting – though not necessarily significant – to find an early translation in German of *aule milites* as 'chamara chnechta' (servants of the hall) in a

Reichenau document of *c.*790 × 820: see K.-F. Werner, *La naissance de noblesse* (2nd edn, Paris, 1998), 139. Under this heading it should be noted how surviving English prelates as much as lay magnates were required by Archbishop Lanfranc in 1085 to hire and maintain troops of *milites* with cash payments and board in their households so as to be prepared to resist a threatened Danish invasion: William of Malmesbury, *Vita Wulfstani*, in *Saints' Lives*, eds and trans. M. Winterbottom and R.M. Thomson (Oxford, 2002), 130.

13. Stenton, *First Century*, 133–6, and see now for its origins, D. Pelteret, *Slavery in Early Medieval England* (Woodbridge, 1995), 266–7. It may be worth noting here the panel of the Bayeux Tapestry 'Where Duke Harold of the English and his *milites* ride to Bosham'. In *c.*1070, the idea that a pre-Conquest earl had household 'knights' was clearly current.

14. J.M.W. Bean, ' "Bachelor" and Retainer', *Medievalia et Humanistica*, new ser., iii (1972), 117–31; J. Flori, 'Qu'est-ce qu'un bacheler?', *Romania*, xcvi (1975), 289–314; Crouch, *Image of Aristocracy*, 130 and n.

15. *Textus Roffensis*, pt 2, ed. P. Sawyer (Copenhagen, 1962), fo. 188r. For comment, see Abels, *Lordship and Military Obligation*, 138. Note the reverse translation by Osbern of Canterbury, who talks in Latin *c.*1090 of the *milites* of Cnut's household, 'which in Danish they call huscarles (*mandans omnibus familiae suae militibus, quos lingua Danorum huscarles vocant*': *Vita et translatio sancti Elphegi*, in H. Wharton, *Anglia Sacra* (2 vols, London, 1691), ii, 145, as noted in Hooper, 'Housecarls', 12. For a suggestion of an equivalency between 'cniht' and 'huscarl', see Williams, *The World before Domesday*, 63.

16. Notably, S. Harvey, 'The Knight and the Knight's Fee in England', *PP*, 49 (1970), 3–43, as criticised in D. Fleming, 'Landholding by *Milites* in Domesday Book', *ANS*, xiii, ed. M. Chibnall (Woodbridge, 1991), 83–98, whose minimalist stance on the subject I favour here.

17. *Domesday Book* i, fo. 180c; ii, fo. 372a.

18. Abels, *Lordship and Military Obligation*, 134–8, considers the possible permutations of meaning. For further discussion of *milites Anglici*, see A. Williams, *The English and the Norman Conquest* (Woodbridge, 1995), 196. There is some comparison here with the idea of 'Welsh knights' (*milites Gualenses*) as it developed in the Welsh March in the twelfth century: Crouch, *Image of Aristocracy*, 158–9.

19. M. Winterbottom, 'An Edition of Faricius, *Vita S. Aldhelmi*', *Journal of Medieval Latin*, 15 (2005), 127.

20. *The Domesday Monachorum of Christ Church Canterbury*, ed. D.C. Douglas (London, 1944), 105. I am half-inclined to wonder whether these men were the reason why William Rufus berated Archbishop Anselm in 1097 for sending him inexperienced, ill-trained and substandard knights for a campaign in Wales; Eadmer, *Historia Novorum*, ed. M. Rule (Rolls Series, 1884), 37.

21. E. King, 'The Peterborough "Descriptio Militum" (Henry I)', *EHR*, 84 (1969), 84–101, text at 97–101.

22. A. Williams, 'The Knights of Shaftesbury Abbey', *ANS*, viii, ed. R.A. Brown (Woodbridge, 1985), 214–42. The date she suggests depends on the evident disintegration of full fees in the survey by the time they were recorded in the abbey's *carta* of 1166. She links the survey with litigation the abbey was carrying on in the first half of Henry I's reign. For another early post-Conquest instance of 'manreda', in an act of Earl Ralph de Gael of East Anglia dating to *c.*1070 × 75, as meaning homage, and involving rights of sake and soke over a tenant, see Cartulary of St Benet of Hulme, BL, ms Cotton Galba, E ii, fo. 35v. For *mannredenne* before the Conquest, which he equates with the Latin term *commendatio*, see S. Baxter, *The Earls of Mercia: Lordship and Power in Late Anglo-Saxon England* (Oxford, 2007), 204–6.

23. JW iii, 24.

24. *ASC s.a.* 1079.

25. Simeon of Durham, *Historia ecclesiae Dunelmensis*, in *Omnia Opera*, ed. T. Arnold (2 vols, Rolls Series, 1882–5), i, 131.

26. For Edgar Ætheling, see N. Hooper, 'Edgar the Ætheling: Anglo-Saxon Prince, Rebel and Crusader', *Anglo-Saxon England*, 14, eds P. Clemoes et al. (Cambridge, 1985), 197–214.

27. BL, Cotton Charter xxii, 3.

28. See the discussion in D. Crouch, *Tournament* (London, 2005), 40–1, 163.

29. OV ii, 266; WM, *GRA* i, 470.

30. R. Fleming, *Kings and Lords in Conquest England* (Cambridge, 1991), 107–13, 183–8; Williams, *English and the Norman Conquest*, 98–107.

31. Williams, *English and the Norman Conquest*, 71–97, offers case studies at this level from four very different counties.

32. *Inquisitio Comitatus Cantabrigiensis and Inquisitio Eliensis*, ed. N.E.S.A. Hamilton (London, 1876).

33. C.P. Lewis, 'Domesday Jurors', *HSJ*, 5 (1993), 24–34.

34. R. Bartlett, *England under the Norman and Angevin Kings, 1075–1225* (Oxford, 2000), 539. The boy later became a hermit on Farne Island and reinvented himself once more, as Bartholomew.

35. *ASC s.a.* 1126; L.L. Huneycutt, *Matilda of Scotland: A Study in Medieval Queenship* (Woodbridge, 2003), 26.

36. Williams, *English and the Norman Conquest*, 198.

37. *Domesday Book* ii, fo. 148b; *Cartularium prioratus de Colne*, ed. J.L. Fisher (Essex Archaeological Society, Occasional Publication, no. 1, 1946), 45.

38. *Charters of the Redvers Family and the Earldom of Devon, 1090–1217*, ed. R. Bearman (Devon and Cornwall Record Society, new ser., 37, 1994), 126–7, 183. Bashley in 1086 was a demesne manor of the canons of Twynham: *Domesday Book* i, fo. 44b.

39. TNA, KB26/169, m. 27.

40. *Curia Regis Rolls* ix, 318–19 and see also *Bracton's Notebook*, ed. F.W. Maitland (3 vols, London, 1887), iii, 706–7. For the English name Stanard, Stonard or Stanheard, see O. von Feilitzen, *The Pre-Conquest Personal Names of Domesday Book* (Uppsala, 1937), 371–2.

41. D. Crouch, 'The Local Influence of the Earls of Warwick, 1088–1242: A Study in Decline and Resourcefulness', *Midland History*, xxi (1996), 20: Appendix A, 'The Romance of Gui de Warewic and the Earls of Warwick.'

42. N. Denholm-Young, 'An Early Thirteenth-Century Anglo-Norman MS', *Bodleian Library Record*, 6 (1921–31), 225–30.

43. G. Garnett, *Conquered England: Kingship, Succession and Tenure 1066–1166* (Oxford, 2007), 120 and n.

44. As, for instance, the colonisation of Warwickshire by the Norman followers of the incoming lord of Kenilworth, Geoffrey de Clinton, in the 1120s; see D. Crouch, 'Geoffrey de Clinton and Roger Earl of Warwick: New Men and *Curiales* in the Reign of Henry I', *BIHR*, lv (1982), 118–19.

45. WM, *GRA* i, 716. For Henry I, with his taste for English lovers and appeals to an English constituency in his troubles with his brother, see H.M. Thomas, *The English and the Normans: Ethnic Hostility, Assimilation and Identity, 1066–c.1220* (Oxford, 2003), 157–8, 275.

46. *Le Roman de Thèbes*, ed. F. Mora-Lebrun (Paris, 1995), lines 7231–44.

47. The 'exceptionality' of English 'feudal' society was an article of faith amongst both French and British historians in the nineteenth century, a view that was transferred to twentieth-century historiography, but I am not endorsing that view in this section; see Crouch, *Birth of Nobility*, 268–9.

48. Crouch, *Birth of Nobility*, 280–92.

49. *The Shrewsbury Cartulary*, ed. U. Rees (2 vols, Aberystwyth, 1975), ii, 318. See also his letter of 1127 addressed 'omnibus baronibus de comitatu Seropesberiensi', ibid. ii, 319. Between 1108 and 1118, the *Leges Henrici Primi* likewise refers to the *barones comitatus* as the leaders of the shire courts (cc. 29.1, 30.1).

50. H.M. Cam, 'An East Anglian Shire Moot of Stephen's Reign', *EHR*, 39 (1924), 569.

51. Crouch, *Image of Aristocracy*, 107–11.

52. OV vi, 26–8 and 26n. The interpretation of *pagenses milites* has caused a lot of debate and been interpreted variously as the levies of the English fyrd, as mercenaries or as feudal knights. Since *pagus* commonly means 'shire', however, the obvious translation is 'county knights'. The number of three thousand such men in Orderic's account would either indicate that their status was very low, or that he was exaggerating numbers for effect.
53. *Monasticon Anglicanum* vi, 345.
54. For the rise in the status of barons, see Crouch, *Image of Aristocracy*, 112–14, and above, p. 49.
55. Stubbs, *Select Charters*, 173, 176, 179.
56. Cartulary of Malmesbury abbey, BL, ms Lansdowne 417, fo. 80v.
57. *Curia Regis Rolls* vii, 158–9.
58. *Rotuli Litterarum Clausarum* i, 132; Stubbs, *Select Charters*, 282.
59. J.C. Holt, 'The Prehistory of Parliament', in *The English Parliament in the Middle Ages* eds R.G. Davies and J.H. Denton (Manchester, 1981), 5–6.
60. There have been two serious published efforts to deduce the number of knights when the panels listed in *curia regis* and eyre rolls allow us a chance after 1200 to attempt county totals: J. Quick, 'The Number and Distribution of Knights in Thirteenth-Century England', in *Thirteenth-Century England* i, eds P.R. Coss and S.D. Lloyd (Woodbridge, 1986), 114–23; K. Faulkner, 'The Transformation of Knighthood in Early Thirteenth-Century England', *EHR* (1996), 1–23. Faulkner points out the reasons why accurate totals are impossible, but demonstrates the underestimation in Quick's figures, suggesting a misleadingly precise figure of 3,453 knights involved in county courts at any one time in John's reign. Her total does not, of course, include landless knights retained in magnate households (and therefore ineligible) or magnate knights themselves. Her own figures are given critical scrutiny in P.R. Coss, *The Origins of the English Gentry* (Cambridge, 2003), 91–7.
61. Faulkner, 'Transformation of Knighthood', 15–16; Coss, *Lordship, Knighthood and Locality*, 244–8.
62. N. Denholm-Young, 'Feudal Society in the Thirteenth Century: The Knights', in *Collected Papers* (Cardiff, 1969), 86–7. It is worth noting the 1309 list of knights attending a tournament at Dunstable, to which six great magnates brought their retinues (*retenaunces*), along with a further seventy unattached knights. In all, 235 English knights were present, which, if Denholm-Young were correct, would mean that just over one in five English knights was present that day; A. Tomkinson, 'Retinues at the Tournament of Dunstable, 1309', *EHR*, 74 (1959), 70–89. The likelihood is that Denholm-Young underestimates the number of knights in England in Edward II's reign; see the contrasting analysis in D. Simpkin, *The English Aristocracy at War* (Woodbridge, 2008), 22–3.
63. Denholm-Young, 'Feudal Society in the Thirteenth Century', 84.
64. There have been other ideas entertained: for a résumé, see P.R. Coss, *The Knight in Medieval England, 1000–1400* (Stroud, 1993), 62. Denholm-Young suggested that the rising cost of military equipment pushed out would-be knights: 'Feudal Society in the Thirteenth Century: The Knights', 89–90. A related explanation is that the inflation of the late twelfth century impoverished many knightly families and led to their disappearance; P.R. Coss, 'Sir Geoffrey de Langley and the Crisis of the Knightly Class in Thirteenth-Century England', *PP*, 68 (1975), 3–37. Professor Coss has subsequently revisited and distanced himself from that stark economic conclusion in *idem, The Origins of the English Gentry*, 99–107, concluding that rising costs, not income, were the principal issue in the shrinkage of what he calls *milituli*.
65. Crouch, *Image of Aristocracy*, 147–8.
66. On distraint and its significances, see M.R. Powicke, 'Distraint of Knighthood and Military Obligation under Henry III', *Speculum*, 25 (1950), 457–70; S.L. Waugh, 'Reluctant Knights and Jurors: Respites, Exemptions and Public Obligations in the Reign of Henry III', *Speculum*, 58 (1983), 937–86.
67. *Documents*, 88.

68. *Close Rolls, 1247–51*, 564; *Close Rolls, 1251–53*, 425.
69. See the conclusion in Waugh, 'Reluctant Knights and Jurors', 986.
70. *Calendar of Patent Rolls, 1247–58*, 536, 646, 655; TNA, KB26/173, m 19d. See, generally, Crouch, *Image of Aristocracy*, 146–7.
71. P.R. Coss, 'Knighthood and the Early Thirteenth-Century County Court', in *Thirteenth-Century England* ii, eds P.R. Coss and S.D. Lloyd (Woodbridge, 1988), 50–2.
72. Crouch, 'Local Influence of the Earls of Warwick', 12–13, 21–2.
73. Crouch, *Image of Aristocracy*, 144–52, part 2, passim.
74. P.A. Brand, 'Oldcotes v. d'Arcy', in *Medieval Legal Records Edited in Memory of C.A.F. Meekings*, eds R.F. Hunnisett and J.B. Post (London, 1978), 64–70.

CHAPTER TWO: MILITARY CULTURE

1. J.O. Prestwich, 'Anglo-Norman Feudalism and the Problem of Continuity', *PP*, 26 (1963), 41–2.
2. Cartulary of Binham priory, BL, MS Cotton Claudius, D xiii, fo. 121r. The charter dates to after the death of Earl William III de Warenne (1148) but possibly before Henry II's reign. His grandfather may have been the Ralph Faeto who held land of Peter de Valognes at Ryburgh: *Domesday Book* i, fo. 257a. Compare the William de Gisney whose 'long and ancient tenure' of his estates referred to in the 1140s was recalled as going back to his father's day, 'tempore regis Willelmi blundi' (viz. William Rufus): *Stoke by Clare Cartulary, Pt 1*, eds C. Harper-Bill and R. Mortimer (Suffolk Charters, 4, 1981), 7 (a writ of Stephen overlooked in *Regesta*).
3. To say this is not to subscribe to the view of G. Garnett, *Conquered England: Kingship, Succession and Tenure 1066–1166* (Oxford, 2007), esp. 31, which would derive the pragmatic view of such twelfth-century people as Ralph from a central Diktat of the Conqueror himself. For a devastating critique of Garnett's views, see the review by N. Vincent, *History*, 95 (2010), 106–8.
4. So William of Colechurch informed Henry II that he held a half-fee in Norfolk 'de antiquo tenemento a conquestu Anglie': *The Red Book of the Exchequer*, ed. H. Hall (3 vols, Rolls Series, 1896), i, 400. On this and the uncertainty of the position in 1166, see H.G. Richardson and G.O. Sayles, 'The Shadow of Feudalism', in *idem, The Governance of Medieval England from the Conquest to Magna Carta* (Edinburgh, 1963), 88–90.
5. The archaeological approach of Sir James Holt to the 1166 returns is the most satisfactory to date. He finds decimal quotas at the root of many baronial honors, including those created after 1100, thus supporting but modifying J.H. Round's basic thesis ('The Introduction of Knight Service into England', in *Feudal England* [repr. London, 1964], 182–245) and affirming that tinkering with them can be proven to have occurred over several decades after 1070: J.C. Holt, 'The Introduction of Knight-Service in England', *ANS*, vi, ed. R.A. Brown (Woodbridge, 1984), 89–106.
6. *Red Book of the Exchequer*, i, 300–1.
7. Holt, 'Introduction of Knight-Service', 104–5.
8. WP, 70. S. Reynolds, *Fiefs and Vassals: The Medieval Evidence Reinterpreted* (Oxford, 1994), 127–30, 370–3; J. le Goff, 'The Symbolic Ritual of Vassalage', in *idem, Time, Work and Culture in the Middle Ages*, trans. A. Goldhammer (Chicago, 1980), 237–87, for contrasting surveys.
9. *Le Roman de Thèbes*, ed. F. Mora-Lebrun (Paris, 1995), lines 9981–10,064.
10. *Red Book of the Exchequer*, i, 368.
11. Westminster Abbey Muniments, no. 3122.
12. TNA, C115/G/30/4371. For the identification of Hurstley, see *Reading Abbey Cartularies*, ed. B.R. Kemp (2 vols, Camden Society, 4th ser., xxxi, xxxiii, 1986–7), i, 283–4.
13. Register of Sheen priory (Inventory of deeds of Ware priory), BL, ms Cotton Otho B xiv, fo. 115v ('Item, carta Petronille comitisse Leyc' de homagio recepto').

14. *The Cartulary of Haughmond Abbey*, ed. U. Rees (Cardiff, 1985), 244. See Stenton, *First Century*, 163n, for context.

15. Braybrooke Cartulary, BL, ms Stowe 986, fo. 74v: 'teste domino Ricardo rege Anglie et Baldewyno comite de Flaundres coram quibus facta fuit istud homagium et ista donatio quando idem Ricardus rex reuersus est de Berry et cepit Virson.' For the date of this campaign, see J. Gillingham, *Richard I* (New Haven, 1999), 310–11. This hitherto unnoticed evidence confirms Gillingham's suggested dating of the fall of Vierzon to July 1197.

16. 'Estate Records of the Hotot Family', ed. E. King, in *A Northamptonshire Miscellany*, ed. *idem* (Northamptonshire Record Society, xxxii, 1983), 41.

17. TNA, E368/5, m. 14d. The *Cartae Baronum* of 1166 appears to make reference to this plea between Robert and Godfrey, showing the two at odds about the service owed for Godfrey's lands (which Robert claimed as eight fees), with the outcome pending a suit in the *curia regis: Red Book of the Exchequer* i, 245.

18. *Domesday Book* i, fo. 381b.

19. See the analysis in *Early Yorkshire Charters*, iv, 11–12, 15–16, and passim for location of fees. See also commentary in Stenton, *First Century*, 194–5. A similar relationship can be seen in 1215 between the castle of Chester and the earl's far-flung *milites de Anglia*, that is, the knights who owe him service across the Midlands and south of England: *Charters of the Anglo-Norman Earls of Chester, c.1071–1237*, ed. G. Barraclough (Lancashire and Cheshire Record Society, cxxvi, 1988), 390.

20. TNA, DL27/1; *Earldom of Gloucester Charters*, ed. R.B. Patterson (Oxford, 1973), 98.

21. Stenton, *First Century*, 208–9, 208n. For the Tourville barony within the earldom, see D. Crouch, *The Beaumont Twins: The Roots and Branches of Power in the Twelfth Century* (Cambridge, 1986), 134–5, 218–19. See also the comparable example of Pulford, Cheshire, in the honor of Chester: Stenton, *First Century*, 211.

22. D. Crouch, 'A Norman "Conventio" and Bonds of Lordship in the Middle Ages', in *Law and Government in Medieval England and Normandy* eds G. Garnett and J.G. Hudson (Cambridge, 1994), 323–4.

23. See F. Suppe, 'Castle Guard and the Castlery of Clun', *HSJ*, 1 (1989), 123–34.

24. *Early Yorkshire Charters* v, 15–16. The erosion of actual service at a baronial castle is assumed in the intelligent survey in S. Painter, 'Castle Guard', *AmHR*, 40 (1935), 450–9. The total raised for Richmond's commutation of castle guard compares very favourably with the sixty shillings raised for the private castle of Skipsea in Yorkshire in the 1260s, which also drew on fees from Lincolnshire: B. English, *The Lords of Holderness, 1086–1260* (Oxford, 1979), 174.

25. J.C. Holt, *Magna Carta* (2nd edn, Cambridge, 1992), 435.

26. TNA, JUST1/696, m. 13d (plea dated 1241).

27. *Rotuli Litterarum Patentium* i, 79.

28. Gerald of Wales, *Itinerarium Kambriae*, in *Opera* vi, ed. J.F. Dimock (Rolls Series, 1868), 63.

29. *HWM* i, lines 40–2. See also Matthew Paris's comment on William de Valence's housebreaking and pillaging of the bishop of Ely's manor of Hatfield in 1252, leaving the house 'as if it had been gutted in war time hostilities (*quasi in hostili guerra conquassata*)': MP, *CM* v, 234.

30. H.E.J. Cowdrey, 'Bishop Ermenfrid of Sion and the Penitential Ordinance Following the Battle of Hastings', *Journal of Ecclesiastical History*, 20 (1969), 235, 239–41, and for comparison see M. Keen, *The Laws of War in the Late Middle Ages* (London, 1965), 63–72.

31. *Red Book of the Exchequer* i, 401–2. See other references to disseisin *per gwerram* by Earl Patrick of Salisbury in Gloucestershire, ibid., i, 298. Also William de Montfichet recalled, 'when I was a boy', how his guardian Earl Gilbert of Pembroke (died 1148) *in gwerra* gave a fee away over which he was in 1166 at law with the beneficiary's son: ibid., i, 351. Hugh de Douvres in Cambridgeshire recalled how his predecessor *post mortem Henrici regis in guerra* gave half a fee to the steward of the honor 'so he could better keep up his service of two knights': ibid. i, 368, 369. William Blund of Suffolk recalled that in

tempore gwerrae his father, Gilbert, was disseised of five of the twelve fees he had before 1135 in Wiltshire: ibid., i, 408. For the bishop of Norwich in 1166, the death of Henry I was followed by 'the time of war': ibid., i, 392. Note, however, how Earl William de Roumare of Lincoln could already talk, well before the end of Stephen's reign, of how the *tempus werre* was in the past: *Documents Illustrative of the Social and Economic History of the Danelaw*, ed. F.M. Stenton (London, 1920), 375.

32. H.M. Thomas, 'Violent Disorder in King Stephen's England', in *King Stephen's Reign, 1135–1154* eds P. Dalton and G.J. White (Woodbridge, 2008), 151.

33. BL, Additional charter 27143; see, N. Vincent, 'More Tales of the Conquest', in *Normandy and its Neighbours, c.950–1250: Essays in Honour of David Bates* eds D. Crouch and K. Thompson (Turnhout, 2010), forthcoming.

34. BL, Additional Charter 19616.

35. *Foedera* i, pt 1, 408–9.

36. *Red Book of the Exchequer* i, 274, as the baron William fitz Alan put it.

37. Key studies here were M. Chibnall, 'Mercenaries and the *Familia Regis* under Henry I', *History*, 62 (1977), 15–23; J.O. Prestwich, 'The Military Household of the Norman Kings', *EHR*, 96 (1981), 1–35; and see for a summary S. Morillo, *Warfare under the Anglo-Norman Kings, 1066–1135* (Woodbridge, 1994), 16–27, 60–6. For the Angevin preference for contracted Welsh, Flemish and Brabazon troops, the pioneering essay is J. Boussard, 'Les Mercenaires au xiiie siècle: Henry II Plantagenêt et les origines de l'armée de métier', *Bibliothèque de l'Ecole des Chartes*, 106 (1945–6), 189–224.

38. *Estoire des Engleis*, lines 5843–50.

39. The best description of the intricacies of knight service at a national level remains I.J. Sanders, *Feudal Military Service in England: A Study of the Constitutional and Military Powers of the* Barones *in Medieval England* (Oxford, 1956). But see Stenton, *First Century*, 152–91; S. Painter, *Studies in the History of the English Feudal Barony* (Baltimore, 1943), 20–72.

40. RT, 202.

41. *Cartulaire de l'abbaye de St-Michel du Tréport*, ed. P. Laffleur de Kermaingant (Paris, 1880), 63–4. The count had pledged the abbey's treasure to raise a cash loan, without first asking.

42. *Red Book of the Exchequer* ii, pp. cclxvii–cclxxiii. See T. Keefe, *Feudal Assessments and the Political Community under Henry II and his Sons* (Berkeley, CA, 1983), 105–6. Those sums given to the earl by individuals in Norfolk 'by the king's writ from beyond the sea' were likely to represent reimbursements claimed from royal debtors.

43. *Regesta: William I*, 449–52. Professor Bates notes the reasons for doubting the Evesham writ's authenticity, but equivocates on the ground that its uniqueness is largely what condemns it. To me it would seem to be compromised by its ostentatious support for the abbey's assessment as owed in the 1159 aid and the 1166 royal inquisition on service owed the crown. The only text is to be found in a late thirteenth-century cartulary of the abbey. J.H. Round noted grounds for suspecting it, but dismissed them by saying that there was not 'anything to be gained by forging a document which admits, by placing on record, the abbey's full liability': 'Introduction of Knight Service into England', 238. But there were many reasons why the abbey should do so, especially if a later king were attempting to argue the assessment upwards.

44. *Regesta*, 261.

45. *The Langley Cartulary*, ed. P.R. Coss (Dugdale Society, 32, 1980), 10.

46. I refer to the serjeantry granted by Osbert of Arden to Thurkil Fundu: original in BL, Cotton Charter xxii, 3, translated with commentary in D. Crouch, *Tournament* (London, 2005), 163.

47. *Le Couronnement de Louis*, ed. E. Langlois (Classiques Français du moyen age, 1984), line 1997.

48. *La Chanson d'Aspremont*, ed. L. Brandin (2 vols, Classiques Français du moyen age, 1923–4), i, line 1512.

49. *HWM*, i, lines 8248–9.

50. The text and the story of its discovery are in N. Vincent, 'William Marshal, King Henry II and the Honour of Châteauroux', *Archives*, xxv (2000), 15. The translation is that offered in D. Crouch, *William Marshal: Knighthood, War and Chivalry, 1147–1219* (2nd edn, London, 2002), 61.

51. H.M. Chew, *The English Ecclesiastical Tenant-in-Chief and Knight Service* (Oxford, 1932), 75, makes this point, even though she did not know of the evidence mentioned here.

52. Ralph de Diceto, *Ymagines Historiarum*, in *Opera Historica*, ed. W. Stubbs (2 vols, Rolls Series, London, 1876), ii, pp. lxxix–lxxx.

53. Stenton, *First Century*, 177–8.

54. G. Duby, 'Les "jeunes" dans la société aristocratique dans la France du nord-ouest au xiie siècle', in *idem*, *La Société chevaleresque* (Paris, 1988), 129–42; trans. C. Postan in *The Chivalrous Society* (London, 1977), 112–22.

55. *Monasticon Anglicanum*, vi, 127.

56. D. Crouch, *The Birth of Nobility: Constructing Aristocracy in England and France, 1000–1300* (Harlow, 2005), 56–68.

57. *Le Roman de Thèbes*, ed. F. Mora-Lebrun (Paris, 1995), lines 6891–934 (on the death of Duke Atys).

58. Vincent, 'More Tales of the Conquest'.

59. Crouch, *Tournament*, 137–44, deploying the hitherto unused commentary on the knightly armour of *c.*1180 offered by Ralph Niger, *De re militari et triplici via peregrinationis Ierosolimitane*, ed. L. Schmugge (Beitrage zür Geschichte und Quellenkunde des Mittelalters, 6, Berlin, 1977), 98–105. See also F. Lachaud, 'Armour and Military Dress in Thirteenth- and Early Fourteenth-Century England', in *Armies, Chivalry and Warfare in Medieval Britain and France*, ed. M. Strickland (Stamford, 1998), 344–69.

60. Crouch, *William Marshal*, 36–7.

61. F. Lachaud, 'Liveries of Robes in England, *c.*1200–*c.*1330', *EHR*, 111 (1996), 281–4, notes the absence of early evidence for this practice, but also regards the clothing of dependants as a universal phenomenon. Her discussion implies at one point that nobles were imitating royal practice and at another that they were reflecting a practice found in twelfth-century romances.

62. *De Nugis Curialium*, 470. It is worth noting here that in an epic of *c.*1130 the granting of fur-lined robes was a way for Count William of Orange to demonstrate his lordship (*La Prise d'Orange*, ed. C. Regnier [Paris, 1967], lines 1883–4), though the beneficiaries in this case were not knights. But see Wace's observations in the 1160s on the granting of cloth to barons and knights by Dukes Richard I and Richard II of Normandy: *Roman de Rou* i, pt 2, lines 4127–8; pt 3, lines 809–10.

63. *HWM* i, lines 53–5; ii, lines 18,685–716. For Robert de Ros 'quondam cissor Ranulphi bone memorie quondam comitis Cestrie', Cartulary of the Earldom of Cornwall, TNA E36/57, fos 30v–31r. And see also the reference in 1282 to the shop of Hugh *cissor* of Henry de Lacy, earl of Lincoln, on Milk Street in the City of London: Corporation of London Record Office, Husting Roll 13 (81).

64. *Curia Regis Rolls* xv, 502.

65. *Rolls of the Justices in Eyre for Yorkshire in 3 Henry III (1218–19)*, ed. and trans. D.M. Stenton (Selden Society, lvi, 1937), 424–5; N. Denholm-Young, *Seignorial Administration in England* (London, 1937), 117; and see Lachaud, 'Liveries of Robes in England', 283–5. See robes granted to lesser retainers by the count of Eu in 1212. *Red Book* ii, 624; and the officers of the honor of Holderness in the 1260s, English, *The Lords of Holderness*, 227–34.

66. Crouch, *The Reign of King Stephen, 1135–1154* (London, 2002), 52–4.

67. *HWM* i, lines 1531–50. 'Vavassor' here means a county landowner outside the knightly milieu.

68. J. Barthélemy Hauréau, 'Un poème inédit de Pierre Riga', *Bibliothèque de l'École de Chartes*, 44 (1883), 7–11, at lines 72–9.

69. *De re militari*, 114.

70. For the tournament in twelfth-century England, see Crouch, *Tournament*, 52–4.

71. C. Bonnier, 'List of English Towns in the Fourteenth Century', *EHR*, 16 (1901), 502. Bonnier misdated the list by a century.

72. *The Book of the Foundation of Walden Abbey*, eds and trans. D.E. Greenway and L. Watkiss (Oxford, 1999), 44, 80. *HWM* i, lines 7610–13.

73. *Cartulaire d'Affligbem*, ed. E. de Marneffe, in *Analectes pour servir à l'histoire de la Belgique*, iie section, *Série des cartulaires et des documents étendus*, pt 1 (Louvain, 1894), 218.

74. *Complete Peerage* xii, pt 1, 764n.

75. Rouen, Bibliothèque municipale, Collection Leber, carton 4, no. 142. The witnesses of this undated charter are identifiable as the count's followers in the earlier part of his career.

76. *Gui de Warewic: roman du xiiie siècle*, ed. A. Ewert (2 vols, Classiques Français du moyen age, 1932), i, lines 1128–74.

77. *Roman de Ham*, in *Histoire des ducs de Normandie et des rois d'Angleterre*, ed. F. Michel (Paris, 1840) 215.

78. See the reconstruction of the Clare foreign tours in Crouch, *Tournament*, 42.

79. MP, *CM* v, 557; *Annales de Dunstaplia*, in *Annales Monastici* iii, 218–19; M. Prestwich, *Edward I* (London, 1988), 34–5.

80. For the list of 'Les Anglois', the English bannerets, see A. de Behault de Dornon, 'La noblesse hennuyère au tournoi de Compiègne de 1238', *Annales du cercle archéologique de Mons*, xxii (1890), 87–8. For the correct dating of the Compiègne roll published by de Dornon, see M.L. Carolus-Barré, 'Les grands tournois de Compiègne et de Senlis en l'honneur de Charles, prince de Salerne (mai 1279)', *Bullétin de la Société Nationale des Antiquaires de France* (1978–9), 87–100.

CHAPTER THREE: THE SHIFTING BORDERS OF NOBILITY

1. A stimulating essay is D. Cannadine, *Class in Britain* (New Haven, 1998), though it is a study very much of its day, and sees 'class' as an essentially early modern phenomenon.

2. This is a digest of an argument presented in more detail in D. Crouch, *The Birth of Nobility: Constructing Aristocracy in England and France, 900–1300* (Harlow, 2005), 173–87.

3. See on these antecedents S. Keynes, *The Diplomas of King Aethelred 'the Unready', 978–1016: A Study in their Use as Historical Evidence* (Cambridge, 1980), 197–8, 197n, 206–7n; C. Hart, 'Athelstan "Half-King" and his Family', in *Anglo-Saxon England* ii, eds P. Clemoes et al., (Cambridge, 1973), 122–3; D. Crouch, *The Image of Aristocracy in Britain, 1000–1300* (London, 1992), 46–8; A. Williams, *The World before Domesday: The English Aristocracy, 900–1066* (London, 2008), 11–24.

4. C.P. Lewis, 'The Early Earls of Norman England', *ANS*, xiii, ed. M. Chibnall (Woodbridge, 1990), 211–22.

5. *Regesta: William I*, 286 (1068). The latter act is revealing in that the 'eorlas' present are *duces*, whereas Robert of Mortain, a count, is not identified by title but as the king's brother, perhaps to avoid a confusion of status.

6. *Sir Christopher Hatton's Book of Seals*, eds L.C. Loyd and D.M. Stenton (Oxford, 1950), no. 431; *Regesta: William I*, no. 139.

7. *Godefridi prioris Wintoniensis epigrammata historica*, in *The Anglo-Latin Satirical Poets and Epigrammatists of the Twelfth Century*, ed. T. Wright (2 vols, Rolls Series, 1872), ii, 152–3. Note the parallel case of Morcar of Northumbria, called *comes* in a charter of his gaoler in Normandy in 1086: F. Lot, *Etudes critiques sur l'abbaye de St-Wandrille* (Paris, 1913), 95–6.

8. *Domesday Book* i, fos 247c, 301d. Likewise Geoffrey Gaimar retrospectively made Nidi, wife of Earl Tostig, a *cuntesse*: *L'Estoire des Engleis*, lines 5093–4; and see Crouch, *Image of Aristocracy*, 75–7.

9. *Le Grand Cartulaire de Conches et sa copie: transcription et analyse*, ed. C. de Haas (Le Mesnil-sur-l'Estrée, 2005), 64. For the date of Robert's accession to Meulan, see S. Vaughn,

'Robert of Meulan and *Raison d'Etat* in the Anglo-Norman State, 1093–1118', *Albion*, 10 (1978), 355 and n.

10. For his career and seal, see D. Crouch, 'Robert of Beaumont, Count of Meulan and Leicester: His Lands, his Acts and his Self-Image', in *Henry I and the Anglo-Norman World: Studies in Memory of C. Warren Hollister* eds D. Fleming and J.M. Pope (Woodbridge, 2006), 91–9, 103. For the seal, see University of Keele, Robert Richards Collection 72/46/1(1). The legend was partly readable in the eighteenth century, for which see a drawing in J. Nichols, *The History and Antiquities of the County of Leicester* (4 vols in 8, London, 1795–1815), i, pt 1, App. p. 48.

11. Durham D & C muniments, charter no. 1.3 Ebor. 12: *A. comes Brit' et Angl'*; this is far and away the commonest style he took, accounting for ten of the fifteen of his acts collected in *Early Yorkshire Charters* iv, 15–30. TNA, 31/8/140B, pt 3, p. 88 has him as 'Alanus comes Anglie et indigena comesque Britannie'. In another instance he is found more specifically as 'Alan by the grace of God, count of Brittany, Cornwall and Richmond': *The Cartulary of St Michael's Mount*, ed. P.L. Hull (Devon and Cornwall Record Society, new ser., v, 1962), 6. Alan III too rejoiced in a double-sided seal (attached to the Durham act). I owe to Richard Sharpe the suggestion that Alan's vague styles and eventual adoption of Richmond as the seat of his county reflect his assertion of his comital status in a land where otherwise earls were attached to shires.

12. MP, *CM* v, 86.

13. On this formula and its implications, see Crouch, *Image of Aristocracy*, 13–14, 67–8; *idem, Birth of Nobility*, 71–6; G. Koziol, *Begging Pardon and Favor: Ritual and Political Order in Early Medieval France* (Ithaca, 1992), 258–67.

14. Cartulary of Durford, BL, ms Cotton Vespasian, E xxiii, fo. 26v: *Willelmus dei gratia comes Sussex tertius; Les chartes de St-Bertin*, ed. D. Haigneré (4 vols, St-Omer, 1886–90), i, 144, 160.

15. *Le Grand Cartulaire de Conches et sa copie*, 227.

16. *Rouleaux des morts du ixe au xve siècle*, ed. L. Delisle (Paris, 1866), 288.

17. On profession generally, see G. Constable, 'The Ceremonies and Symbolism of Entering Religious Life and Taking the Monastic Habit, from the Fourth to the Twelfth Century', in *idem, Segni e riti nella chiesa altomedioevale occidentale* (Spoleto, 1987), 771–834. For comparison, see Stephen de Rouen's lament for Count Waleran II of Meulan, who also ended his days in Préaux, *Chronicles of the Reigns of Stephen, Henry II and Richard I* ii, ed. Richard Howlett (Rolls Series, 1885), 768, line 71: 'once a count, now a monk, once rich, now an empty-handed pauper.' But Stephen also goes on to lament him thus: 'Waleran, *adorned with the great dignity of a count*, rests with the monks, as the beam of star, so may he shine bright in the world' (p. 770, lines 121–2), my italics.

18. Simeon of Durham, *Historia Regum*, in *Opera Omnia*, ed. T. Arnold (2 vols, Rolls Series, 1882–5), ii, 199 (talking of the deprivation of Earl Gospatric of Northumbria by King William); OV v, 246–8 (referring to the deprivation of Count Elias of Maine).

19. For the three tracts, see *De Obsessione Dunelmi*, in *Opera Omnia* i, 215–20; *Historia Regum*, in *Opera Omnia* ii, 196–200; *De Northymbrorum comitibus*, in *Opera Omnia* ii, 382–4.

20. See the sketch in K.S.B. Keats-Rohan, 'The Bretons and Normans of England, 1066–1154', *Nottingham Medieval Studies*, xxxvi (1992), 46–9.

21. J.A. Everard, 'The Foundation of an Alien Priory at Linton, Cambridgeshire', *Proceedings of the Cambridge Antiquarian Society*, lxxxvi (1997), 173. For a redating of the death of Alan Rufus to 1093, see R. Sharpe, 'King Harold's Daughter', *HSJ*, 19 (2007), 7–10. Later tradition asserted that the Conqueror had granted the earldom in Yorkshire of Edwin to Count Alan Rufus in 1070, and later earls forged a charter to prove it: see Cartulary of the Honor of Richmond, BL, ms Cotton Faustina, B vii, fo. 72v. Alan had acquired his principal Yorkshire estate centres of Gilling and Catterick (North Riding, Yorkshire) from Edwin before 1086: *Domesday Book* i, fos 309a, 310c; and on this see P. Dalton, *Conquest, Anarchy and Lordship: Yorkshire 1066–1154* (Cambridge, 1994), 73–4. But there were numerous other contributors to his honor, including Edwin's brother, Earl Morcar.

22. The entity of 'Richmondshire' like many other such 'shires' in the North of England had no standing at the exchequer and no royal sheriff. It was simply a discrete estate block with a court under private control.

23. *Regesta* iii, nos 204, 949. For the date of his father's death and his succession, wrongly given as 1137 by the *Complete Peerage*, see *Early Yorkshire Charters* iv, 87. As well as being *comes Bretanni et Cornub' et Richemontis* in the 1140 Bodmin charter, Alan is *comes Britannie et Richemont'* in a charter of 1144 x 46 to Alexander, bishop of Lincoln: *Registrum Antiquissimum of the Cathedral Church of Lincoln* ii, 6.

24. Count Brian held land in England at some time in the late 1060s, but clearly did not stay long in the country: see generally M. Jones, 'Notes sur quelques familles bretonnes en Angleterre après la conquête normande', *Mémoires de la Société d'Histoire et d'Archéologie de Bretagne*, 58 (1981), 73–97. For Brian and Cornwall, see Keats-Rohan, 'Bretons and Normans', 48; *eadem*, 'William I and the Breton Contingent in the Non-Norman Conquest, 1060–1087', *ANS*, xiii, ed. M Chibnall (Woodbridge, 1991), 160–1. See also J.E. Powell and K. Wallis, *The House of Lords in the Middle Ages* (London, 1968), 28.

25. *The Cartulary of St Michael's Mount*, 6.

26. Cartulary of Nostell priory, BL, ms Cotton Vespasian E xix, fo. 110r, 'de tertio denario qui pertinet ad comitatum meum'. For the third penny, see pioneering studies in J.H. Round, *Geoffrey de Mandeville* (London, 1892), 287–96; *Complete Peerage* iv, 658–9; G. Ellis, *Earldoms in Fee* (London, 1963), 80–4. The earliest mention of the 'third penny of pleas' as a Norman earl's prerogative comes in charters of creation dating to 1141, though it has to be older: *Regesta* iii, nos 274, 393, 634; the earl of Gloucester received something comparable from Gloucestershire in 1130, *Pipe Roll of 31 Henry I*, 77 (*et comiti Gloec' .xx. li. numero. pro parte sua comitatus*). Round saw the third penny as attached as revenue to a particular comital manor as far back as Domesday Book. S. Baxter, *The Earls of Mercia: Lordship and Power in Late Anglo-Saxon England* (Oxford, 2007), 89–97, successfully argues for it on the evidence of Cheshire as established in pre-Conquest society as the normal (if not universal) expectation of an earl. Williams, *The World before Domesday*, 22–3, interprets the Domesday evidence more freely.

27. For the third penny in Henry II's charters of creation, see N. Vincent, 'Did Henry II Have a Policy towards the Earls?', in *War, Government and Aristocracy in the British Isles, c.1150–1500: Essays in Honour of Michael Prestwich*, eds C. Given-Wilson, A. Kettle and L. Scales (Woodbridge, 2008), 3–4. It long features in subsequent creations of earls. Hence, at Christmas 1239, Simon de Montfort was granted the third penny 'just as Simon de Montfort his father, once earl of Leicester, used to receive the said third penny in his day': TNA, E159/17, m. 6.

28. For Robert III of Leicester, see *Pipe Roll of 27 Henry II*, 79. Note Earl Roger Bigod II's anxiety *c*.1218 to get the twenty-five marks he was owed from Norfolk so as to help pay off the ransom of 800 marks for his son Sir Ralph Bigod of Settrington (died 1253): TNA, SC1/1/60. For Ralph, see M. Morris, *The Bigod Earls of Norfolk in the Thirteenth Century* (Woodbridge, 2005), 205–6. A writ from the barons of the exchequer, 28 January 1242, orders the sheriff of Warwickshire and Leicestershire to refrain from distraining Earl Thomas of Warwick to reclaim £10 which the earl had a right to receive annually 'for the third penny of the earl of Warwick': TNA, E159/20, m. 8d. In December 1274, King Edward I was negotiating terms for the payment to Earl Robert II de Vere of the twenty marks 'for the third penny of the county of Oxford which [Robert's] predecessors have been accustomed to receive of old as earls (*sub nomine comitum*)': Cartulary of the Vere earls of Oxford, Bodl. Libr., ms Rawlinson B 248, fo. 6r.

29. For Earl Arnulf, see V. Chandler, 'The Last of the Montgomerys: Roger the Poitevin and Arnulf', *Historical Research*, lxii (1989), 1–14. For his comital status after 1102, see Eadmer, *Life of St Anselm*, ed. R.W. Southern (Oxford 1962), 146, 153–4; *Chronica monasterii de Hida iuxta Wintoniam*, in *Liber monasterii de Hyda*, ed. E. Edwards (Rolls Series, 1866), 306.

30. *Cartulary of Worcester Cathedral Priory*, ed. R.R. Darlington (Pipe Roll Society, 1968), 134.

31. For the fate of Pembroke and Earl Richard after 1154, see M.T. Flanagan, 'Strongbow, Henry II and Anglo-Norman Intervention in Ireland', in *War and Government in the Middle Ages: Essays in Honour of J.O. Prestwich* eds J. Gillingham and J.C. Holt (Cambridge, 1984), 62–77, for Aoife's styles, 70–1.

32. Crouch, *Image of Aristocracy*, 64–5. For Simon's various styles, see BL, Additional Charter 47630 (*Comes Simon nepos Roberti comitis Legrec'*): here *nepos* might be translated as 'grandson' or 'nephew' since Robert II of Leicester was his mother's father, and Robert III of Leicester was his uncle; Cartulary of St Andrew Northampton, BL, ms Royal 11 B ix, fo. 10r (*Comes Simon*); Cartulary of Bardney, BL, ms Cotton Vespasian, E xx, fos 63v–64r, 73v (*Comes Simon filius Simonis comitis Norhamton'*).

33. For the Marshal and his title, see Crouch, *Image of Aristocracy*, 69–70.

34. Bodl. Libr., ms Dugdale 17, p. 71.

35. Cartulary of Launceston Priory, Lambeth Palace Library ms 719, fo. 199r–v: *Henricus filius comitis Raginaldi comes Cornubie.*

36. He is *dominus de Penbrok* in his own acts as late as 2 August 1284, *Eynsham Cartulary*, ed. H.E. Salter (2 vols, Oxford Historical Society, xlix, li, 1907–8), i, 367–8; March 1285, Bodl. Libr., ms Dodsworth 30, fo. 115r; and 27 August 1285, *Calendar of Ancient Correspondence concerning Wales*, cal. J.G. Edwards (Cardiff, 1935), 132–3. However, in a receipt dated 1283, his Pembrokeshire tenant Nicholas of Carew calls William 'earl': BL, ms Stowe 666, fo. 6r. In 1288–9, in a letter to the earl of Cornwall, his nephew, *Calendar of Ancient Correspondence concerning Wales*, 170, William calls himself 'earl', and in April 1295 he is 'earl', ibid., 153, in his correspondence with the royal chancery. On 31 January 1289, a cirograph of a fine calls him 'earl', TNA, E40/1438. Finally, an act of King Edward himself, dated 21 October 1292, refers to William as 'our beloved and faithful uncle, William de Valence, earl of Pembroke', TNA, E40/15195.

37. Famously, K.B. McFarlane, 'Had Edward I a "Policy" towards the Earls?', in *The Nobility of Later Medieval England* (Oxford, 1973), 248–67, who was in fact arguing against the idea of Edward I's preference for the 'murder' of earldoms proposed in T.F. Tout, 'The Earldoms under Edward I', *TRHS*, new ser., viii (1894), 129–55. For McFarlane, Edward I's abiding concern was to aggrandise his close relatives, and other people's earldoms were prizes to award them.

38. R.H.C. Davis, *King Stephen* (3rd edn, London, 1990), 125–41; G.J. White, 'Earls and Earldoms during King Stephen's Reign', in *War and Society in Medieval and Early Modern Britain*, ed. D. Dunn (Liverpool, 2000), 76–95; D. Crouch, *The Reign of King Stephen, 1135–1154* (London, 2000), 85–90.

39. Vincent, 'Did Henry II Have a Policy towards the Earls?', 8–13, prefigured by White, 'Earls and Earldoms during King Stephen's Reign', 89–91.

40. G.J. White, *Restoration and Reform, 1153–1165: Recovery from Civil War in England* (Cambridge, 2000), 88–91.

41. Ralph de Diceto, *Ymagines Historiarum*, in *Opera Historica*, ed. W. Stubbs (2 vols, Rolls Series, 1876). ii, 3.

42. Crouch, *Image of Aristocracy*, 73–4, 190–5.

43. *Regesta* iii, no. 437.

44. *Facsimiles of the National Manuscripts of Scotland*, ed. H. James (3 vols, London, 1869–71), i, no. 50.

45. Thus Earl Hugh de Lacy of Ulster in 1209 × 10, ending a charter 'Apud Dublin, octauo die martis. comitatus nostri. anno quinto', Cartulary of St Thomas, Dublin, Bodl. Libr., ms Rawlinson B 500, fo. 8v.

46. Aymer de Valence, earl of Pembroke after 1296, possessed a gold crown, according to the inventory of his chattels compiled after his death in 1324: J. Selden, *Titles of Honor* (2nd edn, London, 1631), 680. For a discussion of the diffusion of the coronet amongst non-royal princes, dukes and counts, see Crouch, *Image of Aristocracy*, 198–211. See for the association of crown and *seignorie, The Song of Songs: A Twelfth-Century Version*, ed. C.E. Pickford (Oxford, 1974), p. 48, lines 1699–1700.

47. Ralph Niger, *De re militari et triplici via peregrinationis Ierosolimitane*, ed. L. Schmugge (Berlin, 1977), 130, 'de virga habet imperium . . .'. See also Crouch, *Image of Aristocracy*, 211–14.

48. Note the phrase 'cingulum militiae comites gestare decet', *De diversis ordinibus hominum*, in *The Latin Poems Commonly Attributed to Walter Mapes*, ed. T. Wright (Camden Society, 1841), p. 232, line 97, an English poem of 1220 × 40.

49. For the French word generally, see Crouch, *Image of Aristocracy*, 107. For *baruns chevaliers*, see *Jordan Fantosme's Chronicle*, ed. and trans. R.C. Johnston (Oxford, 1981), 38.

50. *Estoire des Engleis*, lines 3671–2. For *chasez* (Lat. *casati*), see O. Guillotjeannin, *Episcopus et Comes* (Geneva, 1987), 96–100.

51. *Sir Christopher Hatton's Book of Seals*, 102.

52. *The Cartulary of St Augustine's Abbey, Bristol*, ed. D. Walker (Gloucestershire Record Series, 10, 1998), 43. For Sandwich, see D.M. Stenton, *English Justice between the Norman Conquest and the Great Charter, 1066–1215* (London, 1965), 116–22. For the *barones* of the Cinque Ports in 1257, see the Cartulary of the see of Canterbury, Lambeth Palace Library ms 1212, fos 42v, 43r.

53. *The Cartulary of Shrewsbury Abbey*, ed. U. Rees (2 vols, Aberystwyth, 1975), ii, 318–19. The *Leges Henrici Primi*, ed. L.J. Downer (Cambridge, 1972), *c.* 29.1, refers likewise to *barones comitatus*.

54. *Ibid., c.* 7.7. For Stenton's model, see *First Century*, 84–97, and for a critique, Crouch, *Image of Aristocracy*, 112–13. Curiously, this general sense of 'baron' simply as a local leader, introduced into Scotland, persisted there, while it narrowed in England to mean a magnate: see A. Grant, 'Franchises North of the Border: Baronies and Regalities in Medieval Scotland', in *Liberties and Identities in the Medieval British Isles*, ed. M. Prestwich (Woodbridge, 2008), 191.

55. *Le Roman de Toute Chevalerie*, ed. B. Foster (2 vols, Anglo-Norman Text Society, 1976–7), i, lines 46–7, 446, 451, 1744.

56. William fitz Stephen, 'A Description of the Most Noble City of London', trans. H.E. Butler, in F.M. Stenton, *Norman London: An Essay* (London, 1934), 27; *Histoire des ducs*, 118; MP, *CM* v, 22.

57. *Book of Fees* i, 144.

58. Developments summarised from S. Painter, *Studies in the History of the English Feudal Barony* (Baltimore, 1943), 59–63; Crouch, *Image of Aristocracy*, 22.

59. MP, *CM* v, 617. The king also recalled for Matthew the names of the electors of the Empire and eleven of the canonised kings of the English.

60. For the individual summons to royal councils, see G.B. Adams, *Councils and Courts in Anglo-Norman England* (repr. New York, 1965), 39, 110–11, 117. It is first evident in sources from the 1140s, notably *Gesta Stephani*, eds and trans. K.R. Potter and R.H.C. Davis (Oxford, 1976), 22, 24; *Letters and Charters of Gilbert Foliot*, eds A. Morey and C.N.L. Brooke (Cambridge, 1967), 63. For Pommeraye's oath, see *Curia Regis Rolls* vii, 170.

61. *Rolls of the Justices in Eyre for Yorkshire in 3 Henry III* (1218–19), ed. and trans. D.M Stenton (Selden Society, lvi, 1937), 424–5; for the Thornton family, see *Early Yorkshire Charters* v, 17–26. For some discussion of this incident, see F. Lachaud, 'Liveries of Robes in England, *c.*1200–*c.*1330', *EHR*, 111 (1996), 282–3.

62. *Foedera* i, pt 1, 65.

63. As in the early formulary in Bodl. Libr., ms Fairfax 27, fos 1r–6v, a product of the 1230s, which features letters *comes comiti, comes baroni, baro comiti, baro baroni, miles militi* and *vicecomes militibus et libere tenentibus sui comitatus*. A French formulary of a decade before this also perceives noble society as hierarchically arranged, in the degrees of *comes, baro, miles* and, intriguingly, *serviens*, the last status level being noble, as a sample letter shows such a man negotiating release from captivity, and we might identify this *serviens* as a synonym for squire: see L. Delisle, *Notice sur une* Summa Dictaminis *jadis conservée à Beauvais* (Paris, 1898).

64. Bodl. Libr. ms Fairfax 27, fo. 1r.

65. Key works here are G. Duby, 'Situation de la noblesse en France au début de xiiie siècle', *Tijdschrift voor Geschiedenis*, 82 (1969), 309–15, trans. by C. Postan as 'The Transformation of the Aristocracy', in *The Chivalrous Society* (London, 1977), 178–85; J. Flori, *L'Essor de Chevalerie, xie-xiie siècles* (Geneva, 1986); and see also, particularly on this view, *idem, Chevaliers et chevalerie au moyen âge* (Paris, 1998), 64–85.

66. Andrew the Chaplain, *Tractatum Amoris*, ed. and trans. P.G. Walsh (London, 1982), 78.

67. D. Crouch, 'Courtliness and Chivalry: Colliding Constructs', in *Soldiers, Nobles and Gentlemen: Essays in Honour of Maurice Keen*, eds P.R. Coss and C. Tyerman (Woodbridge, 2009), 44–7.

68. *The Red Book of the Exchequer*, ed. H. Hall (3 vols, Rolls Series, 1896), i, 200–1. It was 'before monks, clerks, laypeople *et militibus meis*' that Earl Simon III of Northampton took an oath on the gospels: Cartulary of St Andrew, Northampton, BL, ms Royal 11 B, ix, fo. 9v.

69. Cartulary of St Mary York, BL, ms Lansdowne 402, fo. 107v; Worcestershire Record Office, Lechmere Deeds, 1531/1/72/2; *Shrewsbury Cartulary* i, 17. For other such examples before 1200, see BL, Additional charter 47573 (charter of Robert IV, earl of Leicester); *Monasticon Anglicanum* iv, 492, where the knights are called *domini ... milites* (charter of Roger of Sandford); *Cartularium Monasterii de Rameseia*, eds W.H. Hart and P.A. Lyons (3 vols, Rolls Series, 1884–93), i, 256–7 (time of Abbot William, 1161–77).

70. *Basset Charters c.1120 to 1250*, ed. W.T. Reedy (Pipe Roll Society, lxxxviii, 1995), 21–2.

71. 'ex illustri satis ordine militari duxit originem', William of Wycombe, *Speculum vitae viri venerabilis Rotberti episcopi Herefordiae*, in H. Wharton, *Anglia Sacra* (2 vols, London, 1691), ii, 299.

72. *Dialogus de Scaccario*, ed. and trans. E. Amt (Oxford, 2007), 176 (my translation).

73. *Roman de Rou* i pt 2, line 2888.

74. For the concept of 'habitus' as a body of accepted, if unstated, social norms, see Crouch, *Birth of Nobility*, 52–6.

75. *The Chronicle of Battle Abbey*, ed. and trans. E. Searle (Oxford, 1980), 214. For commentary, see Crouch, *Image of Aristocracy*, 138–9, 242–4.

76. *De re militari*, ed. Schmugge, 140. Note the comment of Wace, *c.*1170, that the barons at Hastings were distinguished by their gonfanons, the common knights by penons: *Roman de Rou* ii, pt 3, lines 6504–6. For comment, see M. Bennett, 'Wace and Warfare', *ANS*, ed. R.A. Brown, xi (Woodbridge, 1988), 46.

77. *Oeuvres de Rigord et de Guillaume le Breton*, ed. F. Delaborde (2 vols, Société de l'Histoire de France, Paris, 1882–5), i, 290.

78. In general see Crouch, *Image of Aristocracy*, 114–17.

79. This elision appears in the early fourteenth century: *Dictionary of Medieval Latin from British Sources, s.v. baronettus.*

80. See *Close Rolls, 1259–61*, 315, for one of the earliest examples. See additionally for the banneret's later dimension, N. Saul, *Knights and Esquires: The Gloucestershire Gentry in the Fourteenth Century* (Oxford, 1981), 7–10; D. Simpkin, *The English Aristocracy at War: From the Welsh Wars of Edward I to the Battle of Bannockburn* (Woodbridge, 2008), 60–7.

81. His 'esperons' are regarded as the particular sign of a knight by Stephen de Fougères in the late 1150s or early 1160s: *LM*, lines 625–8. William of Orange's 'esperons d'or mier' were a feature of his knightly equipment *c.*1130: *Le Couronnement de Louis*, ed. E. Langlois (Classiques Français du Moyen Age), line 2143.

82. D. Crouch, 'William Marshal and the Mercenariat', in *Mercenaries and Paid Men: The Mercenary Identity in the Middle Ages*, ed. J. France (Woodbridge, 2008), 15–32.

83. *Chronica Majora* v, 367.

84. *Le Livre des manières*, ed. R.A. Lodge (Geneva, 1979), 88–91.

85. *Le Conte de Graal*, ed. F. Lecoy (2 vols, Classiques Français du moyen age, 1972–5), i, lines 5024–58.

86. J.H. Round, 'Gervase of Cornhill', in *Geoffrey de Mandeville*, 304–12.

87. For a study of such upward mobility, see Crouch, *Birth of Nobility*, 213–21.

88. *De diversis ordinibus hominum*, 229–36.
89. On this see M. Bennett, 'The Status of the Squire: The Northern Evidence', in *The Ideals and Practice of Medieval Knighthood* i, eds C. Harper-Bill and R. Harvey (Woodbridge, 1986), 1–11.
90. B. O'Brien, *God's Peace and King's Peace: The Laws of Edward the Confessor* (Philadelphia, 1999), p. 180, ch.2. 1; *Regesta* ii, no. 1364.
91. *Charters of the Earls of Chester*, no. 147; Bodl. Libr., ms Ashmole 833, fo. 248v. For a later definition of the fee of a squire as equal to half a knight's fee, see Saul, *Knights and Esquires*, 16.
92. Cartulary of Kenilworth Priory, BL, ms Harley 3650, fo. 19r.
93. TNA E164/1, p. 478; Bodl. Libr., ms Dugdale 13, pp. 521–2. For salaried 'squires of the household' in the imaginary household of an earl of Oxford in the 1230s, see Philip de Remy, *Jehan et Blonde*, ed. S. Lécuyer (Classiques Français du Moyen Age, 1984), lines 148–9.
94. *HWM* i, lines 772–3; for a discussion, see ibid. iii, p. 61.
95. *Facetus*, pp. 225–6, lines 69–72, and comments, in N. Orme, *From Childhood to Chivalry: The Education of the English Kings and Aristocracy, 1066–1530* (London, 1984), 136–7.
96. *Chanson d'Aspremont* ii, lines 7255–73; O'Brien, *God's Peace and King's Peace*, p. 196, c. 35.1c.
97. J. De Cauna, *L'Ensenhamen ou code du parfait chevalier* (Mounenh en Biarn, 2007), pp. 64, 82, lines 11, 371–88.
98. For the initial diagnosis of the development, see P. Guilhiermoz, *Essai sur la noblesse du moyen âge* (Paris, 1902), 485, refined as to chronology in P. Contamine, 'Points du vue sur la chevalerie en France à la fin du moyen âge', *Francia*, 4 (1976), 255–8; Crouch, *Image of Aristocracy*, 169. For case studies quoted, see D. Barthélemy, *Les Deux Ages de la seigneurie banale: Coucy (xie-xiiie siècle)* (Paris, 1984), 201–2; T. Evergates, *The Aristocracy in the County of Champagne, 1100–1300* (Philadelphia, 2007), 52–3.
99. Crouch, *Image of Aristocracy*, 169 and n.
100. *Les Quatre Ages de l'homme*, ed. M. de Fréville (Paris, 1888), pp. 38–9, c. 66 (emphasis added).
101. P. Adam-Even, 'Les sceaux d'écuyers au xiiie siècle', *Archives héraldiques suisses*, 66 (1951), 19–23.
102. For the prohibition on squires carrying any heraldry other than their lord's, see *Statuta Armorum*, BL, Harley ms 69, fo. 17r. For the uptake of heraldry by non-knights in England, see P.R. Coss, 'Knights, Squires and the Origins of Social Gradation', *TRHS*, 6th ser., 5 (1995), 173–7.
103. C. Dyer, *Standards of Living in the Later Middle Ages: Social Change in England, c.1200–1520* (Cambridge, 1989), 38–41, summarises this view.
104. *Walter of Henley and Other Treatises on Estate Management and Accounting*, ed. and trans. D.M. Oschinsky (Oxford, 1971), 402.
105. *HWM* i, lines 767–8.
106. A. Långfors, 'Le *dit des hérauts* par Henri de Laon', *Romania*, 43 (1914), 224.
107. *Calendar of Patent Rolls, 1232–47*, 84.
108. P.R. Coss, *The Origins of the English Gentry* (Cambridge, 2003), 217 and n, points out that a Northamptonshire sheriff's return of 1297 lists forty-one *armigeri* after the *milites* of the shire amongst those whose income exceeded £20, though (p. 218) he doubts whether this was sufficient to define squires as a social group.
109. F. Lachaud, 'La "Formation de la *Gentry*", xie–xive siècle: un nouveau concept historiographique?', in *Histoires de'Outre-Manche: tendances récentes de l'historiographie britannique*, eds F. Lachaud, I. Lescent-Giles and F-J. Ruggiu (Paris, 2001), 15–16. For the historiographical background to this usage, see Crouch, *Birth of Nobility*, 183. Note the observation of John Gillingham on the lack of a gentry construct generally in European social history: 'Thegns and Knights in Eleventh-Century England: Who Was Then the Gentleman?', *TRHS*, 6th ser., 5 (1995), 131 and n.
110. C. Richmond, 'The Rise of the English Gentry, 1150–1350', *The Historian*, 26 (1990), 14–17, who talks of the 'proto-gentry' before 1300; J. Scammell, 'The Formation of the English Social Structure: Freedom, Knights and Gentry, 1066–1300', *Speculum*, 68 (1993), 601–18, defines the gentry as being local knights, despite the title of the article.

Likewise, K.S. Naughton, *The Gentry of Bedfordshire in the Thirteenth and Fourteenth Centuries* (Leicester, 1976) is entirely about Bedfordshire knights. J. Gillingham, 'Thegns and Knights', 144, goes further, concluding that a common military culture 'allows us to see the "lesser nobility" as a gentry' from the tenth to the thirteenth century. But see a dissenting view in H.M. Thomas, *Vassals, Heiresses, Crusaders and Thugs: The Gentry of Angevin Yorkshire, 1154–1216* (Philadelphia, 1993), 4–13, which offers an equally contestable categorisation based on subtenancy in a supposed feudal hierarchy.

111. Of the twenty-nine lay *domini* given for thirty-one manors in Stoneleigh hundred in Warwickshire in 1279–80, two were women, and at least five (Silvester of Hunningham, John of Wileby, Robert Masse, Roger Gopil and John Benet), though visible in other sources, do not appear as knights in the shire: *The Warwickshire Hundred Rolls of 1279–80: Stoneleigh and Kineton Hundreds*, ed. T. John (British Academy Records of Social and Economic History, new ser., xix, 1992), 25–165, passim. Of the others named in 1279–80, John Peche and William de Semilly had respites from being knighted in 1256: see P.R. Coss, *Lordship, Knighthood and Locality: A Study in English Society, c.1180–c.1280* (Cambridge, 1991), 258–63, for lists of Warwickshire knightly families.

112. P.R. Coss, *Lordship, Knighthood and Locality*, especially ch. 5. Anne Polden's work on Buckinghamshire offers numerous points of comparison with Coss, and eschews the identification of gentry with knights: see 'A Crisis of the Knightly Class? Inheritance and Office among the Gentry of Thirteenth-Century Buckinghamshire', in *Regionalism and Revisionism: The Crown and its Provinces in England, 1200–1650*, eds P. Fleming, A. Gross and J.E. Lander (London, 1998), 29–57; 'The Social Networks of the Buckinghamshire Gentry in the Thirteenth Century', *JMH*, 32 (2006), 371–94.

113. For the relatively more hierarchical social structure of a local society around 1400, with some broader comparison, see C. Carpenter, *Locality and Polity: A Study in Warwickshire Landed Society, 1401–1499* (Cambridge, 1992), 35–95.

114. Coss, *Origins of the English Gentry*, 2–3.

115. It is worth noting here the example of the English boy Orm of Howden, who in the 1120s played with the daughter of his Yorkshire neighbour, Stephen the knight: 'the Vision of Orm', ed. H. Farmer, in *Analecta Bollandiana*, 75 (1957), 79.

116. *Roman de Rou* i, pt 2, lines 758–9.

117. *Curia Regis Rolls* xii, nos 2142, 2312; J.R. Maddicott, 'Magna Carta and the Local Community, 1215–1259', *PP*, no. 102 (1984), 33–4.

118. BL, ms Additional 8167, fo. 106r.

CHAPTER FOUR: THE RISE OF CONCILIARISM

1. E.A. Freeman's discourse of the 'constitution' of the Norman 'parliament' in 1066 is only one of the more obviously lunatic results of the constitutionalist perspective on medieval history: *The History of the Norman Conquest of England* (5 vols, Oxford, 1870–9), iii, 289–90.

2. *Regesta: William I*, 210, 442. This mechanism is equally evident in William's acts as duke of Normandy, where he notes in 1050, for instance, that it is by the 'intercession of our sworn men (*fidelium*)' that he has confirmed the grants to the abbey of St-Evroult: *Recueil des actes des ducs de Normandie de 911 à 1066*, ed. M. Fauroux (Caen, 1961), 289.

3. William of Poitiers, *Gesta Guillelmi*, eds and trans. R.H.C. Davis and M. Chibnall (Oxford, 1998), 100–2. The later and expanded accounts of this council (supposedly held at Lillebonne) by William of Malmesbury and Orderic Vitalis can have very little value as historical evidence, being written over half a century after the event.

4. William's figure of 200 senators, inaccurate for the later republic (when it totalled 900 members), was Livy's figure for the Senate at the time of King Lucius: *Ab Urbe Condita*, Bk 1, *c.* 58. Livy is not mentioned in the list of *fontes* for direct Classical quotations in the 1998 edition of the *Gesta Guillelmi*.

5. The memorandum of the mid-1070s which records the members of the Norman aristocracy who contributed ships and knights to the expedition includes almost every count and major baron of the duchy, which indicates compliance to the council's decision: E.M.C. van Houts, 'The Ship List of William the Conqueror', in *ANS*, x (1987), ed. R.A. Brown (Woodbridge, 1988), 176. But, despite being a contributor of sixty ships and his son Robert being at Hastings, the great baron Roger de Beaumont was apparently given or accepted few lands in England after the Conquest, which tallies with William of Malmesbury's comment (made over thirty years after his death) that Roger 'refused many invitations from William I to come to England and receive as much land as he wanted in return, saying that he would rather look to the inheritance of his fathers than go soliciting or snatching possessions overseas to which he had no claim': WM, *GRA* i, 736.

6. See the reasoned account in C.W. Hollister, *Henry I* (New Haven, 2001), 102–9, which deals effectively with some of the theories that have gathered round the events following Rufus's death.

7. I have employed the text as edited in F. Liebermann, 'The Text of Henry I's Coronation Charter', *TRHS*, new ser., 8 (1894), 21–48; see also J.C. Holt, *Magna Carta* (2nd edn, Cambridge, 1992), 418–28. G. Garnett, *Conquered England: Kingship, Succession and Tenure 1066–1166* (Oxford, 2007), 105–20, stresses the speed with which the 'edict', as he calls it, was drawn up, but sees it as a document attempting to consolidate a mythical view of tenure, rather than an adroit political appeal to a dissatisfied aristocratic constituency.

8. P. Stafford, 'The Laws of Cnut and the History of Anglo-Saxon Promises', in *Anglo-Saxon England*, 10, eds P. Clemoes et al. (Cambridge, 1982), 173–90, suggests parallels between Henry I's charter and the promises of Cnut on his accession, as summed up in the code called II Cnut, which does in fact touch on succession dues (heriot), marriageability and unrestrained royal exactions, but amongst a wealth of other concerns: the text amounts to eighty-four chapters in Liebermann's edition, *Die Gesetze de Angelsachsen* (3 vols, Halle, 1903–16), i, 308–71. Though Henry's charter was certainly extant in legal circles in 1100, the parallels with II Cnut are perhaps more of a testament to the relentless unoriginality of rapacious royal officials than to an aristocratic agenda of protest spanning the Conquest in a teleological trajectory towards Magna Carta, as Stafford goes so far as to propose (p. 190). Stafford's view is adopted, though with some modification, in J.A. Green, ' "A Lasting Memorial": The Charter of Liberties of Henry I', in *Charters and Charter Scholarship in Britain and Ireland*, eds J.A. Green and M.T. Flanagan (Basingstoke, 2005), 55–62.

9. JW iii, 94.

10. For the basic sorting of the provenance of the several remaining versions, see F. Liebermann, 'The Text of Henry I's Coronation Charter', 21–48. I have much profited here from the advice and expertise of Professor Richard Sharpe.

11. Eadmer, *Vita sancti Anselmi*, ed. and trans. R.W. Southern (repr. Oxford, 1972), 126. Henry I's letter to Anselm says, however, that he 'was elected by the clergy and *people* of England', in a common canonical formula: *Sancti Anselmi Omnia Opera*, ed. F.S. Schmitt, iii–v (Edinburgh, 1946–51), no. 212.

12. J.G. Hudson, 'Henry I and Counsel', in *The Medieval State: Essays Presented to James Campbell*, eds J.R. Maddicott and D.M. Palliser (London, 2000), 116, points out that c. 10 alone of the coronation charter, which retains the forest as a royal prerogative, is keen to state that it is done 'with the common consent of my barons'.

13. *ASC s.a.* 1101; John of Worcester, *Chronicle*, eds R.R. Darlington and P. McGurk, ii (Oxford, 1995), iii (Oxford, 1998) ii, 98.

14. Significant studies are in C.W. Hollister, 'Magnates and "Curiales" in Early Norman England', *Viator*, 4 (1973), 115–22; *idem, Henry I*, ch. 8.

15. *The History of the Church of York, 1066–1127*, ed. and trans. C. Johnson (London, 1961), 37.

16. For this troublesome sector of the Anglo-Norman aristocracy, see D. Crouch, 'Normans and Anglo-Normans: A Divided Aristocracy', in *England and Normandy in the Middle Ages*, eds D. Bates and A. Curry (London, 1994), 59–61.

17. C.W. Hollister, 'The Taming of a Turbulent Earl: Henry I and William of Warenne', in *Monarchy Magnates and Institutions in the Anglo-Norman World* (London, 1986), 137–44.

18. 'He had a register (*scriptos*) of all the earls and barons of his realm, appointed for them ... certain presents with which he honoured them': *De Nugis Curialium*, 470. Map refers elsewhere to the customs of Henry I's court, called the *Constitutio Domus Regis*, as a different document to the *scripti* mentioned here: ibid, 438.

19. G.B. Adams, *Councils and Courts in Anglo-Norman England* (repr. New York, 1965), 39, 110–11, 117; D. Crouch, *The Reign of King Stephen, 1135–1154* (Harlow, 2000), 39n.

20. Though note that Orderic Vitalis – writing in his reign – implies that Henry tried to accommodate all the *optimates* of his kingdom into his rule: OV v, 296.

21. A point made in Hudson, 'Henry I and Counsel', 119 and n. See *Regesta* ii, no. 959; B. O'Brien, *God's Peace and King's Peace: The Laws of Edward the Confessor* (Philadelphia, 1999), 168.

22. See, most recently, E. King, 'Stephen of Blois, Count of Mortain and Boulogne', *EHR* 115 (2000), 288–90; J.A. Green, *Henry I: King of England and Duke of Normandy* (Cambridge, 2006), 193–5.

23. J.E.A. Jolliffe, *Angevin Kingship* (2nd edn, London, 1963), 170. Jolliffe did not see it as a reality until nearly a century after these events.

24. Crouch, *Reign of King Stephen*, 30–49.

25. *Regesta* iii, no. 270. The concession is to 'baronibus et hominibus meis de Anglia'.

26. See analyses in E. King, 'King Stephen and the Anglo-Norman Aristocracy', *History*, lix (1974), 180–94; K.J. Stringer, *The Reign of Stephen: Kingship, Warfare and Government in Twelfth-Century England* (Routledge, 1993), 49–55; Crouch, *Reign of King Stephen*, 74–83, 155–65.

27. R.H.C. Davis, *King Stephen* (3rd edn, London, 1990), 108–24. The dating of this is refined in Crouch, *Reign of Stephen*, 234–9.

28. D. Crouch, *The Birth of Nobility: Constructing Aristocracy in England and France, 950–1300* (Harlow, 2005), 71–9.

29. *Gesta Stephani*, ed. and trans. K.R. Potter, revised R.H.C. Davis (Oxford, 1976), 238. Note the parallels in the independent comments in RT, 173–4. Robert de Torigny talks of 'certain ecclesiastics' from the king's army acting as secret intermediaries with the 'leading men' (*summates*) of the ducal army in reaching conditions for a mutual withdrawal, and of the anger of Duke Henry when his army withdrew. One should note here also Graeme White's view, drawn from Henry of Huntingdon's account, that the magnates refused battle because an outright victory by either side would have led to forfeitures by the losers: 'The End of Stephen's Reign', *History*, 75 (1990), 9.

30. A view found in E. Amt, *The Accession of Henry II in England: Royal Government Restored, 1149–1159* (Woodbridge, 1993), 16.

31. Crouch, *Reign of Stephen*, 264 and nn, 267.

32. *Regesta* iii, no. 709, where the earl features at Eu as 'qui in hoc et aliis negotiis meis locum meum tenet in Anglia'. Note, however, that the earl had crossed to Normandy with the duke, which hardly indicates he had much to do.

33. F. West, *The Justiciarship in England, 1066–1232* (Cambridge, 1966), 31–53.

34. Crouch, *Beaumont Twins*, 74–6.

35. Gervase of Canterbury i, 160.

36. RT, 186. A dating clause to a charter of Count John of Eu (1140–70), 'at Winchester in the year in which there was a discussion about conquering Ireland', shows how the curial nobility was caught up in the plan and validates Robert's chronicle, for which see M.T. Flanagan, *Irish Society, Anglo-Norman Settlers, Angevin Kingship: Interactions in Ireland in the Late 12th century* (Oxford, 1989), 39–40, 305–6.

37. For the fall of Count William, see P. Dalton, 'William Earl of York and Royal Authority in Yorkshire in the Reign of Stephen', *HSJ*, 2 (1990), 164–5; idem, *Conquest, Anarchy and Lordship: Yorkshire, 1066–1154* (Cambridge, 1994), 156–7. For the date of the king's action, see Gervase of Canterbury, *Opera Historica*, ed. W. Stubbs (2 vols, Rolls Series, 1879–80). i, 161–2.

38. See the reconstruction and re-evaluation of this highly significant incident in D. Crouch, 'The March and the Welsh Kings', in *The Anarchy of King Stephen's Reign*, ed. E. King (Oxford, 1994), 284–6. This disputes the interpretation placed on it in W. Stubbs, *The Constitutional History of England* (3 vols, Oxford, 1880), i, 512, and most subsequent studies; cf. A.L. Poole, *From Domesday Book to Magna Carta, 1087–1216* (2nd edn, Oxford, 1955), 322.

39. Hugh's wilfulness and isolation as a rebel is pointed up by the contemporary account in *The Chronicle of Battle Abbey*, ed. and trans. E. Searle (Oxford, 1980), 158–60. The rebellion was apparently Hugh's protest at the impending loss of his custody of the royal castle of Bridgnorth.

40. Cf. Garnier de Pont-Sainte-Maxence, *La Vie de Saint Thomas le Martyr*, ed. E. Walberg (Paris, 1936), lines 914–15.

41. I follow the reconstruction of events in F. Barlow, *Thomas Becket* (London, 1986), 109–14.

42. Garnier de Pont-Sainte-Maxence, *Vie de Saint Thomas le Martyr*, lines 1542–5. Later, Garnier states that Thomas was informed that some had taken an oath that the archbishop should die (lines 1708–10).

43. Ibid., line 1625.

44. Ibid., lines 1659–60, 1691–2.

45. Ibid., lines 1921–37. William fitz Stephen says that Becket was not quite so dignified as he withdrew into the hall, pausing to refute Earl Hamelin and Ranulf, calling one a bastard and the other a mere footman: *Vita sancti Thome*, in *Materials for the History of Thomas Becket*, ed. J.C. Robertson (7 vols, Rolls Series, 1875–85), i, 39.

46. On this, see Crouch, *Birth of Nobility*, 56–62.

47. *The Correspondence of Thomas Becket, Archbishop of Canterbury, 1162–1170*, ed. and trans. A. Duggan (2 vols, Oxford, 2000), i, 150–4. In fact, Garnier credits Earl Robert with persuading the king to let the archbishop leave freely, as it would be shameful to him should such a noble man be harried from the court in that way: *Vie de Saint Thomas le Martyr*, lines 1966–70.

48. See generally J.C. Holt, 'The Assizes of Henry II: the Texts', in *The Study of Medieval Records*, eds D.A. Bullough and R.L. Storey (Oxford, 1971), 85–106, but also now P. Brand, 'Henry II and the Creation of the English Common Law', in *Henry II: New Interpretations*, eds C. Harper-Bill and N. Vincent (Woodbridge, 2007), 215–32, which highlights the 'lost' legislation which can be reconstructed from a variety of sources. It should be noted that J. Boussard, *Le Gouvernement d'Henri II Plantagenêt* (Paris, 1956), 443, sees the assizes by contrast as the manifestation in England of 'gouvernement autocratique'.

49. Brand, 'Henry II and the Creation of the English Common Law', 229–30.

50. *Glanvill*, 2.

51. Stubbs, *Select Charters*, 164.

52. Ibid., 184.

53. *Glanvill*, 28; Brand, 'Henry II and the Creation of the English Common Law', 230–1.

54. *Chronicle of Battle Abbey*, 13–14, 182. For a later thirteenth-century reprise of this view, put in the mouth of Earl John I of Warenne, see *The Chronicle of Walter of Guisborough*, ed. H. Rothwell (Camden Society, 3rd ser., lxxxix, 1957), 216.

55. For Henry's capacity to hold a grudge and some useful observations on absentees, see N. Vincent, 'The Court of Henry II', in *Henry II: New Interpretations*, eds C. Harper-Bill and N. Vincent (Woodbridge, 2007), 287–8; but see also T.K. Keefe, 'King Henry II and the Earls: The Pipe Roll Evidence', *Albion*, 13 (1981), 196–7; *idem, Feudal Assessments and the Political Community under Henry II and his Sons* (Berkeley, 1983), 105–8, pointing out Henry's concern to use certain earls in administration (notably Salisbury, Arundel, Essex and Hertford), even if they appeared infrequently at court. For Henry's antipathy to Richard fitz Gilbert, see M.T. Flanagan, 'Strongbow, Henry II and the Anglo-Norman Intervention in Ireland', in *War and Government in the Middle Ages*, eds J. Gillingham and J.C. Holt (Woodbridge, 1984), 64–6. For William of Gloucester, see D. Crouch, 'Earl William of Gloucester and the End of the Anarchy', *EHR*, 103 (1988), 69–75.

56. For the separation of itinerant court from regional aristocracies, see M. Aurell, *The Plantagenet Empire, 1154–1224*, trans. D. Crouch (Harlow, 2007), 27–30.

57. Jolliffe, *Angevin Kingship*, 175–6.

58. W.L. Warren, *Henry II* (London, 1973), 309–11; N. Vincent, 'King Henry and the Poitevins', in *La Cour Plantagenêt, 1154–1204*, ed. M. Aurell (Poitiers, 2000), 112–13.

59. Brand, 'Henry II and the Creation of the English Common Law', 232.

60. Stubbs, *Select Charters*, 176.

61. For the 'official' list of rebels, excerpted by Howden, see *Gesta Henrici Secundi*, ed. W. Stubbs (2 vols, Rolls Series, 1867), i, 45.

62. Ralph de Diceto i, *Ymagines Historiarum*, in *Opera Historica*, ed. W. Stubbs (2 vols, Rolls Series, 1876), 371, for which see comments in Warren, *Henry II*, 367–9.

63. Aurell, *The Plantagenet Empire*, 110–11.

64. See the reconstruction in D. Crouch, *William Marshal: Knighthood, War and Chivalry, 1147–1219* (2nd edn, Harlow, 2002), 76–80.

65. *Histoire des ducs*, 105.

66. R. Turner, *Men Raised from the Dust: Administrative Service and Upward Mobility in Angevin England* (Philadelphia, 1988), 71–90.

67. S. Duffy, 'John and Ireland: The Origins of England's Irish Problem', in *King John: New Interpretations*, ed. S.D. Church (Woodbridge, 1999), 238–40; M.T. Flanagan, 'Defining Lordships in Angevin Ireland: William Marshal and the King's Justiciar', in *Les Seigneuries dans l'espace Plantagenêt (c.1150–c.1250)*, eds M. Aurell and F. Boutoulle (Bordeaux, 2009), 41–59.

68. Crouch, *William Marshal*, 101–13.

69. Wendover ii, 48–9.

70. *HWM* ii, lines 13,274–6.

71. *HWM* ii, lines 13,385–406, 14,565–78, 14,334–42.

72. *HWM* ii, lines 13,159–82, quotation from lines 13,171–4.

73. *HWM* ii, lines 13,215–56.

74. For the assassination plot by one H., a chamberlain, see Suger, *Vie de Louis VI le Gros*, ed. and trans. (into French) H. Waquet (Paris, 1929), 190. For the consequences and identification, see now R. Sharpe, 'The Last Years of Herbert the Chamberlain: Weaverthorpe Church and Hall', *Historical Research* 83 (2010), 588–601. For the assassination attempt on Stephen at Bedford, see *English Lawsuits from William I to Richard I*, ed. and trans. R.C. van Caenegem (2 vols, Selden Society, 106–7, 1990–1), i, 289.

75. *Memoriale fratris Walteri de Coventria*, ed. W. Stubbs (2 vols, Rolls Series, 1872–3), ii, 207.

76. N. Vincent, 'Hugh de Neville and his Prisoners', *Archives*, xx (1992), 192–4.

77. J.C. Holt, *The Northerners* (Oxford, 1961), 94–7.

CHAPTER FIVE: THE KING AND THE PEERS

1. See the survey in J.C. Holt, 'The Barons and the Great Charter', *EHR*, 70 (1955), 1–2. F.M. Powicke, *Stephen Langton* (Oxford, 1965), 113–22, does justice to the barons' ability to organise themselves and articulate an agenda, however much they benefited from Langton's sagacity.

2. *De Antiquis Legibus Liber. Chronica Maiorum et Vicecomitum Londoniarum*, ed. T. Stapleton (Camden Society, 1846), 201. For the temporary stigmatism of the emerging baronial opposition as *Norenses* or *Aquilonares* in 1213, see J.C. Holt, *The Northerners* (Oxford, 1961), 8–9.

3. In 1213, Pope Innocent III addressed himself to the whole body of 'earls, barons and other magnates to be found in England': *Selected Letters of Pope Innocent III concerning England*, eds and trans. C.R. Cheney and W.H. Semple (London, 1953), 154. For the 'litterae magnatum Angliae' commissioning their agents in Rome early in 1214, see *Foedera* i, pt 1, 120. See also the inventory of the muniments of the kings of Scotland taken by Edward I's army in Edinburgh in 1291, which contained two letters of the *barones*

Anglie to Alexander II of Scotland, probably late in 1215, 'against King John', a writ in their name directed to the citizens of Carlisle, and a letter to the tenants of Westmorland, Cumberland and Northumberland 'against King John'; *Instrumenta et Acta de munimentis regni Scotie*, in *Acts of the Parliaments of Scotland*, eds T. Thomson and C. Innes (12 vols, Edinburgh, 1814–75), i, 111. My thanks to Dr Hugh Doherty for this reference, and see also Holt, *The Northerners*, 131–3.

4. For instance, John talks in 1214 of the 'barones nobis adversantes': see *Foedera* i, pt 1, 121.
5. Holt, *Magna Carta*, 224–5.
6. BL, ms Harley 458. This agrees with the comment by the contemporary Béthune chronicler that at a *parlement* early in 1215 the barons 'decided to demand of the king that he should maintain the charters that his great-grandfather King Henry gave their ancestors and which King Stephen had confirmed to them, and if he would not they would all defy him and make war on him with all their power': *Histoire des ducs*, 145–6.
7. Holt, *Magna Carta*, 418–28.
8. Ibid., 347–8.
9. *Histoire des ducs*, 150–1, quotation at 51.
10. *Select Charters*, 335–9, 340–51. On the date of the reissue of 1217, see D.A. Carpenter, *The Minority of Henry III* (London, 1990), 60n.
11. See the considered verdict on his standing in the 1240s in N.C. Vincent, *The Holy Blood: King Henry III and the Westminster Blood Relic* (Cambridge, 2001), 188–9.
12. For the *pares* of the seigneurie of Coucy in the Laonnais in 1138 and their identity as the principal *barones* of the lordship, see D. Barthélemy, *Les Deux Ages de la seigneurie banale, Coucy, xie–xiiie siècle* (Paris, 1984), 153–7; for a comparable and contemporary use of the term in the English honor of the abbey of Bury, see F.M. Stenton, *The First Century of English Feudalism, 1066–1166* (2nd edn, Oxford, 1961), 60–1.
13. *Estoire des Engleis*, lines 3701, 3747.
14. *Wace's Roman de Brut: A History of the British. Text and Translation*, ed. and trans. J. Weiss (Exeter, 2002), lines 921–5 (my translation). See also line 10,316. For the 'peers' of the Vermandois region in a late twelfth-century source, see *Raoul de Cambrai*, ed. S. Kay (Oxford, 1992), line 2278.
15. J.P. Poly and E. Bournazel, *The Feudal Transformation, 900–1200*, trans. C. Higgitt (New York, 1991), 201. The ecclesiastical peers held the sees of Reims, Laon, Langres, Châlons, Beauvais and Noyon; the princes were Flanders, Aquitaine, Burgundy, Normandy, Toulouse and Champagne. The study by P. Feuchère, 'Pairs de principauté et pairs de château: essai sur l'institution des pairies en Flandre. Etude géographique et institutionelle', *Revue belge de philologie et d'histoire*, 31 (1953), 973–1002, contains some conceptual and chronological difficulties.
16. Earl William Marshal II appealed to the judgement of his *pares* in his lawsuit over Caerleon with Morgan ap Hywel, *Patent Rolls, 1225–32*, 82, for which suit see D. Crouch, 'The Transformation of Medieval Gwent', in *Gwent County History* ii, *The Age of Marcher Lords, c.1075–1536*, eds R.A. Griffiths, A. Hopkins and R. Howell (Cardiff, 2008), 34–5. For Peter des Roches's comment on Earl Richard Marshal's plea, Wendover iv, 276; MP, *CM* iii, 252. See the discussion of this passage in N. Vincent, *Peter des Roches: An Alien in English Politics, 1205–1238* (Cambridge, 1996), 409.
17. TNA, KB26/141, m. 25d. On this see Crouch, *Image of Aristocracy*, 105, 330.
18. *Documents*, 92.
19. I differ here from the view that the 1290s was the crucial decade, as expressed in J.R. Maddicott, *The Origins of the English Parliament, 924–1327* (Oxford, 2010), 350–1.
20. D. Crouch, 'William Marshal and the Mercenariat', in *Mercenaries and Paid Men: The Mercenary Identity in the Middle Ages*, ed. J. France (Leiden, 2008), 27–30. It might be noted that Richard's captain, Mercadier, was openly admired for his nobility in the early 1200s by the Occitan poet Raimon Vidal de Besalú: *Nouvelles occitanes du moyen âge*, ed. and trans. J.-C. Huchet (Paris, 1992), p.71, lines 590–2.

21. N. Vincent, 'The Court of Henry II', in *Henry II: New Interpretations*, eds C. Harper-Bill and N. Vincent (Woodbridge, 2007), 296–7; *idem*, 'King Henry and the Poitevins', in *La Cour Plantagenêt, 1154–1204*, ed. M. Aurell (Poitiers, 2000), 122.

22. Gerald of Wales, *Opera*, eds J.S. Brewer, J.F. Dimock and G.F. Warner (8 vols, Rolls Series, 1861–91), ii, 348. See the analysis in H.M Thomas, *The English and the Normans: Ethnic Hostility, Assimilation and Identity, 1066–c.1220* (Oxford, 2003), 328–31, noting the fiction propagated by Nonant that Longchamp was of French peasant descent, making him even more foreign in origin.

23. The London chronicler writes of him in 1223 as 'a foreigner called Faulkes de Bréauté whom King John brought to the kingdom of England along with other foreigners': *De Antiquis Legibus Liber*, 204. The animus was apparently returned. William Longespée, earl of Salisbury, wrote to the justiciar in 1224 accusing Faulkes of publicly inveighing against all native Englishmen as 'traitors': *Royal Letters* i, 221.

24. Ibid., 121–2.

25. *The Chronicle of Richard of Devizes*, ed. J.T. Appleby (London, 1963), 31.

26. Wendover iii, 51; Vincent, *Peter des Roches*, 33–5. On this phenomenon generally, see M.T. Clanchy, *England and its Rulers, 1066–1307* (3rd edn, Oxford, 2006), 178ff.

27. J. Maddicott, *Simon de Montfort* (Cambridge, 1994), 1–7, 75–6.

28. M.L. Colker, 'The "Margam Chronicle" in a Dublin Manuscript', *HSJ*, 4 (1992), 134.

29. Wendover ii, 320–2. See the analysis of Wendover's account in N. Denholm-Young, *Richard of Cornwall* (Oxford, 1947), 11–13, though one has to dispute his contention that the earls had 'no constructive programme' (p. 13).

30. S.N. Mitchell, *Studies in Taxation under John and Henry III* (New Haven, 1914), 208–14; R.C. Stacey, *Politics, Policy and Finance under Henry III, 1216–1245* (Oxford, 1987), 98–9.

31. *Select Documents*, 357.

32. *Treaty Rolls* i, *1234–1325*, ed. P. Chaplais (London, 1955), no. 15 (my translation). For comment, see D.A. Carpenter, 'King, Magnates and Society: The Personal Rule of King Henry III, 1234–1258', *Speculum*, 60 (1985), 41.

33. BL, ms Additional 8167, fo. 105r–v. The identity of the senders of the letter quoted is inferred from the subsequent letter of the bishops in support of its position.

34. BL, Additional ms 8167, fos 105v–106r. On the subject of the use of Magna Carta as an agenda against the king, particularly at a local knightly level, as here, see J.R. Maddicott, 'Magna Carta and the Local Community, 1215–1259', *PP*, 102 (1984), 25–65, especially 48–50.

35. 'Estate Records of the Hotot Family', ed. E. King, in *A Northamptonshire Miscellany*, ed. *idem* (Northamptonshire Record Society, xxxii, 1983), 32.

36. Carpenter, 'Personal Rule', 44–5.

37. MP, *CM* v, 594.

38. Carpenter, 'Personal Rule', 46–7. As some confirmation that the favoured party, William de Montacute, was one of the earl's affinity, see his appearance as a knight in the earl's court at Cranborne on 25 March 1251: Cartulary of the Mortimer family, BL, ms Harley 1240, fos 90v–91r.

39. *Documents of the Baronial Movement*, 96–112.

40. *Select Documents*, 387–8: 'thaet loandes folk on ure kuneriche.' See on this S. Reynolds, *Kingdoms and Communities in Western Europe, 900–1300* (Oxford, 1984), 270–1.

41. *Political Songs of England*, ed. and trans. T. Wright (1839), revised P.R. Coss (Cambridge, 1996), 59–63.

42. As in T.F. Tout, 'The "Communitas Bacheleriae Angliae" ', *EHR*, 17 (1902), 89–95, a line followed by historians such as Denholm-Young. However, a subsequent deeper reflection on the nature of the 'bachelery' of 1259 came to a different conclusion, that the 'bachelers' were local men of affairs up from the shires: see E.F. Jacob, *Studies in the Period of Baronial Reform and Rebellion, 1258–1267* (Oxford Studies in Social and Legal History, viii, 1925), 126–43. esp. 133–4. This view is itself defective on several grounds, for which see on.

43. *Annales Monastici* i, 471. A *baccelarius* can be a young knight, and also betokens a retained knight, as in *Rotuli Litterarum Patentium*, 190–1, where King John awards Thomas Malesmains a money fee of 60 *li* to be one of his *baccelarii*. Thomas of Kent around 1180 uses *bachelerie* to denote the manpower of a retained military household, as in *Le Roman de toute chevalerie*, ed. B. Foster (2 vols, ANTS, 1976–7) i, lines 1111, 1768. A town list of the middle of the thirteenth century reckons that Northampton, England's prime tournament site, was famous for its *bachelerie*; and the nobles who frequented a tournament at Brackley in 1249 described themselves as *bachelarii*, according to Matthew Paris: C. Bonnier, 'List of English Towns in the Fourteenth Century', *EHR*, 16 (1901), 502; MP, *CM* v, 83. Note the bull of Pope Gregory IX of 1228 which inveighed against the magnates and barons of England who assembled 'on the excuse of a tournament' to set on foot plots and conspiracies against Henry III: *Foedera* i, pt 1, 189. See generally for its household application J.M.W. Bean, ' "Bachelor" and Retainer', *Medievalia et Humanistica*, new ser., iii (1972), 117–31.

Chapter Six: Local Violence

1. T.N. Bisson, *The Crisis of the Twelfth Century: Power, Lordship, and the Origins of European Government* (Princeton, 2009), especially 574. The concept of lordship and violence is quite differently treated in D. Crouch, *The Birth of Nobility: Constructing Aristocracy in England and France, 900–1300* (Harlow, 2005), 187–98, which favours more the standpoint of Stephen D. White, especially his 'Feuding and Peace-Making in the Touraine around the Year 1000', *Traditio*, 42 (1986), 195–263.
2. I follow the reconstruction of his career in C.P. Lewis, 'The King and Eye: A Study in Anglo-Norman Politics', *EHR*, 104 (1989), 571–84; but see also V. Chandler, 'The Last of the Montgomerys: Roger the Poitevin and Arnulf', *Historical Research*, lxii (1989), 1–14; K. Thompson, 'Arnoul de Montgomery', *Annales de Normandie*, 45 (1995), 49–53.
3. Geoffrey of Burton, *Life and Miracles of St Modwenna*, ed. and trans. R. Bartlett (Oxford, 2002), 192. The ultimate cause of the problem might have been William the Conqueror's supposed grant or confirmation to Burton of 'all the land beyond the river Dove', a vaguely expressed and soon-forgotten endowment that may have been responsible for local difficulties, especially since Roger the Poitevin had in the 1090s only recently acquired his estates in Drakelow and the Repton area at the confluence of the rivers Dove and Trent: see *Annales de Burton*, in *Annales Monastici* i, 185. For some comment on the extra-legal context of this incident, see J.G. Hudson, 'Maitland and Anglo-Norman Law', in *Proceedings of the British Academy*, 89 (1996), 35–7.
4. For 'distraint' or 'distress' (*districtio*), see F. Pollock and F.W. Maitland, *The History of English Law* (2nd edn, 2 vols, Cambridge, 1898), i, 353–5, where it is regarded as a recent innovation in the thirteenth century. For a consideration of the historiography of the question and a differing conclusion, that 'extra-judicial' distraint was well established by 1200, see P. Brand, 'Lordship and Distraint in Thirteenth-Century England', in *The Making of the Common Law* (London, 1992), 301–24. J.G. Hudson, *Land, Law and Lordship in Anglo-Norman England* (Oxford, 1994), 22–44, considers earlier examples, however, going back to the reign of Henry I. By the 1170s, there was some attempt to restrict the right of 'judicial' distraint to sheriffs and their officers, presumably to avoid incidents like this: Richard fitz Nigel, *Dialogus de Scaccario*, ed. and trans. E. Amt (Oxford, 2007), 158.
5. *Liber de Llan Dâv*, ed. J.G. Evans (Oxford, 1893), 272–3. Dated in W. Davies, *The Llandaff Charters* (Aberystwyth, 1979), 129, to *c*.1072.
6. Translation from a charter of the abbey of Notre-Dame de Noyers in White, 'Feuding and Peace-Making', 241, where it is dated to *c*.1090.
7. On the 'feudal transformation', see the classic statement in J.-P. Poly and E. Bournazel, *The Feudal Transformation, 900–1200*, trans. C. Higgitt (New York, 1999), 10ff; and the extensive critique of the idea of 'the descent of the *ban*' in Crouch, *The Birth of Nobility*, 191–8.

8. D. Barthélemy, *Chevaliers et miracles: la violence et le sacré dans la société féodale* (Paris, 2004), especially p. 13, defining it as 'un type de guerre revendicatrice de biens'. See also M. Chibnall, *The World of Orderic Vitalis* (Oxford, 1984), 133–8; P.R. Hyams, *Rancor and Reconciliation in Medieval England* (Ithaca, NY, 2003), 128–9.

9. *The Letters of Lanfranc, Archbishop of Canterbury*, eds and trans. H.M. Clover and M. Gibson (Oxford, 1979), 118–22. The archbishop on more than one occasion contrasted the loyalty of Earl Roger's father with the faithlessness of his son, choosing to treat Roger's defiance as self-interested treachery. For a general account of Earl Roger's defiance, see D. Bates, *William the Conqueror* (London, 1989), 154–6.

10. OV iv, 278–80.

11. WM, *GRA* ii, 564, 'orta inter eum et regem non modica controversia verborum' (my translation).

12. RH, 146–7, says that Baldwin resented that he had been denied an 'honor' (a possession or distinction) by the king. See the reconstruction of this incident in R. Bearman, 'Baldwin de Redvers: Some Aspects of a Baronial Career in the Reign of Stephen', *ANS* xviii, ed. C. Harper-Bill (Woodbridge, 1996), 20–4. For the siege of Exeter and its significance, see D. Crouch, *The Reign of King Stephen, 1135–1154* (London, 2000), 57–8.

13. HH, 706. Hugh later turned up in the royal army besieging Exeter, so his seizure of Norwich was soon forgiven: *Regesta* iii, no. 592.

14. *Royal and Other Historical Letters Illustrative of the Reign of Henry III from the Originals in the Public Record Office*, ed. W.W. Shirley (2 vols, Rolls Series, 1862–6), i, 222.

15. For the early stages of the dispute, see B.W. Holden, 'King John, the Braoses and the Celtic Fringe, 1207–1216', *Albion*, 33 (2001), 10–11.

16. For John's *querimonia* about Briouze (written up *c.*September 1210), see *Foedera* i, pt 1, 107–8, and for an analysis see D. Crouch, 'The Complaint of King John against William de Briouze (*c.*September 1210): The Black Book of the Exchequer Text', in *Magna Carta and the England of King John*, ed. J. Loengard (Woodbridge, 2010), 168–79.

17. *HWM* ii, lines 14,157–64. To other contemporaries, such as the chronicler of Neath abbey, it seemed that John 'took over William de Briouze's lands determined to disinherit him, saying he was a traitor (*proditor*)': F.R. Lewis, 'A History of the Lordship of Gower from the Missing Cartulary of Neath Abbey', *Bulletin of the Board of Celtic Studies*, xi (1937–9), 151.

18. N. Vincent, *Peter des Roches: An Alien in English Politics, 1205–1238* (Cambridge, 1996), 327.

19. For an analysis of Gilbert's career, see *Basset Charters*, ed. W.T. Reedy (Pipe Roll Society, new ser., 50, 1995), pp. xxvii–xxviii. In 1230, Gilbert's father, Alan Basset, was described as a member of Earl William Marshal II's household (*familia*): TNA, C72/5. Alan's son and Gilbert's elder brother, Thomas (died 1230), was a leading follower of both the elder and younger Earl William Marshal: *Basset Charters*, p. xxxiv; Crouch, *William Marshal*, 171–2. Gilbert's connection with the Marshal affinity can be deduced from his involvement in the marriage of his first cousin, Countess Philippa Basset of Warwick, to Richard Siward, a Marshal banneret, and from the evidence of the Dunstable annalist: *Annales Monastici* iii, 136. See also the evidence marshalled in Vincent, *Peter des Roches*, 337n. There is no evidence to support the assertion by Björn Weiler that Gilbert Basset was a 'close kinsman' of Earl Richard Marshal: *Kingship, Rebellion and Political Culture: England and Germany, c.1215–c.1250* (Basingstoke, 2007), 15.

20. Vincent, *Peter des Roches*, 334–9.

21. Ibid., 399ff; D. Crouch, 'The Last Adventure of Richard Siward', *Morgannwg*, xxxv (1991), 11–17; R.F. Walker, 'The Supporters of Richard Marshal, Earl of Pembroke, in the Rebellion of 1233-1234', *Welsh History Review*, xvii (1994), 41–65.

22. OV iii, 158–60, 296–300. A critical assessment of Orderic's rhetoric is to be found in K. Thompson, 'Orderic Vitalis and Robert of Bellême', *JMH*, 20 (1994), 133–41. For a reasoned account of Robert's career, see *eadem*, 'Robert of Bellême Reconsidered', *ANS*, xiii, ed. M. Chibnall (Woodbridge, 1990), 263–86.

23. OV vi, 20 talks of forty-five offences alleged against him in the royal court, while the Welsh chronicles refer to his building of Bridgnorth castle (presumably to extend his power in the Midlands) as the trigger for the king's accusations of treachery: *Brut y Tywysogyon: Red Book of Hergest Version*, ed. and trans. T. Jones (Cardiff, 1955), *s.a.* 1102.

24. OV vi, 26–8. For a discussion of knights who were *pagenses* or *stipendarii*, and their relationship, see M. Chibnall, 'Mercenaries and the *Familia Regis* under Henry I', *History*, 62 (1977), 15–23.

25. F.M. Stenton, St Benet of Holme and the Norman Conquest', *EHR*, 37 (1922), 225–7. In one instance, Roger had taken land from another Frenchman, one Walter, who had taken it from the abbey.

26. *Life and Miracles of St Modwenna*, liii–lv. For some reflection on the context of such *conventiones*, see M. Chibnall, 'Anglo-French Relations in the Work of Orderic Vitalis', in *Documenting the Past: Essays in Honour of G.P. Cuttino*, eds J.S. Hamilton and P.J. Bradley (Woodbridge, 1989), 5–19; E. King, 'Dispute Settlement in Anglo-Norman England', *ANS*, xiv, ed. M. Chibnall (Woodbridge, 1992), 115–30. One might point here to the mingled flattery and intimidation by which the Oxfordshire baron and sheriff Robert d'Oilly (died *c.*1094) obtained an estate at Tadmarton from Abingdon abbey in the 1080s. The king had to be motivated to intervene to restore the estate to the abbey, and even then d'Oilly's naked threats of violence obliged the abbey to buy him off with an annual monetary fee of ten pounds, *Historia Ecclesiae Abbendonensis*, ed. and trans. J.G. Hudson (2 vols, Oxford, 2002), lxx, 10, 32. A further comparison is the account of the settlement between William Peverel himself and Thorney abbey, *c.*1115 × 24, brokered as in the Burton case by a third party, Earl David I of Huntingdon, before a baronial assembly: *Regesta Regum Scottorum* i, *The Acts of Malcolm IV*, ed. G.W.S. Barrow (Edinburgh, 1960), 133.

27. *Domesday Book* i, fos 375r–377v. For some comment on the Domesday *clamores* and *invasiones*, see P. Wormald, 'Domesday Lawsuits: A Provisional List and Preliminary Comments', in *England in the Eleventh Century*, ed. C. Hicks (Stamford, 1992), 61–102; D. Roffe, *Domesday: The Inquest and the Book* (Oxford, 2000), 165–8.

28. *Domesday Book* i, fo. 151v; ii, fo. 447r; R. Fleming, *Domesday Book and the Law: Society and Legal Custom in Early Medieval England* (Cambridge, 1998), 68–9. Richard fitz Gilbert's father, Count Gilbert of Brionne, was characterised by Gilbert Crispin in the 1090s as an aggressive magnate apt to lead his military household against his neighbours to avenge slights to his honour in the Normandy of the 1030s (*Vita sancti Herluini*, in, *PL* 150, col. 696), which might indicate the epithet 'malveisin' was hereditary. For the Verdun family and its lands, see R. Dace, 'Bertran de Verdun: Royal Service, Land and Family in the Late Twelfth Century', *Medieval Prosopography*, 20 (1999), 76–7; M.S. Hagger, *The Fortunes of a Norman Family: The De Verduns in England, Ireland and Wales, 1066–1316* (Dublin, 2001).

29. We might recall here the confessions of the king's justice Nigel d'Aubigny on what he thought was his deathbed early in the 1110s. He urged William, his brother and heir, to restore lands to seventeen men or their heirs whom he had 'disinherited', presumably not so much by violence as by distortion of legal process and aggressive exploitation of wardships: *Charters of the Honour of Mowbray, 1107–1191*, ed. D.E. Greenway (London, 1972), 7–9.

30. E. King, 'Mountsorrel and its Region in King Stephen's Reign', *Huntington Library Quarterly*, 44 (1980), 1–10; D. Crouch, 'Earls and Bishops in Twelfth-Century Leicestershire', *Nottingham Medieval Studies*, 37 (1993), 9–14.

31. D. Crouch, 'Geoffrey de Clinton and Roger, Earl of Warwick: Magnates and *Curiales* in the Reign of Henry I', *BIHR*, 55 (1982), 113–24. For the Warwick-Clinton *conventio*, see *idem*, 'A Norman *Convenio* and Bonds of Lordship in the Middle Ages', in *Law and Government in Medieval England and Normandy*, eds G. Garnett and J.G. Hudson (Cambridge, 1994), 323–4.

32. For Suger's verdict on England under Henry I's rule, see *Vita Ludovici Grossi*, ed. and trans. H. Waquet (Paris, 1929), 100; for that of Pope Innocent II in 1136, see RH, 147–8; for that of the Anglo-Saxon Chronicle, *s.a.* 1135.

33. *Chronica monasterii de Melsa*, ed. E.A. Bond (3 vols, Rolls Series, 1866–8), i, 356–8; H.M. Thomas, *Vassals, Heiresses, Crusaders and Thugs: The Gentry of Angevin Yorkshire, 1154–1216* (Philadelphia, 1993), 64–5, takes the abbey's part.

34. *Jordan Fantosme's Chronicle*, ed, and trans. R.C. Johnston (Oxford, 1981), 52, 58, 72–4, 86–8. The incompetence in arms of the English in the 1160s is also alleged by William Marshal's biographer: *HWM* i, lines 1526–50.

35. The most accessible version of this story is in *English Lawsuits* ii, 414–19. One might note here the comparable conduct in the 1190s of Geoffrey fitz Peter towards Walden abbey and Hamelin, earl of Warenne, towards Lewes priory, who for several years both conducted campaigns of threat, minor violence and intimidation against those houses as a way of getting them to acknowledge their rights as patrons: *Book of the Foundation of Walden Abbey*, eds and trans. D.E. Greenway and L. Watkiss (Oxford, 1999); *English Episcopal Acta* iii, *Canterbury 1193–1205*, eds C.R. Cheney and E. John (London, 1986), no. 524.

36. *Calendar of Inquisitions Post Mortem* i, 67. A series of Lancashire fines at Le Mans in September and October 1199 show John coming to grips with the problems of dispossession caused by Theobald, who had clearly traded on his position as John's butler and the brother of Hubert Walter, archbishop of Canterbury and justiciar: *Rotuli Chartarum*, 25–8. For John and Theobald, see M.T. Flanagan, *Irish Society, Anglo-Norman Settlers, Angevin Kingship* (Oxford, 1989), 131–3. For Theobald's repeated acknowledgement of Ranulf de Glanville as his 'dear friend' (*carus*), see *Chartae Privilegia et Immunitates* (Irish Records Commission, 1829), 11; *The Cockersand Chartulary*, ed. W. Farrer (3 vols in 7, Chetham Society, 1898–1909), ii, pt 1, 375. Archbishop Hubert's impatience with his brother's high-handedness is noted in his intervention in the quarrel between his brother and Bishop Felix of Ossory: *Calendar of Ormond Deeds* i, *1172–1350 AD*, ed. E. Curtis (Dublin, 1932), 11.

37. *Curia Regis Rolls* xi, 388–93.

38. Shirley, *Royal Letters* i, 178–9.

39. For the case of Henry Basset and Earl William, TNA, KB26/40, m. 8, see *Curia Regis Rolls* xix, 326–9. The account of the jury is partly confirmed by a series of fines in *Basset Charters*, 93–4, 98, 106–9. For the place of North Moreton as a fee of Warwick in 1242, see *Calendar of Inquisitions Post Mortem* i, 3. The fee of North Moreton had originally been held by the Corbezun family, but the fees had been sold back by the Corbezuns to the earl, who was therefore the direct overlord. The expulsion of Henry's nephew from North Moreton cannot easily be dated, but since his father, Jordan, was in possession of it in the late 1190s (see *Pleas before the King and his Justices* i, 418) and Henry was outlawed after his father's death and then exiled for over a decade, it would seem that the incident must belong late in John's reign or early in Henry III's.

40. The most extensive account of this incident is in *Chronicon Thomae Wykes*, in *Annales Monastici* iv, 234, which maintains that the dispute must have broken out at the south end of Westminster Hall, where the courts of the chancellor and king's bench met, after which the wounded Zouches fled southwards through a passage west of St Stephen's chapel and thence into the White Hall, seeking refuge in the Painted Chamber – where the king was – which opened off the White or New Hall; see for the topography of Henry III's palace *The History of the King's Works*, eds H.M. Colvin et al. (3 vols, London, 1963), i, 494–504. The account of the events in F.M. Powicke, *King Henry III and the Lord Edward* (2 vols, Oxford, 1966) ii, 584–5, is concise but painstaking in its accuracy.

41. *Flores Historiarum*, ed. H. R. Luard (3 vols, Rolls Series, 1890), iii, 17–18; *Cal Patent Rolls, 1266–72*, 438, 451; *Close Rolls, 1268–72*, 282–3. The earl's letter is dated 9 September 1270.

42. The same earl's later violent inroads on Selby abbey's moorlands are noted in *The Coucher Book of Selby*, ed. J.T. Fowler (2 vols, Yorkshire Archaeological Society Record Series, x, xiii, 1891–3), i, 83–4; for his war in Bromfield, see *Calendar of Ancient Correspondence Concerning Wales*, ed. J.G. Edwards (Cardiff, 1935), 170–1.

43. MP, *CM* v, 234. Since his depredations were carried out against the king's peace, they were doubtless focused on Herefordshire rather than across the border in Wales.

44. R. Hilton, *A Medieval Society: The West Midlands at the End of the Thirteenth Century* (repr. Cambridge, 1983), 248–61; N. Saul, *Knights and Esquires: The Gloucestershire Gentry in the Fourteenth Century* (Oxford, 1981), 168–204.

45. E.L.G. Stones, 'The Folvilles of Ashby-Folville, Leicestershire, and their Associates in Crime, 1326–1347', *TRHS*, 5th ser., 7 (1957), 117–36.

46. The relationship is established by a charter in Cartulary of Woodford of Brentingby, BL, ms Cotton Claudius, A xii, fo. 244r–v.

47. For Eustace's activities, see *Cal Patent Rolls, 1266–1272*, 149, 521; *Cal Patent Rolls, 1272–1281*, 115.

48. *Close Rolls, 1247–1251*, 28.

49. *Close Rolls, 1268–1272*, 375.

50. J.B. Given, *Society and Homicide in Thirteenth-Century England* (Stanford, CA, 1977), 121–2.

51. M.T. Clanchy, 'Highway Robbery and Trial by Battle in the Hampshire Eyre of 1249', in *Medieval Legal Records Edited in Memory of C.A.F. Meekings*, eds R.F. Hunnisett and J.B. Post (London, 1978), 26–61.

52. *Rolls of the Justices in Eyre for Gloucestershire, Warwickshire and Staffordshire, 1221–1222*, ed. D.M. Stenton (Selden Society, lix, 1940), 167. The existence of Robert of Shuckburgh, whose daughter Warin abducted, is attested by sources from the 1140s to the 1160s: BL, Additional charter 48304; *Formulare Anglicanum*, ed. T. Madox (London, 1702), no. 77; *Monasticon Anglicanum* iv, 92.

CHAPTER SEVEN: PERSONAL VIOLENCE

1. A point neatly made and illustrated in J.B. Given, *Society and Homicide in Thirteenth-Century England* (Stanford, CA, 1977), 78–9.

2. *Histoire des ducs*, 116–17.

3. *Epistolae*, in *PL*, 207, col. 48. Wace of Bayeux around 1160 notes just such regimentation at the idealised, fictional court of King Arthur, which might be taken as a further reflection on the contemporary Angevin court: *Wace's Roman de Brut: A History of the British. Text and Translation*, ed. and trans. J. Weiss (Exeter, 2002), lines 10,339–58.

4. MP, *CM* v, 266–7.

5. WM *HN*, 26–7, 31. For another account, see *GS*, 76–8. See contextualisations of this incident in E. Kealey, *Roger of Salisbury, Viceroy of England* (Berkeley, CA, 1972), 180–9; Crouch, *The Reign of King Stephen, 1135–1154* (Harlow, 2000), 93–7.

6. G. Koziol, *Begging Pardon and Favour: Ritual and Political Order in Early Medieval France* (Ithaca, NY, 1992), 289–321, writing in the light of Pierre Bourdieu's works, presents a case for the ritualised politics of the time, without going so far as to see it as, on the one hand, emotionless or, on the other, entirely sincere. More recent studies argue for the reality and even necessity of medieval anger: see particularly R.E. Barton, ' "Zealous Anger" and the Renegotiation of Aristocratic Relationships in Eleventh- and Twelfth-Century France', in *Anger's Past: The Social Uses of an Emotion in the Middle Ages*, ed. B.H. Rosenwein (Ithaca, NY, 1998), 153–70, and S.D. White, 'The Politics of Anger', in ibid., 127–52, who provides (pp. 127–31) valuable socio-historical background.

7. R. Kaeuper, *Chivalry and Violence in Medieval Europe* (Oxford, 1999), 199.

8. Thomas Walsingham, *Gesta abbatum monasterii sancti Albani*, ed. H.T. Riley (3 vols, Rolls Series, 1867–9), i, 316–18, an incident dated only by its being within the episcopate of William of York, bishop of Salisbury (1247–56). Geoffrey features from the 1240s to the 1260s as a middle-ranking royal knight, noted as receiving robes in 1261: *Cal Close Rolls, 1259–1261*, 394. He died *c.*1271, leaving Richard his brother as his heir to Childwick, Hertfordshire, and a mass of debt: *Cal Patent Rolls, 1266–72*, 511, 635. His manors of Childwick and Redbourne, Hertfordshire, held of St Albans, and Mugginton and Hulland, Derbyshire, held of the honor of Tutbury, are mentioned in 1249: *Cal Charter Rolls* i, 342.

9. *HWM* i, lines 6677–6852.

10. *Crown Pleas of the Devon Eyre of 1238*, ed. H.T. Summerson (Devon and Cornwall Record Society, new ser., 28, 1985), 9–13 for Axminster hundred. As a loose comparison with modern times, the Devon and Cornwall constabulary recorded thirteen homicides for both counties in the year May 2005–April 2006, *http://www.crimestatistics.org.uk*, with a much higher general population than the Devon of the 1230s. Given, *Society and Homicide*, 87, reckons that nationally 9.6 per cent of thirteenth-century murder victims were vagabonds or unidentifiable strangers.

11. Given, *Society and Homicide*, 40. I may not be typical, but I have had personal contact with at least two murderers and one man who was subsequently murdered.

12. *Pipe Roll of 31 Hen I*, 86 (Leicestershire): 'Radulfus pincerna reddet compotum de .xl. libris pro plegio hominis qui interfecit hominem episcopi Wintonensis.'

13. *Gesta Henrici Secundi* i, 155–6.

14. TNA, SC1/1/149.

15. MP, *CM* v, 318–19.

16. *HWM* i, lines 1623–1710, 6448–58, ii, lines 16,764–8.

17. *HWM* i, lines 8585–772.

18. *HWM* ii, lines 16,859–69.

19. Jacques Bretel, *Le Tournoi de Chauvency*, ed. G. Hecq (Société des Bibliophiles Belges, no. 31, Mons, 1898), 32.

20. OV vi, 240. For a full treatment of this issue, see the forthcoming study M. Strickland, 'Henry I and the Battle of the Two Kings: Brémule 1119', in *Normandy and its Neighbours, c.900–1250: Essays for David Bates*, eds D. Crouch and K. Thompson (Turnhout, 2010).

21. D. Crouch. 'William Marshal and the Mercenariat', in *Mercenaries and Paid Men: The Mercenary Identity in the Middle Ages*, ed. J. France (Leiden, 2008), 29–30; for the encounter between Map and Briouze, see *De Nugis Curialium*, trans. M.R. James, eds C.N.L. Brooke and R.B. Mynors (Oxford, 1983), 146.

22. *Chronicon abbatiae Ramseiensis*, ed. W. Dunn Macray (Rolls Series, 1886), 332.

23. The best account seems to be in M.L. Colker, 'The "Margam Chronicle" in a Dublin Manuscript', *HSJ*, 4 (1992), 139–40. For comment, see N. Vincent, *Peter des Roches: An Alien in English Politics, 1205–1238* (Cambridge, 1996), 438–40.

24. See now O. de Laborderie, J.R. Maddicott and D.A. Carpenter, 'The Last Hours of Simon de Montfort: A New Account', *EHR*, 115 (2000), 378–412, esp. 403, 409.

25. *Erec et Enide*, ed. M. Roquez (Classiques Français du Moyen Age: Paris, 1952), lines 3848–55.

26. *Jordan Fantosme's Chronicle*, ed. and trans. R.C. Johnston (Oxford, 1981), 70.

27. *The Historia Regum Britanniae of Geoffrey of Monmouth* i, *Bern, Burgerbibliothek, MS 568*, ed. N. Wright (Cambridge, 1984), xiii–xiv.

28. BL, ms Additional 8167, fo. 101r.

29. *Foedera* i, pt 1, 65. The way that personal antagonism could lead to animus and unacceptable violence on the tournament ground is noted in Matthew Paris's account of the *torneamentum aculeatum* (the 'needle match') at Rochester in December 1251, where the native knights routed the 'aliens', who were then taken prisoner and beaten up by the squires of the English side before they could reach the refuge of the city: *MP, CM* v, 265.

30. *Le très ancien coutumier de Normandie*, in *Coutumiers de Normandie* i, ed. E.-J. Tardif (Rouen, 1881), 27.

31. For the European background, see R. Bartlett, *'Mortal Enmities': The Legal Aspect of Hostility in the Middle Ages* (Aberyswyth, 1998), 1–8. Bartlett seems to assume, however, that 'mortal enmity' usually meant an intention to pursue an enemy to death.

32. Goscelin of Canterbury, *Historia translationis sancti Augustini episcopi*, in *PL*, 155, col. 19.

33. *La Geste des Engleis en Yrlande*, ed. and trans. E. Mullally (Dublin, 2002), lines 2143–4.

34. *Le Roman de Toute Chevalerie*, ed. B. Foster (2 vols, Anglo-Norman Text Society, 1976–7), i, lines 7357–60.

35. *Gui de Warewic: roman du xiii*ᵉ *siècle*, ed. A. Ewert (2 vols, Classiques Français du moyen age, 1932), i, lines 3593–4: 'mes mortels enemis a nul jur ne me serrunt amis'.

36. *Histoire des ducs*, 156.

37. *Somersetshire Pleas to 41 Henry III*, ed. C.E.H. Chadwycke-Healey (Somersetshire Record Society, xi, 1897), 237.

38. See M. Strickland, 'Slaughter, Slavery or Ransom: The Impact of the Conquest on Conduct in Warfare', in *England in the Eleventh Century*, ed. C. Hicks (Stamford, 1992), 41–60; J. Gillingham, 'Thegns and Knights in Eleventh-Century England', *TRHS*, 6th ser., 5 (1995), 150–1; and, for an overview, D. Crouch, *The Birth of Nobility: Constructing Aristocracy in England and France, 950–1300* (Harlow, 2005), 63–6. For a view that a violent 'feud mentality' was embedded in pre-Conquest English social and political life, not to mention its legal processes, see P.R. Hyams, 'Feud and the State in Anglo-Saxon England', *Journal of British Studies*, 40 (2001), 1–43, especially 9–10. T.N. Bisson, *The Crisis of the Twelfth Century: Power, Lordship, and the Origins of European Government* (Princeton, 2009), 574, talks more accurately of a 'vengeance' mentality, but assumes that feuding was both violent and 'ubiquitous' in high medieval Europe.

39. J. Gillingham, 'Fontenoy and After: Pursuing Enemies to Death in France between the Ninth and Eleventh Centuries', in *Frankland: The Franks and the World of the Early Middle Ages*, eds P. Fouracre and D. Ganz (Manchester, 2008), 242–65.

40. A point made in P.R. Hyams, *Rancor and Reconciliation in Medieval England* (Ithaca, NY, 2003), 137–9.

41. *Leges Henrici Primi*, 258 (82.8), 260 (83.6), 276 (88.19).

42. See the royalist rhetoric in R. Sharpe, 'The Prefaces of "Quadripartitus" ', in *Law and Government in Medieval England and Normandy: Essays in Honour of Sir James Holt*, eds G. Garnett and J.G. Hudson (Cambridge, 1992), 165–6.

43. Thomas of Chobham, *Summa Confessorum*, ed. F. Broomfield (Analecta Mediaevalia Namurcensia, 25, Louvain, 1968), 192.

44. As noted in R. Bartlett, *England under the Norman and Angevin Kings, 1075–1225* (Oxford, 2000), 568.

45. O. Padel, 'Geoffrey of Monmouth and Cornwall', *Cambridge Medieval Celtic Studies*, 8 (1984), 20–7.

46. A reconstruction of this notorious aristocratic slaughter is in R. Fletcher, *Bloodfeud: Murder and Revenge in Anglo-Saxon England* (London, 2002).

47. RH, 140; *Regesta* iii, no. 428. For comment, see W.E. Wightman, *The Lacy Family in England and Normandy, 1066–1194* (Oxford, 1966), 66–74. This excuse, that an act of violence between succession and coronation could not offend the king, appears to have been used by gentry involved in a Cornish housebreaking plea just after King Richard's death in 1199: Hyams, *Rancor and Reconciliation*, 288–9.

48. *Fouke le Fitz Waryn*, eds E.J. Hathaway et al. (Anglo-Norman Text Society, 26–8, 1975), xxvii–xxxii, 32–3.

49. OV vi, 214–16.

50. WM, *HN*, 42–3. For aspects of this incident, see Crouch, *The Reign of King Stephen*, 76–7, 77n; *idem, Birth of Nobility*, 60–1.

51. TNA, JUST1/734, m. 15 (my translation). For edition and comment, see *The Roll of the Shropshire Eyre of 1256*, ed. A. Harding (Selden Society, 96, 1981), xxvii–xxviii, 137–8. For the relations between Corbets and fitz Warins, see J. Meisel, *Barons of the Welsh Frontier: The Corbet, Pantulf and fitz Warin Families, 1066–1272* (Lincoln, NE, 1980), 91–2. The necessity of a man enfeoffed with an estate returning it if he renounces the homage he did for it is noted in Edmund of Lancaster's indenture of agreement with Dafydd ap Meilyr of 1277: TNA, DL25/2048.

CHAPTER EIGHT: DOMINATING LOCALITIES

1. D. Barthélemy, *Les Deux Ages de la seigneurie banale: Coucy xie–xiiie siècle* (2nd edn, Paris, 2000).
2. For the formation of castellanries on either side of 1000 in the Grand-Caux, an area framed by the ducal centres of Rouen, Fécamp and Arques, see J. le Maho, 'L'apparition des seigneuries châtelaines dans la Grand-Caux à l'époque ducale', *Archéologie Mediévale*, 6 (1976), 5–148, and see *idem*, 'Châteaux d'époque franque en Normandie', *Archéologie Mediévale*, 10 (1980), 153–65. However, the process went much further in the principalities surrounding Normandy than it did within the duchy: see the comment in D. Power, 'Le régime seigneurial en Normandie', in *Les Seigneuries dans l'espace Plantagenêt (c.1150–c.1250)*, eds M. Aurell and F. Boutoulle (Bordeaux, 2009), 121.
3. *Domesday Book* i, fo. 62b.
4. For the significance of the *antecessor* in the Conquest period, see P. Sawyer, '1066–1086: A Tenurial Revolution', in *Domesday Book: A Reassessment*, ed. *idem* (London, 1983), 71–85; R. Fleming, 'Domesday Book and the Tenurial Revolution', *ANS*, ix, ed. R.A. Brown (Woodbridge, 1986), 87–102; *eadem, Kings and Lords in Conquest England* (Cambridge, 1991), ch. 6; J.A. Green, *The Aristocracy of Norman England* (Cambridge, 1997), ch. 2.
5. Fleming, *Kings and Lords*, 113–15.
6. Fleming, 183–214, gives plenty of examples of such 'private enterprise', though her characterisation of a Norman 'kleptocracy' is played down by Green, *The Aristocracy of Norman England*, 49, 78–9, who subscribes to a more Stentonian idea of order and continuity.
7. P.A. Clarke, *The English Nobility under Edward the Confessor* (Oxford, 1994), 18–23, 61–4, 94–8. For a study of commendation in action, see S. Baxter, 'The Earls of Mercia and their Commended Men in the Mid Eleventh Century', *ANS*, xxiii, ed. J. Gillingham (Woodbridge, 2001), 23–46; and, in more detail, *idem, The Earls of Mercia: Lordship and Power in Late Anglo-Saxon England* (Oxford, 2007), 109–18, 204–15, 266–9.
8. A. Williams, 'The Estates of Harold Godwinsson', *ANS*, iii, ed. R.A. Brown (Woodbridge, 1980), 171–87; Fleming, *Kings and Lords*, 60–7, though Baxter, *The Earls of Mercia*, 12–13, disputes the extent of Godwinsson land.
9. The nearest thing to a comprehensive survey of the creation of English honors in the Conquest period is Green, *The Aristocracy of Norman England*, ch. 2.
10. Ibid., 58–9, 85; P. Dalton, *Conquest, Anarchy and Lordship: Yorkshire, 1066–1154* (Cambridge, 1994), 33–4.
11. R. Liddiard, *Landscapes of Lordship: Norman Castles and the Countryside in Medieval Norfolk, 1066–1200* (BAR British Series, 309, 2000), 28–33.
12. Cf. Stenton, *First Century*, 193–4, followed by most subsequent commentators.
13. B. English, *The Lords of Holderness, 1086–1260* (Oxford, 1979), 6–9, 173–4.
14. J.F.A. Mason, *William I and the Sussex Rapes* (St Leonards, 1966).
15. For Dudley, see J. Hunt, *Lordship and the Landscape: A Documentary and Archaeological Study of the Honor of Dudley, c.1066–1322* (BAR British Series, 264, 1997), 14–28. For the *castellaria* reference, see *Domesday Book* i, fo. 177b. For the ineffectual nature of Edwin's rising, see *ASC s.a.*, 1071.
16. Lambert of Ardres, *The History of the Counts of Guines and Lords of Ardres*, trans. L. Shopkow (Philadelphia, 2001), 98–100.
17. See on this generally, *Leicestershire Survey, c.AD 1130*, ed. C.F. Slade (Leicester, 1956).
18. OV vi, 18–20.
19. D. Crouch, 'The Foundation of Leicester Abbey and Other Problems', *Midland History*, 11 (1987), 9. In 'Earls and Bishops in Twelfth-Century Leicestershire', *Nottingham Medieval Studies*, 37 (1993), 12–14, I presented arguments as to which of the first two Earl Roberts had seized Knighton, and favoured the idea that it was Robert II on the basis of later evidence deriving from Leicester abbey.
20. E. King, 'Mountsorrel and its Region in King Stephen's Reign', *Huntington Library Quarterly*, 44 (1980), 3–7.

21. D. Crouch, *The Beaumont Twins: The Roots and Branches of Power in the Twelfth Century* (Cambridge, 1986), 82–5. For the likely date of the Chester-Leicester treaties, see *idem*, *The Reign of King Stephen, 1135–1154* (London, 2000), 253–4.

22. See studies in Stenton, *First Century*, 250–6; King, 'Mountsorrel', 2–8; Crouch, *Beaumont Twins*, 80–5; *idem*, *Reign of King Stephen*, 238–9, 253–4. For Belvoir, see ibid., 144–5; E. King, 'The Foundation of Pipewell Abbey, Northamptonshire', *HSJ*, 2 (1990), 171–3.

23. King, 'Mountsorrel', 8–9.

24. Crouch, 'Earls and Bishops', 16–20.

25. For Frederick (died 1070) as brother-in-law of William I de Warenne, see *Early Yorkshire Charters* viii, 40–3.

26. For the castle and its associated developments, see R. Liddiard, *Castles in Context: Power, Symbolism and Landscape, 1066 to 1500* (Macclesfield, 2005), 134–9.

27. For Thetford in 1086, then over half the size of the city of Norwich, with multiple churches and a former cathedral, see *Domesday Book* ii, fos 118b–119a. The grant to the Warennes is mentioned in William III's charter: BL Harley charter 57 E 32. This can be dated as after William II's death in 1138 and before 1141, since Countess Isabel, his mother, is noted as still alive. See for her death Crouch, *Beaumont Twins*, 12–13. The dating in *Early Yorkshire Charters* viii, 93–4, is in error. The charter records that William III had received Thetford from the king, and was able to grant liberties and fairs within the town to his new priory, which indicates complete dominance there. He refers to 'villa mea de Tieford' in an act in favour of Stoneleigh abbey before 1147: Cartulary of Stoneleigh Abbey, Shakespeare Birthplace Trust, ms DR10/1406, pp. 222–3.

28. *Regesta* iii, no. 272.

29. A. Wareham, 'The Motives and Politics of the Bigod Family, *c*.1066–1177', in *ANS*, xvii, ed. C. Harper-Bill (Woodbridge, 1994), 227–8, suggests an earlier outbreak of Warenne-Bigod hostilities in 1101, also centred on Thetford.

30. See Crouch, *Reign of King Stephen*, 118–20.

31. For the Bigod Domesday share of Thetford, see *Domesday Book* ii, fo. 173a. For the Bigods and St Mary's priory, Thetford, see BL, ms Lansdowne 229, fo. 148r.

32. William, son of King Stephen, issued a charter in Thetford between 1153 and 1159: *Early Lancashire Charters*, ed. W. Farrer (Liverpool, 1902), 306–7. RT, 192–3, says William lost Norwich in 1157, but the king must have reclaimed it earlier owing to its appearance in the sheriff's accounts for Michaelmas 1156: *Pipe Roll of 2 Henry II*, 8. He may have lost Thetford at the same time, though it first appears in the Michaelmas 1159 account: *Pipe Roll of 5 Henry II*, 12. William died in October 1159. See also G.J. White, *Restoration and Reform 1153–1165: Recovery from Civil War in England* (Cambridge, 2000), 115.

33. *Liber Niger Scaccarii*, ed. T. Hearne (2 vols, London, 1771–4), i, 371. The Michaelmas 1191 account first mentions Thetford as *terra data* to Earl Hamelin 'in escambio de Columbar' et aliarum terrarum Turon': *Pipe Roll of 3 Richard I*, 33. Thetford was still in the king's hands at Michaelmas 1190: *Pipe Roll of 2 Richard I*, 92, 94, 100. See also *Early Yorkshire Charters* viii, 124–5. The Thetford confirmation is in an inspeximus of Earl John II de Warenne dated 1315: BL, Harley charter 57 E 32. The grant guarantees a revenue of £35 annually from the town at the exchequer. Earl Hamelin made several subsequent grants in Thetford: Cartulary of Castle Acre, fo. 6v (witnessed by Abbot Roger of Le Valasse); Cartulary of Waltham Abbey, BL, ms Harley 391, fos 143v–144r; BL, Harley charter 57 E 32; Cartulary of Walden Abbey, BL, ms Harley 3697, fo. 232 (*villa mea de Thetford*). See also *Book of Fees* i, 128.

34. For John Marshal's lineage, see N.E. Stacy, 'Henry of Blois and the Glastonbury Connection', *EHR*, 114 (1999), 32–3 and nn.

35. For his lands, see D. Crouch, *William Marshal: Knighthood, War and Chivalry, 1147–1219* (2nd edn, London, 2002), 13–14.

36. For John at Marlborough and Ludgershall, 1136–9, see *Regesta* iii, no. 868; JW iii, 268, 284–90; *GS*, 104–8. In the mid-1140s, Gilbert Foliot, abbot of Gloucester, refers to him

as 'John of Marlborough' troubling the peace of Wiltshire: *The Letters and Charters of Gilbert Foliot*, eds A. Morey and C.N.L. Brooke (Cambridge, 1967), 71–2. For the war between John and Earl Patrick of Salisbury, c.1145, see Crouch, *William Marshal*, 17–19.

37. *Pipe Roll of 4 Henry II*, 116; *Pipe Roll of 10 Henry II*, 14; see White, *Restoration and Reform*, 115 and n. 116.

38. TNA, C52/21/9.

39. For the reconstruction of these events, see Crouch, *William Marshal*, 78–81. See for the evidence *HWM* ii, lines 10,023–48; RH iii, 237, 238; *WN*, *HRA* i, 406.

40. *Histoire des ducs*, 175.

41. For William's presence in Marlborough at the beginning of April 1220, see *Receipt Rolls, 4, 5, 6 Henry III*, ed. N. Barratt (Pipe Roll Society, 2003), 11; Shirley, *Royal Letters* i, 100–1. For the marriage negotiations, see *Calendar of Entries in the Papal Registers Relating to Great Britain and Ireland, 1198–1304*, cal. W.H. Bliss (London, 1893), 88; *Diplomatic Documents Preserved in the Public Record Office* i, *1101–1272*, ed. P. Chaplais (London, 1964), 96. See the discussion in D.A. Carpenter, *The Minority of Henry III* (London, 1990), 239, 243–4. A revised dating is offered in D. Crouch, 'Mothers, Sons and Executors: The Brief Widowhood of Isabel, Countess of Pembroke, May 1219–March 1220', forthcoming.

42. D.A. Carpenter, 'The Struggle to Control the Peak: An Unknown Letter Patent from 1217', in *Foundations of Medieval Scholarship: Records Edited in Honour of David Crook*, eds P. Brand and S. Cunningham (Heslington, 2008), 35–49.

43. P. Dalton, 'William Earl of York and Royal Authority in Yorkshire in the Reign of Stephen', *HSJ*, 2 (1990), 155–65; *idem*, 'Aiming at the Impossible: Ranulf II of Chester and Lincolnshire in the reign of Stephen', in *The Earldom of Chester and its Charters*, ed. A.T. Thacker (Journal of the Chester Archaeological Society, 71, 1991), 109–34. For Bungay, see above, p. 141.

44. For the Montfort of Beaudesert lineage, see *Complete Peerage* viii, 120; F.W. Evans, 'Beaudesert and the De Mountfords', in *Transactions of the Birmingham Archaeological Society*, xxxii (1907), 24–40; D. Crouch, 'From Stenton to McFarlane: Models of Societies of the Twelfth and Thirteenth Centuries', *TRHS*, 6th ser., 5 (1995), 199–200. For the honor of Warwick and its baronies, see D. Crouch, 'The Local Influence of the Earls of Warwick, 1088–1242: A Study in Decline and Resourcefulness', *Midland History*, 21 (1996), 3–5. For the allegiance, borough and estates at Beaudesert and Henley-in-Arden, see *Regesta* iii, no. 597; *Inquisitions post mortem* ii, 225 (Beaudesert); 225 (Henley). Henley is likely to have been part of the Stafford Domesday estate of Ullenhall (*Domesday Book* i, fo. 242c), where Peter de Montfort I made a grant to the Stafford priory of Wootton Wawen as *dominus de Bellodeserto*. Bodl. Libr., ms Dugdale 12, p. 363.

45. R. Mortimer, 'Land and Service: The Tenants of the Honour of Clare', *ANS*, viii, ed. R.A. Brown (Woodbridge, 1986), 177–97. His conclusions are supported by studies in Crouch, *The Beaumont Twins*, 127–32; Hunt, *Lordship and the Landscape*, 66–7; K.J. Stringer, *Earl David of Huntingdon: A Study in Anglo-Scottish History* (Edinburgh, 1985), 128–32.

46. See Crouch, 'From Stenton to McFarlane', 179–200, for a lot of what follows.

47. See Crouch, *Birth of Nobility*, 265–70.

48. William fitz Stephen, *Vita sancti Thomae*, in *Materials for a History of Thomas Becket* iii, 20–1; *Poésies complètes de Bertran de Born*, ed. A. Thomas (Toulouse, 1888), 25; Arnault-Guilhem de Marsan, *L'Ensenhamen*, lines 137–42.

49. *L'Ensenhamen*, lines 433–54. The Prose Lancelot praises Arthur for dining publicly amongst his knights and bachelers: *Lancelot do Lac*, ed. E. Kennedy (2 vols, Oxford, 1980), i, lines 28–30. See the corresponding advice to the countess of Lincoln in the 1240s: *Walter of Henley and Other Treatises on Estate Management*, ed. D.M. Oschinsky (Oxford, 1971), 407.

50. Cartulary of Thorney abbey, Cambridge University Library, Additional ms 3021, fo. 233r.

51. B.G. Charles, 'An Early Charter of the Abbey of Cymhir', *The Transactions of the Radnorshire Society*, 40 (1970), 68–73. For a comparable instance from Leicestershire in

Stephen's reign, where William de Launay granted a six-shilling rent to Kenilworth priory for the souls of members of the Luzerne family killed in his service, see Cartulary of Kenilworth priory, BL, ms Harley 3650, fo. 28r. The Durham *Liber Vitae* contains clumps of names that appear to commemorate members of at least one household in prayer, notably a group of early thirteenth-century names associated with the household of Earl William Marshal II (1219–31): *The Durham Liber Vitae*, eds D. and L. Rollason (3 vols, London, 2007), i, 185 (his cousins the Marshals of Hingham, Robert de Braiboeuf, Adam de Novomercato).

52. E. Baumgartner, 'Trouvères et losengiers', *Cahiers de civilisation médiévale*, 25 (1982), 171–8; S. Kay, 'The Contradictions of Courtly Love and the Origins of Courtly Poetry: The Evidence of the *Lauzengiers*', *Journal of Medieval and Early Modern Studies*, 26 (1996), 209–53; M. Faure, 'Le losengier dans la chanson des trouvères des xiie et xiiie siècles', in *Félonie, trahison, reniements au moyen âge: actes du troisième colloque international de Montpellier, 24–26 novembre 1995* (Montpellier, 1997), 189–95.

53. Crouch, *William Marshal*, 47–50.

54. RH, 140; W.E. Wightman, *The Lacy Family in England and Normandy, 1066–1194* (Oxford, 1966), 68–73.

55. Cartulary of the Counts of Eu, Bibliothèque Nationale, ms Latin 13,904, fo. 45r–v.

56. Hunt, *Lordship and Landscape*, 66; and compare Stringer, *Earl David of Huntingdon*, 25–6, 132.

57. J.C. Holt, *The Northerners* (Oxford, 1961), 43–4.

58. See especially the integrity of the Marcher honorial community of Glamorgan into the fourteenth century: J. Beverley Smith, 'The Kingdom of Morgannwg and the Norman Conquest of Glamorgan', in *Glamorgan County History* iii, *The Middle Ages*, ed. T.B. Pugh (Cardiff, 1971), 16–18, and more generally R.R. Davies, *Lordship and Society in the March of Wales, 1282–1400* (Oxford, 1978), 77–9.

59. Crouch, *Image of Aristocracy*, 238–40; P.R. Coss, *The Knight in Medieval England, 1000–1400* (Stroud, 1993), 80–1.

60. P.R. Coss, *Lordship, Knighthood and Locality: A Study in English Society, c.1180–c.1280* (Cambridge, 1991), 5–8.

61. Crouch, 'Local Influence of the Earls of Warwick', 12.

62. Crouch, *Birth of Nobility*, 287, and see for the sale of the wardship TNA, KB26/131, m. 8d.

63. Crouch, 'Local Influence of the Earls of Warwick', 5, 16, 17. See also the sheriffs of Derby and Nottingham who were tenants of the dominant Nottinghamshire magnates, the Peverels, for much of Henry I's reign: J.A. Green, *The Government of England under Henry I* (Cambridge, 1986), 211.

64. W.A. Morris, *The Medieval English Sheriff to 1300* (Manchester, 1927), 58–60; J.A. Green, *English Sheriffs to 1154* (HMSO, 1990), 16.

65. *Historia et Cartularium monasterii sancti Petri de Gloucestria*, ed. W. Hart (3 vols, Rolls Series, 1896), i, 188 (Adeliza widow of Durand de Pitres), and see for other examples Crouch, *Image of Aristocracy*, 101–2.

66. Morris, *The Medieval English Sheriff*, 77–9. Green, *Government of England under Henry I*, 205, favours fiscal imperatives.

67. Crouch, *William Marshal*, 89, 102.

68. P.R. Coss, 'Knighthood and the Early Thirteenth-Century County Court', in *Thirteenth-Century England* ii, eds P.R. Coss and S.D. Lloyd (Woodbridge, 1987), 45–58; D.A. Carpenter, 'The Decline of the Curial Sheriff in England, 1194–1258', *EHR*, 91 (1976), 1–32.

69. Crouch, 'Local Influence of the Earls of Warwick', 13, 22; M. Morris, *The Bigod Earls of Norfolk in the Thirteenth Century* (Woodbridge, 2005), 70–2.

70. Crouch, *William Marshal*, 147–50, 166–70, 217–25.

71. For the Bigod council in the 1270s and 1280s under Earl Roger IV, see Morris, *The Bigod Earls of Norfolk*, 144–6. N. Denholm-Young, *Seignorial Administration in England* (London,

1937), 26–7, notes twelfth-century antecedents but sees seigneurial *concilia* as developing a new legal expertise in the mid-thirteenth century. However, the *concilium* of William Marshal I self-evidently operated on that level, as the surviving business correspondence of Abbot David of Bristol, one of its members and a Marshal executor, reveals: see BL, Cotton Roll iv, 28, with a rare printed edition in *Ecclesiastical Letter Books of the Thirteenth Century*, ed. R. Hill (Oxford, 1936), 218–41.

72. D. Crouch, 'The March and the Welsh Kings', in *The Anarchy of Stephen's Reign*, ed. E. King (Oxford, 1994), 281–6.

73. G.G. Simpson, 'The *Familia* of Roger de Quincy, Earl of Winchester and Constable of Scotland', in *Essays on the Nobility of Medieval Scotland*, ed. K.J. Stringer (Edinburgh, 1985), 102–27.

74. J.R. Maddicott, *Simon de Montfort* (Cambridge, 1994), 61–71, quotation at 71. For earlier and complementary explorations of the Montfort affinity, see D. Williams, 'Simon de Montfort and his Adherents', in *England in the Thirteenth Century*, ed. W.M. Ormrod (Grantham, 1985), 74–6; D.A. Carpenter 'Simon de Montfort: The First Leader of a Political Movement in English History', *History*, 76 (1991), 10–13.

75. The recent study by C. Burt, 'A "Bastard Feudal" Affinity in the Making? The Followings of William and Guy Beauchamp, Earls of Warwick, 1268–1315', *Midland History*, 34 (2009), 156–80, though badly flawed both methodologically (based on too small a sample of available acta) and conceptually (unable to think beyond a 'bastard feudal' model of society), cannot put much meaning into tenurial connections between Earl William (died 1298) and his men (pp. 171–2).

76. For a discussion of early indentures and their context, see D. Crouch, 'A Norman "Conventio" and Bonds of Lordship in the Middle Ages', in *Law and Government in Medieval England and Normandy: Essays in Honour of Sir James Holt* (Cambridge, 1994), 299–324.

77. *Littere Baronum: The Earliest Cartulary of the Counts of Champagne*, ed. T. Evergates (Toronto, 2003), nos 34, 46. See also the alliance between the counts of Macon and Champagne, expressed by a money charge on the fairs of Champagne: ibid., no. 49. Comparison can be made with the indentures entered into with neigbouring magnates by Duke Matthew II of Lorraine (died 1251), some of which are renewals of relationships made by his father: *Actes de Mathieu II duc de Lorraine (1220–1251)*, ed. M. le Mercier de Morière (Recueil des Documents sur l'Histoire de Lorraine, 17, 1893), 256–7, 260–1, and for comment and context see Crouch, *Birth of Nobility*, 299–301.

78. TNA, DL25/2240. *Documents Illustrative of the Social and Economic History of the Danelaw*, ed. F.M. Stenton (London, 1920), 361, dates the document to the 1170s, though the grounds are not given. Compare the rent charge of 5 *li* owed to successive butlers of the counts of Meulan in the 1130s, first on their Dorset estate of Charlton Marshall and then on the markets of Pont Audemer: Crouch, *Beaumont Twins*, 148.

79. *Cartularium prioratus de Colne*, ed. J.L. Fisher (Essex Archaeological Society, Occasional Publications, 1, 1946), 26: 'non iure hereditario sed in vita sua tantummodo tenendas ... et sciatis quod talo cirografum recepit prefatus Petrus in presentia mea a priore de Colum.'

80. *Calendar of Charter Rolls* i, 189–90, 252.

81. Wiltshire Record Office, 1300/159.

82. TNA, JUST1/81, m. 6; CP25(1)/122/21/366.

83. TNA, KB26/143, m. 17, for which see S.L. Waugh, 'From Tenure to Contract: Lordship and Clientage in Thirteenth-Century England', *EHR*, 101 (1986), 823.

84. 'Private Indentures for Life Service in Peace and War, 1278–1476', eds M. Jones and S. Walker, in *Camden Miscellany*, xxxii (Camden 5th ser., 3, 1994), 13–16, regards the mention of military service in indentures to be a new thing at the end of Henry III's reign, but that is arguing from silence.

85. H. Ridgeway. 'William de Valence and his *Familiares*, 1247–72', *Historical Research*, 65 (1992), 254–7. His prominence in the English tournaments of the 1250s is notable and

he retained in his affinity Roger of Leyburn, one of the most famous tourneyers of his day: ibid., 248; MP, *CM* v, 318–19.

86. N. Vincent, 'William Marshal, King Henry II and the Honour of Châteauroux', *Archives*, xxv (2000), 15.

87. *HWM* ii, lines 13,488–502; *Layettes du trésor des chartes*, ed. A. Teulet (5 vols, Paris, 1863–1909), i, no. 1354. In 1229, five knights of the *familia* of Earl William Marshal II were recorded as having exemption from scutage for crossing with him to Poitou, TNA, C72/5, but there might have been more who had no scutage obligation. Three (Baldwin de Béthune, John III of Earley and Alan Basset) are identifiable as regular members of his entourage.

88. *HWM* i, lines 1314–17.

89. BL, ms Additional 8167, fo. 128r.

90. A. Tomkinson, 'Retinues at the Tournament of Dunstable 1309', *EHR*, 74 (1959), 78–9.

CHAPTER NINE: THE SEIGNEURIAL COURT

1. F. Pollock and F.W. Maitland, *The History of English Law* (2 vols, repr. Cambridge, 1968), i, 571–94. See comment in P. Wormald, *The Making of English Law: King Alfred to the Twelfth Century* (Oxford, 1999), 18–19, 327, and the case study in *idem*, 'Lordship and Justice in the Early English Kingdom: Oswaldlow Revisited', in *Property and Power in the Early Middle Ages*, eds W. Davies and P. Fouracre (Cambridge, 1995), 114–36. Some parts of this chapter have appeared elsewhere: see D. Crouch, 'La cour seigneuriale en Angleterre aux xiie–xiiie siècles', in *Les seigneuries dans l'espace Plantagenêt (c.1150–c.1250)*, eds M. Aurell and F. Boutoulle (Bordeaux, 2009), 31–40.

2. For Maitland's still-relevant observations about the distinction between honorial and manorial courts, see *Select Pleas in Manorial and Other Seignorial Courts* i, *Reigns of Henry III and Edward I*, ed. F.W. Maitland (Selden Society, ii, 1888), pp. xlii–xlvii. *Leges Henrici Primi*, cc. 9.6, 25.1, 33, 55.1.

3. J. Laporte, '*Epistulae Fiscannenses*: lettres d'amitié, de gouvernement et d'affaires (xie–xiie siècles)', *Revue Mabillon*, lxiii (1953), 29–31.

4. Ibid., pp. 128, 172. (The translations are mine.) The definition of *homo ligius* in c. 55.2 is difficult, but in this instance it would seem to mean that the status of a 'liege' man reflected the principal allegiance he swore and acknowledged.

5. Stubbs, *Select Charters*, 122.

6. B.R. O'Brien, *God's Peace and King's Peace: The Laws of Edward the Confessor* (Philadelphia, 1999), p. 167, cc. 9:1–3. On this royal oversight of seigneurial courts, see the king's assertion of his right in 1170 to regulate their practices in the so-called Assize of Essoiners: *Pleas before the King or his Justices, 1198–1202*, ed. D.M. Stenton (Selden Society, 67, 1948), 153.

7. *Early Yorkshire Charters* ix, no. 157.

8. *The Treatise on the Law and Customs of the Realm of England Commonly Called Glanvill*, ed. G.D.G. Hall (London, 1965), 136–7, 139–41. P. Brand, 'Henry II and the Creation of the English Common Law', in *Henry II: New Interpretations*, eds C. Harper-Bill and N. Vincent (Woodbridge, 2007), 220, also considers briefly the process of 'tolt' begun under Henry II by which a case could be transferred from a private to a royal court for failure of justice.

9. This is not the same as saying, as Alan Harding did, that 'the pyramidial shape of English feudalism meant that the *curia regis* was one court the jurisdiction of which none could escape': *The Law Courts of Medieval England* (London, 1973), 38.

10. D. Crouch, *The Beaumont Twins: The Roots and Branches of Power in the Twelfth Century* (Cambridge, 1986), 159. For the Croft charter, see BL, Additional charter 48299.

11. TNA, E210/173; Cartulary of Sele priory, Oxford, Magdalen College, ms 274, fos 26v, 27r.

12. The reason for this further step may be revealed by a plea in the *curia regis* of 1224, when the king's justices refused to take steps to enforce a final concord made in Somerset in the years 1190–2 as it had been drawn up in the court of John, count of Mortain, not that of the king: *Curia Regis Rolls* xi, 303.

13. *Luffield Priory Charters*, ed. G.R. Elvey (2 vols, Northamptonshire Record Society, xxii, xxvi, 1968–75), i, 118–20. Compare the diplomatic of another final concord reached in a seigneurial court, that of Roger de Lacy at Clitheroe in 1195 × 96: *Early Yorkshire Charters* iii, 211–12.

14. For the text, see Cartulary of Plympton priory, Oxford, Bodl. Libr., ms James 23, pp. 159–60, published in *English Lawsuits* ii, no. 452, pp. 487–8. For other documents arising from the same Roger's honor court, a *conventio* between himself and Totnes priory, see Devon Record Office, 312M/TY7 (Hole of Park Deeds), and another between himself and Buckfast abbey; see *The Register of John de Grandison, Bishop of Exeter* iii, *1360–1369*, ed. F.C. Hingeston-Randolph (London, 1899), 1572–3.

15. The monks of Tewkesbury produced their charters to justify a claim in the honor court of Earl William of Gloucester at some time between 1155 and 1183: *Monasticon Anglicanum* ii, 73.

16. Use of a judicial duel in the court of the earl of Leicester is noted in the mid-1160s: Crouch, *Beaumont Twins*, 161–2. The text in *English Lawsuits* i, 265, misidentifies the place in contention and dates the case twenty years too early. A land plea in Wiltshire came to a final concord after a combat in the court of Earl William Marshal at Marlborough some time between 1215 and 1221: *Basset Charters c.1120 to 1250*, ed. W.T. Reedy (Pipe Roll Society, lxxxviii, 1995), 151 (the date established by the temporary possession of Marlborough by the Marshals). A plea over a landed estate of fourteen bovates was fought in the court of Earl William de Warenne at Conisbrough (West Riding, Yorkshire) in or soon before 1219 in the presence of the earl's seneschal and bailiffs, who then arranged a fine: *Bracton's Note Book*, ed. F.W. Maitland (3 vols, London, 1887), ii, 23. In the 1250s, Bracton still gives extensive guidance on the conduct of duels as an active part of the legal process: *Bracton on the Laws and Customs of England*, ed. G.E. Woodbine and trans. S.E. Thorne (2 vols, Cambridge, MA, 1968), ii, 385–92.

17. *Feet of Fines in the Public Record Office of the 10th Year of King Richard I, also a Roll of the King's Court in the Reign of King Richard I*, ed. anon. (Pipe Roll Society, xxiv, 1900), 239–40. For another use of summons, essoin and confiscation, this time in the court of Hugh de Mortemer, see *Monasticon Anglicanum* vi, 345. A comparable case can be seen from the court of Nigel de Luvetot in Northamptonshire in 1217, when a defendant was summoned in three successive courts, and on failure to appear was disseised: *Bracton's Note Book* iii, 306–7.

18. Cartulary of St Andrew Northampton, BL, ms Royal 11 B ix, fo. 19r; 'veritatem diligenter inquisiui et recognitum est per antiquos homines curie mee.'

19. Cartulary of St-Evroult, Bibliothèque Nationale de France, ms Latin 11055, fo. 35v. For a jury used in the honor court of Earl Hamelin of Warenne, 1173 × 81, see *Early Yorkshire Charters*, viii, 103–4, and for a recognition of darrein presentment before Earl Reginald of Cornwall, 1161 × 70, see H.P.R. Finberg, 'Some Early Tavistock Charters', *EHR*, 62 (1947), 360.

20. *Three Rolls of the King's Court in the Reign of Richard I, AD 1194–1195*, ed. F.W. Maitland (Pipe Roll Society, xiv, 1891), 17.

21. H.M. Cam, *The Hundred and the Hundred Rolls* (London, 1963), 137–45.

22. *Monasticon Anglicanum* vi, 345.

23. *Curia Regis Rolls* i, 370.

24. Ibid. xvii, 261–2.

25. TNA, KB26/156 m. 13.

26. *History of English Law* i, 153–6. See the observations on this historiographical tradition in R.C. van Caenegem, *The Birth of the English Common Law* (Cambridge, 1973), 23–8;

P. Brand, '*Multis Vigiliis Excogitatam et Inventam*: Henry II and the Creation of the English Common Law', in *The Making of the Common Law* (London, 1992), 79–86, especially 86. S.F.C. Milsom, *Historical Foundations of the Common Law* (London, 1969), 11–12, 15ff., supposed that justice had been centralised in England before 1250, with the corollary that seigneurial courts had '*perished*' (my italics).

27. D.M. Stenton, *English Justice between the Norman Conquest and the Great Charter, 1066–1215* (London 1965), 77–8.

28. Stenton, *First Century*, 45, developed this argument in 1929. Stenton believed that the English honor was a 'feudal state in miniature' that had been subverted by royal authority before the 1170s; ibid., 51–4. Stenton was followed by Sidney Painter, *Studies in the English Feudal Barony* (Baltimore, 1943), 137. See the further development of this idea in the work of the jurists Van Caenegem, *Birth of the English Common Law*, 24, 54, and S.F.C. Milsom, *The Legal Framework of English Feudalism* (Cambridge, 1976), 8. The two take Stenton's thesis of honorial decline as gospel, for which see J.G. Hudson, *The Formation of the English Common Law* (London, 1996), 53–4. P.R. Coss, 'Bastard Feudalism Revised', *PP*, 125 (1989), 27–64, esp. 41, developed a theory from Stenton's idea of a consequent noble reaction against the Angevin reforms of English law.

29. J. Hudson, *Land, Law and Lordship in Anglo-Norman England* (Cambridge, 1994), 263–5.

30. *Glanvill*, ed. Hall, 179–80.

31. J. Biancalana, 'For Want of Justice: The Legal Reforms of Henry II', *Columbia Law Review*, 88 (1988), 509–11.

32. *Histoire des ducs*, 150: 'Toutes hautes justices vaurrent-il avoir en lor tierres.' See on this M.T. Clanchy, 'Magna Carta, Clause Thirty-Four', *EHR*, 79 (1964), 542–8; Hudson, *Formation of the English Common Law*, 224–6.

33. Cartulary of Sele Priory, Oxford, Magdalen College ms 274, fos 26v–27r (1269), fo. 27r (1272).

34. *Curia Regis Rolls* xiv, 484–5.

35. TNA E40/9420, deed dated 1272.

36. *Records of the Barony and Honour of the Rape of Lewes*, ed. A.J. Taylor (Sussex Record Society, 44, 1939), esp. 37, 48, for the seigneurial *quo warranto* proceedings.

37. Ibid., 2.

38. *The Cartulary of St Mary's Collegiate Church, Warwick*, ed. C. Fonge (Woodbridge, 2004), 20. This example seems to tell against Maitland's argument that the sake and soke of the burgesses of Warwick in Domesday Book did not involve jurisdiction but only 'house-peace': F.W. Maitland, 'Sake and Soke', in *Domesday Book and Beyond: Three Essays in the Early History of England* (repr. Cambridge, 1987), 98–9. Burgage land often went along with estates outside the walls.

39. *The Thurgarton Cartulary*, ed. T. Foulds (Stamford, 1994), 349.

40. M. Bailey, *The English Manor, c.1200–c.1500* (Manchester, 2002), 167–83.

41. For the *vicecomites* of Lewes and Wakefield, see *Early Yorkshire Charters* viii, 74, 83. Payn *vicecomes de Lewes* paid a sum to the Jews of Warwick for Earl Hamelin's debt in 1182 × 83; TNA E210/10868. For private 'sheriffs' or 'vicomtes' in England and Normandy, see W.A. Morris, *The Medieval English Sheriff* (Manchester, 1927), 108–9; Crouch, *Beaumont Twins*, 170–3. With the exception of Cheshire, the English private *vicecomites* most resemble Franco-Norman honorial *vicomtes*, who were primarily judical officers. For a revealing recent survey of the Norman evidence, see M.S. Hagger, 'The Norman *Vicomte, c.*1035–1135: What Did He Do?', *ANS*, xxix, ed. C.P. Lewis (Woodbridge, 2007), 65–83, and for a much broader series of studies, see *Vicomtes et vicomtés dans l'Occident médiéval*, ed. H. Débax (Toulouse, 2008). The 'sheriff' of Holderness presided over his lord's private wapentake court of Hedon: B. English, *The Lords of Holderness, 1086–1260* (Oxford, 1979), 70–6.

42. *Early Yorkshire Charters* viii, 220. The earl appears to have regarded his lands in Yorkshire as part of his wider honor in England, rather than as simply jurisdictional sokes, such as

Conisbrough or Wakefield, for which see ibid., 103. For another example of a concord being sworn on gospels in a Yorkshire honor court, this time the Lacy court at Pontefract in 1201, see *Early Yorkshire Charters* iii, 213–14.

43. D. Crouch, 'The Local Influence of the Earls of Warwick, 1088–1242: A Study in Decline and Resourcefulness', *Midland History*, xxi (1996), 11–13. A notice of the surrender of the fees of the barony of Corbezun to Earl Waleran by William son of Peter Corbezun II is to be found in BL, ms Cotton Julius C vii, fo. 218v. No detail is given, but the likeliest explanation is that the Corbezuns were disseised of the fees for non-performance of service.

44. D.A. Carpenter, 'King, Magnates and Society: The Personal Rule of King Henry III, 1234–1258', *Speculum*, 60 (1985), 63–4.

45. *Documents*, 138–40.

46. *Basset Charters*, 102–3. For Guy fitz Robert, see D.A. Carpenter, 'Was There a Crisis of the Knightly Class in the Thirteenth Century? The Oxfordshire Evidence', *EHR*, 95 (1980), 733. Guy was sometime sheriff, coroner and escheator of Oxfordshire. A plea to enforce suit at the court of Hugh Talemasch at Bentley, Suffolk, also mentions that suit ought to be made 'when a royal writ should come into the court' and when a thief was to be judged there: *Curia Regis Rolls* xi, 339.

47. *Descriptive Catalogue of the Charters and Muniments at Berkeley Castle*, ed. I.H. Jeayes (Bristol, 1892), 10–11.

48. *Leges Henrici Primi, c.* 7.7a–b. This is made explicit in the case of shire or hundred courts for the prior of Wenlock in a charter of King Stephen dated 1138: See D.C. Cox, 'Two Charters of King Stephen for Wenlock Priory', *Transactions of the Shropshire Archaeological and Historical Society*, lxvi (1989), 56–8, where the *dapifer* or *magistralis serviens* of the prior can discharge the suits, except for pleas of the crown.

49. D.A. Carpenter, 'The Second Century of English Feudalism', *PP*, 168 (2000), 53–4.

50. *Rolls of the Justices in Eyre for Worcestershire, Warwickshire and Staffordshire, 1221–1222*, ed. and trans. D.M. Stenton (Selden Society, lix, 1940), 176–7.

51. For Henry of Tubney as seneschal of Thomas Basset in 1207, see TNA 370/1/4, m. 1. He held Tubney, Berkshire, of the abbey of Abingdon, and his lineage can be traced back through his father, John of Tubney, to the Domesday tenant Rainbald, who was a son-in-law of the then abbot, Reginald: *Historia Ecclesiae Abbendonensis* ii, ed. and trans. J.G. Hudson (Oxford, 2002), lxiii–lxiv.

52. See Crouch, *Birth of Nobility*, 293 and n.

53. For the case of Henry Basset, TNA, KB26/40, m. 8, see *Curia Regis Rolls* xix, 326–9. For the place of North Moreton as a fee of Warwick in 1242, *Cal Inquisitions PM* i, 3. The fee of North Moreton had originally been held of the Corbezun family, but the fees had been sold back by the Corbezuns to the earl (see above, n. 43) who was therefore the direct overlord; for the date of this judgement see above, pp. 112–13.

54. *The Cartulary of Daventry Priory*, ed. M.J. Franklin (Northamptonshire Record Society, xxxv, 1988), 295.

55. *Gui de Warewic: roman du xiii ͤ siècle*, ed. A. Ewert (2 vols, Paris, 1932), i, 6–7. For the date of this romance, see Crouch, 'Local Influence of the Earls of Warwick', 20.

56. *Cal. Inquisitions PM* vii, no. 417.

57. For John Durvassal II of Spernall's office-holding, see Crouch, 'Local Influence of the Earls of Warwick', 22. He was keeper of Warwick castle when Earl Thomas died in 1242: *Cal Patent Rolls*, 299. He was dead by 1257: TNA, KB26/154, m. 23, when his heir was his son William Durvassal II. For their relationship, see Cartulary of Wootton Wawen priory, Cambridge, King's College, mun. no. WOW/231, fo. 23v. A Durvassal first appears in the Warwick acts at the time of Earl Waleran: Shakespeare Birthplace Trust, DR37/5 (Archer of Tanworth deeds).

58. Oxford, Bodl. Libr., ms Dugdale 13, pp. 521–2: a facsimile of an obviously interpolated charter dating to Alan of Woodloes's grandfather's day, fabricated to assert a claim to his perquisites.

CHAPTER TEN: CAPITAL JUSTICE AND THE RISE OF LIBERTIES

1. Lanfranc in 1075 refers to captured soldiers in a rebellion being pardoned penalty of 'life and limbs': *The Letters of Lanfranc Archbishop of Canterbury*, eds and trans. H. Clover and M. Gibson (Oxford, 1979), no. 35, p. 124. In 1154, King Stephen withheld 'justice of life and limbs' from the Templars' exemption for royal pleas in their lands: *Regesta* iii, no. 866. A charter of William III de Briouze dating to 1185 × 90 reserves to himself 'justicia omnium hominum suorum totius . . . tenementi sui *unde pertinet vitam vel menbrum perdere'* (my italics) when confirming his lands in the honor of Brecon to Walter of Clifford: I.W. Rowlands, 'William de Braose and the Lordship of Brecon', *Bulletin of the Board of Celtic Studies*, 30 (1982–3), 123–33, quotation at 133. N.D. Hurnard, 'The Anglo-Norman Franchises', *EHR*, 64 (1949), 289n, views the phrase as dating from the late twelfth century and as only relevant to royal pleas.
2. This is the use found in Hurnard, 'The Anglo-Norman Franchises', 289–327, 433–60. M.T. Clanchy, 'The Franchise of Return of Writs', *TRHS*, 5th ser., 17 (1967), 59n, is more precise.
3. D.W. Sutherland, *Quo Warranto Proceedings in the Reign of Edward I, 1278–1294* (Oxford, 1963), 1–6, gives a good overview.
4. *Gesta Henrici Secundi*, ed. W. Stubbs (2 vols, Rolls Series, 1867), ii, 233.
5. D.A. Carpenter, 'King, Magnates and Society: The Personal Rule of King Henry III, 1234–1258', *Speculum*, 60 (1985), 49–50. It should be noted that magnates themselves might pursue *quo warranto* cases against tenants in their own courts, as Earl John I of Warenne was doing in the 1260s in Sussex: *Records of the Barony and Honour of the Rape of Lewes*, ed. A.J. Taylor (Sussex Record Society, 44, 1939), 37, 48.
6. Cartulary of Launceston priory, Lambeth Palace Library, ms 719, fo. 11r–v.
7. TNA, E159/23, m. 8; KB26/140 m. 12d; KB26/141 m. 9d.
8. TNA, KB26/158, m. 13.
9. BL, Harley charter 55 D 24.
10. For the historiography of this, see D. Crouch, The *Birth of Nobility: Constructing Aristocracy in England and France, 900–1300* (Harlow, 2005), 191–8.
11. Clanchy, 'The Franchise of Return of Writs', esp. 61–2.
12. Dublin, National Library of Ireland, ms D. 50 (Duiske Charters).
13. Register of Bury, BL, ms Harley 743, fo. 141r–v.
14. *Placita de Quo Warranto*, 88–98.
15. *Letters of Lanfranc*, 118–20.
16. C.P. Lewis, 'The Formation of the Honor of Chester', in *The Earldom of Chester and its Charters*, ed. A.T. Thacker (Chester Archaeological Society, 71, 1991), 44–5; D. Crouch, 'The Administration of the Norman Earldom', in ibid., 70–3.
17. *Liber Luciani de laude Cestrie*, ed. M.V. Taylor (Lancashire and Cheshire Record Society, lxiv, 1912), 61–2.
18. Bodl. Libr., ms Dugdale 17, p. 83. Apparently some relics of the office attached to the manor of Dutton survived into the eighteenth century: *Notes & Queries* (29 June 1850), 77.
19. *Charters of the Earls of Chester*, ed. Barraclough, no. 394, pp. 388–91. The charter duplicates the concern of King John's charter, especially over succession, wardship and disparagement.
20. The case of the liberty of the bishop of Durham (another so-called 'palatinate') is not comparable, as the exclusion of royal writs from the bishop's lands was being vigorously disputed in 1204, when it was claimed by a plaintiff that a king's or chief justiciar's writ was needed to initiate actions in the bishop's court in Henry II's reign: *Curia Regis Rolls* iii, 108–9. The place of the bishop's honor within Northumberland and the applicability of royal writs were asserted by King John in 1208 and 1211: see J. Scammell, 'The Origin and Limitations of the Liberty of Durham', *EHR*, 81 (1966), 458–60.
21. It was Sir William Blackstone in the eighteenth century who chose to describe Angevin Chester as a 'palatine earldom' – analogous to privileged counties in medieval France

and the Empire – and his assumptions influenced the generations of Stubbs and Maitland. For this vexed question, see G. Barraclough, *The Earldom and County Palatine of Chester* (Oxford, 1953); J.W. Alexander, 'The Alleged Palatinates of Norman England,' *Speculum*, 56 (1981), 17–27, esp. 18.

22. M. Howell, 'Regalian Right in Wales and the March: The Relation of Theory to Practice', *Welsh History Review*, 7 (1974–5), 269–88.

23. D. Crouch, *The Reign of King Stephen, 1135–1154* (Harlow, 2000), 84–90. The best illustration of the liberties of Stephen's post-1138 earls is the case of Worcester, held by Waleran of Meulan. His forest pleas in the shire and the 'king's geld which belongs to me' are mentioned in a letter to his sheriff and son-in-law, William de Beauchamp: H.W.C. Davis, 'Some Documents of the Anarchy', in *Essays in History Presented to R.L. Poole* (Oxford, 1927), 170–1. See also the settlement of pleas and exemptions between Waleran and the bishop of Worcester: H.A. Cronne, 'An Agreement between Simon, Bishop of Worcester, and Waleran, Earl of Worcester', *University of Birmingham Historical Journal*, ii (1949–50), 201–7.

24. In a charter to Launceston dating after the succession of 1154, he referred to a plea held in his castle of Dunheved 'in pleno comitatu coram me': Cartulary of Launceston priory, fo. 11r–v.

25. Cartulary of Plympton priory, p. 156. S. Painter, *Studies in the History of the English Feudal Barony* (Baltimore, 1943), 110, says otherwise, but his view of baronial immunities ignores too much evidence to be accepted. The fact that the king ordered a magnate to do his will in his lands does not make his barony an immunity for it does not exclude the king, it simply co-opts the baron into becoming a king's officer.

26. N. Denholm-Young, *Richard of Cornwall* (Oxford, 1947), 29, 164. His confirmation of the liberties of the boroughs of Dunheved and Lostwithiel refers to pleas of the crown in his shire, not of his sword: TNA, C52/20, m. 16; C56/50 m. 18. Like Earl Reginald, he presided at a shire court meeting in August 1229 at Bodmin and held an inquisition over presentations to two churches: Cartulary of Launceston, fo. 200v.

27. See his charter dated 1257: BL, Additional charter 1051.

28. Note how Earl Ranulf III of Chester claimed parity in his privileges with two other magnates in the 1220s, the earl of Cornwall and the bishop of Durham, which indicates an emerging idea that some immunities were more absolute than others in England: *Bracton's Notebook*, ed. F.W. Maitland (3 vols, London, 1887), iii, 146–7. Note also how in Richard's reign Count John of Mortain, like the earl of Chester, claimed to have 'pleas of the sword' in his lordship of Lancashire, though they did not exclude those of the crown there: *Coucher Book of Furness Abbey*, ed. J.C. Atkinson (3 vols, Chetham Society, new ser., ix, xi, xiv, 1886–7), iii, 468. For an informative look at the consolidation of a Marcher lordship, see the example of Clun, in M. Lieberman, *The Medieval March of Wales* (Cambridge, 2010) 215–45.

29. *Rolls of the Justices in Eyre for Yorkshire in 3 Henry III (1218–19)*, ed. and trans. D.M. Stenton (Selden Society, 56, 1937), 422; *Calendar of Inquisitions Miscellaneous Preserved in the Public Record Office* (London, HMSO, 1916–2003) i, no. 131. For this, see Clanchy, 'The Franchise of Return of Writs', 60.

30. *Rotuli Hundredorum*, ed. W. Illingworth (2 vols, Record Commission, 1812–18), ii, 12–13. Though the inquisition believed Earl Richard's father acquired the hundred, the hundredal manor of Rothwell was in fact in the hands of his grandfather Earl Richard of Hertford (died 1217) in 1204: *Rotuli Chartarum* i, 117.

31. Cartulary of Pipewell abbey, BL, ms Stowe 937, fo. 19r.

32. *Records of the Barony and Honour of the Rape of Lewes*, ed. A.J. Taylor (Sussex Record Society, 44, 1939), esp. 17, 30, 41.

33. *Rotuli Hundredorum* ii, pt 1, 208–10.

34. L.F. Salzman, 'The Family of Aguillon', *Sussex Archaeological Collections*, 79 (1938), 45–58; H. Ridgeway. 'William de Valence and his *Familiares*, 1247–72', *Historical Research*, 65 (1992), 247.

35. *Rotuli Hundredorum* ii, 209, 210.
36. BL, Additional Charter 21694; Bodl. Libr., ms Dugdale 15, p. 218.
37. Bracton's tendency to identify *potestas* with lordship over peasants made this easy, though in the case of Astley the *potestas* he was referring to was territorial: *Bracton on the Laws and Customs of England* ii, 36–8.
38. *Curia Regis Rolls* vii, 57.
39. The rights are defined in the *Leges Edwardi* of the 1130s, where it is explicitly stated that their possession can be taken as a lord's warrant to do justice on men 'sub suo friborgo', that is, within his jurisdiction for peacekeeping purposes, the mechanism later called 'frankpledge'. See on this O'Brien, *God's Peace and King's Peace*, 84–7, 179–83.
40. Maitland, 'Sake and Soke', 80–9; Stenton, *First Century*, 100–4; cf. Hudson, *Formation of the English Common Law*, 44–5. D. Roffe, 'From Thegnage to Barony: Sake and Soke, Title and Tenants-in-Chief', *Anglo-Norman Studies*, xii, ed. M. Chibnall (Woodbridge, 1990), 157–76, further examines the incidence of the mnemonic in Domesday Book and traces the jurisdictional rights to pre-Conquest days. Nicholas Vincent has pointed out to me a confirmation by Count Stephen of Brittany (died 1137) to one of his men of tol, team etc. as granted to the man's father in the 1080s: see Burghley House, deed 14/32.
41. Stenton, *First Century*, 105–6. It is worth noting in comparison that Ranulf's equally well-documented contemporary Robert II of Leicester made only two known grants of sake, soke, etc. One of those was a grant attached to just ten burgesses in the town of Leicester: *Registrum Antiquissimum* ii, 16–17.
42. *Charters of the Honour of Mowbray, 1107–1191*, ed. D.E. Greenway (London, 1972), nos 343, 354.
43. *Curia Regis Rolls* xi, 208, 494.
44. Stenton, *First Century*, 102n. When the court of Earl Gilbert Marshal at Long Crendon, Buckinghamshire, hanged a horse thief before 1241, the earl's bailiff was challenged for doing so without a king's bailiff present, and also for seizing and selling the thief's chattels without view of the county coroner: TNA, JUST1/55, m. 23d.
45. TNA, JUST1/455, m. 3.
46. Cartulary of the Hospitallers, BL, ms Cotton Nero, E vi, pt 1, fo. 135v.
47. *Placita de Quo Warranto*, 81. The oddity of the charter's phrasing might be suspicious in light of the fact that its original was produced before a *quo warranto* inquisition in 1284 designed to establish just the rights it claimed. Or perhaps I'm being cynical.
48. TNA, JUST1/455, m. 11.
49. TNA, JUST1/58 m 24; JUST1/61, m. 6.
50. *Curia Regis Rolls* xx, 52.
51. TNA, JUST1/951A, mm. 1, 1d. At the time of the murder Peter de Montfort was in wardship to William de Cantilupe, and one of the principals charged. Geoffrey Pauncefot, described as *serviens* of Beaudesert, was also Cantilupe's seneschal: TNA, E159/13, m. 2. The amercements for the offence were not paid off until 1241: TNA, E159/19 m. 1d.
52. MP, *CM* v, 726, 737–9. A.H. Hershey, 'The Rise and Fall of William de Bussey: A Mid Thirteenth-Century Steward', *Nottingham Medieval Studies*, 44 (2000), 116.
53. *The Chronicle of William de Rishanger of the Barons' Wars*, ed. J.O. Halliwell (Camden Soc., xv, 1840), 4–5.
54. There is little space in my interpretation of the idea of judicial liberties for the debate over the nature of the state and its powers which recent publication has tried to impose on the study of the practice of magnate power. See on this K.J. Stringer, 'States, Liberties and Communities in Medieval Britain and Ireland (*c.*1100–1400)', in *Liberties and Identities in the Medieval British Isles*, ed. M. Prestwich (Woodbridge, 2008), 5–36. Even where such debate tries to assert the importance of the periphery against the centre, it asserts a conflictual, top-down dynamic in interpreting magnate power which runs clean counter to the evidence presented here.
55. *The Chronicle of Walter of Guisborough*, ed. H. Rothwell (Camden Society, 3rd ser., lxxxix, 1957), 216.

CHAPTER ELEVEN: CONDUCT

1. R. Fleming, 'The New Wealth, the New Rich, and the New Political Style in Late Anglo-Saxon England', *ANS*, xxiiii, ed. J. Gillingham (Woodbridge, 2000), 1–22. The acquisition and display of status objects in manifestations of lordship were an integral part of Western aristocracy from its very origins and were the basis of the appearance of complex economies in northern Europe, according to the interpretation of C. Wickham, *The Inheritance of Rome: A History of Europe from 400 to 1000* (Harmondsworth, 2009), esp. ch. 23.

2. For this see M. Keen, *Chivalry* (New Haven, 1984), especially 6, 239; D. Crouch, *The Birth of Nobility: Constructing Aristocracy in England and France, 900–1300* (Harlow, 2005), pt 1, especially 52–6, for the idea of habitus, deriving from the French sociologist Pierre Bourdieu.

3. J. Flori, 'La notion de chevalerie dans les chansons de geste du xiie siècle: étude historique de vocabulaire', *Le Moyen Âge*, 81 (1975), 211–44, 407–45, quotation and dating at 437. His views were repeated and elaborated in 'La notion de la chevalerie dans les romans de Chrétien de Troyes', *Romania*, 114 (1996), 289–315.

4. See generally A. Monson, *Les Ensenhamens occitans: essai de définition et délimitation du genre* (Paris, 1981). Monson (pp. 167–8) defines nine such works between the twelfth and early fourteenth centuries in terms of content and six-syllable verse structure, which distinguishes them from the genre of *novas* (pp. 86–93). For an edition and translation (by Gerard Gouiran) into modern French, see J. de Cauna, *L'Ensenhamen ou code du parfait chevalier du troubadour gascon Arnaut Guilhem de Marsan* (Mounenh en Biarn, 2007), pp. 64–95. For a corpus of such texts, see G.E. Sansone, *Testi Didattico-Cortesi di Provenza* (Bari, 1977).

5. M.L. Colker, 'Latin Texts Concerning Gilbert, Founder of Merton Priory', *Studia Monastica*, 12 (1970), 248–61 (passim). See on this source Crouch, *Birth of Nobility*, 41–43.

6. Colker, 'Latin Texts', 254.

7. L. Zatočil, *Cato a Facetus: Zu den deutschen Cato- und Facetusbearbeitungen. Untersuchungen und Texte* (Opera Universitatis Masarykianae Brunensis, Facultas Philosophica, 48, Brno, 1952), 229–37.

8. For teaching avatars, see C.S. Jaeger, *The Envy of Angels: Cathedral Schools and Social Ideals in Medieval Europe, 950–1200* (Philadelphia, 1994), 76–83; *idem*, 'Book-Burning at Don Quixote's: Thoughts on the Educating Force of Courtly Romance', in *Courtly Arts and the Art of Courtliness: Selected Papers from the Eleventh Triennial Congress of the International Courtly Literature* Society, eds K. Busby and C. Kleinhenz (Cambridge, 2006), 20. The concept of emulation of literary avatars of conduct as a way of instructing nobles is tellingly found outside the Francophone world; see H. Fulton, 'The *Mabinogi* and the Education of Princes in Medieval Wales', in *eadem, Medieval Celtic Literature and Society,* ed. (Dublin, 2005), 230–47. Interestingly, Robert Grosseteste, bishop of Lincoln (died 1253), a man of humble background but great courtliness, when supposedly challenged by the earl of Gloucester on this disparity in birth and behaviour, is made by a later source to comment that he had learned his urbanity from biblical characters who were models of prudence, modesty, largesse and virtue: *The Lanercost Chronicle, 1201–1346*, ed. J. Stevenson (Edinburgh, 1839), 44–5.

9. *Facetus*, 230–1.

10. *LM*, 81–3 (my translation).

11. Andrew de Coutances, 'Le *Roman des Franceis*', ed. A.J. Holden, in *Études de langue et de littérature du moyen âge offertes à Félix Lecoy* (Paris, 1973), lines 139–56 (my translation). For this work, see now D. Crouch, 'The *Roman des Franceis*: Text, Translation and Significance', in *Culture and Change: England, Normandy and France, 1000–1250: Essays for David Bates*, eds D. Crouch and K. Thompson (Turnhout, 2010), forthcoming. The reference to an 'Armenian' apparently signifies uncouthness.

12. See Crouch, *Birth of Nobility*, 71–9, for this.

13. OV iv, 143.

14. Baudrey de Bourgeuil, *Historia Hierosolymitina*, in *PL*, 154, col. 368.

15. *The Cartulary and Charters of Notre-Dame of Homblières*, ed. W.M. Newman, revised by T. Evergates and G. Constable (Cambridge, Mass., 1990), 120–1.
16. For an edition and modern French translation, see *Nouvelles occitanes du moyen âge*, ed. and trans. J.-C. Huchet (Paris, 1992), 38–138.
17. Ibid., 71 (lines 590–2).
18. Ibid., 98 (line 1058).
19. For the authorship and construction of the work, see D. Crouch, 'Writing a Biography in the Thirteenth Century: The Construction and Composition of the "History of William Marshal" ', in *Writing a Medieval Biography: Essays in Honour of Frank Barlow*, eds D. Bates, J. Crick and S. Hamilton (Woodbridge, 2006), 221–35.
20. Crouch, *Birth of Nobility*, 58–9. See generally for the context of Marshal's behaviour, D. Crouch, 'Loyalty, Career and Self-Justification at the Plantagenet Court: The Thought-World of William Marshal and his Colleagues', in *Culture politique des Plantagenêt, 1154–1224*, ed. M. Aurell (Poitiers, 2003), 229–40.
21. Crouch, *Birth of Nobility*, 68–71.
22. *HWM* i, lines 5060–108.
23. As in ibid., lines 5214–17, where his *chevalerie* is not Marshal's conduct but his deeds of arms.
24. A possible exception is a vernacular Anglo-Norman *ars amoris* of apparent English provenance, which might date to before 1250: O. Södergård, 'Un art d'aimer anglo-normand', *Romania*, 77 (1956), 289–330.
25. *Le traité de Walter de Bibbesworth sur la langue française*, ed. A. Owen (Paris, 1929); for comments on the difficulties of this text, see W. Rothwell, 'A Mis-judged Author and a Mis-used Text: Walter de Bibbesworth and his *Tretiz*', *Modern Language Review*, 77 (1982), 282–93. For the meagre output of thirteenth-century courtesy literature in England, see N. Orme, *From Childhood to Chivalry: The Education of the English Kings and Aristocracy, 1066–1530* (London, 1984), 137.
26. MP, *CM* v, 85–6.
27. *Jehan et Blonde*, ed. S. Lécuyer (Classiques Français du Moyen Age, 1984), lines 358–9.
28. *HWM* i, lines 5214–20.
29. E. Faral, *Mimes français du xiii* siècle* (Paris, 1910), 42, 45. An earlier edition in *Political Songs of England*, ed. and trans. T. Wright (1839), revised P.R. Coss (Cambridge, 1996), 63–8, is accompanied by a somewhat quaint translation.
30. *Le Roman de Ham*, in *Histoire des ducs de Normandie et des rois d'Angleterre*, ed. F. Michel (Paris, 1840), 225–6; for comment, see J. Vale, 'The Late Thirteenth-Century Precedent: Chauvency, Le Hem and Edward I', in *eadem, Edward III and Chivalry: Chivalric Society and its Context, 1270–1350* (Woodbridge, 1983), 15–16.
31. For Matthew Paris's view that the French still remained terrified of the prowess of King Richard in the 1250s, see MP *CM* v, 478, and see comments on Richard's thirteenth-century reputation as a warrior in J. Gillingham, *Richard I* (New Haven, 1999), 8–9; J. Flori, *Richard Coeur de Lion: le roi-chevalier* (Paris, 1999), 475–82.
32. S.D. Lloyd, 'William Longespee II: The Making of an English Crusading Hero', *Nottingham Medieval Studies*, 35 (1991), 52–8. For Paris's accounts, see MP *CM* v, 147–54; *Historia Anglorum sive historia minor*, ed. F. Madden (3 vols, Rolls Series, 1866–9), iii, 81.
33. See the brief but informative historiographical sketch in K.D. Uitti, 'Remarks on Old French Narratives: Courtly Love and Poetic Form', *Romance Philology*, 26 (1972–3), 78–9.
34. Fauriel in his posthumously published *Histoire de la poésie provençale* (1846) talks of 'amour chevaleresque' where Gaston Paris in 1883 talks of 'amour courtois', for which see Uitti, 'Remarks on Old French Narratives', 78.
35. This is diagnosed by G.S. Burgess, 'Etude sur le terme *cortois* dans le français du xiie siècle', in *Travaux de linguistique et de philologie*, xxxi (1993), 197–8: 'le terme *cortois* appartient à deux catégories: celle des relations humaines où un geste, une salutation, un acte d'hospitalité ou de politesse prennent de l'importance (c'est-à-dire le monde courtois) et celle du champ de bataille où les qualités militaires, l'efficacité et la capacité à bien juger

sont essentielles.' Burgess eschews the word 'chivalry'. See also J. Ferrante, 'The Court in Medieval Literature', in *The Medieval Court in Europe*, ed. E.R. Haymes (Houston German Studies, 6, Munich, 1986), 1–25.

36. C.S. Jaeger, *The Origins of Courtliness: Civilizing Trends and the Formation of Courtly Ideals, 939–1210* (Philadelphia, 1985). This had been preceded by a couple of preliminary studies: 'The Courtier Bishop in *Vitae* from the Tenth to the Twelfth Century', *Speculum*, 58 (1983), 291–325, and 'Beauty of Manners and Discipline: An Imperial Tradition of Courtliness in the German Romance', in *Barocker Lust-Spiegel: Festschrift für Blake Lee Spahr* (Amsterdam, 1984), 27–45.

37. Garin le Brun, *Ensenhamen*, in *Testi Didattico-Cortesi*, lines 445–52, quotation from lines 445–8 (p. 68).

38. See for a discussion of this D. Crouch, 'Chivalry and Courtliness: Colliding Constructs', in *Soldiers, Nobles and Gentlemen: Essays in Honour of Maurice Keen*, eds P.R. Coss and C. Tyerman (Woodbridge, 2009), 32–48.

39. Colker, 'Latin Texts Concerning Gilbert, Founder of Merton Priory', 260–1.

40. M.L. Colker, 'The Life of Guy of Merton by Rainald of Merton', *Medieval Studies*, 31 (1969), 258.

41. For a survey see M. Aurell, *The Plantagenet Empire, 1154–1224*, trans. D. Crouch, (Longman, 2007), 60–82.

42. Flori, *Richard Coeur de Lion*, ch. 15. See also on this the evocative article by Frédérique Lachaud, 'L'Enseignement des bonnes manières en milieu de cour en Angleterre d'après l'*Urbanus magnus* attribué à Daniel de Beccles', in *Erziehung und Bildung bei Hofe*, eds W. Paravicini and J. Wettlaufer (Stuttgart, 2002), 43–53.

CHAPTER TWELVE: EXPECTATIONS AND DEMANDS

1. *Le Jeu d'Adam*, ed. W. van Emden (Société Rencesvals British Branch, British Rencesvals Publications, 1, 1996), 8, lines 93–4: 'Femme dë home n'avra irur, ne home de femme verguine ne freür.' C. Lévi-Strauss, *Les Structures élémentaires de la parenté* (2nd edn, Paris, 1979), 570 ('un monde où l'on pourrait vivre *entre soi*').

2. See particularly in this regard J.C. Holt, 'Feudal Society and the Family in Early Medieval England: IV. The Heiress and the Alien', *TRHS*, 5th ser., 35 (1985), 1–28, and the chapter on women in J.A. Green, *The Aristocracy of Norman England* (Cambridge, 1996), 361–90; likewise *eadem*, 'Aristocratic Women in Early Twelfth-Century England', in *Anglo-Norman Political Culture and the Twelfth-Century Renaissance*, ed. C.W. Hollister (Woodbridge, 1997), 59–82. For broader historiographical surveys, see Crouch, *Birth of Nobility*, 304–19; P. Stafford, 'Women and the Norman Conquest', *TRHS*, 6th ser., 4 (1994), 221–6.

3. K. LoPrete, *Adela of Blois: Countess and Lord, c.1067–1137* (Dublin, 2007).

4. *Chanson d'Aspremont* i, lines 1451–2, when applying the word to a duchess of Burgundy. Note the French tract known as the *Miroir aux preudes femmes*, or *Miroir des bonnes femmes*, which was composed a little later than the period of this book (*c.*1300) and features sketches of over sixty good and bad women as avatar exemplars. For this, see K.M. Ashley, 'Medieval Courtesy Literature and Dramatic Mirrors of Female Conduct', in *The Ideology of Conduct: Essays in Literature and the History of Sexuality*, eds N. Armstrong and L. Tennenhouse (London, 1987), 33–6; *eadem*, 'The *Miroir des Bonnes Femmes*: Not for Women Only?', in *Medieval Conduct*, eds K.M. Ashley and R.L.A. Clark (Minneapolis, 2001), 86–105.

5. For the penetration of twelfth-century genres from Occitan literature to that of northern France and beyond, and the literary unity of the twelfth-century Francophone world, see S. Gaunt, *Gender and Genre in Medieval French Literature* (Cambridge, 1995), 17–19.

6. Cf. Proverbs 10:19, 11:12, 17:28; *Facetus*, 231.

7. Garin le Brun, *Ensenhamen*, in *Testi Didattico-Cortesi*, 43–107. The supposed tendency of women to run off at the mouth is likewise alleged in an English romance of *c.*1218,

where an undiplomatic male ambassador is given the rough edge of a female ruler's tongue, and retorts: 'You're a woman, so you talk nonsense (*Feme estes si dites folie*) and it surprises me not at all that you've replied rashly (*sans consel*)': *The Romance of Fergus*, ed. W. Frescoln (Philadelphia, 1983), lines 5246–8. On the other hand, the courtliness and controlled speech of the noblewoman is the basis of her characterisation (*c*.1180) in the contentious and ironic dialogues of Andrew the Chaplain's *De Amore*, ed. and trans. P.G. Walsh (London, 1982), bk 1.

8. *LM*, 100–1.

9. Ibid., 96–7, 97–8.

10. Ibid., 99. For Anselm's contribution, see M.-T. d'Alverny, 'Comment les théologiens et les philosophes voient la femme', *Cahiers de civilisation médiévale*, 20 (1977), 115.

11. *Carmen elegiacum de Waleranno comite Mellenti*, in *Chronicles of the Reigns of Stephen, Henry II and Richard*, ed. R. Howlett (4 vols, Rolls Series, 1886–9), ii, 767.

12. *Recueil de chartes et documents de St-Martin-des-Champs*, ed. J. Depoin (3 vols, Paris, 1913–17), ii, 307–10. For her seneschal and prévôt of Gournay, see Bibliothéque Nationale, Collection du Vexin, viii, p. 471. For contemporary countesses in control of their husband's lands, see K.F. Werner, 'Les femmes, le pouvoir et la transmission du pouvoir', in *La Femme au moyen âge* (Mauberge, 1990), 365–79; T. de Hemptinne, 'Les épouses des croisés et pèlerins flamands aux xie et xiie siècles: l'exemple des comtesses de Flandre, Clémence et Sibylle' in *Autour de la Première Croisade: actes du colloque de la 'Society for the Study of the Crusades and the Latin East'*, ed. M. Balard (Paris, 1996), 111–37; LoPrete, *Adela of Blois*, chs 2–3.

13. For Agnes in her husband's acts, see *Cartulaire de l'abbaye Bénédictine de Saint-Pierre-de-Préaux*, ed. D. Rouet (Collection de Documents Inédits sur l'Histoire de France, 34, Paris, 2005), 221, 230–1; *Recueil de chartes et documents de St-Martin-des-Champs* ii, 158, 230, 231–2, 235–6, 245–6; Cartulary of the hospital of St-Gilles de Pont Audemer, Rouen, Bibliothèque municipale, Y 200, fos 13v, 27v; Cartulary of the chapter of Évreux, Archives départementales de l'Eure, G 122, fo. 22r. For the Meulan administration, see D. Crouch, 'Between Three Realms: The Acts of Waleran II, Count of Meulan and Worcester', in *Records, Administration and Aristocratic Society in the Anglo-Norman Realm*, ed. N. Vincent (Boydell, 2009), 75–90.

14. S. Johns, *Noblewomen, Aristocracy and Power in the Twelfth-Century Anglo-Norman Realm* (Manchester, 2003), esp. chs 2, 4.

15. OV vi, 38.

16. *Foedera* i, pt 1, 107–8.

17. *Histoire des ducs*, 111.

18. Wendover ii, 48–9.

19. 'Estate Records of the Hotot Family', ed. E. King, in *A Northamptonshire Miscellany*, ed. *idem* (Northamptonshire Record Society, xxxii, 1983), 45. For the not infrequent medieval depiction of women in arms, see M. McLaughlin, 'The Woman Warrior: Gender, Warfare and Society in Medieval Europe', *Women's Studies*, 17 (1990), 193–209, who suggests (p. 199) that the woman in arms is encountered with increasing rarity after 1300. For the famous case of Nicola de la Haie, hereditary castellan and successful wartime commander of Lincoln castle in 1216–17, see Johns, *Noblewomen, Aristocracy and Power*, 22–3.

20. *Jordan Fantosme's Chronicle*, ed. and trans. R.C. Johnston (Oxford, 1981), 72–4, 78.

21. D'Alverny, 'Comment les théologiens et les philosophes voient la femme', 105–29; S. Farmer, 'Clerical Images of Medieval Wives', *Speculum*, 61 (1986), 517–43, esp. 519–20.

22. OV iii, 134–6; iv, 212–15. For comment, see M. Chibnall, 'Women in Orderic Vitalis', *HSJ*, 2 (1990), 107–8.

23. Farmer, 'Clerical Images of Medieval Wives', 520.

24. Ibid., 527.

25. P. Stafford, *Queen Emma and Queen Edith: Queenship and Women's Power in the Eleventh Century* (Oxford, 1997), 150. This topos has become part of current dogma in the emerging genre

of 'queenship studies': see *eadem*, 'The Portrayal of Royal Women in England, Mid Tenth to Mid Twelfth Centuries', in *Medieval Queenship*, ed. J. Carmi Parsons (Stroud, 1994), 146–7; J. Carmi Parsons, 'The Queen's Intercession in Thirteenth-Century England', in *Power of the Weak: Studies on Medieval Woman*, eds J. Carpenter and S.-B. Maclean (Urbana, 1995), 147–77; L.L. Huneycutt, *Matilda of Scotland: A Study of Medieval Queenship* (Woodbridge, 2003), 82–4, who tautologically argues that Matilda was reluctant to intercede with her husband, Henry I, in 1105, yet talks of her 'power' to intercede.

26. *Chanson d'Aspremont* i, lines 1407–1505; my translation, but with acknowledgement to *The Song of Aspremont*, trans. M.A. Newth (Garland Library of Medieval Literature, series B, vol. 61, 1989), 36–9.

27. V.L. Bullough, 'On Being a Male in the Middle Ages', in *Medieval Masculinities: Regarding Men in the Middle Ages* (Minneapolis, 1994), 31–43, demonstrates this very well, though his reductionist argument that masculinity was about 'impregnating women, protecting dependents and serving as provider to one's family' (p. 34) barely scratches the surface of the problem.

28. Crouch, *Birth of Nobility*, 67–8.

29. J. Subrenat, 'e Oliver est proz', in *Études de philologie romane et d'histoire littéraire offertes à Jules Horvent*, eds J.-M. d'Heur and N. Cherubini (Liège, 1980), 461–7; E. Steidl, '*Meilz valt mesure*: Oliver, the Norman Chroniclers and the Model Commander', *Romance Philology*, 45 (1991–2), 251–68.

30. M. Bennett, 'Military Masculinity in England and Northern France, *c.*1150–*c.*1225', in *Masculinity in Medieval Europe*, ed. D.M. Hadley (London, 1999), 85–8. The need to demonstrate 'prowess' to acquire honour, and the embracing of extreme forms of religious asceticism in lay and clerical behaviour, are yet more symptoms of it, for which see R.W. Kaeuper, *Holy Warriors: The Religious Ideology of Chivalry* (Philadelphia, 2009), esp. 57 where Kaeuper demonstrates the universality of male competitiveness.

31. *HWM* i, lines 1677–834.

32. WM, *MP* iv, 135, translation from D. Crouch, *Tournament* (London, 2005), 194–5.

33. P. Noble, 'Anti-clericalism in the Feudal Epic', in *The Medieval Alexander Legend and Romance Epic: Essays in Honour of David J.A. Ross*, eds P. Noble, L. Polak and C. Isoz (Nendeln, 1982), 149–58; R.N. Swanson, 'Angels Incarnate: Clergy and Masculinity from Gregorian Reform to Reformation', in *Masculinity in Medieval Europe*, ed. D.M. Hadley (London, 1999), 160–77.

34. *HWM* i, lines 6677–812. For clerical incontinence and the rhetoric of celibacy, see J.W. Baldwin, 'Five Discourses on Desire: Sexuality and Gender in Northern France around 1200', *Speculum*, 66 (1991), 797–819, and for a later period see H. Cullum, 'Clergy, Masculinity and Transgression in Late Medieval England' in *Masculinity in Medieval Europe*, ed. D.M. Hadley (London, 1999), 178–96. William Marshal himself had to deal with the scandalously military bishop Philip of Beauvais, who led Capetian armies against Norman forces.

35. M. Kuefler, 'Male Friendship and the Suspicion of Sodomy', in *The Boswell Thesis: Essays on Christianity, Social Tolerance and Homosexuality*, ed. *idem* (Chicago, 2006), 179–212, especially 194–6. For the culture of Rufus's court, see F. Barlow, *William Rufus* (London, 1983), 99–119.

36. *Facetus*, 36.

37. *GS*, 118.

38. JB, 68–71.

39. See Crouch, *Birth of Nobility*, 99–116. See in particular on this shift P. Stafford, 'La Mutation Familiale: A Suitable Case for Caution', in *The Community, the Family and the Saint: Patterns of Power in Early Medieval Europe*, eds J. Hill and M. Swan (Turnhout, 1998), 103–25, A. Livingstone, *Out of Love for my Kin: Aristocratic Family Life in the Lands of the Loire, 1000–1200* (Ithaca NY, 2010), 87–119, has recently stressed the diversity of ideas of family in one medieval society.

40. *Estoire des Engleis*, lines 3619–30. For the concept of *parage*, see Crouch, *Birth of Nobility*, 135–48.

41. It has been suggested that the word *disparagacio* was coined in England in the reign of John as a result of the more intensive exploitation of wardships by Richard and John: S.L. Waugh, *The Lordship of England: Royal Wardships and Marriages in English Society and Politics, 1217–1327* (Princeton, 1988), 80n. The sudden appearance of the word in French and Latin forms at the end of the twelfth century has been seen as a consequence of renewed royal exploitation of marriage under John, but chronology tells against this argument. It occurs in the French past participle form *desparagee* in the Anglo-Norman romance *Protheselaus*, which was composed in England between 1180 and 1190; Hue de Roteland, *Protheselaus*, ed. A.J. Holden (3 vols, Anglo-Norman Text Society, 1989–93), ii, p. 118, line 10,734. This would indicate that the word was in use well before the end of the reign of Henry II of England.

42. It should be noted that the first occurrence of the Latin word in English royal records relates to money paid in 1194 for the marriage of a Gloucestershire boy heir 'where he may not be disparaged': It does not concern a girl. *Pipe Roll of 6 Richard I*, p. 238.

43. It would appear that the king's exploitative treatment of female heirs (whether daughters or widows) had antagonised the Anglo-Norman aristocracy as early as the reign of William Rufus (1087–1100), since his brother Henry was so keen to distance himself from the practice in the aftermath of his seizure of the throne. But as commentators have noted, Henry continued to make the most of his rights of wardship throughout his reign, making widows pay if they wished to be free of his control of their marriage, and selling and granting wardships to his favoured officers: see observations in Barlow, *William Rufus*, 255–6, noting Orderic Vitalis's comments about the excessive fines demanded by Rufus from his barons. See also J.A. Green, *The Government of England under Henry I* (Cambridge, 1986), 84–6, and particularly Holt, 'Heiress and the Alien', 24–5, who lists the social disparities between Henry I's servants and the noble brides they were awarded, but does not see significant resistance to the practice at the time.

44. Holt, 'Heiress and the Alien', 26–8.

45. *Histoire des ducs*, 149; The 'Magna Carta of Cheshire' granted by Earl Ranulf III to his tenants in mid-1215 deals with disparagement (*c.* 8): 'Neither a widow nor an heir should be married where disparagement occurs (*disparigetur*), but by permission and gift of their family.' *Charters of the Earls of Chester*, 389.

46. See the review of the issue in S.S. Walker, 'Free Consent and Marriage of Feudal Wards in Medieval England', *JMH*, 8 (1982), 123–34. Those disappointed men who bought the marriages of wards who then refused to accept their selected spouse were offered financial compensation from the ward's estate.

47. S.L. Waugh, 'Marriage, Class and Royal Wardship in England under Henry III', *Viator*, 16 (1985), 181–2, 202–3.

48. P.R. Coss, *The Lady in Medieval England, 1000–1500* (Stroud, 1998), 121–3.

49. Crouch, *Beaumont Twins*, 112–13, 113n.

50. *Sarum Charters and Documents*, eds W.R. Jones and W.D. McCray (Rolls Series, 1891), 34–5. For considerations of the Tosny-Clifford link, see M. Lovatt, 'Archbishop Geoffrey of York: A Problem in Anglo-French Maternity', in *Records, Administration and Aristocratic Society in the Anglo-Norman Realm*, 91–124.

51. 'Matildis comitissa de Clara filia Jam(es) de sancto Hillario', Cartulary of the priory of St Andrew, Northampton, BL, ms Royal ii B ix, fo. 57r.

52. See the pioneering survey in Johns, *Noblewomen, Aristocracy and Power*, 169–73. Cartulary of St Neots priory, BL, ms Cotton Faustina, A iv, fo. 89r. See similar charters in Cartulary of Godstow abbey, TNA, E164/20, fo. 62r; BL, Harley charter, 55 B 5; BL, Harley ms 1400, fo. 35v; Berkeley Castle muniments, Select Charters 171, 236. See also the example of her contemporary Constance, wife of Roger II de Tosny (died 1209), whom her husband calls Constance *de Toeni*; Cartulary of Flamstead priory, Hertfordshire Record Office, ms 17465, fo. 3r. Constance was the sister-in-law of King William of Scotland, a member of the Angevin family of Beaumont-sur-Sarthe, and a

granddaughter and namesake of Constance, illegitimate daughter of King Henry I of England.

53. A fine specimen of an impression of this is attached to the charter: Oxford, Magdalen College Archives, Brackley no. B 180. For an illustration and discussion, see G. Henderson, 'Romance and Politics on Some Medieval English Seals', *Art History*, i (1980), 33–6.

54. For William Longespée's mention of his mother as 'countess Ida', see Cartulary of Bradenstoke priory, BL, ms Stowe 925, fo. 143r. She is generally identified with Ida, wife of Earl Roger Bigod II of Norfolk (died 1221), who was a royal ward in the 1160s: see M. Morris, *The Bigod Earls of Norfolk in the Thirteenth Century* (Woodbridge, 2005), 2, for the marriage.

55. For a reference to her as the king's cousin, see *Cal Charter Rolls* ii, 29.

56. For Ela's first (or second) seal, see Oxford, Merton College mun. no. 646 (charter dated 1267), and an illustration in C.H. Hunter Blair, 'Armorials upon English Seals from the Twelfth to the Sixteenth Centuries', *Archaeologia*, 2nd ser., lxxxix (1943), 45 (e–f). For an extended and illuminating discussion of heraldry and female identity, see Coss, *The Lady in Medieval England*, 39–46, especially his discussion of the identity and lineage of Agnes de Vesci (pp. 43–4).

57. For her second (or possibly third) seal, see the facsimiles in Northamptonshire Record Office, Finch Hatton ms 170, fo. 68v (Sir Christopher Hatton's Book of Seals); BL, ms Lansdowne 203, fo. 100r (dated 1289). These can be compared with a large fragment attached to Oxford, Magdalen College Archives, ms Selborne 52 (dated 1285).

58. *Itinerarium Kambriae*, in *Opera* vi, ed. J.F. Dimmock (Rolls Series, 1868), 132; *The Letters and Charters of Gilbert Foliot*, eds Z.N. Brooke, A. Morey and C.N.L. Brooke (Cambridge, 1967), 214–15.

59. See the digest of the case in C.N.L. Brooke, *The Medieval Idea of Marriage* (Oxford, 1989), 152–7. Another example – though in a different direction – is the divorce of Graecia Briwerre, daughter of King John's favourite, William Briwerre, from Reginald de Briouze following the disgrace and exile of Reginald's father in 1208.

60. D. Crouch, 'A Norman "conventio" and Bonds of Lordship in the Middle Ages', in *Law and Government in Medieval England and Normandy: Essays in Honour of Sir James Holt*, eds G. Garnett and J. Hudson (Cambridge, 1994), 299–324. See also in that regard studies by Paul Dalton, 'Civil Peace and Ecclesiastical Peace in the Reign of King Stephen', in *War and Society in Medieval and Early Modern Britain*, ed. D. Dunn (Liverpool, 2000), 53–75; 'Churchmen and the Promotion of Peace in King Stephen's Reign', *Viator*, 31 (2000), 79–119.

61. *Roman de Brut: A History of the British*, ed. and trans. J. Weiss (revised edn, Exeter, 1999), lines 13,371–4.

CHAPTER THIRTEEN: PIETY

1. J.A. Green, *The Aristocracy of Norman England* (Cambridge, 1997), 391–428. For burial practices, see B. Golding, 'Anglo-Norman Knightly Burials', in *ANS*, 13, ed. M. Chibnall (Woodbridge 1991), 35–48. A recent exception, drawing on a wide range of practices, is H.M. Thomas, 'Lay Piety in England from 1066 to 1215', *ANS*, 29, ed. C.P. Lewis (Woodbridge, 2007), 179–92.

2. On the mass and lay participation and reaction to it, see J. Bossy, 'The Mass as a Social Institution, 1200–1700', *PP*, 100 (1983), 30–2; M. Rubin, *Corpus Christi: The Eucharist in Late Medieval Culture* (Cambridge, 1991), 55–60, 72–4; E. Saxon, *The Eucharist in Romanesque France: Iconography and Theology* (Woodbridge, 2006) 40–1.

3. Thomas of Chobham, subdean of Salisbury, writing around 1216, gave as his opinion that laypeople only needed to take communion once a year, though in the twelfth century three times a year had been recommended. The devout and the professed religious might take it weekly, but he thought that excessive: *Summa Confessorum*, ed. F. Broomfield (Analecta Mediaevalia Namurcensia, 25, 1968), xxxvii–xxxxviii, 106, 122.

The ladies for whom the 'Ancrene Riwle' was written some time in the 1210s were warned to take communion no more than fifteen times a year on particular feasts: *The Latin Text of the Ancrene Riwle*, ed. C. D'Evelyn (Early English Text Society, no. 216, 1944), 164–5.

4. WM, *GRA* i, 458, 492.

5. 'The Vision of Orm', ed. H. Farmer, *Analecta Bollandiana*, 75 (1957), 76–7.

6. J. de Cauna, *L'Ensenhamen ou code du parfait chevalier*, trans. G. Gouiran (Mounenh en Biarn, 2007), lines 147–53.

7. WN, *HRA* i, 36–8. We might note in this regard the story told of Henry I's chaplain, Bernard son of Ailsi, who accompanied the king on campaign in Wales, celebrating mass before him in a tent which was nearly burnt down when fire swept the royal camp; Peter of Cornwall, 'The Visions of Ailsi and his Sons', eds R. Easting and R. Sharpe, *Mediaevistik*, 1 (1988), 226–7. This would imply that the king's day started with mass wherever he was.

8. See, for instance, *Ami et Amile*, ed. P.F. Dembowski (Classiques Français du moyen age, 1987), lines 233–5, 321–2, 1643–4, 2322–4. It may be revealing for the level of piety that the villains of this mystical romance of *c.*1200 hear mass at dawn as much the heroes.

9. WP, 80. The fact that William was schooled as a boy and had some claims to literacy, and did indeed have his sons educated is significant for his ability to follow the mass and daily offices; on this see D. Bates, 'The Conqueror's Adolescence', *ANS*, 25, ed. J. Gillingham (Woodbridge, 2002), 1–18; W.M. Aird, *Robert Curthose, Duke of Normandy* (Woodbridge, 2008), 36–40.

10. On the Domesday evidence, see D. Crouch, *The Normans: The History of a Dynasty* (London, 2002), 126, 324; on Simon's lay piety, see *Vita beati Simonis comitis Crespiensis*, in *PL*, 156, col. 213.

11. As shown in the 1170s romance-epic *Garin le Loherenc*, ed. A. Iker-Gittleman (3 vols, Classiques Français du moyen age, 1996–7), ii, lines 10,726–36.

12. *Le Roman de Rou*, ed. A.J. Holden (3 vols, Société des Anciens Textes Français, 1970–3), i, pt 3, lines 2312–14. Cardinal James de Vitry liked to tell the tale of a knight whose firm belief it was that priests said the mass just so as to be able to collect the offertory: *The Exempla of Jacques de Vitry*, ed. and trans. T.F. Crane (New York, 1890), 62.

13. *Urbanus Magnus Danielis Becclesiensis*, ed. J.G. Smyly (Dublin, 1939), 9. For an actual case of this happening in Istria in 1226, see Ulrich von Liechtenstein, *Service of Ladies*, trans. J.W. Thomas (Chapel Hill, 1969), 110–11.

14. H.M. Colvin, 'The Origin of Chantries', *JMH*, 26 (2000), 163–73.

15. OV ii, 10.

16. Thus Stephen of Rouen memorialises the abbey of Préaux around 1167: 'the noble monastery possesses, houses and preserves the distinguished corpse of Count Waleran [of Meulan], providing obsequies worthy of him': *Carmen elegiacum*, in *Chronicles of the Reigns of Stephen, Henry II and Richard*, ed. R. Howlett (4 vols, Rolls Series, 1886–9), ii, 770.

17. For some reflections on Gundrada's tomb and its epitaph, see G. Zarnecki, 'Gundrada's Tombstone', in *English Romanesque Art, 1066–1200* (London, 1984), 181–2; E.M.C. van Houts, 'The Epitaph of Gundreda of Warenne', in *Nova de veteribus: mittel und neulateinische Studien für Paul Gergard Schmidt*, eds A. Bihrer and E. Stein (Leipzig, 2004), 366–78. I follow the drift of Zarnecki's translation of the epitaph (deriving from Christopher Brooke), rather than that of van Houts. For the location of the founders' burials, see *Victoria County History of Sussex* vii, 49.

18. See for this consensus Green, *Aristocracy of Norman England*, 393–414; R. Bartlett, *England under the Norman and Angevin Kings, 1075–1225* (Oxford, 2000), 417–34.

19. *The Cartulary of Shrewsbury Abbey*, ed. U. Rees (2 vols, Cardiff, 1975), ii, 337.

20. Between 1162 and 1173, Earl Hugh II of Chester granted a manor to Bordesley abbey for the services of all of six monks, for the souls of himself, his father, Earl Ranulf II (died 1153), his grandfather, Earl Robert of Gloucester, and others of his family: *Charters of the Earls of Chester*, no. 148. For other examples, see Colvin, 'Origin of Chantries'. 170–1; D. Crouch, 'The Origin of Chantries: Some Further Anglo-Norman Evidence', *Journal of Medieval History*, 27 (2001), 167–9.

21. University of Kansas, Kenneth Spencer Research Library, ms 191:1, edited in Crouch, 'Origin of Chantries', 179–80.
22. Cartulary of Rouen Cathedral, Bibliothèque Municipale de Rouen, Y44, fos 58r, 73r–v, 141r.
23. Cartulary of Lichfield cathedral, ms Harley 4799, fo. 5r.
24. *Actes des évêques de Laon des origines à 1151*, ed. A. Dufour-Malbézin (Paris, 2001), 288–9.
25. For a number of early twelfth-century examples of household chaplains and clerks as clergy of collegiate churches under their lord's patronage, see D. Crouch, *The Beaumont Twins: The Roots and Branches of Power in the Twelfth Century* (Cambridge, 1986), 148–55. Nicholas Vincent has pointed out to me how this fact would create a more personal link between lords and the intercession such colleges offered.
26. Cartulary of Évreux cathedral, Archives départementales de l'Eure, G 122, fos 19v–20r, a charter datable to the episcopate of John, bishop of Évreux (1182–92).
27. Cartulary of the see of Dublin (Liber Niger), Dublin, Representative Church Body Library, ms C.6.1.1, fo. 20r–v.
28. Cartulary of Wymondham priory, BL, ms Cotton Titus, C viii, fo. 48v. A comparable instance comes from between 1226 and 1243 when Sir Maurice Butler of Oversley came to an agreement with the rector of Wixford, Warwickshire, over presentation to his perpetual chantry altar in Wixford church: Cartulary of Kenilworth priory, BL, ms Additional 47677, fo. 208r.
29. D. Crouch, *The Image of Aristocracy in Britain, 1000–1300* (London, 1992), 269–70.
30. For this debate, see the exploration in J. Blair, *The Church in Anglo-Saxon Society* (Oxford, 2005), 368ff.
31. For an early example at Market Bosworth, Leicestershire, see *Sir Christopher Hatton's Book of Seals*, eds L.C. Loyd and D.M. Stenton (Oxford, 1950), 31. The dispute resurfaced before 1225 under Bertram's son Nicholas: *Rotuli Hugonis de Welles*, eds W.P.W. Phillimore and F.N. Davis (3 vols, Canterbury and York Society, 1907–9), ii, 294. For some general comments, see J.R.H. Moorman, *Church Life in England in the Thirteenth Century* (Cambridge, 1946), 15–16. For Robert fitz Ivo de Harcourt, see Crouch, *Beaumont Twins*, 126–7, 220–1. For Earley, see Bodl. Libr., ms Berkshire a.1. no. 17.
32. *Charters of the Earls of Chester*, no. 254. For William Marshal of Coventry (no relation to the Pembroke Marshals), see P.R. Coss, *Lordship, Knighthood and Locality: A Study in English Society, c.1180–c.1280* (Cambridge, 1991), 34–6.
33. For a classic example, at Noseley, Leicestershire, see Crouch, *Birth of Nobility*, 320–1; H. Hartopp, 'Some Unpublished Documents Relating to Noseley co. Leics.', *Associated Architectural Societies: Reports and Papers*, xxv, pt 2 (1900), 433–4. G. Farnham, 'The Manor of Noseley', *Transactions of the Leicestershire Archaeological Society*, xii (1922), 233–8.
34. C. Harper-Bill, 'The Piety of the Anglo-Norman Knightly Class', *ANS*, ii, ed. R.A. Brown (Woodbridge, 1980), 71–5.
35. R. Mortimer, 'Religious and Secular Motives for Some English Monastic Foundations', *Studies in Church History*, xv (1978), 77–81.
36. *Cartulaire de l'église de la Sainte-Trinité de Beaumont-le-Roger*, ed. E. Deville (Paris, 1912), 10.
37. See the analysis of the *Chronique des comtes d'Eu* in *RHF* xxiii, 439, in Crouch, *Image of Aristocracy*, 311–13, 321. The status of any great church as a dynastic 'mausoleum' in England needs to be approached with caution. Generations of a magnate family tended to shift their allegiance from church to church; see D. Crouch, *The Birth of Nobility: Constructing Aristocracy in England and France, 900–1300* (Harlow, 2005), 162–7, and for a similar conclusion relating to the Low Countries see M. Lauwers, *La Mémoire des ancêtres. Le souci des morts. Morts, rites et société au moyen âge* (Paris, 1996), 294–301.
38. Crouch, *Image of Aristocracy*, 329–30.
39. *Tractatus de adventu fratrum minorum in Angliam*, ed. A.G. Little (Manchester, 1951), 20.
40. *Prima fundatio fratrum minorum Londoniae*, in *Monumenta Franciscana*, ed. J.S. Brewer (Rolls Series, 1858), 499, 500.

41. *Brut y Tywysogyon: Red Book of Hergest Version*, ed. T. Jones (Cardiff, 1955), 234.

42. MP, *CM* v, 235–6.

43. *Tractatus de adventu fratrum minorum*, 62–4.

44. H. Ridgeway, 'William de Valence and his *familiares*, 1247–72', *Historical Research*, 65 (1992), 253.

45. C.H. Lawrence, *The Friars* (Harlow, 1994), 170–3.

46. J.R. Maddicott, *Simon de Montfort* (Cambridge, 1994), 91–2.

47. *Epistolae*, in *Monumenta Franciscana*, ed. J.S. Brewer (Rolls Series, 1858), 260–301, 330–1, 336–7. Marsh also had connections to lesser aristocrats, such as Eva de Tracy, ibid., 98–9, for whom he sought permission to make a home in Godstow abbey.

48. Marsh, *Epistolae*, 286. For the will, see the *Register of Godfrey Giffard, 1268–1301*, ed. J. Willis Bund (2 vols, Worcester Historical Society, 1902), 8. There is a notable absence of any patronage by William of traditional monasticism, other than compositions over minor difficulties with the abbeys and priories of the Severn valley; see *The Beauchamp Cartulary Charters, 1100–1268*, ed. E. Mason (Pipe Roll Society, new ser., xliii, 1980), 30–1 (Worcester cathedral priory), 33–39 (Evesham), 40–1 (Little Malvern), 41–3 (Pershore), 49 (Bruern). Only the Bruern settlement stipulates he wanted the prayers of the monks for his soul and those of his predecessors.

49. MP, *CM* iv 579–80.

50. E.J. Dobson, 'The Date and Composition of *Ancrene Wisse*', *Proceedings of the British Academy*, lii (1966), 181–206, though Dobson's idea that 'Ancrene Riwle' is closely linked with the consequences of Fourth Lateran is not particularly convincing in the light of the devotional context I am offering here, since most of its concerns are prefigured in the twelfth century. For the anchorites' routine of prayer, see *The English Text of the Ancrene Riwle: Cotton Cleopatra C vi*, ed. E.J. Dobson (Early English Text Society, no. 267, 1972), 15ff.

51. Dobson, 'The Date and Composition of *Ancrene Wisse*', 187. For a recent such statement of this presupposition, see E. Duffy, *Marking the Hours: English People and their Prayers, 1240–1570* (New Haven, 2006), 6.

52. T. Webber, 'The Books of Leicester Abbey', in *Leicester Abbey: Medieval History, Archaeology and Manuscript Studies*, eds J. Story et al. (Leicester, 2006), 137.

53. WM, *GRA* i, 554.

54. *Genealogia regum Anglorum*, in *PL*, 195, col. 715.

55. Peter of Blois, *Dialogus inter regem Henricum II et abbatem Bonevallis*, in *PL*, 207, col. 983.

56. *Close Rolls, 1231–34*, 161; M.L. Colker, 'The "Margam Chronicle" in a Dublin Manuscript', *HSJ*, 4 (1992), 135. See comments on Hubert's spirituality in N. Vincent, 'King Henry III and the Blessed Virgin Mary', in *The Church and Mary*, ed. R.N. Swanson (Studies in Church History, 39, Woodbridge, 2004), 143–4.

57. Duffy, *Marking the Hours*, 8–10.

58. *The English Text of the Ancrene Riwle*, 254.

59. L.L. Huneycutt, *Matilda of Scotland: A Study in Medieval Queenship* (Woodbridge, 2003), 175–6.

60. *Self and Society in Medieval France*, ed. and trans. J.F. Benton (Toronto, 1984), 75. A. Murray, 'Confession before 1215', *TRHS*, 6th ser., 3 (1993), 77–8, sees the school of Laon as important in propagating the discipline of auricular confession, noting its connections with clergy at Henry I's court.

61. *Vita beati Vitalis*, ed. E.P. Sauvage, in *Analecta Bollandiana* i (1882), 363–4.

62. *The Cartulary of Holy Trinity Aldgate*, ed. G.A.J. Hodgett (London Record Society, 7, 1971), 230. For a general consideration of piety, confession and penance at Henry I's court, see D. Crouch, 'The Troubled Deathbeds of Henry I's Servants: Death, Confession and Secular Conduct in the Twelfth Century', *Albion*, 34 (2002), 24–36, and Huneycutt, *Matilda of Scotland*, 106–11. It might be noted that a late source (*c*.1220) credits King William Rufus with a confessor, the bishop of Winchester, but says that the king was little influenced by him: *Histoire des ducs*, 53.

63. RT, 123.

64. *Cartulary of Holy Trinity Aldgate*, 232.

65. *Cartularium prioratus de Colne*, ed. J.L. Fisher (Essex Archaeological Society, Occasional Publication, no. 1, 1946), 30.

66. *Curia Regis Rolls* ix, 142–3. Thomas Becket as Henry II's chancellor also took an Augustinian confessor, Robert, canon of Merton: see William fitz Stephen, *Vita sancti Thome*, in *Materials for the History of Thomas Becket, Archbishop of Canterbury*, ed. J.C. Robertson (7 vols, Rolls Series, 1875–85), iii, 21. Thanks to Hugh Doherty for help with this.

67. Peter of Blois, *Dialogus*, cols 975–87.

68. W. Hinnebusch, *The Early English Friars Preacher* (Rome, 1951), 72–85, for royal interest in the Dominicans.

69. For Cecilia, her marriages and lands, see principally D. Walker, 'The "Honours" of the Earls of Hereford in the Twelfth Century', *Transactions of the Bristol and Gloucestershire Archaeological Society*, lxxix (1960), pt 2, 186–9.

70. *LM*, 100–1. There is a literary parallel in the idealised piety of the heroine of the romance of *c.*1240 *La Manekine*, who earns the love of her people in giving generously to the poor, conferring dowries on poor gentlewomen, frequenting churches and saying the hours with her psalter; *La Manekine*, ed. H. Suchier (Société des Anciens Textes Français, 1884), lines 2429–40.

71. M.L. Colker, 'Latin Texts concerning Gilbert, Founder of Merton Priory', *Studia Monastica*, 12 (1970), 260–1, 269. For another instance of wearing heavy chains as penance (in this case from 1132), see Thomas of Monmouth, *Life and Miracles of St William of Norwich*, eds A. Jessopp and M.R. James (Cambridge, 1896), 2–13. For an even more dramatic instance in a collection of saint's *miracula*, where a German who had murdered his brother had the blade by which he did the deed forged tightly round his waist and was sent into exile, eventually arriving in England, see R. Sharpe, 'Some Medieval Miracula from Llandegley', *Bulletin of the Board of Celtic Studies*, 37 (1990), 171–2. My thanks to Richard Sharpe for the last reference.

72. D. Crouch, *The Reign of King Stephen, 1135–1154* (Harlow, 2000), 18 and n.

73. *The Letters and Charters of Gilbert Foliot*, eds Z.N. Brooke, A. Morey and C.N.L. Brooke (Cambridge, 1967), 159–60, 265–7.

74. Crouch, *Birth of Nobility*, 71–9.

75. William of Malmesbury, *Vita Wulfstani* in *Saints' Lives*, eds and trans. M. Winterbottom and R.M. Thomson (Oxford, 2002), 116–18.

76. For Count Robert's dole table, see *Chartes de l'abbaye de Jumièges* (2 vols, Rouen, 1916), ii, 207–9. For the Meulan almoners, see Crouch, *Beaumont Twins*, 155; for the fashion for Templar almoners around 1200, see Crouch, *William Marshal*, 155. Walter de Bibbesworth's *Tretiz* (*c.*1250–1300), an Anglo-Norman language manual that describes many daily household activities, says that the 'parings' of bread – that is, the burned bits cut off loaves – should be sliced and the parings given as alms ('Taillez ceo pain que est paré; / Les bisseaus seient pur Deu doné'): Walter de Bibbesworth, *Le Tretiz*, ed. W. Rothwell, (Anglo-Norman Text Society, Plain Texts Series 6, London, 1990), lines 1055–6. My thanks to Martha Carlin for that reference.

77. *HWM* ii, lines 18,468–96.

78. See Crouch, *William Marshal*, 207–16.

79. P. Noble, 'Anticlericalism in the Feudal Epic', in *The Medieval Alexander Legend and Romance Epic: Essays in Honour of David J.A. Ross*, eds P. Noble, L. Polak and C. Isoz (Nendeln, 1982), 149–58.

80. *Liber Poenitentialis*, in *PL*, 210, cols 283–4.

81. C. Bémont, *Simon de Montfort*, trans. E.F. Jacob (2nd edn, Oxford, 1930), 277. See comment in Maddicott, *Simon de Montfort*, 176.

82. There survives a fragment of a bond of one Peter Norreys of Leicester to the earl of Leicester, in return for forty-four shillings, recognising a penalty of twenty shillings in case of a default on his payment and pledging his possessions, which would agree with

the accusatory evidence of Montfort's own will: see Huntington Library, San Marino, CA, HAD 775a [49]. The bond was cut down to provide a seal tag for a Leicester deed of the 1290s.

83. Maddicott, *Simon de Montfort*, 84–6.
84. Ibid., 90–1.
85. MP, *CM* v, 48.
86. Each day Louis heard a requiem and a mass of the day, said an office of the dead with his chaplain and concluded the day with vespers and compline, in which Joinville imitated him: *Vie de Saint Louis*, ed. J. Monfrin (Paris, 1995), 28, 248.
87. *De naturis rerum libri duo*, ed. T. Wright (Rolls Series, 1863), 326.
88. For the French antecedents of this, see Crouch, *Image of Aristocracy*, 180–7. For the Mortain example, see *The Cartulary of St Michael's Mount*, ed. P.L. Hull (Devon and Cornwall Record Society, new ser., v, 1962), 1, an interpolated early twelfth-century version of an original act, for which see further *The Cartulary of the Abbey of Mont-Saint-Michel*, ed. K.S.B. Keats-Rohan (Donington, 2006), 89–90, 213–14.
89. Cartulary of St Mary York, BL, ms Additional 38816, fo. 22v.
90. *Annals and Memorials of St Edmunds Abbey*, ed. T. Arnold (2 vols, Rolls Series, 1890), i, 261–2; *Jordan Fantosme's Chronicle*, ed. and trans. R.C. Johnston (Oxford, 1981), 25; JB, 57.
91. N. Rogers, 'The Waltham Abbey Relic-list', in *England in the Eleventh Century*, ed. C. Hicks (Stamford, 1992), 157–81, see especially 175, for a collection of unidentified relics, *sub sigillo Lefwi ducis*.
92. D. Bethell, 'The Making of a Twelfth-Century Relic Collection', in *Popular Belief and Practice*, eds G.J. Cuming and D. Baker (Studies in Church History, 8, Cambridge, 1972), 61–72.
93. Cartulary of Wymondham priory, BL, ms Cotton Titus, C viii, fos 70v–71r.
94. D. Walker, 'Ralph Son of Pichard', *BIHR*, 33 (1960), 201.
95. *Annales de Theokesberia*, 113–14.
96. *La Manekine*, lines 5359–66.
97. Ibid., lines 5611–5716.
98. Vincent, 'King Henry III and the Blessed Virgin Mary', 126–46.
99. Colker, 'The "Margam Chronicle"', 137, cited in Vincent, 'King Henry III and the Blessed Virgin Mary', 144, who also notes the Marian dedication of the hospital Hubert founded at Dover. The celestial voice is probably an allusion to Daniel 6:16, 'Thy God whom thou servest continually, he will deliver thee,' Daniel being another unjustly persecuted royal servant.
100. Vincent, 'King Henry III and the Blessed Virgin Mary', 135, 143.
101. The description of the chapel and its building is given in *HWM* ii, lines 18,989–90.
102. Oxford, Christ Church muniments, DY13 (a), m. 3.
103. Ibid., m. 7. Earl Gilbert endowed two perpetual lamps in the chapel in the 1230s for the soul of his brother Earl Richard, and in due course Countess Margaret, Earl Gilbert's widow, endowed a lamp to burn before the image of the Virgin at Caversham for her husband's soul; ibid., m. 5.
104. Cartulary of Durford priory, BL, ms Cotton Vespasian E xxiii, fo. 27r.
105. D. Crouch, 'Early Charters and Patrons of Leicester Abbey', in *Leicester Abbey*, ed. Story, 251.
106. Cartulary of Wymondham priory, fo. 18r; TNA, 3/8/140B, pt 3, p. 38.
107. *De miraculis sanctae Frideswidae*, in *Acta Sanctorum*, 8 Oct., 570.
108. R.W. Kaeuper, *Holy Warriors: The Religious Ideology of Chivalry* (Philadelphia, 2009), 68–93.
109. Odo of Deuil, *De profectione Ludovici VII in orientem*, ed. and trans. V.G. Berry (New York, 1948), 114–22.
110. *Rufford Abbey Charters*, ed. C.J. Holdsworth (4 vols, Thoroton Society Record Series, 29–30, 32, 34, 1972–81), ii, 167–8. See generally C. Tyerman, *The English and the Crusades, 1095–1588* (Chicago, 1988); S.D. Lloyd, *English Society and the Crusade, 1216–1307* (Oxford, 1988).

111. *LM*, 96.
112. *Vie de Saint Louis*, 146–8.
113. So, according to Alan of Lille in the 1180s, piety teaches the layman 'to defend widows, console the unhappy, support the needy, feed the destitute and befriend orphans': *Anticlaudianus*, trans. J.J. Sheridan (Toronto, 1973), 184.
114. *Carmen elegiacum*, 768. For several examples of twelfth-century laments for counts and princes that labour the point of *contemptus mundi*, see D.A. Traill, 'More Poems by Philip the Chancellor', *Journal of Medieval Latin*, 16 (2006), 164–81.

CONCLUSION

1. C.S. Jaeger, *The Origins of Courtliness: Civilizing Trends and the Formation of Courtly Ideals, 939–1210* (Philadelphia, 1985), 224–6. For the Marbod reference, see *Vita sancti Magnobodi Andegavensis episcopi*, in *PL*, 171, col. 1549.
2. For the literacy of Fulk le Réchin, J. Martindale, 'Secular Propaganda and Aristocratic Values: The Autobiographies of Count Fulk le Réchin and Count William of Poitou, Duke of Aquitaine', in *Writing Medieval Biography*, 143–59; *Ordines Coronationis Franciae*, ed. R.A. Jackson (Philadelphia, 1995), 230–2.
3. *Eracle*, ed. G. Raynaud de Lage (Classiques Français du moyen age, 1976), lines 252–8.
4. Philip of Harvengt, *Epistolae*, in *PL*, 203, col. 149; *De institutione clericorum*, in ibid., 816. In the latter case, Clanchy portrays Philip as deploring the way knights were crossing boundaries, but my reading is that he was deploring the illiteracy of contemporary clergy: *Memory to Written Record*, 227.
5. *De principis instructione*, in *Giraldi Cambrensis Opera*, eds J.S. Brewer, J.F. Dimock and G.F. Warner (8 vols, Rolls Series, 1861–91), viii, 7.

BIBLIOGRAPHY

This is arranged without distinction between primary and secondary sources. Manuscript sources are cited in full in the relevant notes.

Abels, R. *Lordship and Military Obligation in Anglo-Saxon England* (Berkeley, CA, 1988).
Actes de Mathieu II duc de Lorraine (1220–1251), ed. M. le Mercier de Morière (Recueil des Documents sur l'Histoire de Lorraine, 17, 1893).
Actes des évêques de Laon des origines à 1151, ed. A. Dufour-Malbézin (Paris, 2001).
Adam-Even, P. 'Les sceaux d'écuyers au xiiie siècle', *Archives héraldiques suisses*, 66 (1951), 19–23.
Adams, G.B. *Councils and Courts in Anglo-Norman England* (repr. New York, 1965).
Ailred of Rievaulx. *Genealogia regum Anglorum*, in *PL*, 195.
Aird, W.M. *Robert Curthose, Duke of Normandy* (Woodbridge, 2008).
Alan of Lille, *Anticlaudianus*, trans. J.J. Sheridan (Toronto, 1973).
—— *Liber Poenitentialis*, in *PL* 210.
Alexander Neckham, *De naturis rerum libri duo*, ed. T. Wright (Rolls Series, 1863).
Alexander, J.W. 'The Alleged Palatinates of Norman England,' *Speculum*, 56 (1981), 17–27.
Ami et Amile, ed. P.F. Dembowski (Classiques Français du moyen age, 1987).
Amt, E. *The Accession of Henry II in England: Royal Government Restored, 1149–1159* (Woodbridge, 1993).
Andrew de Coutances, 'Le *Roman des Franceis*', ed. A.J. Holden, in *Études de langue et de littérature du moyen âge offertes à Félix Lecoy* (Paris: H. Champion, 1973), 213–25.
Andrew the Chaplain, *De Amore*, ed. and trans. P.G. Walsh (London, 1982).
Anglo-Latin Satirical Poets and Epigrammatists of the Twelfth Century, ed. T. Wright (2 vols, Rolls Series, 1872).
Annales Monastici, ed. H.R. Luard (5 vols, Rolls Series, 1864–9).
Annals and Memorials of St Edmunds Abbey, ed. T. Arnold (2 vols, Rolls Series, 1890).
Ashley, K.M. 'Medieval Courtesy Literature and Dramatic Mirrors of Female Conduct', in *The Ideology of Conduct: Essays in Literature and the History of Sexuality*, eds N. Armstrong and L. Tennenhouse (London, 1987), 25–38.
—— 'The *Miroir des Bonnes Femmes*: Not for Women Only?', in *Medieval Conduct*, eds K.M. Ashley and R.L.A. Clark (Minneapolis, 2001), 86–105.
Aurell, M. *The Plantagenet Empire, 1154–1224*, trans. D. Crouch (Harlow, 2007).
Bailey, M., *The English Manor, c.1200–c.1500* (Manchester, 2002).
Baldwin, J.W. 'Five Discourses on Desire: Sexuality and Gender in Northern France around 1200', *Speculum*, 66 (1991), 797–819.
Barlow, F. *William Rufus* (London, 1983).
—— *Thomas Becket* (London, 1986).
Barraclough, G. *The Earldom and County Palatine of Chester* (Oxford, 1953).
Barthélemy, D. *Les Deux Ages de la seigneurie banale: Coucy (xie–xiiie siècle)* (Paris, 1984).

—— *Chevaliers et miracles: la violence et le sacré dans la société féodale* (Paris, 2004).

—— *La Chevalerie: de la Germanie antique à la France du xiie siècle* (Paris, 2007).

Bartlett, R. *'Mortal Enmities': The Legal Aspect of Hostility in the Middle Ages* (Aberyswyth, 1998).

—— *England under the Norman and Angevin Kings, 1075–1225* (Oxford, 2000).

Barton, R.E. ' "Zealous Anger" and the Renegotiation of Aristocratic Relationships in Eleventh- and Twelfth-Century France', in *Anger's Past: The Social Uses of an Emotion in the Middle Ages*, ed. B.H. Rosenwein (Ithaca, NY, 1998), 153–70.

Basset Charters c.1120 to 1250, ed. W.T. Reedy (Pipe Roll Society, lxxxviii, 1995).

Bates, D. 'The Conqueror's Adolescence,' *ANS*, xxv, ed. J. Gillingham (Woodbridge, 2002), 1–18.

—— *William the Conqueror* (London, 1989).

Baudrey de Bourgeuil, *Historia Hierosolymitina*, in *PL*, 154.

Baumgartner, E. 'Trouvères et losengiers', *Cahiers de civilisation médiévale*, 25 (1982), 171–8.

Baxter, S. 'The Earls of Mercia and their Commended Men in the Mid Eleventh Century', *ANS*, xxiii, ed. J. Gillingham (Woodbridge, 2001), 23–46.

—— *The Earls of Mercia: Lordship and Power in Late Anglo-Saxon England* (Oxford, 2007).

Bean, J.M.W. ' "Bachelor" and Retainer', *Medievalia et Humanistica*, new ser., iii (1972), 117–31.

Bearman, R. 'Baldwin de Redvers: Some Aspects of a Baronial Career in the Reign of Stephen', *ANS*, xviii, ed. C. Harper-Bill (Woodbridge, 1996), 19–46.

Beauchamp Cartulary Charters, 1100–1268, ed. E. Mason (Pipe Roll Society: new ser., xliii, 1980).

Bémont, C. *Simon de Montfort, Earl of Leicester*, trans. E.F. Jacob (Oxford, 1930).

Bennett, M. 'The Status of the Squire: The Northern Evidence', in *The Ideals and Practice of Medieval Knighthood* i, eds C. Harper-Bill and R. Harvey (Woodbridge, 1986), 1–11.

—— 'Wace and Warfare', *ANS*, xi, ed. R.A. Brown (Woodbridge, 1988), 37–57.

—— 'Military Masculinity in England and Northern France, c.1150–c.1225', in *Masculinity in Medieval Europe*, ed. D.M. Hadley (London, 1999), 85–8.

Bethell, D. 'The Making of a Twelfth-century Relic Collection', in *Popular Belief and Practice*, eds G.J. Cuming and D. Baker (Studies in Church History, 8, Cambridge, 1972), 61–72.

Biancalana, J. 'For Want of Justice: The Legal Reforms of Henry II', *Columbia Law Review*, 88 (1988), 433–536.

Bisson, T. *The Crisis of the Twelfth Century: Power, Lordship, and the Origins of European Government* (Princeton, 2009).

Blair, J. *The Church in Anglo-Saxon Society* (Oxford, 2005).

Bonnier, C. 'List of English Towns in the Fourteenth Century', *EHR*, 16 (1901), 501–3.

Book of Fees, Commonly Called Testa de Nevill, ed. H.C. Maxwell-Lyte (3 vols, HMSO, 1920–31).

Book of the Foundation of Walden Abbey, eds and trans. D.E. Greenway and L. Watkiss (Oxford, 1999).

Bossy, J. 'The Mass as a Social Institution, 1200–1700,' *PP*, 100 (1983), 29–61.

Boussard, J. 'Les mercenaires au xiiie siècle: Henry II Plantagenêt et les origines de l'armée de métier', *Bibliothèque de l'Ecole des Chartes*, 106 (1945–6), 189–224.

—— *Le Gouvernement d'Henri II Plantagenêt* (Paris, 1956).

Bracton on the Laws and Customs of England, eds G.E. Woodbine and trans. S.E. Thorne (2 vols, Cambridge, MA, 1968).

Bracton's Notebook, ed. F.W. Maitland (3 vols, London, 1887).

Brand, P.A. 'Oldcotes v. d'Arcy', in *Medieval Legal Records Edited in Memory of C.A.F. Meekings*, eds R.F. Hunnisett and J.B. Post (London, 1978), 64–70.

—— 'Lordship and Distraint in Thirteenth-Century England', in *The Making of the Common Law* (London, 1992), 301–24.

—— '*Multis Vigiliis Excogitatam et Inventam*: Henry II and the Creation of the English Common Law', in *The Making of the Common Law* (London, 1992), 79–86.

—— 'Henry II and the Creation of the English Common Law', in *Henry II: New Interpretations*, eds C. Harper-Bill and N. Vincent (Woodbridge, 2007), 215–32.

Brooke, C.N.L. *The Medieval Idea of Marriage* (Oxford, 1989).

Brut y Tywysogyon: Red Book of Hergest Version, ed. and trans. T. Jones (Cardiff, 1955).

Bullough, V.L. 'On Being a Male in the Middle Ages', in *Medieval Masculinities: Regarding Men in the Middle Ages* (Minneapolis, 1994), 31–43.

Bumke, J. *The Concept of Knighthood in the Middle Ages*, trans. W.T.H. and E. Jackson (New York, 1982).

Burgess, G.S. 'Etude sur le terme *cortois* dans le français du xiie siècle', in *Travaux de linguistique et de philologie*, xxxi (1993), 195–210.

Burt, C. 'A "Bastard Feudal" Affinity in the Making? The Followings of William and Guy Beauchamp, Earls of Warwick, 1268–1315', *Midland History*, 34 (2009), 156–80.

Calendar of Ancient Correspondence concerning Wales, cal. J.G. Edwards (Cardiff, 1935).

Calendar of the Charter Rolls Preserved in the Public Record Office (6 vols, London, HMSO, 1923–7).

Calendar of the Close Rolls Preserved in the Public Record Office (London, HMSO, 1892–).

Calendar of Entries in the Papal Registers Relating to Great Britain and Ireland, 1198–1304, cal. W.H. Bliss (London, 1893).

Calendar of Inquisitions Miscellaneous Preserved in the Public Record Office (8 vols, London, HMSO, 1916–2003).

Calendar of Inquisitions Post Mortem and Other Analogous Documents Preserved in the Public Record Office (London, HMSO, 1904–).

Calendar of Ormond Deeds i, *1172–1350 AD*, ed. E. Curtis (Dublin, 1932).

Calendar of Patent Rolls Preserved in the Public Record Office (London, HMSO, 1891–).

Cam, H.M. 'An East Anglian Shire Moot of Stephen's Reign', *EHR*, 39 (1924), 568–71.

—— *The Hundred and the Hundred Rolls* (London, 1963).

Campbell, J. 'Observations on English Government from the Tenth Century to the Twelfth Century', *TRHS*, 5th ser., 25 (1975), 39–54.

Cannadine, D. *Class in Britain* (New Haven, 1998).

Carolus-Barré, M.L. 'Les grands tournois de Compiègne et de Senlis en l'honneur de Charles, prince de Salerne (mai 1279)', *Bullétin de la Société Nationale des Antiquaires de France* (1978–9), 87–100.

Carpenter, C. *Locality and Polity: A Study in Warwickshire Landed Society, 1401–1499* (Cambridge, 1992).

Carpenter, D.A. 'The Decline of the Curial Sheriff in England, 1194–1258', *EHR*, 91 (1976), 1–32.

—— 'Was There a Crisis of the Knightly Class in the Thirteenth Century? The Oxfordshire Evidence'. *EHR*, 95 (1980), 751–72.

—— 'King, Magnates and Society: The Personal Rule of King Henry III, 1234–1258', *Speculum*, 60 (1985), 39–70.

—— *The Minority of Henry III* (London, 1990).

—— 'Simon de Montfort: The First Leader of a Political Movement in English History', *History*, 76 (1991), 3–23.

—— 'The Second Century of English Feudalism', *PP*, 168 (2000), 30–71.

—— 'The Struggle to Control the Peak: An Unknown Letter Patent from 1217', in *Foundations of Medieval Scholarship: Records Edited in Honour of David Crook*, ed. P. Brand and S. Cunningham (Heslington, 2008), 35–49.

—— ' "In Testimonium Factorum Brevium": The Beginnings of the English Chancery Rolls', in *Records, Administration and Aristocratic Society in the Anglo-Norman Realm*, eds D. Crook and N. Vincent (Woodbridge, 2009), 1–28.

Cartulaire de l'abbaye Bénédictine de Saint-Pierre-de-Préaux, eds D. Rouet (Collection de Documents Inédits sur l'Histoire de France, 34, Paris, 2005).

Cartulaire de l'abbaye de St-Martin de Pontoise, ed. J. Depoin (Pontoise, 1895).

Cartulaire de l'abbaye de St-Michel du Tréport, ed. P. Laffleur de Kermaingant (Paris, 1880).

Cartulaire d'Afflighem, ed. E. de Marneffe, in *Analectes pour servir à l'histoire de la Belgique*, iie section, *Série des cartulaires et des documents étendus*, pt 1 (Louvain, 1894).

Cartulaire de l'église de la Sainte-Trinité de Beaumont-le-Roger, ed. E. Deville (Paris, 1912).

Cartularium Monasterii de Rameseia, eds W.H. Hart and P.A. Lyons (3 vols, Rolls Series, 1884–93).

Cartularium prioratus de Colne, ed. J.L. Fisher (Essex Archaeological Society, Occasional Publication, no. 1, 1946).

Cartulary of the Abbey of Mont-Saint-Michel, ed. K.S.B. Keats-Rohan (Donington, 2006).

Cartulary and Charters of Notre-Dame of Homblières, ed. W.M. Newman, revised by T. Evergates and G. Constable (Cambridge, MA., 1990).

Cartulary of the Cistercian Abbey of Flaxley, ed. A.W. Crawley-Boevey (Exeter, 1887).

Cartulary of Daventry Priory, The ed. M.J. Franklin (Northamptonshire Record Society, xxxv, 1988).

Cartulary of Haughmond Abbey, ed. U. Rees (Cardiff, 1985).

Cartulary of Holy Trinity Aldgate, ed. G.A.J. Hodgett (London Record Society, 7, 1971).

Cartulary of Shrewsbury Abbey, ed. U. Rees (2 vols, Cardiff, 1975).

The Cartulary of St Augustine's Abbey, Bristol, ed. D. Walker (Gloucestershire Record Series, 10, 1998).

Cartulary of St Mary's Collegiate Church, Warwick, ed. C. Fonge (Woodbridge, 2004).

Cartulary of St Michael's Mount, ed. P.L. Hull (Devon and Cornwall Record Society, new ser., v, 1962).

Cartulary of Worcester Cathedral Priory, ed. R.R. Darlington (Pipe Roll Society, 1968).

Chandler, V. 'The Last of the Montgomerys: Roger the Poitevin and Arnulf', *Historical Research*, lxii (1989), 1–14.

Chanson d'Aspremont, ed. L. Brandin (2 vols, Classiques Français du Moyen Âge, 1923–4).

Charles, B.G. 'An Early Charter of the Abbey of Cymhir', *The Transactions of the Radnorshire Society*, 40 (1970), 68–73.

Chartae Privilegia et Immunitates (Irish Records Commission, 1829).

Charters of the Anglo-Norman Earls of Chester, c.1071–1237, ed. G. Barraclough (Lancashire and Cheshire Record Society, cxxvi, 1988).

Charters of the Honour of Mowbray, 1107–1191, ed. D.E. Greenway (London, 1972).

Charters of the Redvers Family and the Earldom of Devon, 1090–1217, ed. R. Bearman (Devon and Cornwall Record Society, new ser., 37, 1994).

Chartes de l'abbaye de Jumièges (2 vols, Rouen, 1916).

Chartes de St-Bertin, ed. D. Haigneré (4 vols, St-Omer, 1886–90).

Chassel, J.-L. 'L'essor du sceau au xie siècle', *Bibliothèque de l'Ecole de Chartes*, 155 (1997), 221–34.

Chew, H.M. *The English Ecclesiastical Tenant-in-Chief and Knight Service* (Oxford, 1932).

Chibnall, M. 'Mercenaries and the *Familia Regis* under Henry I', *History*, 62 (1977), 15–23.

—— 'Anglo-French Relations in the Work of Orderic Vitalis', in *Documenting the Past: Essays in Honour of G.P. Cuttino*, eds J.S. Hamilton and P.J. Bradley (Woodbridge, 1989), 5–19.

—— 'Women in Orderic Vitalis', *HSJ*, 2 (1990), 105–21.

—— *The World of Orderic Vitalis* (Oxford, 1984).

Chrétien de Troyes, *Erec et Enide*, ed. M. Roquez (Classiques Français du Moyen Âge: Paris, 1952).

—— *Le Conte de Graal*, ed. F. Lecoy (2 vols, Classiques Français du Moyen Âge, 1972–5).

Chronica monasterii de Hida iuxta Wintoniam, in *Liber monasterii de Hyda*, ed. E. Edwards (Rolls, Series, 1866).

Chronica monasterii de Melsa, ed. E.A. Bond (3 vols, Rolls Series, 1866–8).

Chronica Rogeri de Wendover liber qui dicitur Flores Historiarum, ed. H.G. Hewlett (3 vols, Rolls Series, 1886–9).

Chronicle of Battle Abbey, ed. and trans. E. Searle (Oxford, 1980).

Chronicle of Richard of Devizes, ed. J.T. Appleby (London, 1963).

Chronicle of Walter of Guisborough, ed. H. Rothwell (Camden Society, 3rd ser., lxxxix, 1957).

Chronicle of William de Rishanger of the Barons' Wars, ed. J.O. Halliwell (Camden Soc., xv, 1840).

Chronicles of the Reigns of Stephen, Henry II and Richard I, ed. R. Howlett (Rolls Series, 1885).

Chronicon abbatiae Ramseiensis, ed. W. Dunn Macray (Rolls Series, 1886).

Chronique des comtes d'Eu, in *RHF*, 23.

Clanchy, M.T. 'Magna Carta, Clause Thirty-Four', *EHR*, 79 (1964), 542–8.

—— 'The Franchise of Return of Writs', *TRHS*, 5th ser., 17 (1967), 59–82.

—— 'Highway Robbery and Trial by Battle in the Hampshire Eyre of 1249', in *Medieval Legal Records Edited in Memory of C.A.F. Meekings*, eds R.F. Hunnisett and J.B. Post (London, 1978), 26–61.

—— *From Memory to Written Record: England, 1066–1307* (2nd edn, London, 1993).

—— *England and its Rulers, 1066–1307* (3rd edn, Oxford, 2006).

Clapham, J.H. 'The Horsing of the Danes', *EHR*, 25 (1910), 287–93.

Clarke, P.A. *The English Nobility under Edward the Confessor* (Oxford, 1994).

Close Rolls of the Reign of Henry III (14 vols, London, HMSO, 1902–38).

Cockersand Chartulary, ed. W. Farrer (3 vols in 7, Chetham Society, 1898–1909).

Colker, M.L. 'The Life of Guy of Merton by Rainald of Merton', *Medieval Studies*, 31 (1969), 250–61.

—— 'Latin Texts concerning Gilbert, Founder of Merton Priory', *Studia Monastica*, 12 (1970), 248–61.

—— 'The "Margam Chronicle" in a Dublin Manuscript', *HSJ*, 4 (1992), 123–48.

Colvin, H.M. 'The Origin of Chantries', *JMH*, 26 (2000), 163–73.

Complete Peerage of England, Scotland, Ireland and Great Britain, ed. V. Gibbs (13 vols in 14, London, 1910–59).

Constable, G. 'The Ceremonies and Symbolism of Entering Religious Life and Taking the Monastic Habit, from the Fourth to the Twelfth Century', in *Segni e riti nella chiesa altomedioevale occidentale* (Spoleto, 1987), 771–834.

Contamine, P. 'Points du vue sur la chevalerie en France à la fin du moyen âge', *Francia*, 4 (1976), 255–86.

Correspondence of Thomas Becket, Archbishop of Canterbury, 1162–1170, ed. and trans. A. Duggan (2 vols, Oxford, 2000).

Coss, P.R. 'Sir Geoffrey de Langley and the Crisis of the Knightly Class in Thirteenth-Century England', *PP*, 68 (1975), 3–37.

—— 'Knighthood and the Early Thirteenth-Century County Court', in *Thirteenth-Century England*, ii, eds P.R. Coss and S.D. Lloyd (Woodbridge, 1987), 45–58.

—— 'Bastard Feudalism Revised', *PP*, 125 (1989), 27–64.

—— 'Knights, Squires and the Origins of Social Gradation', *TRHS*, 6th ser., 5 (1995), 155–78.

—— *Lordship, Knighthood and Locality: A Study in English Society, c.1180–c.1280* (Cambridge, 1991).

—— *The Knight in Medieval England, 1000–1400* (Stroud, 1993).

—— *The Lady in Medieval England, 1000–1500* (Stroud, 1998)

—— *The Origins of the English Gentry* (Cambridge, 2003).

Coucher Book of Furness Abbey, ed. J.C. Atkinson (3 vols, Chetham Society, new ser., ix, xi, xiv, 1886–7).

Coucher Book of Selby, ed. J.T. Fowler (2 vols, Yorkshire Archaeological Society Record Series, x, xiii, 1891–3).

Couronnement de Louis, Le ed. E. Langlois (Classiques Français du Moyen Âge, 1984).

Cowdrey, H.E.J. 'Bishop Ermenfrid of Sion and the Penitential Ordinance Following the Battle of Hastings', *Journal of Ecclesiastical History*, 20 (1969), 225–42.

Cox, D.C. 'Two Charters of King Stephen for Wenlock Priory', *Transactions of the Shropshire Archaeological and Historical Society*, lxvi (1989), 56–9.

Cronne, H.A. 'An Agreement between Simon, Bishop of Worcester, and Waleran, Earl of Worcester', *University of Birmingham Historical Journal*, ii (1949–50), 201–7.

Crouch, D. 'Geoffrey de Clinton and Roger, Earl of Warwick: Magnates and *Curiales* in the Reign of Henry I', *BIHR*, 55 (1982), 113–24.

—— 'The Foundation of Leicester Abbey and Other Problems', *Midland History*, 11 (1987), 1–13.

—— 'Earl William of Gloucester and the End of the Anarchy', *EHR*, 103 (1988), 69–75.

—— 'The Last Adventure of Richard Siward', *Morgannwg*, xxxv (1991), 7–30.

—— 'Earls and Bishops in Twelfth-Century Leicestershire', *Nottingham Medieval Studies*, 37 (1993), 9–20.

—— 'A Norman "Conventio" and Bonds of Lordship in the Middle Ages', in *Law and Government in Medieval England and Normandy*, eds G. Garnett and J.G. Hudson (Cambridge, 1994), 299–324.

—— 'The March and the Welsh Kings', in *The Anarchy of King Stephen's Reign*, ed. E. King (Oxford, 1994), 255–89.

—— 'Normans and Anglo-Normans: A Divided Aristocracy', in *England and Normandy in the Middle Ages*, eds D. Bates and A. Curry (London, 1994), 59–61.

—— 'From Stenton to McFarlane: Models of Societies of the Twelfth and Thirteenth Centuries', *TRHS*, 6th ser., 5 (1995), 179–200.

—— 'The Local Influence of the Earls of Warwick, 1088–1242: A Study in Decline and Resourcefulness', *Midland History*, xxi (1996), 1–22.

—— 'The Origin of Chantries: Some Further Anglo-Norman Evidence', *Journal of Medieval History*, 27 (2001), 159–80.

—— 'The Troubled Deathbeds of Henry I's Servants: Death, Confession and Secular Conduct in the Twelfth Century', *Albion*, 34 (2002), 24–36.

—— 'Loyalty, Career and Self-Justification at the Plantagenet Court: The Thought-World of William Marshal and his Colleagues', in *Culture Politique des Plantagenêt, 1154–1224*, ed. M. Aurell (Poitiers, 2003), 229–40.

—— 'Early Charters and Patrons of Leicester Abbey', in *Leicester Abbey: Medieval History, Archaeology and Manuscript Studies*, eds J. Story et al. (Leicester, 2006), 225–87.

—— 'Writing a Biography in the Thirteenth Century: The Construction and Composition of the "History of William Marshal" ', in *Writing Medieval Biography: Essays in Honour of Frank Barlow*, eds D. Bates, J. Crick and S. Hamilton (Woodbridge, 2006), 221–35.

—— 'Robert of Beaumont, Count of Meulan and Leicester: His Lands, his Acts and his Self-Image', in *Henry I and the Anglo-Norman World: Studies in Memory of C. Warren Hollister*, eds D. Fleming and J.M. Pope (Woodbridge, 2006), 91–116.

—— 'William Marshal and the Mercenariat', in *Mercenaries and Paid Men: The Mercenary Identity in the Middle Ages*, ed. J. France (Woodbridge, 2008), 15–32.

—— 'The Transformation of Medieval Gwent', in *Gwent County History* ii, *The Age of Marcher Lords, c.1075–1536*, eds R.A. Griffiths, A. Hopkins and R. Howell (Cardiff, 2008), 1–45.

—— 'La cour seigneuriale en Angleterre aux xiie–xiiie siècles', in *Les Seigneuries dans l'espace Plantagenêt (c.1150–c.1250)*, eds M. Aurell and F. Boutoulle (Bordeaux, 2009), 31–40.

—— 'Between Three Realms: The Acts of Waleran II, Count of Meulan and Worcester', in *Records, Administration and Aristocratic Society in the Anglo-Norman Realm*, eds D. Crook and N. Vincent (Woodbridge, 2009), 75–90.

—— 'Chivalry and Courtliness: Colliding Constructs', in *Soldiers, Nobles and Gentlemen: Essays in Honour of Maurice Keen*, eds P.R. Coss and C. Tyerman (Woodbridge, 2009), 32–48.

—— 'The *Roman des Franceis* of Andrew de Coutances: Significance, Text and Translation', in *Normandy and its Neighbours, c.900–1250: Essays for David Bates*, eds D. Crouch and K. Thompson (Turnhout, 2010).

—— 'The Complaint of King John against William de Briouze (*c.*September 1210): The Black Book of the Exchequer Text', in *Magna Carta and the England of King John*, ed. J. Loengard (Woodbridge, 2010), 169–78.

—— 'Mothers, Sons and Executors: The Brief Widowhood of Isabel, Counters of Pembroke, May 1219–March 1220', forthcoming.

—— *The Beaumont Twins: The Roots and Branches of Power in the Twelfth Century* (Cambridge, 1986).

—— *The Image of Aristocracy in Britain, 1000–1300* (London, 1992).

—— *The Reign of King Stephen, 1135–1154* (London, 2000).

—— *The Normans: the History of a Dynasty* (London, 2002).

—— *William Marshal: Knighthood, War and Chivalry, 1147–1219* (2nd edn, London, 2002).

—— *Tournament* (London, 2005).

—— *The Birth of Nobility: Constructing Aristocracy in England and France, 900–1300* (Harlow, 2005).

Crown Pleas of the Devon Eyre of 1238, ed. H.T. Summerson (Devon and Cornwall Record Society, new ser., 28, 1985).

Cullum, H. 'Clergy, Masculinity and Transgression in Late Medieval England', in *Masculinity in Medieval Europe*, ed. D.M. Hadley (London, 1999), 178–96.

Curia Regis Rolls Preserved in the Public Record Office (20 vols, London, HMSO, 1922–2007).

Dace, R. 'Bertran de Verdun: Royal Service, Land and Family in the Late Twelfth Century', *Medieval Prosopography*, 20 (1999), 75–93.

Dalton, P. 'William Earl of York and Royal Authority in Yorkshire in the Reign of Stephen', *HSJ*, 2 (1990), 155–65.

—— 'Aiming at the Impossible: Ranulf II of Chester and Lincolnshire in the Reign of Stephen', in *The Earldom of Chester and its Charters*, ed. A.T. Thacker (Journal of the Chester Archaeological Society, 71, 1991), 109–34.

—— 'Civil Peace and Ecclesiastical Peace in the Reign of King Stephen', in *War and Society in Medieval and Early Modern Britain*, ed. D. Dunn (Liverpool, 2000), 53–75.

—— 'Churchmen and the Promotion of Peace in King Stephen's Reign', *Viator*, 31 (2000), 79–119.

—— *Conquest, Anarchy and Lordship: Yorkshire 1066–1154* (Cambridge, 1994).

D'Alverny, M.-T. 'Comment les théologiens et les philosophes voient la femme', *Cahiers de civilisation médiévale*, 20 (1977), 15–40.

Davies, R.R. *Lordship and Society in the March of Wales, 1282–1400* (Oxford, 1978).

Davies, W. *The Llandaff Charters* (Aberystwyth, 1979).

Davis, H.W.C. 'Some Documents of the Anarchy', in *Essays in History Presented to R.L. Poole* (Oxford, 1927), 168–72.

Davis, R.H.C. *King Stephen* (3rd edn, London, 1990).

De Antiquis Legibus Liber. Chronica Maiorum et Vicecomitum Londoniarum, ed. T. Stapleton (Camden Society, 1846).

De Cauna, J. *L'Ensenhamen ou code du parfait chevalier* (Mounenh en Biarn, 2007).

De diversis ordinibus hominum, in *The Latin Poems Commonly Attributed to Walter Mapes*, ed. T. Wright (Camden Society, 1841).

De Dornon, A. de Behault, 'La noblesse hennuyère au tournoi de Compiègne de 1238', *Annales du cercle archéologique de Mons*, xxii (1890), 61–114.

De Hemptinne, T. 'Les épouses des croisés et pèlerins flamands aux xie et xiie siècles: l'exemple des comtesses de Flandre, Clémence et Sibylle', in *Autour de la Première Croisade: actes du colloque de la 'Society for the Study of the Crusades and the Latin East'*, ed. M. Balard (Paris, 1996), 111–37.

De Laborderie, O., J.R. Maddicott and D.A. Carpenter. 'The Last Hours of Simon de Montfort: A New Account,' *EHR*, 115 (2000), 378–412.

Debord, A. *Aristocratie et pouvoir: le rôle du château dans la France médiévale* (Paris, 2000).

Delisle, L. *Notice sur une* Summa Dictaminis *jadis conservée à Beauvais* (Paris, 1898).

Denholm-Young, N. 'An Early Thirteenth-Century Anglo-Norman MS', *Bodleian Library Record*, 6 (1921–31), 225–30.

—— 'Feudal Society in the Thirteenth Century: The Knights', in *Collected Papers* (Cardiff, 1969).

—— *Seignorial Administration in England* (London, 1937).

—— *Richard of Cornwall* (Oxford, 1947).

Descriptive Catalogue of the Charters and Muniments at Berkeley Castle, ed. I.H. Jeayes (Bristol, 1892).

Dialogus de Scaccario, ed. and trans. E. Amt (Oxford, 2007).

Die Gesetze de Angelsachsen, ed. F. Liebermann (3 vols, Halle, 1903–16).

Diplomatic Documents Preserved in the Public Record Office i, *1101–1272*, ed. P. Chaplais (London, 1964).

Dobson, E.J. 'The Date and Composition of *Ancrene Wisse*', *Proceedings of the British Academy*, lii (1966), 181–206.

Documents of the Baronial Movement of Reform and Rebellion, 1252–1267, eds and trans. R.F. Treharne and I.J. Sanders (Oxford, 1973).

Documents Illustrative of the Social and Economic History of the Danelaw, ed. F.M. Stenton (London, 1920).

Domesday Book seu Liber Censualis Willelmi primi regis Angliae, eds A. Farley et al. (4 vols, London, 1783–1816).

Domesday Monachorum of Christ Church Canterbury, ed. D.C. Douglas (London, 1944).

Duby, G. 'Les "Jeunes" dans la société aristocratique dans la France du nord-ouest au xiie siècle', in *La Société chevaleresque* (Paris, 1988), 129–42; trans. in *The Chivalrous Society*, trans. C. Postan (London, 1977), 112–22.

—— 'Situation de la noblesse en France au début de xiiie siècle', *Tijdschrift voor Geschiedenis*, 82 (1969), 309–15, trans. as 'The Transformation of the Aristocracy', in *The Chivalrous Society*, trans. C. Postan (London, 1977), 178–85.

Duffy, E. *Marking the Hours: English People and their Prayers, 1240–1570* (New Haven, 2006).

Duffy, S. 'John and Ireland: The Origins of England's Irish Problem', in *King John: New Interpretations*, ed. S.D. Church (Woodbridge, 1999), 221–45.

Durham Liber Vitae, The, eds D. and L. Rollason (3 vols, London, 2007).

Dyer, C. *Standards of Living in the Later Middle Ages: Social Change in England, c.1200–1520* (Cambridge, 1989).

Eadmer, *Historia Novorum*, ed. M. Rule (Rolls Series, 1884).

—— *Life of St Anselm*, ed. R.W. Southern (Oxford 1962).

Earldom of Gloucester Charters, ed. R.B. Patterson (Oxford, 1973).

Early Lancashire Charters, ed. W. Farrer (Liverpool, 1902).

Early Yorkshire Charters i–iii, ed. W. Farrer (Edinburgh, 1914–16); iv–xii, ed. C.T. Clay (Huddersfield, Leeds and Wakefield, 1935–65).

Ecclesiastical Letter Books of the Thirteenth Century, ed. R. Hill (Oxford, 1936).

Elliott, A.G. 'The *Facetus* or the Art of Courtly Loving', *Allegorica*, 2 (1977), 27–57.

Ellis, G. *Earldoms in Fee* (London, 1963).

English, B. *The Lords of Holderness, 1086–1260* (Oxford, 1979).

English Episcopal Acta iii, *Canterbury 1193–1205*, eds C.R. Cheney and E. John (London, 1986).

English Lawsuits from William I to Richard I, ed. and trans. R.C. van Caenegem (2 vols, Selden Society, 106–7, 1990–1).

English Romanesque Art, 1066–1200, eds G. Zarnecki et al. (London, 1984).

English Text of the Ancrene Riwle: Cotton Cleopatra C vi, ed. E.J. Dobson (Early English Text Society, no. 267, 1972).

Eracle, ed. G. Raynaud de Lage (Classiques Français du Moyen Age, 1976).

Evans, F.W. 'Beaudesert and the De Mountfords', in *Transactions of the Birmingham Archaeological Society*, xxxii (1907), 24–40.

Everard, J.A. 'The Foundation of an Alien Priory at Linton, Cambridgeshire', *Proceedings of the Cambridge Antiquarian Society*, lxxxvi (1997), 169–74.

Evergates, T. *The Aristocracy in the County of Champagne, 1100–1300* (Philadelphia, 2007).

Exempla of Jacques de Vitry, ed. and trans. T.F. Crane (New York, 1890).

Eynsham Cartulary, ed. H.E. Salter (2 vols, Oxford Historical Society, xlix, li, 1907–8).

Facsimiles of the National Manuscripts of Scotland, ed. H. James (3 vols, London, 1869–71).

Faral, E. *Mimes français du xiiie siècle* (Paris, 1910).

Farmer, S. 'Clerical Images of Medieval Wives', *Speculum*, 61 (1986), 517–43.

Farnham, G. 'The Manor of Noseley', *Transactions of the Leicestershire Archaeological Society*, xii (1922), 233–8.

Faulkner, K. 'The Transformation of Knighthood in Early Thirteenth-Century England', *EHR* (1996), 1–23.

Faure, M. 'Le losengier dans la chanson des trouvères des xiie et xiiie siècles', in *Félonie, trahison, reniements au moyen âge: actes du troisième colloque international de Montpellier, 24–26 novembre 1995* (Montpellier, 1997), 189–95.

Fauriel, M. *Histoire de la poésie provençale* (2 vols, Paris, 1846).

Feet of Fines in the Public Record Office of the 10th Year of King Richard I, also a Roll of the King's Court in the Reign of King Richard I, ed. anon. (Pipe Roll Society, xxiv, 1900).

Ferrante, J. 'The Court in Medieval Literature', in *The Medieval Court in Europe*, ed. E.R. Haymes (Houston German Studies, 6, Munich, 1986), 1–25.

Feuchère, P. 'Pairs de principauté et pairs de château: essai sur l'institution des pairies en Flandre. Etude géographique et institutionelle', *Revue belge de philologie et d'histoire*, 31 (1953), 973–1002.

Finberg, H.P.R. 'Some Early Tavistock Charters', *EHR*, 62 (1947), 352–77, 1103–1235.

Flanagan, M.T. 'Strongbow, Henry II and Anglo-Norman Intervention in Ireland', in *War and Government in the Middle Ages: Essays in Honour of J.O. Prestwich*, eds J. Gillingham and J.C. Holt (Cambridge, 1982), 62–77.

—— 'Defining Lordships in Angevin Ireland: William Marshal and the King's Justiciar', in *Les Seigneuries dans l'espace Plantagenêt (c.1150–c.1250)*, eds M. Aurell and F. Boutoulle (Bordeaux, 2009), 41–59.

—— *Irish Society, Anglo-Norman Settlers, Angevin Kingship: Interactions in Ireland in the Late 12th century* (Oxford, 1989).

Fleming, D. 'Landholding by *Milites* in Domesday Book', *ANS*, xiii, ed. M. Chibnall (Woodbridge, 1991), 83–98.

Fleming, R. 'Domesday Book and the Tenurial Revolution', *ANS*, ix, ed. R.A. Brown (Woodbridge, 1986), 87–102.

—— 'The New Wealth, the New Rich, and the New Political Style in Late Anglo-Saxon England', *ANS*, xxiiii, ed. J. Gillingham (Woodbridge, 2000), 1–22.

—— *Kings and Lords in Conquest England* (Cambridge, 1991).

—— *Domesday Book and the Law: Society and Legal Custom in Early Medieval England* (Cambridge, 1998).

Fletcher, R. *Bloodfeud: Murder and Revenge in Anglo-Saxon England* (London, 2002).

Flores Historiarum, ed. H.R. Luard (3 vols, Rolls Series, 1890).

Flori, J. 'La Notion de chevalerie dans les chansons de geste du xiie siècle: étude historique de vocabulaire', *Le Moyen Age*, 81 (1975), 211–44, 407–45.

—— 'Qu'est-ce qu'un bacheler?', *Romania*, xcvi (1975), 289–314.

—— 'La notion de la chevalerie dans les romans de Chrétien de Troyes', *Romania*, 114 (1996), 289–315.

—— *L'Essor de Chevalerie, xie–xiie siècles* (Geneva, 1986).

—— *Chevaliers et chevalerie au moyen âge* (Paris, 1998).

—— *Richard Coeur de Lion: le roi-chevalier* (Paris, 1999).

Formulare Anglicanum, ed T. Madox (London, 1702).

Fouke le Fitz Waryn, eds E.J. Hathaway et al. (Anglo-Norman Text Society, 26–8, 1975).

Freeman, E.A. *The History of the Norman Conquest of England* (5 vols, Oxford, 1870–9).

Frithegodi monachi Breuiloquium Vitae Beati Wilfredi et Wulfstani Cantoris Narratio Metrica de Sancto Swithuno, ed. A. Campbell (Zurich, 1950).

Fulton, H. 'The *Mabinogi* and the Education of Princes in Medieval Wales', in *Medieval Celtic Literature and Society*, ed. *eadem* (Dublin, 2005), 230–47.

Garin le Brun, *Ensenhamen*, in *Testi Didattico-Cortesi di Provenza* ed. G.E. Sansone (Bari, 1977), 53–107.

Garin le Loherenc, ed. A. Iker-Gittleman (3 vols, Classiques Français du Moyen Âge, 1996–7).

Garnett, G. *Conquered England: Kingship, Succession and Tenure 1066–1166* (Oxford, 2007).

Garnier de Pont-Sainte-Maxence, *La Vie de Saint Thomas le Martyr*, ed. E. Walberg (Paris, 1936).

Gaunt, S. *Gender and Genre in Medieval French Literature* (Cambridge, 1995).

Geoffrey of Burton, *Life and Miracles of St Modwenna*, ed. and trans. R. Bartlett (Oxford, 2002).

Geoffrey Gaimar, *Estoire des Engleis*, ed. and trans. I. Short (Oxford, 2009).

Gerald of Wales, *De principis instructione*, in *Giraldi Cambrensis Opera*, eds J.S. Brewer, J.F. Dimock and G.F. Warner (8 vols, Rolls Series, 1861–91), viii.

—— *Itinerarium Kambriae*, in *Giraldi Cambrensis Opera*, eds J.S. Brewer, J.F. Dimock and G.F. Warner (8 vols, Rolls Series, 1861–91), vi.

Gesta Henrici Secundi, ed. W. Stubbs (2 vols, Rolls Series, 1867).

Gesta Stephani, eds and trans. K.R. Potter and R.H.C. Davis (Oxford, 1976).

Geste des Engleis en Yrlande, ed. and trans. E. Mullally (Dublin, 2002).

Gillingham, J. 'Thegns and Knights in Eleventh-Century England: Who Was Then the Gentleman?', *TRHS*, 6th ser., 5 (1995), 129–53.

—— 'Fontenoy and After: Pursuing Enemies to Death in France between the Ninth and Eleventh Centuries', in *Frankland: The Franks and the World of the Early Middle Ages. Essays in Honour of Dame Jinty Nelson*, eds P. Fouracre and D. Ganz (Manchester, 2008), 242–65.

—— *Richard I* (New Haven, 1999).

Given, J.B. *Society and Homicide in Thirteenth-Century England* (Stanford, CA, 1977).

Golding, B. 'Anglo-Norman Knightly Burials', *ANS*, xiii, ed. M. Chibnall (Woodbridge, 1991), 35–48.

Goscelin of Canterbury, *Historia translationis sancti Augustini episcopi*, in *PL*, 155.

Grand Cartulaire de Conches et sa copie: transcription et analyse, ed. C. de Haas (Le Mesnil-sur-l'Estrée, 2005).

Grant, A. 'Franchises North of the Border: Baronies and Regalities in Medieval Scotland', in *Liberties and Identities in the Medieval British Isles*, ed. M. Prestwich (Woodbridge, 2008), 155–99.

Green, J.A. 'Aristocratic Women in Early Twelfth-Century England', in *Anglo-Norman Political Culture and the Twelfth-Century Renaissance*, ed. C.W. Hollister (Woodbridge, 1997), 59–82.

—— ' "A Lasting Memorial": The Charter of Liberties of Henry I', in *Charters and Charter Scholarship in Britain and Ireland*, eds J.A. Green and M.T. Flanagan (Basingstoke, 2005), 55–62.

—— *The Government of England under Henry I* (Cambridge, 1986).

—— *English Sheriffs to 1154* (HMSO, 1990).

—— *The Aristocracy of Norman England* (Cambridge, 1997).

—— *Henry I: King of England and Duke of Normandy* (Cambridge, 2006).

Gui de Warewic: roman du xiii siècle*, ed. A. Ewert (2 vols, Classiques Français du Moyen Âge, 1932).

Guilhiermoz, P. *Essai sur la noblesse du moyen âge* (Paris, 1902).

Guillotjeannin, O. *Episcopus et Comes* (Geneva, 1987).

Hagger, M.S. 'The Norman *Vicomte*, c.1035–1135: What Did he Do?', *ANS*, xxix, ed. C.P. Lewis (Woodbridge, 2007), 65–83.

—— *The Fortunes of a Norman Family: The De Verduns in England, Ireland and Wales, 1066–1316* (Dublin, 2001).

Harding, A. *The Law Courts of Medieval England*, (London, 1973).

Harper-Bill C. 'Herluin, Abbot of Bec, and his Biographer', in *Studies in Church History*, xv, ed. D. Baker (Ecclesiastical History Society, Oxford, 1978), 15–25.

—— 'The Piety of the Anglo-Norman Knightly Class', *ANS*, ii, ed. R.A. Brown (Woodbridge, 1980), 63–77.

Hart, C. 'Athelstan "Half-King" and his Family', in *Anglo-Saxon England* ii, eds P. Clemoes et al. (Cambridge, 1973), 122–3.

Hartopp, H. 'Some Unpublished Documents Relating to Noseley co. Leics.' *Associated Architectural Societies: Reports and Papers*, xxv, pt 2 (1900).

Harvey, S. 'The Knight and the Knight's Fee in England', *PP*, 49 (1970), 3–43.

Hauréau, J. Barthélemy. 'Un poème inédit de Pierre Riga', *Bibliothèque de l'École de Chartes*, 44 (1883), 7–11.

Henderson, G. 'Romance and Politics on Some Medieval English Seals', *Art History*, i (1980), 26–42.

Henry of Huntingdon, *Historia Anglorum*, ed. and trans. D. Greenway (Oxford, 1996).

Hershey, A.H. 'The Rise and Fall of William de Bussey: A Mid Thirteenth-Century Steward', *Nottingham Medieval Studies*, 44 (2000), 104–22.

Heslop, T.A. 'English Seals from the Mid Ninth Century to 1100', *Journal of the British Archaeological Association*, 133 (1980), 1–16.

Hilton, R. *A Medieval Society: The West Midlands at the End of the Thirteenth Century* (repr. Cambridge, 1983).

Hinnebusch, W. *The Early English Friars Preacher* (Rome, 1951).

Historia Ecclesiae Abbendonensis, ed. and trans. J.G. Hudson (2 vols, Oxford, 2002).

Historia et Cartularium monasterii sancti Petri de Gloucestria, ed. W. Hart (3 vols, Rolls Series, 1896).

Historia Regum Britanniae of Geoffrey of Monmouth i, Bern, Burgerbibliotehek, MS 568, ed. N. Wright (Cambridge, 1984).

History of the King's Works, The, eds H.M. Colvin et al. (3 vols, London, 1963).

History of William Marshal, eds A.J. Holden and D. Crouch, trans. S. Gregory (3 vols, Anglo-Norman Text Society, Occasional Publications Series, 4–6, 2002–7).

Holden, B.W. 'King John, the Braoses and the Celtic Fringe, 1207–1216', *Albion*, 33 (2001), 1–23.

Hollister, C.W. 'Magnates and "Curiales" in Early Norman England', *Viator*, 4 (1973), 115–22.

—— 'The Taming of a Turbulent Earl: Henry I and William of Warenne', in *Monarchy Magnates and Institutions in the Anglo-Norman World* (London, 1986), 137–44.

—— *Anglo-Saxon Military Institutions on the Eve of the Norman Conquest* (Oxford, 1962).

—— *Henry I* (New Haven, 2001).

Holt, J.C. 'The Barons and the Great Charter', *EHR*, 70 (1955), 1–24.

—— 'The Assizes of Henry II: The Texts', in *The Study of Medieval Records*, eds D.A. Bullough and R.L. Storey (Oxford, 1971), 85–106.

—— 'The Prehistory of Parliament', in *The English Parliament in the Middle Ages*, eds R.G. Davies and J.H. Denton (Manchester, 1981).

—— 'The Introduction of Knight-Service in England', *ANS*, vi, ed. R.A. Brown (Woodbridge, 1984), 89–106.

—— 'Feudal Society and the Family in Early Medieval England: IV. The Heiress and the Alien', *TRHS*, 5th ser., 35 (1985), 1–28.

—— *The Northerners* (Oxford, 1961).

—— *Magna Carta* (2nd edn, Cambridge, 1992).

Hooper, N. 'Anglo-Saxon Warfare on the Eve of the Conquest: A Brief Survey', *ANS*, i, ed. R.A. Brown (Woodbridge, 1978), 84–93.

—— 'Edgar the Ætheling: Anglo-Saxon Prince, Rebel and Crusader', *Anglo-Saxon England*, 14, eds P. Clemoes et al. (Cambridge, 1985), 197–214.

—— 'The Housecarls in England in the Eleventh Century', *ANS*, vii, ed. R.A. Brown (Woodbridge, 1985), 161–76.

Howell, M. 'Regalian Right in Wales and the March: The Relation of Theory to Practice', *Welsh History Review*, 7 (1974–5), 269–88.

Hudson, J.G. 'Maitland and Anglo-Norman Law', in *Proceedings of the British Academy*, 89 (1996), 21–46.

—— *The Formation of the English Common Law* (London, 1996).

—— *Land, Law and Lordship in Anglo-Norman England* (Oxford, 1994).

—— 'Henry I and Counsel', in *The Medieval State: Essays Presented to James Campbell*, eds J.R. Maddicott and D.M. Palliser (London, 2000), 109–26.

Hue de Roteland, *Protheselaus*, ed. A.J. Holden (3 vols, Anglo-Norman Text Society, 1989–93).

Hugh the Chanter, *The History of the Church of York, 1066–1127*, ed. and trans. C. Johnson (London, 1961).

Huneycutt, L.L. *Matilda of Scotland: A Study in Medieval Queenship* (Woodbridge, 2003).

Hunt, J. *Lordship and the Landscape: A Documentary and Archaeological Study of the Honor of Dudley, c.1066–1322* (BAR British Series, 264, 1997).

Hunter Blair, C.H. 'Armorials upon English Seals from the Twelfth to the Sixteenth Centuries', *Archaeologia*, 2nd ser., lxxxix (1943), 1–26.

Hurnard, N.D. 'The Anglo-Norman Franchises', *EHR*, 64 (1949), 289–327, 433–60.

Hyams, P.R. 'Feud and the State in Anglo-Saxon England', *Journal of British Studies*, 40 (2001), 1–43.

——— *Rancor and Reconciliation in Medieval England* (Ithaca, NY, 2003).

Inquisitio Comitatus Cantabrigiensis and Inquisitio Eliensis, ed. N.E.S.A. Hamilton (London, 1876).

Instrumenta et Acta de munimentis regni Scotie, in *Acts of the Parliaments of Scotland*, eds T. Thomson and C. Innes (12 vols, Edinburgh, 1814–75).

Jacob, E.F. *Studies in the Period of Baronial Reform and Rebellion, 1258–1267* (Oxford Studies in Social and Legal History, viii, 1925).

Jacques Bretel, *Le Tournoi de Chauvency*, ed. G. Hecq (Société des Bibliophiles Belges, no. 31, Mons, 1898).

Jaeger, C.S. 'The Courtier Bishop in *Vitae* from the Tenth to the Twelfth Century', *Speculum*, 58 (1983), 291–325.

——— 'Beauty of Manners and Discipline: An Imperial Tradition of Courtliness in the German Romance', in *Barocker Lust-Spiegel: Festschrift für Blake Lee Spahr* (Amsterdam, 1984), 27–45.

——— 'Book-Burning at Don Quixote's: Thoughts on the Educating Force of Courtly Romance', in *Courtly Arts and the Art of Courtliness: Selected Papers from the Eleventh Triennial Congress of the International Courtly Literature* Society, eds K. Busby and C. Kleinhenz (Cambridge, 2006), 3–27.

——— *The Origins of Courtliness: Civilizing Trends and the Formation of Courtly Ideals, 939–1210* (Philadelphia, 1985).

——— *The Envy of Angels: Cathedral Schools and Social Ideals in Medieval Europe, 950–1200* (Philadelphia, 1994).

Jean de Joinville, *Vie de Saint Louis*, ed. J. Monfrin (Paris, 1995).

Jehan et Blonde, ed. S. Lécuyer (Classiques Français du Moyen Age, 1984).

Jeu d'Adam, ed. W. van Emden (Société Rencesvals British Branch, British Rencesvals Publications, 1, 1996).

John of Worcester, *Chronicle*, eds R.R. Darlington and P. McGurk, ii (Oxford, 1995), iii (Oxford, 1998).

Johns, S. *Noblewomen, Aristocracy and Power in the Twelfth-Century Anglo-Norman Realm* (Manchester, 2003).

Jolliffe, J.E.A. *Angevin Kingship* (2nd edn, London, 1963).

Jones, M. 'Notes sur quelques familles bretonnes en Angleterre après la conquête normande', *Mémoires de la Société d'Histoire et d'Archéologie de Bretagne*, 58 (1981), 73–97.

Jordan Fantosme's Chronicle, ed. and trans. R.C. Johnston (Oxford, 1981).

Kaeuper, R.W. *Chivalry and Violence in Medieval Europe* (Oxford, 1999).

——— *Holy Warriors: The Religious Ideology of Chivalry* (Philadelphia, 2009).

Kay, S. 'The Contradictions of Courtly Love and the Origins of Courtly Poetry: The Evidence of the *Lauzengiers*', *Journal of Medieval and Early Modern Studies*, 26 (1996), 209–53.

Kealey, E. *Roger of Salisbury, Viceroy of England* (Berkeley, CA, 1972).

Keats-Rohan, K.S.B. 'William I and the Breton Contingent in the Non-Norman Conquest, 1060–1087', *ANS*, xiii, ed. M. Chibnall (Woodbridge, 1991), 157–72.

—— 'The Bretons and Normans of England, 1066–1154', *Nottingham Medieval Studies*, 36 (1992), 42–78.

Keefe, T.K. 'King Henry II and the Earls: The Pipe Roll Evidence', *Albion*, 13 (1981), 191–222.

—— *Feudal Assessments and the Political Community under Henry II and his Sons* (Berkeley, 1983).

Keen, M. *The Laws of War in the Late Middle Ages* (London, 1965).

—— *Chivalry* (New Haven, 1984).

Keynes, S. *The Diplomas of King Aethelred 'the Unready', 978–1016: A Study in their Use as Historical Evidence* (Cambridge, 1980).

King, E. 'The Peterborough "Descriptio Militum" (Henry I)', *EHR*, 84 (1969), 84–101.

—— 'King Stephen and the Anglo-Norman Aristocracy', *History*, 59 (1974), 180–94.

—— 'Mountsorrel and its Region in King Stephen's Reign', *Huntington Library Quarterly*, 44 (1980), 1–10.

—— 'Estate Records of the Hotot Family', in *A Northamptonshire Miscellany*, ed. *idem* (Northamptonshire Record Society, xxxii, 1983).

—— 'The Foundation of Pipewell Abbey, Northamptonshire', *HSJ*, 2 (1990), 167–77.

—— 'Dispute Settlement in Anglo-Norman England', *ANS*, xiv, ed. M. Chibnall (Woodbridge, 1992), 115–30.

—— 'Stephen of Blois, Count of Mortain and Boulogne', *EHR*, 115 (2000), 271–96.

Koziol, G. *Begging Pardon and Favor: Ritual and Political Order in Early Medieval France* (Ithaca, 1992).

Kuefler, M. 'Male Friendship and the Suspicion of Sodomy', in *The Boswell Thesis: Essays on Christianity, Social Tolerance and Homosexuality*, ed. *idem* (Chicago, 2006), 179–212.

Lachaud, F. 'Liveries of Robes in England, *c*.1200–*c*.1330', *EHR*, 111 (1996), 279–98.

—— 'Armour and Military Dress in Thirteenth- and Early Fourteenth-Century England', in *Armies, Chivalry and Warfare in Medieval Britain and France*, ed. M. Strickland (Stamford, 1998), 344–69.

—— 'La "Formation de la *Gentry*", xie–xive siècle: un nouveau concept historiographique?', in *Histoires d'Outre-Manche: tendances récentes de l'historiographie britannique*, eds F. Lachaud, I. Lescent-Giles and F.-J. Ruggiu (Paris, 2001), 13–36.

—— 'L'Enseignement des bonnes manières en milieu de cour en Angleterre d'après l'*Urbanus magnus* attribué à Daniel de Beccles', in *Erziehung und Bildung bei Hofe*, eds W. Paravicini and J. Wettlaufer (Stuttgart, 2002), 43–53.

Lambert of Ardres, *The History of the Counts of Guines and Lords of Ardres*, trans. L. Shopkow (Philadelphia, 2001).

Lancelot do Lac, ed. E. Kennedy (2 vols, Oxford, 1980).

Lanercost Chronicle, 1201–1346, ed. J. Stevenson (Edinburgh, 1839).

Långfors, A. 'Le *Dit des hérauts* par Henri de Laon', *Romania*, 43 (1914), 216–25.

Langley Cartulary, ed. P.R. Coss (Dugdale Society, 32, 1980).

Laporte, J. '*Epistulae Fiscannenses*: lettres d'amitié, de gouvernement et d'affaires (xie–xiie siècles)', in *Revue Mabillon*, lxiii (1953), 5–31.

Latin Text of the Ancrene Riwle, ed. C. D'Evelyn (Early English Text Society, no. 216, 1944).

Lauwers, M. *La Mémoire des ancêtres. Le souci des morts. Morts, rites et société au moyen âge* (Paris, 1996).

Lawrence, C.H. *The Friars* (Harlow, 1994).

Layettes du trésor des chartes, ed. A. Teulet (5 vols, Paris, 1863–1909).

Le Goff, J. 'The Symbolic Ritual of Vassalage', in *idem, Time, Work and Culture in the Middle Ages*, trans. A. Goldhammer (Chicago, 1980), 237–87.

Le Maho, J. 'L'Apparition des seigneuries châtelaines dans la Grand-Caux à l'époque ducale', *Archéologie mediévale*, 6 (1976), 5–148.

—— 'Châteaux d'époque franque en Normandie', *Archéologie Mediévale*, 10 (1980), 153–65.

Leges Henrici Primi, ed. L.J. Downer (Cambridge, 1972).

Leicestershire Survey, c.AD 1130 ed. C.F. Slade (Leicester, 1956).

Letters and Charters of Gilbert Foliot, eds Z.N. Brooke, A. Morey and C.N.L. Brooke (Cambridge, 1967).

Letters of Lanfranc, Archbishop of Canterbury, eds and trans H.M. Clover and M. Gibson (Oxford, 1979).

Lévi-Strauss, C. *Les Structures élémentaires de la parenté* (2nd edn, Paris, 1979).

Lewis, C.P. 'The King and Eye: A Study in Anglo-Norman Politics', *EHR*, 104 (1989), 571–84.

—— 'The Early Earls of Norman England', *ANS*, xiii, ed. M. Chibnall (Woodbridge, 1990), 211–22.

—— 'The Formation of the Honor of Chester', in *The Earldom of Chester and its Charters*, ed. A.T. Thacker (Chester Archaeological Society, 71, 1991), 37–66.

—— 'Domesday Jurors', *HSJ*, 5 (1993), 24–34.

Lewis, F.R. 'A History of the Lordship of Gower from the Missing Cartulary of Neath Abbey', *Bulletin of the Board of Celtic Studies*, xi (1937–9), 149–54.

Liber de Llan Dâv, ed. J.G. Evans (Oxford, 1893).

Liber Luciani de laude Cestrie, ed. M.V. Taylor (Lancashire and Cheshire Record Society, lxiv, 1912).

Liber Niger Scaccarii, ed. T. Hearne (2 vols, London, 1771–4).

Liddiard, R. *Landscapes of Lordship: Norman Castles and the Countryside in Medieval Norfolk, 1066–1200* (BAR British Series, 309, 2000).

—— *Castles in Context: Power Symbolism and Landscape, 1066 to 1500* (Macclesfield, 2005).

Lieberman, M. *The Medieval March of Wales: The Creation and Perception of a Frontier 1066–1283* (Cambridge, 2010).

Liebermann, F. 'The Text of Henry I's Coronation Charter', *TRHS*, new ser., 8 (1894), 21–48.

Littere Baronum: The Earliest Cartulary of the Counts of Champagne, ed. T. Evergates (Toronto, 2003).

Livingstone, A. *Out of Love for my Kin: Aristocratic Family Life in the Lands of the Loire* (Ithaca NY, 2010).

Lloyd, S.D. 'William Longespee II: The Making of an English Crusading Hero', *Nottingham Medieval Studies*, 35 (1991), 41–79.

—— *English Society and the Crusade, 1216–1307* (Oxford, 1988).

LoPrete, K. *Adela of Blois: Countess and Lord, c.1067–1137* (Dublin, 2007).

Lot, F. *Etudes critiques sur l'abbaye de St-Wandrille* (Paris, 1913).

Lovatt, M. 'Archbishop Geoffrey of York: A Problem in Anglo-French Maternity', in *Records, Administration and Aristocratic Society in the Anglo-Norman Realm*, ed. N. Vincent (Woodbridge, 2009), 91–124.

Luffield Priory Charters, ed. G.R. Elvey (2 vols, Northamptonshire Record Society, xxii, xxvi, 1968–75).

Maddicott, J.R. 'Magna Carta and the Local Community, 1215–1259', *PP*, 102 (1984), 25–65.

—— *Simon de Montfort* (Cambridge, 1994).

—— *The Origins of the English Parliament, 924–1327* (Oxford, 2010).

Magnum rotulum scaccarii vel magnum rotulum pipæ de anno tricesimo-primo regni Henrici Primi (ut videtur), ed. J. Hunter (Record Commission, 1833).

Maitland, F.W. *Domesday Book and Beyond: Three Essays in the Early History of England* (repr. Cambridge, 1987).

Manekine, Le, ed. H. Suchier (Société des Anciens Textes Français, 1884).

Martindale, J. 'Secular Propaganda and Aristocratic Values: The Autobiographies of Count Fulk le Réchin and Count William of Poitou, Duke of Aquitaine', in *Writing Medieval Biography: Essays in Honour of Frank Barlow*, eds D. Bates, J. Crick and S. Hamilton (Woodbridge, 2006), 143–59.

Mason, J.F.A. *William I and the Sussex Rapes* (St Leonards, 1966).

Materials for the History of Thomas Becket, eds J.C. Robertson and J.B. Sheppard (7 vols, Rolls Series, 1872–83).

Matthew Paris, *Historia Anglorum sive historia minor*, ed. F. Madden (3 vols, Rolls Series, 1866–9).

—— *Chronica Majora*, ed. H.R. Luard (7 vols, Rolls Series, 1872–84).

McFarlane, K.B. 'Had Edward I a "Policy" towards the Earls?', in *The Nobility of Later Medieval England* (Oxford, 1973), 248–67.

McLaughlin, M. 'The Woman Warrior: Gender, Warfare and Society in Medieval Europe', *Women's Studies*, 17 (1990), 193–209.

Meisel, J. *Barons of the Welsh Frontier: The Corbet, Pantulf and fitz Warin Families, 1066–1272* (Lincoln, NE, 1980).

Memoriale fratris Walteri de Coventria, ed. W. Stubbs (2 vols, Rolls Series, 1872–3).

Milsom, S.F.C. *Historical Foundations of the Common Law* (London, 1969).

—— *The Legal Framework of English Feudalism* (Cambridge, 1976).

Mitchell, S.N. *Studies in Taxation under John and Henry III* (New Haven, 1914).

Monasticon Anglicanum, eds J. Caley et al. (8 vols, Record Commission, 1817–30).

Monson, A. *Les Ensenhamens occitans: essai de définition et délimitation du genre* (Paris, 1981).

Monumenta Franciscana, ed. J.S. Brewer (Rolls Series, 1858).

Moorman, J.R.H. *Church Life in England in the Thirteenth Century* (Cambridge, 1946).

Morel-Fatio, A. 'Mélanges de littérature Catalane', *Romania*, 15 (1886), 224–35.

Morillo, S. *Warfare under the Anglo-Norman Kings, 1066–1135* (Woodbridge, 1994).

Morris, M. *The Bigod Earls of Norfolk in the Thirteenth Century* (Woodbridge, 2005).

Morris, W.A. *The Medieval English Sheriff to 1300* (Manchester, 1927).

Morsel, J. *L'aristocratie médiévale, v^e–xve siècle* (Paris, 2004).

Mortimer, R. 'Religious and Secular Motives for Some English Monastic Foundations', *Studies in Church History*, xv (1978), 77–85.

—— 'Knights and Knighthood in Germany in the Central Middle Ages', in *The Ideals and Practice of Medieval Knighthood* i, eds C. Harper-Bill and R. Harvey (Woodbridge, 1986), 86–103.

—— 'Land and Service: The Tenants of the Honour of Clare', *ANS*, viii, ed. R.A. Brown (Woodbridge, 1986), 177–97.

Murray, A. 'Confession before 1215', *TRHS*, 6th ser., 3 (1993), 51–81.

Naughton, K.S. *The Gentry of Bedfordshire in the Thirteenth and Fourteenth Centuries* (Leicester, 1976).

Nichols, J. *The History and Antiquities of the County of Leicester* (4 vols in 8, London, 1795–1815).

Noble, P. 'Anti-clericalism in the Feudal Epic', in *The Medieval Alexander Legend and Romance Epic: Essays in Honour of David J.A. Ross*, eds P. Noble, L. Polak and C. Isoz (Nendeln, 1982), 149–58.

Nouvelles occitanes du moyen âge, ed. and trans. J.-C. Huchet (Paris, 1992).

O'Brien, B. *God's Peace and King's Peace: The Laws of Edward the Confessor* (Philadelphia, 1999).

Odo of Deuil, *De profectione Ludovici VII in orientem*, ed. and trans. V.G. Berry (New York, 1948).

Oeuvres de Rigord et de Guillaume le Breton, ed. F. Delaborde (2 vols, Société de l'Histoire de France, Paris, 1882–5).

Orderic Vitalis, *The Ecclesiastical History*, ed. M. Chibnall (6 vols, Oxford, 1969–80).

Ordines Coronationis Franciae, ed. R.A. Jackson (Philadelphia, 1995).

Orme, N. *From Childhood to Chivalry: The Education of the English Kings and Aristocracy, 1066–1530* (London, 1984).

Osbern of Canterbury, *Vita et translatio sancti Elphegi*, in H. Wharton, *Anglia Sacra* (2 vols, London, 1691), 2.

Padel, O. 'Geoffrey of Monmouth and Cornwall', *Cambridge Medieval Celtic Studies*, 8 (1984), 1–28.

Painter, S. 'Castle Guard', *AmHR*, 40 (1935), 450–9.

—— *Studies in the History of the English Feudal Barony* (Baltimore, 1943).

Parsons, J. Carmi, 'The Queen's Intercession in Thirteenth-Century England', in *Power of the Weak: Studies on Medieval Woman*, eds J. Carpenter and S.-B. Maclean (Urbana, 1995), 147–77.

Patent Rolls of the Reign of Henry III (6 vols, London, HMSO, 1901–13).

Patrologiae cursus completus: series Latina, ed. J.-P. Migne (221 vols, Paris, 1847–67).

Pelteret, D. *Slavery in Early Medieval England* (Woodbridge, 1995).

Peter of Blois, *Dialogus inter regem Henricum II et abbatem Bonevallis*, in *PL*, 207.

Peter of Cornwall, 'The Visions of Ailsi and his Sons', eds R. Easting and R. Sharpe, *Mediaevistik*, 1 (1988), 206–62.

Peterborough Chronicle, 1070–1154, ed. and trans. C. Clark (2nd edn, Oxford, 1970).

Philip de Novara, *Les Quatre Ages de l'Homme*, ed. M. de Fréville (Paris, 1888).

Philip de Remy, *Jehan et Blonde*, ed. S. Lécuyer (Classiques Français du Moyen Age, 1984).

Philip of Harvengt, *De institutione clericorum*, in *PL*, 203.

—— *Epistolae*, in *PL*, 203.

Philip the Prior, *Miraculis sanctae Frideswidae*, in *Acta Sanctorum*, 8 Oct.

Pipe Roll identified by regnal year (Pipe Roll Society, 1884–).

Pleas before the King or his Justices, 1198–1202, ed. D.M. Stenton (Selden Society, 67, 1948).

Poésies complètes de Bertran de Born, ed. A. Thomas (Toulouse, 1888).

Polden, A. 'A Crisis of the Knightly Class? Inheritance and Office among the Gentry of Thirteenth-Century Buckinghamshire', in *Regionalism and Revisionism: The Crown and its Provinces in England, 1200–1650*, eds P. Fleming, A. Gross and J.E. Lander (London, 1998), 29–57.

—— 'The Social Networks of the Buckinghamshire Gentry in the Thirteenth Century', *JMH*, 32 (2006), 371–94.

Political Songs of England, ed. and trans. T. Wright (1839), revised P.R. Coss (Cambridge, 1996).

Pollock, F. and F.W. Maitland, *The History of English Law* (2nd edn, 2 vols, Cambridge, 1898).

Poly, J.P. and E. Bournazel, *The Feudal Transformation, 900–1200*, trans. C. Higgitt (New York, 1991).

Poole, A.L. *From Domesday Book to Magna Carta, 1087–1216* (2nd edn, Oxford, 1955).

Powell, J.E. and K. Wallis, *The House of Lords in the Middle Ages* (London, 1968).

Power, D. 'Le régime seigneurial en Normandie', in *Les Seigneuries dans l'espace Plantagenêt (c.1150–c.1250)*, eds M. Aurell and F. Boutoulle (Bordeaux, 2009), 117–36.

—— *The Norman Frontier in the Twelfth and Early Thirteenth Centuries* (Cambridge, 2004).

Powicke, F.M. *King Henry III and the Lord Edward* (2 vols, Oxford, 1947).

—— *Stephen Langton* (Oxford, 1965).

Powicke, M.R. 'Distraint of Knighthood and Military Obligation under Henry III', *Speculum*, 25 (1950), 457–70.

Prestwich, J.O. 'Anglo-Norman Feudalism and the Problem of Continuity', *PP*, 26 (1963), 39–57.

—— 'The Military Household of the Norman Kings', *EHR*, 96 (1981), 1–35.

Prestwich, M. *Edward I* (London, 1988).

Prise d'Orange, ed. C. Regnier (Paris, 1967).

Private Indentures for Life Service in Peace and War, 1278–1476, eds M. Jones and S. Walker, in *Camden Miscellany*, xxxii (Camden, 5th ser., 3, 1994).

Protheselaus, ed. F. Kluckow (Göttingen, 1924).

Quick, J. 'The Number and Distribution of Knights in Thirteenth-Century England', in *Thirteenth-Century England* i, eds P.R. Coss and S.D. Lloyd (Woodbridge, 1986), 114–23.

Ralph de Diceto, *Opera Historica*, ed. W. Stubbs (2 vols, Rolls Series, London, 1876).

Ralph Niger, *De re militari et triplici via peregrinationis Ierosolimitane*, ed. L. Schmugge (Beitrage zür Geschichte und Quellenkunde des Mittelalters, 6, Berlin, 1977).

Raoul de Cambrai, ed. S. Kay (Oxford, 1992).

Reading Abbey Cartularies, ed. B.R. Kemp (2 vols, Camden Society, 4th ser., xxxi, xxxiii, 1986–7).

Receipt Rolls, 4, 5, 6 Henry III, ed. N. Barratt (Pipe Roll Society, 2003).

Records of the Barony and Honour of the Rape of Lewes, ed. A.J. Taylor (Sussex Record Society, 44, 1939).

Recueil des actes des ducs de Normandie de 911 à 1066, ed. M. Fauroux (Caen, 1961).

Recueil de chartes et documents de St-Martin-des-Champs, ed. J. Depoin (3 vols, Paris, 1913–17).

Recueil des historiens des Gaules et de la France, eds M. Bouquet et al. (24 vols, Paris, 1864–1904).

Red Book of the Exchequer, ed. H. Hall (3 vols, Rolls Series, 1896).

Regesta Regum Anglo-Normannorum, eds H.W.C. Davis et al. (4 vols, Oxford, 1913–69).

Regesta Regum Anglo-Normannorum: The Acta of William I, 1066–1087, ed. D.R. Bates (Oxford, 1998).

Regesta Regum Scottorum i, *The Acts of Malcolm IV*, ed. G.W.S. Barrow (Edinburgh, 1960).

Register of Godfrey Giffard, 1268–1301, ed. J. Willis Bund (2 vols, Worcester Historical Society, 1902).

Register of John de Grandison, Bishop of Exeter iii, *1360–1369*, ed. F.C. Hingeston-Randolph (London, 1899).

Registrum Antiquissimum of the Cathedral Church of Lincoln, eds C.W. Foster and K. Major (10 vols, Lincoln Record Society, 1931–73).

Reynolds, S. *Kingdoms and Communities in Western Europe, 900–1300* (Oxford, 1984).

—— *Fiefs and Vassals: The Medieval Evidence Reinterpreted* (Oxford, 1994).

Richard fitz Nigel, *Dialogus de Scaccario*, ed and trans. E. Amt (Oxford, 2007).

Richard of Hexham, *De gestis regis Stephani*, in *Chronicles of the Reigns of Stephen, Henry II and Richard*, ed. R. Howlett (4 vols, Rolls Series, 1886–9), iii.

Richardson, H.G. and G.O. Sayles. *The Governance of Medieval England from the Conquest to Magna Carta* (Edinburgh, 1963).

Richmond, C. 'The Rise of the English Gentry, 1150–1350', *The Historian*, 26 (1990), 14–17.

Ridgeway. H. 'William de Valence and his Familiares, 1247–72', *Historical Research*, 65 (1992), 239–57.

Robinson, W.A. *Gilbert Crispin, Abbot of Westminster* (Cambridge, 1911).

Roffe, D. 'From Thegnage to Barony: Sake and Soke, Title and Tenants-in-Chief', *Anglo-Norman Studies*, xii, ed. M. Chibnall (Woodbridge, 1990), 157–176.

—— *Domesday: The Inquest and the Book* (Oxford, 2000).

Roger of Howden, *Gesta Henrici Secundi*, ed. W. Stubbs (2 vols, Rolls Series, 1867).

Rogers, N. 'The Waltham Abbey Relic-list', in *England in the Eleventh Century*, ed. C. Hicks (Stamford, 1992), 157–81.

Roll of the Shropshire Eyre of 1256, ed. A. Harding (Selden Soc, 96, 1981).

Rolls of the Justices in Eyre for Gloucestershire, Warwickshire and Staffordshire, 1221–1222, ed. D.M. Stenton (Selden Society, lix, 1940).

Rolls of the Justices in Eyre for Yorkshire in 3 Henry III (1218–19), ed. and trans. D.M Stenton (Selden Society, lvi, 1937).

Roman de Ham, in *Histoire des ducs de Normandie et des rois d'Angleterre*, ed. F. Michel (Paris, 1840).

Roman de Thèbes, ed. F. Mora-Lebrun (Paris, 1995).

Roman de toute chevalerie, Le, ed. B. Foster (2 vols, Anglo-Norman Text Society, 1976–7).

Romance of Fergus, ed. W. Frescoln (Philadelphia, 1983).

Rothwell, W. 'A Mis-judged Author and a Mis-used Text: Walter de Bibbesworth and his *Tretiz*', *Modern Language Review*, 77 (1982), 282–93.

Rotuli Chartarum, ed. T.D. Hardy (Record Commission, 1837).

Rotuli Hugonis de Welles, eds W.P.W. Phillimore and F.N. Davis (3 vols, Canterbury and York Society, 1907–9).

Rotuli Hundredorum, ed. W. Illingworth (2 vols, Record Commission, 1812–18).

Rotuli Litterarum Clausarum, 1204–27 i, ed. T.D. Hardy (Record Commission, 1833).

Rouleaux des morts du ix au xv* siècle*, ed. L. Delisle (Paris, 1866).

Round, J.H. 'The Introduction of Knight Service into England', in *Feudal England* (1891) (repr. London, 1964), 182–245.

—— *Geoffrey de Mandeville* (London, 1892).

Rowlands, I.W. 'William de Braose and the Lordship of Brecon', *Bulletin of the Board of Celtic Studies*, 30 (1982–3), 123–33.

Royal and Other Historical Letters Illustrative of the Reign of Henry III, ed. W.W. Shirley (2 vols, Rolls Series, 1862–6).

Rubin, M. *Corpus Christi: The Eucharist in Late Medieval Culture* (Cambridge, 1991).

Rufford Abbey Charters, ed. C.J. Holdsworth (4 vols, Thoroton Society Record Series, 29–30, 32, 34, 1972–81).

Rymer, T. *Foedera, Conventiones, Litterae et Acta Publica*, eds A. Clarke and F. Holbrooke (7 vols, London, 1816–69).

Salzman, L.F. 'The Family of Aguillon', *Sussex Archaeological Collections*, 79 (1938), 45–58.

Sancti Anselmi Omnia Opera, ed. F.S. Schmitt, iii–v (Edinburgh, 1946–51).

Sanders, I.J. *Feudal Military Service in England: A Study of the Constitutional and Military Powers of the* Barones *in Medieval England* (Oxford, 1956).

Sansone, G.E. *Testi Didattico-Cortesi di Provenza* (Bari, 1977).

Sarum Charters and Documents, eds W.R. Jones, and W.D. McCray (Rolls Series, 1891).

Saul, N. *Knights and Esquires: The Gloucestershire Gentry in the Fourteenth Century* (Oxford, 1981).

Sawyer, P. '1066–1086: A Tenurial Revolution', in *Domesday Book: A Reassessment*, ed. *idem* (London, 1983), 71–85.

Saxon, E. *The Eucharist in Romanesque France: Iconography and Theology* (Woodbridge, 2006).

Scammell, J. 'The Origin and Limitations of the Liberty of Durham', *EHR*, 81 (1966), 449–73.

—— 'The Formation of the English Social Structure: Freedom, Knights and Gentry, 1066–1300,' *Speculum*, 68 (1993), 601–18.

Selden, J. *Titles of Honor* (2nd edn, London, 1631).

Select Pleas in Manorial and Other Seignorial Courts i, *Reigns of Henry III and Edward I*, ed. F.W. Maitland (Selden Society, 1888).

Selected Letters of Pope Innocent III concerning England, eds and trans. C.R. Cheney and W.H. Semple (London, 1953).

Self and Society in Medieval France, ed. and trans. J.F. Benton (Toronto, 1984).

Sharpe, R. 'Some Medieval Miracula from Llandegley', *Bulletin of the Board of Celtic Studies*, 37 (1990), 166–76.

—— 'The Prefaces of "Quadripartitus" ', in *Law and Government in Medieval England and Normandy: Essays in Honour of Sir James Holt*, eds G. Garnett and J.G. Hudson (Cambridge, 1992), 148–72.

—— *Norman Rule in Cumbria, 1092–1136* (Cumberland and Westmorland Antiquarian and Archaeological Society, Tract Series, xxi, 2006).

—— 'King Harold's Daughter', *HSJ*, 19 (2007), 1–27.

—— 'The Last Years of Herbert the Chamberlain: Weaverthorpe Church and Hall', *Historical Research* 83 (2010), 588–601.

Shrewsbury Cartulary, ed. U. Rees (2 vols, Aberystwyth, 1975).

Sigar of Newbold, 'The Vision of Orm', ed. H. Farmer, *Analecta Bollandiana*, 75 (1957), 72–82.

Simeon of Durham, *Historia ecclesiae Dunelmensis*, in *Opera Omnia*, ed. T. Arnold (2 vols, Rolls Series, 1882–5).

Simeon of Durham, *Historia Regum*, in *Opera Omnia*, ed. T. Arnold (2 vols, Rolls Series, 1882–5).

Simpkin, D. *The English Aristocracy at War: From the Welsh Wars of Edward I to the Battle of Bannockburn* (Woodbridge, 2008).

Simpson, G.G. 'The *Familia* of Roger de Quincy, Earl of Winchester and Constable of Scotland', in *Essays on the Nobility of Medieval Scotland*, ed. K.J. Stringer (Edinburgh, 1985), 102–27.

Sir Christopher Hatton's Book of Seals, eds L.C. Loyd and D.M. Stenton (Oxford, 1950).

Smith, J. Beverley, 'The Kingdom of Morgannwg and the Norman Conquest of Glamorgan', in *Glamorgan County History* iii, *The Middle Ages*, ed. T.B. Pugh (Cardiff, 1971), 1–43.

Södergård, O. 'Un Art d'aimer anglo-normand', *Romania*, 77 (1956), 289–330.

Somersetshire Pleas to 41 Henry III, ed. C.E.H. Chadwycke-Healey (Somersetshire Record Society, xi, 1897).

Song of Aspremont, trans. M.A. Newth (Garland Library of Medieval Literature, series B., vol. 61, 1989).

Song of Songs: A Twelfth-Century Version, ed. C.E. Pickford (Oxford, 1974).

Stacey, R.C. *Politics, Policy and Finance under Henry III, 1216–1245* (Oxford, 1987).

Stacy, N.E. 'Henry of Blois and the Lordship of Glastonbury', *EHR*, 114 (1999), 1–33.

Stafford, P. 'The Laws of Cnut and the History of Anglo-Saxon Promises', in *Anglo-Saxon England*, 10, eds P. Clemoes et al. (Cambridge, 1982), 173–90.

—— 'The Portrayal of Royal Women in England, Mid Tenth to Mid Twelfth Centuries', in *Medieval Queenship*, ed. J. Carmi Parsons (Stroud, 1994), 143–67.

—— 'Women and the Norman Conquest,' *TRHS*, 6th ser., 4 (1994), 221–49.

—— 'La Mutation Familiale: A Suitable Case for Caution', in *The Community, the Family and the Saint: Patterns of Power in Early Medieval Europe*, eds J. Hill and M. Swan (Turnhout, 1998), 103–25.

—— *Queen Emma and Queen Edith: Queenship and Women's Power in the Eleventh Century* (Oxford, 1997).

Steidl, E. '*Meilz valt mesure*: Oliver, the Norman Chroniclers and the Model Commander', *Romance Philology*, 45 (1991–2), 251–68.

Stenton, D.M. *English Justice between the Norman Conquest and the Great Charter, 1066–1215* (London, 1965).

Stenton, F.M. 'St Benet of Holme and the Norman Conquest', *EHR*, 37 (1922), 225–35.

—— *The First Century of English Feudalism, 1066–1166* (2nd edn, Oxford, 1960).

Stephen de Fougères, *Le Livre des Manières*, ed. R.A. Lodge (Geneva, 1979).

Stoke by Clare Cartulary, pt 1, eds C. Harper-Bill and R. Mortimer (Suffolk Charters, 4, 1981).

Stones, E.L.G. 'The Folvilles of Ashby-Folville, Leicestershire, and their Associates in Crime, 1326–1347', *TRHS*, 5th ser., 7 (1957), 117–36.

Strickland, M. 'Slaughter, Slavery or Ransom: The Impact of the Conquest on Conduct in Warfare', in *England in the Eleventh Century*, ed. C. Hicks (Stamford, 1992), 41–60.

—— 'Henry I and the Battle of the Two Kings: Brémule 1119', in *Normandy and its Neighbours, c.900–1250: Essays for David Bates*, eds D. Crouch and K. Thompson (Turnhout, 2010).

Stringer, K.J. 'States, Liberties and Communities in Medieval Britain and Ireland (*c.*1100–1400)', in *Liberties and Identities in the Medieval British Isles*, ed. M. Prestwich (Woodbridge, 2008), 5–36.

—— *Earl David of Huntingdon: A Study in Anglo-Scottish History* (Edinburgh, 1985).

—— *The Reign of Stephen: Kingship, Warfare and Government in Twelfth-Century England* (Routledge, 1993).

Stubbs, W. *The Constitutional History of England* (3 vols, Oxford, 1880).

—— *Select Charters and Other Illustrations of English Constitutional History*, ed. H.W.C. Davis (9th edn, Oxford, 1913).

Subrenat, J. 'e Oliver est proz', in *Études de philologie romane et d'histoire littéraire offertes à Jules Horvent*, eds J.-M. d'Heur and N. Cherubini (Liège, 1980), 461–7.

Suger, *Vie de Louis VI le Gros*, ed. and trans. (into French) H. Waquet (Paris, 1929).

Suppe, F. 'Castle Guard and the Castlery of Clun', *HSJ*, 1 (1989), 123–34.

Sutherland, D.W. *Quo Warranto Proceedings in the Reign of Edward I, 1278–1294* (Oxford, 1963).

Swanson, R.N. 'Angels Incarnate: Clergy and Masculinity from Gregorian Reform to Reformation', in *Masculinity in Medieval Europe*, ed. D.M. Hadley (London, 1999), 160–77.

Textus Roffensis, pt 2, ed. P. Sawyer (Copenhagen, 1962).

Thomas of Chobham, *Summa Confessorum*, ed. F. Broomfield (Analecta Mediaevalia Namurcensia, 25, Louvain, 1968).

Thomas of Monmouth, *Life and Miracles of St William of Norwich*, eds A. Jessopp and M.R. James (Cambridge, 1896).

Thomas Walsingham, *Gesta abbatum monasterii sancti Albani*, ed. H.T. Riley (3 vols, Rolls Series, 1867–9).

Thomas, H.M. 'Lay Piety in England from 1066 to 1215', in *ANS*, 29, ed. C.P. Lewis (Woodbridge, 2007), 179–92.

—— 'Violent Disorder in King Stephen's England', in *King Stephen's Reign, 1135–1154*, eds P. Dalton and G.J. White (Woodbridge, 2008), 139–70.

—— *Vassals, Heiresses, Crusaders and Thugs: the Gentry of Angevin Yorkshire, 1154–1216* (Philadelphia, 1993).

—— *The English and the Normans: Ethnic Hostility, Assimilation and Identity, 1066–c.1220* (Oxford, 2003).

Thompson, K. 'Robert of Bellême Reconsidered', *ANS*, xiii, ed. M. Chibnall (Woodbridge, 1990), 263–86.

—— 'Orderic Vitalis and Robert of Bellême', *JMH*, 20 (1994), 133–41.

—— 'Arnoul de Montgomery,' *Annales de Normandie*, 45 (1995), 49–53.

—— 'Affairs of State: The Illegitimate Children of Henry I', *Journal of Medieval History*, 29 (2003).

Three Rolls of the King's Court in the Reign of Richard I, AD 1194–1195, ed. F.W. Maitland (Pipe Roll Society, xiv, 1891).

Thurgarton Cartulary, ed. T. Foulds (Stamford, 1994).

Tomkinson, A. 'Retinues at the Tournament of Dunstable, 1309', *EHR*, 74 (1959), 70–89.

Tout, T.F. 'The Earldoms under Edward I', *TRHS*, new ser., viii (1894), 129–55.

—— 'The "Communitas Bacheleriae Angliae" ', *EHR*, 17 (1902), 89–95.

Tractatus de adventu fratrum minorum in Angliam, ed. A.G. Little (Manchester, 1951).

Traill, D.A. 'More Poems by Philip the Chancellor,' *Journal of Medieval Latin*, 16 (2006), 164–81.

Traité de Walter de Bibbesworth sur la langue française, ed. A. Owen (Paris, 1929).

Treatise on the Law and Customs of the Realm of England Commonly Called Glanvill, ed. G.D.G. Hall (London, 1965).

Treaty Rolls i, *1234–1325*, ed. P. Chaplais (London, 1955).

Très ancien coutumier de Normandie, in *Coutumiers de Normandie* i, ed. E.-J. Tardif (Rouen, 1881).

Turner, R. *Men Raised from the Dust: Administrative Service and Upward Mobility in Angevin England* (Philadelphia, 1988).

Tyerman, C. *The English and the Crusades, 1095–1588* (Chicago, 1988).

Uitti, K.D. 'Remarks on Old French Narratives: Courtly Love and Poetic Form', *Romance Philology*, 26 (1972–3), 77–93.

Ulrich von Liechtenstein, *Service of Ladies*, trans. J.W. Thomas (Chapel Hill, 1969).

Urbanus Magnus Danielis Becclesiensis, ed. J.G. Smyly (Dublin, 1939).

Vale, J. 'The Late Thirteenth-Century Precedent: Chauvency, Le Hem and Edward I', in *eadem Edward III and Chivalry: Chivalric Society and its Context, 1270–1350* (Woodbridge,1983), 4–24.

Van Caenegem, R.C. *The Birth of the English Common Law* (Cambridge, 1973).

Van Houts, E.M.C. 'The Epitaph of Gundrada de Warenne', in *Nova de veteribus: mittel und neulateinische Studien für Paul Gergard Schmidt*, eds A. Bihrer and E. Stein (Leipzig, 2004), 366–78.

—— 'The Ship List of William the Conqueror', in *ANS*, x, ed. R.A. Brown (Woodbridge, 1988), 159–83.

Vaughn, S.N. 'Robert of Meulan and *Raison d'Etat* in the Anglo-Norman State, 1093–1118', *Albion*, 10 (1978), 352–73.

—— *The Abbey of Bec and the Anglo-Norman State, 1034–1136* (Woodbridge, 1981).

Vicomtes et vicomtés dans l'Occident médiéval, ed. H. Débax (Toulouse, 2008).

Vincent, N. 'Hugh de Neville and his Prisoners', *Archives*, xx (1992), 190–7.

—— *Peter des Roches: An Alien in English Politics, 1205–1238* (Cambridge, 1996).

—— 'King Henry and the Poitevins', in *La Cour Plantagenêt, 1154–1204*, ed. M. Aurell (Poitiers, 2000), 103–35.

—— 'William Marshal, King Henry II and the Honour of Châteauroux', *Archives*, xxv (2000), 1–15.

—— *The Holy Blood: King Henry III and the Westminster Blood Relic* (Cambridge, 2001).

—— 'King Henry III and the Blessed Virgin Mary', in *The Church and Mary*, ed. R.N. Swanson (Studies in Church History, 39, Woodbridge, 2004), 126–46.

—— 'The Court of Henry II', in *Henry II: New Interpretations*, eds C. Harper-Bill and N. Vincent (Woodbridge, 2007), 278–334.

——— 'Did Henry II Have a Policy towards the Earls', in *War, Government and Aristocracy in the British Isles, c.1150–1500: Essays in Honour of Michael Prestwich*, eds C. Given-Wilson, A. Kettle and L. Scales (Woodbridge, 2008), 1–25.

——— 'More Tales of the Conquest', in *Normandy and its Neighbours, c.950–1250: Essays in Honour of David Bates*, eds D. Crouch and K. Thompson (Turnhout, 2010), forthcoming.

'The Vision of Orm', ed. H. Farmer, in *Analecta Bollandiana*, 75 (1957), 76–82.

Vita beati Simonis comitis Crespiensis, in *PL*, 156.

Vita beati Vitalis, ed. E.P. Sauvage, in *Analecta Bollandiana*, 1 (1882).

Vita Herluini, in *The Works of Gilbert Crispin, Abbot of Westminster*, eds A.S. Abulafia and G.R. Evans (Auctores Britannici Medii Aevi, viii, British Academy, London, 1986).

Vita sancti Magnobodi Andegavensis episcopi, in *PL* 171.

Vita sancti Waldevi, in *Chroniques Anglo-Normandes*, ed. F. Michel (3 vols, Paris, 1831–40).

Von Feilitzen, O. *The Pre-Conquest Personal Names of Domesday Book* (Uppsala, 1937).

Wace's Roman de Brut: A History of the British. Text and Translation, ed. and trans. J. Weiss (Exeter, 2002).

Wace, *Roman de Rou*, ed. A.J. Holden (3 vols, Société des Anciens Textes Français, 1970–3).

Walker, D. 'Ralph Son of Pichard', *BIHR*, 33 (1960), 195–202.

——— 'The "Honours" of the Earls of Hereford in the Twelfth Century', *Transactions of the Bristol and Gloucestershire Archaeological Society*, lxxix (1960), pt 2, 174–211.

Walker, R.F. 'The Supporters of Richard Marshal, Earl of Pembroke, in the Rebellion of 1233–1234', *Welsh History Review*, xvii (1994), 41–65.

Walker, S.S. 'Free Consent and Marriage of Feudal Wards in Medieval England', *JMH*, 8 (1982), 123–34.

Walter of Henley and Other Treatises on Estate Management and Accounting, ed. and trans. D.M. Oschinsky (Oxford, 1971).

Walter Map, *De Nugis Curialium or Courtiers' Trifles*, ed. and trans. M.R. James, revised C.N.L. Brooke and R.A.B. Mynors (Oxford, 1983).

Wareham, A. 'The Motives and Politics of the Bigod Family, c.1066–1177', *ANS*, xvii, ed. C. Harper-Bill (Woodbridge, 1994), 223–42.

Warren, W.L. *Henry II* (London, 1973).

Warwickshire Hundred Rolls of 1279–80: Stoneleigh and Kineton Hundreds, ed. T. John (British Academy Records of Social and Economic History, new ser., xix, 1992).

Waugh, S.L. 'Reluctant Knights and Jurors: Respites, Exemptions and Public Obligations in the Reign of Henry III', *Speculum*, 58 (1983), 937–86.

——— 'Marriage, Class and Royal Wardship in England under Henry III', *Viator*, 16 (1985), 181–207.

——— 'From Tenure to Contract: Lordship and Clientage in Thirteenth-Century England', *EHR*, 101 (1986), 811–39.

——— *The Lordship of England: Royal Wardships and Marriages in English Society and Politics, 1217–1327* (Princeton, 1988).

Webber, T. 'The Books of Leicester Abbey', in *Leicester Abbey: Medieval History, Archaeology and Manuscript Studies*, eds J. Story et al. (Leicester, 2006), 127–46.

Werner, K.-F. 'Les femmes, le pouvoir et la transmission du pouvoir', in *La femme au moyen âge* (Mauberge, 1990), 365–79.

——— *La naissance de noblesse* (2nd edn, Paris, 1998).

West, F. *The Justiciarship in England, 1066–1232* (Cambridge, 1966).

Wharton, H. *Anglia Sacra* (2 vols, London, 1691).

White, G.J. 'The End of Stephen's Reign', *History*, 75 (1990), 3–22.

——— 'Earls and Earldoms during King Stephen's Reign', in *War and Society in Medieval and Early Modern Britain*, ed. D. Dunn (Liverpool, 2000), 76–95.

——— *Restoration and Reform 1153–1165: Recovery from Civil War in England* (Cambridge, 2000).

White, S.D. 'Feuding and Peace-Making in the Touraine around the Year 1000', *Traditio*, 42 (1986), 195–263.

—— 'The Politics of Anger', in *Anger's Past: The Social Uses of an Emotion in the Middle Ages*, ed. B.H. Rosenwein (Ithaca, NY, 1998), 127–52.

Wickham, C. *Framing the Early Middle Ages: Europe and the Mediterranean, 400–800* (Oxford, 2005).

—— *The Inheritance of Rome: A History of Europe from 400 to 1000* (Harmondsworth, 2009).

Wightman, W.E. *The Lacy Family in England and Normandy, 1066–1194* (Oxford, 1966).

William fitz Stephen, 'A Description of the Most Noble City of London', trans. H.E. Butler, in F.M. Stenton, *Norman London: An Essay* (London, 1934).

—— *Vita sancti Thome*, in *Materials for the History of Thomas Becket*, ed. J.C. Robertson (7 vols, Rolls Series, 1875–85).

William of Malmesbury, *Gesta regum Anglorum*, eds R.A.B. Mynors, R.M. Thomson and M. Winterbottom (2 vols, Oxford, 1998–9).

—— *Historia Novella*, trans. K.R. Potter, ed. and revised E. King (Oxford, 1998).

—— *Vita Wulfstani*, in *Saints' Lives*, eds and trans. M. Winterbottom and R.M. Thomson (Oxford, 2002).

William of Newburgh, *Historia rerum Anglicarum*, in *Chronicles of the Reigns of Stephen, Henry II and Richard I*, ed. Richard Howlett (Rolls Series, 1885), i–ii.

William of Poitiers, *Gesta Guillelmi*, eds and trans. R.H.C. Davis and M. Chibnall (Oxford, 1998).

William of Wycombe, *Speculum vitae viri venerabilis Rotberti episcopi Herefordiae*, in H. Wharton, *Anglia Sacra* (2 vols, London, 1691).

Williams, A. 'The Estates of Harold Godwinsson', *ANS*, iii, ed. R.A. Brown (Woodbridge, 1980), 171–87.

—— 'The Knights of Shaftesbury Abbey', *ANS*, viii, ed. R.A. Brown (Woodbridge, 1985), 214–42.

—— 'The King's Nephew: Ralph, Earl of Hereford', in *Studies in Medieval History Presented to R. Allen Brown*, eds C. Harper-Bill, C. Holdsworth and J.L. Nelson (Woodbridge, 1989), 327–43.

—— *The English and the Norman Conquest* (Woodbridge, 1995).

—— *The World before Domesday: The English Aristocracy, 900–1066* (London, 2008).

Williams, D. 'Simon de Montfort and his Adherents', in *England in the Thirteenth Century*, ed. W.M. Ormrod (Grantham, 1985), 166–77.

Winterbottom, M. 'An Edition of Faricius, *Vita S. Aldhelmi*', *Journal of Medieval Latin*, 15 (2005), 93–147.

Wormald, P. 'Domesday Lawsuits: A Provisional List and Preliminary Comments', in *England in the Eleventh Century*, ed. C. Hicks (Stamford, 1992), 61–102.

—— 'Lordship and Justice in the Early English Kingdom : Oswaldlow Revisited', in *Property and Power in the Early Middle Ages*, eds W. Davies and P. Fouracre (Cambridge, 1995), 114–36.

—— *The Making of English Law: King Alfred to the Twelfth Century* (Oxford, 1999).

Zatočil, L. *Cato a Facetus: Zu den deutschen Cato- und Facetusbearbeitungen. Untersuchungen und Texte* (Opera Universitatis Masarykianae Brunensis, Facultas Philosophica, 48, Brno, 1952).

INDEX